The Essence of Japanese Architecture I

First published in Japan on September 21, 2016
Second published on July 20, 2018

TOTO Publishing (TOTO LTD.)	TOTO Nogizaka Bldg. 2F 1–24–3, Minami-Aoyama, Minato-ku Tokyo 107-0062, Japan [Sales] Telephone: +81-3-3402-7138 Facsimile: +81-3-3402-7187 [Editorial] Telephone: +81-3-3497-1010 [URL] https://jp.toto.com/publishing
Copyright	©2016 Yutaka Saito
Photograph Copyright	©2016 Yutaka Saito
Author	Yutaka Saito
Publisher	Toru Kato
Editor	Naomi Miwa
Book Designer	Tsuyokatsu Kudo
Printing	TOSHO Printing Co., Ltd.

This book may not be reproduced, in whole or in part, in any form or by any means, including photocopying, scanning, digitizing, or otherwise, without prior permission. Scanning or digitizing this book through a third party, even for personal or home use, is also strictly prohibited.
The list price is indicated on the cover.

ISBN978-4-88706-361-7

The Essence of
Japanese Architecture

Text and Photographs by Yutaka Saito

I

日本建築の形

著・写真 齋藤 裕

TOTO出版

日本建築の形 I　The Essence of Japanese Architecture I

目次　Contents

008　日本建築の形──祈りの空間　文：齋藤 裕
　　　The Essence of Japanese Architecture: Spaces for the Divine　Essay by Yutaka Saito

026　伊勢神宮
　　　Ise Jingu Shrine

046　法隆寺 金堂・五重塔・廻廊
　　　Horyuji Temple Kondo, Five-story Pagoda, and Corridors

074　正倉院 正倉
　　　Shosoin Repository

086　唐招提寺 金堂
　　　Toshodaiji Temple Kondo

098　新薬師寺 本堂
　　　Shin Yakushiji Temple Hondo

110　元興寺 極楽坊禅室
　　　Gangoji Temple Gokurakubo Zenshitsu Hall

122　室生寺 五重塔・金堂・灌頂堂
　　　Murouji Temple Five-story Pagoda, Kondo, and Kanjodo Hall

142　醍醐寺 五重塔
　　　Daigoji Temple Five-story Pagoda

152　三徳山三佛寺 奥院（投入堂）
　　　Mitokusan Sanbutsuji Temple Okunoin (Nageiredo Hall)

160　平等院 鳳凰堂
　　　Byodoin Temple Phoenix Hall

182　法界寺 阿弥陀堂
　　　Hokaiji Temple Amida Hall

194　宇治上神社
　　　Ujigami Shrine

220	**嚴島神社**	
	Itsukushima Shrine	
240	**春日大社 摂社若宮神社**	
	Kasuga Taisha Auxiliary Wakamiya Shrine	
254	**高山寺 石水院**	
	Kosanji Temple Sekisui-in	
264	**石山寺 多宝塔**	
	Ishiyamadera Temple Tahoto	
276	**興福寺 北円堂・東金堂・三重塔**	
	Kofukuji Temple Hokuendo, Tokondo, and Three-story Pagoda	
304	**浄土寺 浄土堂**	
	Jodoji Temple Jododo Hall	
322	**東大寺 金堂**	
	Todaiji Temple Kondo	
340	**東大寺 南大門**	
	Todaiji Temple Nandaimon	
352	**東大寺 法華堂**	
	Todaiji Temple Hokkedo Hall	
364	**東大寺 大湯屋**	
	Todaiji Temple Oyuya	
382	**東大寺 二月堂**	
	Todaiji Temple Nigatsudo Hall	
392	掲載建造物データ	
	Data of the Buildings	
394	注・参考文献	
	Notes/References	
396	謝辞	
	Acknowledgements	
397	著者紹介	
	About the Author	

Book Design: Tsuyokatsu Kudo

日本建築の形——祈りの空間

齋藤 裕

日本は木の国である。古代の日本人は深い緑に取り囲まれ、山や森とともに生きてきた。そして、木を使って住居や宮殿、宗教建築を建ててきた。今や当たり前の鉄やガラス、コンクリートが普及したのは、せいぜいこの100年の話である。どの国もどの民族も、周囲にある自然資源を利用しながら、その土地の自然条件に適応した技術を培い、特徴ある建築の形を生みだしてきた。今も昔も、自然条件の差異は個々の文化に反映され、独自性を育むもっとも大きな推進力である。

日本では、地震は不可避である。また、初夏から晩秋には必ず台風に襲われる。さらに、降水量が多い。温暖湿潤な気候のため、植物が旺盛に成長する。森林率は今でも国土の約7割を占めている。このような自然条件を利用し、あるいは適応しつつ、日本建築の形はどのように育まれ、成立してきたのだろうか。

二つの永遠——伊勢神宮と法隆寺

日本建築の歴史は、木造建築の歴史である。おとぎ話『三匹の子豚』では、藁や木の枝でつくった家は吹き飛ばされ、煉瓦造の家だけが残る。一方、日本では、台風や地震で何度倒壊しようとも、火災で焼失しようとも、ふたたび木で建てなおしてきた。それはひとえに、森林資源が豊富で、手近にある材料だったからである。

石や煉瓦ではなく、木を使った建物に恒久性を求めるとき、日本では古来二つの方法が併存してきた。一つには、世界最古の木造建築・法隆寺のように、1,000年以上の歳月に耐える建物をつくる方法である。もう一つは、伊勢神宮のように、定期的に造替することで、半永久的にその原形を伝え残していく方法である。方法は違っても、こうして法隆寺や伊勢神宮は1,300年以上の命脈をつないできた。

まず、1,000年の建築を可能にしたのが、素材である。法隆寺以下、本書に収められている建築には、ほとんどにヒノキが使われている。そ

The Essence of Japanese Architecture: Spaces for the Divine

Yutaka Saito

Japan is a land of wood. Surrounded by dense forests and lush vegetation, people have felt close to the mountains and woodlands since antiquity. And for centuries they built their homes, palaces, and religious edifices out of wood. The use of steel, glass, concrete, and other materials began to spread only about 100 years ago. The people of every country in the world used the natural resources around them to develop technologies suited to their local natural conditions and to build distinctive types of architecture. Today and long ago, natural conditions reflected in each culture have been the driving force of distinctiveness.

Japan is, too, a land of earthquakes, and it is buffeted over and over from early summer to late fall by typhoons. Annual rainfall is high. Vegetation flourishes in the warm and humid climate. Even today about 70 percent of Japan's land is covered with forests. What is particular about Japanese architecture then, is how it grew and developed making use of and adapting to specific natural conditions.

Two Approaches to the Eternal: Ise Jingu Shrine and Horyuji Temple

The history of Japanese architecture is essentially a history of architecture in wood. In the Western children's tale of the *Three Little Pigs*, the houses two of the little pigs build of straw and twigs are blown away by the wolf, but the house built of bricks by the third little pig remains standing despite the exertions of the wolf. In Japan, however, no matter how many times people's homes are blown away by typhoons, toppled by earthquakes, or burned to the ground, they have always rebuilt them with wood. They could do so because it is such an abundant resource; wood has always been close by and in ample supply.

Two methods were adopted in ancient Japan in the effort to make buildings last as long as possible. One was to build structures capable of enduring for more than a thousand years, as is the case of Horyuji temple, the world's oldest standing wooden structure. The other was to pass down and preserve original buildings semi-permanently by the method of rebuilding them at regular intervals, as is still done at Ise Jingu shrine. The method by which they are preserved differs, but architectural continuity has been maintained at both Horyuji and Ise Jingu for 1,300 years.

The key factor that made durability of 1,000 years possible was the kind of wood used. Horyuji and almost all the other buildings included in this book are built with Japanese cypress (*hinoki*). The fact that good quality cypress was available and used for architecture is without doubt the preeminent reason that Japan's ancient architecture has endured to this day. It was not until medieval times,

もそもヒノキの良材が手に入り、それで建ててきたことが、日本の古建築が持ちこたえてきた第一条件といっても過言ではない。寺社建築にヒノキ以外の材木、ケヤキなどが使われるようになるのは、その大径材が少なくなった中世、特に大鋸や台鉋などの道具が発達した桃山時代以降である。

ヒノキは九州から福島まで分布し、日本と台湾にしかない木で、腐朽菌に強いフェノール成分を多く含む。腐りにくく、白蟻といった虫害にも強くて、優れた強度と耐久性を持つ。さらには、加工がしやすい。ヒノキは真っ直ぐに木目が通っているので、斧やクサビを打ち、山で割ってから引き下ろすことができた。それを手斧や槍鉋できれいに仕上げたのである。産地によって特徴に差はあるが、色味がよく、木目は緻密で肌に光沢があり、芳香がある。

古代には樹齢1,000年以上、直径2m以上、高さ40m以上もあるようなヒノキの大木が、西日本を中心に少なからず生育していたことは想像に難くない。法隆寺の金堂や五重塔では、樹齢1,500年は下らないヒノキの心去り材が用いられている。心去り材とは、年輪の中心まわり（樹心）をはずした材のことで、この木取りで大きな板や太い柱を取るのは、かなりの大径木に限られる。たとえば直径30cmの円柱を取るのに、心持ち材であれば直径40cmの丸太があれば取れるが、心去り材であれば1mは必要となる。同じ生育条件下と仮定して、心去り材と心持ち材の樹齢は3倍も違ってくる。法隆寺金堂の裳階扉は幅1m、高さ2.7m、厚み8.4cmの一枚板（p. 63参照）だが、これに使われたヒノキの直径は、辺材（白太）部分を除いているから、少なくとも1.3m以上はあったはずだ。樹齢が高くなればなるほど年輪幅は密になり、腐りにくい心材部分が多くを占め、強度は増す。その心去り材は強靭で腐らず、干割れが少ない。だからこそ法隆寺の、あの見事な一枚板の扉が成り立つ。今見ると、扉に塗られていた丹の塗装は剥落し、細かく美しい中杢が槍鉋の削り跡とともに浮かび上がっている。1mmにも満たない木目を見ていると、その巨木の立ち姿や太古の森を想像することができる。

素材と技術

法隆寺の西院伽藍は、大陸、とくに朝鮮半島の影響が強いといわれるが、ヒノキの大径木を心去り材で使うのは、日本だけで可能となった手段である。大陸由来の様式や建造技術を踏襲しても、素材が違えば、当然その特長を活かすかたちで改変したところがあったはずである。

法隆寺の金堂や五重塔では、のちの唐様式に倣った薬師寺東塔や唐招提寺金堂の三手先斗栱のように、小部材に分けた組物を用いず、一

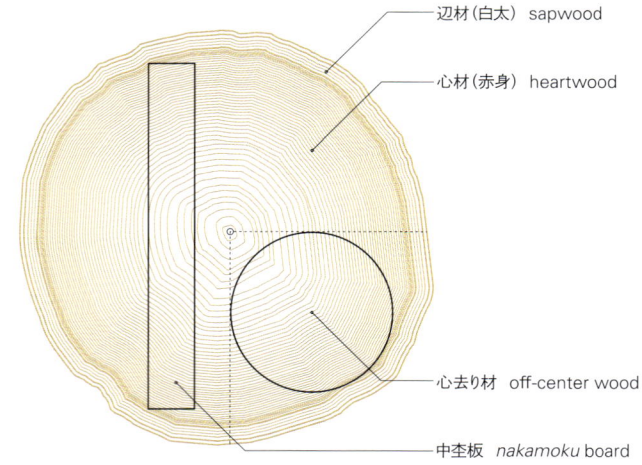

辺材（白太）　sapwood
心材（赤身）　heartwood
心去り材　off-center wood
中杢板　nakamoku board

法隆寺五重塔の雲斗雲肘木
A cloud-shaped bracket complex, Horyuji Five-story Pagoda

particularly from the late sixteenth century when use of the two-man saw (*oga*) and the plane (*daiganna*) developed and large cypress trees became harder to obtain, that temples and shrines began to be built of other types of wood, like zelkova (*keyaki*).

In Asia, *hinoki* cypress grows widely only on the Japanese archipelago from Fukushima in the north to Kyushu in the south as well as on Taiwan. The wood contains large quantities of phenol, which protects it against rot and against the predations of termites and other insects, making it both extremely strong and durable. The wood is moreover easy to shape. The grain runs perfectly straight, so the trees were split using axes and wedges right where they were felled before carrying the wood out of the mountains. The lumber was then smoothed using adzes and spear planes (*yariganna*). *Hinoki* wood varies slightly from one area to another but in general has a rich color, dense grain, smooth surface, and fine aroma.

In ancient times, it is not difficult to imagine that the forests, especially of western Japan, were filled with massive cypress trees that had been growing for more than 1,000 years, were more than two meters in diameter, and towered to heights of 40 meters or more. For the Kondo and Five-story Pagoda at Horyuji, cypress timbers no less than 1,500 years old, cut to avoid the central core (*shinsari*), were used. To obtain large boards and thick posts using *shinsari* lumber requires trees of quite immense diameter. For example, in order to obtain a pillar 30 centimeters in diameter, if wood with the central core (*shinmochi*) is to be used, a tree of only 40 centimeters in diameter is needed; but to obtain the same pillar with *shinsari* wood a log of at least one meter in diameter is required. The age of the tree needed to obtain pillars from *shinsari* wood will thus be three times that of the tree that is needed for pillars taken from *shinmochi* wood. The doors of the *mokoshi* enclosure of the Horyuji Kondo (see p. 63) are made of solid slabs of wood; they are each one meter wide, 8.4 centimeters thick, and 2.7 meters high. Since the outer sapwood is removed, that means that the cypress tree used to make them must have been more than 1.3 meters across. The older the tree, the denser the tree rings and the greater the proportion of heartwood that is resistant to decay, thereby increasing its strength. *Shinsari* wood is quite hard and does not rot; it is also less likely to split when it dries. That is why those splendid *mokoshi* doors at Horyuji could be made. Looking closely, now that the vermillion paint with which the doors were coated has worn off, we can see the beautiful, dense *nakamoku* grain of the surface together with the traces of *yariganna* planing. Gazing at the wood grain showing rings less than one millimeter wide, we can imagine the massive trees that grew in the forests of primeval times.

Materials and Technology

The architecture of the Western Precinct of Horyuji is said to have been greatly influenced by continental, especially Korean building techniques, but the use of the *shinsari* wood of massive cypress trees was a means that was possible only in Japan. While the builders may have followed styles and architectural techniques introduced from the continent, they were using different and local materials, so it was likely that they made changes taking advantage of the features of their materials.

The Horyuji Kondo and Five-story Pagoda did not use bracket complexes made up of smaller parts like the three-stepped bracket complexes used in the later Yakushiji East Pagoda and Toshodaiji Kondo in emulation of Tang style, but used cloud-shaped bearing blocks/bracket arms made of a single piece of wood. Whether or not similar kinds of bracket complexes were being made in China or Korea at that time cannot be confirmed for lack of preserved remains. All we can say is that the

木造の斗栱(雲斗雲肘木)とする。同時代の中国や朝鮮にこれと同じ形の組物があったかどうかは、比較できる遺構がないのでわからない。ここでいえるのは、大径材が採れる環境にあったからこそ、斗と肘木を一体化する発想につながったことである。小さな部材を組み合わせてつくる三手先斗栱は、力を分散させつつ荷重を柱へ伝える方法で、大径材の少ない大陸で発達した方法である。他方、法隆寺金堂の雲斗雲肘木をつくるには、直径1.5mはある大木が必要となってくる。そんな雲斗雲肘木が表わす力の流れは、じつに簡潔明瞭である。昭和の大修理の際、隅垂木、尾垂木などの軒を支える材が屋根の重みで湾曲し、垂れ下がっていたのを、瓦や屋根土を降ろすと垂木がもとの姿にもどったという話がある。*1 創建時の工匠は、ヒノキが持つ独特の粘りやしなやかさをよくわかっていたのであろう。西院伽藍は607年に創建され、670年に焼失し、その後710年までの間に再建されたと考えると、そこにはほぼ100年、四代、五代ほどの世代交代がある。最初の建造に朝鮮渡来系の職工集団が関わったにしても、日本特有の素材であるヒノキを扱う経験値は、少なくとも再建時にはすでに十分に積み重ねられていたのではないか。

一方、伊勢神宮のヒノキは樹齢200年から800年のものが主要部分に使われているであろう。塗装をしない素木造とするため、遷宮された社殿のヒノキの瑞々しさ、清潔感は神々しいばかりで、いつの頃からか日本人のヒノキ信奉を象徴するものになっている。柱などの太い材は心持ち材である。柱は掘立式で地中に埋めこまれており、ここにも腐りにくいヒノキが選ばれる理由がある。だが、時とともに、いくらヒノキであろうとも腐食は進む。それでも20年で建てかえ時期が来るのかといえば、建物の寿命としてはまだ持つであろう。一方、屋根の萱葺の耐久性は20年が限度である。屋根が腐って雨漏りすれば、建物は急激に傷む。それでは屋根だけ葺きかえればよいではないか、となる。だがそこには、人を育て、形を伝えるというもう一つの目的がある。

20年で1サイクルというのは、もとの形を維持するのに有効な制度である。形の存続は、人と素材の育成と表裏一体であり、技術や信仰の継承でもある。若くして造替にかかわれば、その後、複数の造替を経験する機会はあるし、一族の二代、三代で知識や技術が共有される。それを30以上ある式年遷宮の「祭」を通して、大勢の人が関わりを持ちながら、信仰、しきたり、型、形、技術などが伝えられる。若いときは小さな社の建造から始まり、経験を積むにつれて大きな社を任されるという具合であろう。

ただ20年ごとの造替は、木材の豊富な日本だからこそ発想され、長

伊勢神宮内宮、風日祈宮
Kazahinomi-no-miya, Inner shrine, Ise Jingu

削り立てのヒノキの肌合い
The freshly planed texture of *hinoki* cypress, Ise Jingu

unification of the bearing blocks and bracket arms must have become possible because large-diameter trees were available in Japan. The three-stepped bracket complexes composed by assembling small parts was a method of distributing load and transmitting weight to pillars that was developed on the continent where large-diameter timber was in short supply. The cloud-shaped bearing blocks/bracket arms used in the Horyuji Kondo were possible because the carpenters had large trees 1.5 meters in diameter at their disposal. The flow of forces expressed in these cloud-shaped bracket complexes is very clear. The story is often told how, at the time of the major repairs for the Kondo and Five-story Pagoda conducted in 1940–1954, the corner rafters and tail rafters supporting the eaves had become bent and sagging because of the weight of the roof; but when the tiles and earth on the roof were removed, the rafters reverted to their original shape.[*1] The carpenters who built the buildings were no doubt well aware of the characteristic elasticity and flexibility of the cypress wood they were using. The Western Precinct was originally built in 607 but was burned down in 670. The buildings were later reconstructed, as we see today, by at least 710, and in that time about 100 years passed, a span of about four or five generations. While it may have been that craftsmen from the Korean peninsula or their descendants were the first builders, at least by the time of the reconstruction quite a good deal of experience with the handling of cypress wood, a material specific to Japan, would have been accumulated.

For Ise Jingu shrine, it is likely that cypress timber of between 200 and 800 years was used for the main members. The wood is not painted, so the freshness and immaculate feel of the cypress wood of the newly replaced buildings exudes the very presence of the divine, and has long been considered a symbol of Japanese devotion to *hinoki*. The stouter pillars and thick beams are made of cuts including the central core. Since the pillars are buried directly in the ground using the *hottate-shiki* method, this is a further reason that *hinoki*, which is strong against rot, is used there. Of course, even cypress will rot with the passage of time. After 20 years, when the time comes for the buildings to be replaced, they are actually still in quite good shape and would continue to serve for some time. The thatch of the roofs, however, will not last much more than 20 years, and if the roof should begin to leak, the building would quickly deteriorate. It might be possible to get by with just rethatching the roof. But there is another factor: the need to train younger people to build the shrines and to pass on to them the shapes and forms.

The system of replacing buildings after an interval of 20 years has been effective in maintaining the original forms. Passing down continuity of form goes hand in hand with the nurture of skilled craftsmen and of needed materials, the transmission of technology and of religious faith. A person who is first involved in the rebuilding while young has the chance to experience the replacement several times in his lifetime, and one particular family or workshop may be able to share knowledge and technology over two or three generations simultaneously. Through the replacement of many buildings during the *shikinen sengu* (transfer of the deity from old to new buildings at regular intervals), quite a large number of people will be involved, assuring the transmission of beliefs, customs, patterns and forms, as well as technology. Those who are young begin with the small shrines, and by the time they have grown older can be entrusted with the work for the large shrines. The whole notion of replacement every 20 years, however, would not even have been imaginable without abundant resources of wood. Some proportion of the materials are recycled in the rebuilding. The ridgepole-supporting pillars of the Inner and Outer shrines are replaned and used to replace the great

年にわたって実現してきたものである。そのなかには再生材も何割か含まれる。両宮正殿の棟持柱は削りなおされて宇治橋の大鳥居となり、さらに末社などで再利用されることはよく知られている。それをどのようなかたちでどの程度使うかは、時代時代の状況によって変化するだろう。だが、幾度にもわたって材が活用できるのは、やはりそこにヒノキが適切に使われているからであり、遷宮を支えてきたのがヒノキという木であった。

屋根裏から始まる日本化

日本では、6世紀半ばに朝鮮の百済から仏教が伝えられ、飛鳥から奈良時代のおよそ200年間、朝鮮や中国の建築様式で次々と寺院が建てられた。仏教の隆盛は教義の信仰とともに大陸文明を日本にもたらし、建築においても大陸の水準を目指して計画法、構造、意匠、技術が吸収され、日本建築の基礎が築かれた。

では、日本古来の建築と大陸様式の寺院建築との大きな違いは何だったのだろうか。それは屋根である。大陸様式は屋根に瓦を葺く。その構造技術は、瓦屋根の重い荷重を支えるために編み出されたものである。基壇を築き、礎石を置き、その上に柱を立てる。一方で、屋根荷重は垂木と梁でいったん受けてから柱へと伝えられる。組物は軒を大きく広げて深い軒裏をつくるとともに、垂木にかかる荷重を斗や肘木で何段階かに分散させながら柱に伝える。

ここで、どこまでが大陸式で、どこからが日本的表現なのかを考えるとき、垂木の形式と形態は有力な手掛かりを与えてくれる。一重か二重か、平行か扇状か、円形か角か、軒の荷重を受けているか、受けていないか。さらにいえば、垂木の部材寸法、地垂木と飛檐垂木の長さの差、斗栱の大きさや柱間寸法と垂木寸法との関係、反りのある、なしなど、多くの情報を提供する。

たとえば、唐招提寺金堂を例に挙げよう。寄棟造の大きな瓦屋根が載り、地垂木が円、飛檐垂木が角形断面で、三手先斗栱を組み、唐様式を踏襲した天平時代の金堂形式を残す建物といわれる。創建当時の堂を再現した模型や修理時の写真を見ると、地垂木は見えるところのみを円形断面とし、小屋組のなかは角材のままとする。中国や朝鮮の垂木材は細いマツの丸太を用いるが、木材の豊富な日本では、仏堂を建てるには太い材を割った心去り材を用い、円形断面を得るには、槍鉋を使って削りながら形を整えなければならなかった。日本の素材使いからいえば、角垂木の方が合理的でつくりやすい形だったのである。にもかかわらず、唐招提寺金堂では、見える部分だけであっても円形とし、

興福寺北円堂
Kofukuji Hokuendo

唐招提寺金堂、三手先斗栱と垂木
Bracket complexes and rafters, Toshodaiji Kondo

室生寺五重塔の軒裏
Rafters of Murouji Five-story Pagoda

torii gates at the Ujibashi bridge, and other parts are used by subordinate shrines. In what way and how much of the wood is recycled is likely to change from one period to another. But the fact that wood can thus be used and reused is because the cypress wood is so well-suited to the architecture in question; indeed, cypress is the wood that has sustained the *sengu* tradition.

Japanization Began Under the Roof

In the two hundred years of the Asuka and Nara periods during which Buddhism was introduced starting in the mid-sixth century from Paekche (Korea), numerous temples were built in the then-current architectural styles of China and Korea. Along with the doctrines of the Buddhist faith came the civilization of the continent. With regard to architecture, the foundations of Japanese architecture were laid as methods of layout, structure, design, and ornament, along with the technologies related to these, were absorbed in the endeavor to attain the same standard as found on the continent.

So what was the major difference between architecture as it had been built since ancient times and the continental architecture used for building temples? The roof.

Continental-style architecture was roofed with tiles and its structural technology had been developed in order to support the massive weight of a tiled roof. Building began with compacting a platform, placing foundation stones, and erecting pillars upon them. The weight of the roof, meanwhile, was first transferred to rafters and beams before being passed down to the pillars. Bracket complexes supported a deep eave overhang as well as used bearing blocks and bracket arms to distribute the weight on the rafters in stages as it was transmitted to the pillars.

When we try to determine what parts of the architecture of these buildings were "continental" and what parts were expressions of "Japanese" techniques, the shape and configuration of the rafters offer useful clues. A great deal of information can be obtained by noting whether there are single or double rafters, whether they are laid parallel or in fan shape, whether they are round or square in section, whether they receive the weight of the eaves or not, the measurements of the rafters, and the difference in length between the base rafters and flying rafters, as well as the relationship between the size of the bracket complexes or spacing of the pillars on the one hand and the measurements of the rafters on the other, and whether or not the rafters are curved or not.

The Toshodaiji Kondo, for example, has a huge hipped roof covered with tiles; the base rafters are round in section and the flying rafters are square in section; three-stepped bracket complexes are used. So the building is said to preserve the Tang-style type of *kondo* main hall introduced in the Tenpyo era. When we examine the replica of the Kondo made to show how it was originally built along with photos taken at the time of repairs, we can see that the base rafters are round only where they are visible and square within the structure of the core. Base rafters in China and Korea were laid using slender pine logs, but in Japan with its wealth of timber, rafters for Buddhist halls were made by splitting thick logs. To make the rafters round in section, they had to be painstakingly shaped using a spear plane. So from the point of view of the materials being used in Japan, it was more logical and easier to use square rafters. Nevertheless, for the Toshodaiji Kondo, if only for the parts that were visible, the rafters are rounded so as to be faithful to the "round base [rafter] and square flying [rafter]" model from the continent. We can see these rafters as evidence available even today of the value placed on the Tang style as the ideal of the time. As the Heian period began, circular rafters gradually gave way to square ones, until in due course square rafters were dominant.

「地円飛角」の軒裏をつくっている。この垂木は、唐様式を理想とした時代の価値観を今に物語る証といえる。円形の地垂木は平安時代に入ると方形に近づいていき、やがて角垂木が配置されるようになる。

垂木が軒の荷重を受ける構造材なのか、荷重をほぼ受けない化粧材なのかは、日本建築の大きな転換点となる。なぜなら、それが屋根と軒の形に大きな影響をおよぼしたからである。寺院建築で、法隆寺のように垂木が構造材として機能したのは、大陸様式が伝えられてから平安中期までとなり、さらに、重源（1121-1206）が宋の様式を取り入れて大仏様を導入した鎌倉時代初期となる。

平安時代の中頃、990年に建立された法隆寺の大講堂では、化粧垂木（構造材か否かは関係なく、軒下から見える垂木の総称）とは別に、その上に急勾配の野垂木をかけて屋根を葺き、天井のなかに見えない小屋組（野屋根）をつくる構造とした。これによって屋根荷重を野垂木と地垂木で分担できるようになり、さらに、屋根の勾配を急にして雨仕舞をよくしたり、化粧垂木の勾配を屋根勾配に左右されずに決められるようになり、軒の出を延ばせるようになった。こうして法隆寺の大講堂以降、野屋根をもつ構造が一般化し、日本に独特の深い軒裏空間がつくりだされていく。

さらに平安末期からは、野屋根の空間を利用して「桔木」と呼ばれる太い斜材の片持梁を入れ、てこの原理を利用して軒を支えるようになった。垂木が支えていた屋根荷重は桔木に肩代わりされるようになって、化粧垂木は構造上、ほぼ支持力を持たせなくてもよくなり、文字通り化粧となっていった。また、化粧垂木の勾配はゆるくなり、長くゆるやかに張り出した飛檐垂木は軒先を軽やかにし、軒裏の空間は穏やかな光に満たされて、下方にまわる縁とともに水平線が強調される姿となった。

降水量の多い日本では、大きな傘となる屋根をかけ、深い軒をつくり、風雨にさらされないつくりにしなければならない。そのもっとも洗練された例が、石山寺の多宝塔である。上重は四手先斗栱を組み、塔身とほぼ同じ長さで軒を長く延ばす。勾配はゆるく、軒先は軽快に反り上がり、軒下には「木の華」とでも呼びたくなる美しい組物が放射状に整然と並び、そこには光が射している。これは桔木が小屋組に入っているからこそ可能となった、軽快で伸びやかな屋根であり、軒である。

桔木は日本ならではの着想といわれ、マツ材が使われるが、マツはヒノキより2割ほど曲げ応力に強い。概して木の強度は応力に対し、曲げ、圧縮、引っ張り、剪断の順で弱くなる。適材適所とはよくいわれるが、まずそれよりも各応力に適した形が考案されて、木造建築の部材ができあがっている点が重要である。その部材の基本形には、必ず木の原

興福寺東金堂の軒裏
Underside of the eaves, Kofukuji Tokondo

法隆寺大講堂
Horyuji Lecture Hall

石山寺多宝塔
Ishiyamadera Tahoto pagoda

The question of whether rafters were structural materials to receive the weight of the eaves or were in fact exposed members that did not carry much weight marks a major turning point in Japanese architecture. For in fact, this had an important impact on the shape of the roof and of the eaves. In temple architecture, it was only from the time the continental style was introduced until the mid-Heian period (tenth-eleventh centuries) that rafters functioned as structural materials, as seen at Horyuji temple and in the early Kamakura period (late twelfth to early thirteenth century) in case of the Daibutsuyo style of Song China utilized by Chogen (1121–1206).

Horyuji's Lecture Hall (Daikodo) built in 990, has—in addition to the exposed rafters (a general term for rafters that are visible under the eaves, regardless of whether they are structural members or not)—steeply sloped hidden rafters (*nodaruki*) upon which the roof is laid, creating a hidden roof (*noyane*) that cannot be seen in the ceiling. This creation of a hidden roof made it possible to place the weight of the roof load on the hidden rafters and base rafters. It also made possible a more steeply inclined roof in order to improve rain run-off. By setting the incline of the exposed rafters independently of the slope of the roof, the eaves could be further extended. From the time of the Daikodo on, as structures incorporating a hidden roof became the general practice, the deep eave overhang that is distinctive to Japan gradually developed.

A further development was made in the late Heian period—the insertion of thick diagonal cantilever beams (*hanegi*) using the space of the hidden roof; these beams helped support extended eaves by applying the principle of leverage. Once the cantilever beams came to bear the weight of the roof that had been carried by the rafters, exposed rafters no longer had to structurally carry much weight and they became more like decorative or ornamental members. Also, the slope of the exposed rafters grew more gradual, and the gently sloping, long-extended flying rafters lightened the look of the eaves ends, and allowed more light into the space beneath the eaves and created forms that, along with the verandas that encircled buildings beneath them, accentuated the horizontality of the design.

To cope with the heavy rainfall of Japan, buildings had to be placed under large umbrella-like roofs and the eaves extended as far as possible beyond the walls in order to protect them from the wet. Perhaps one of the most refined examples of how this was achieved can be seen in the Ishiyamadera Tahoto pagoda built in 1194. The upper story has four-stepped bracket complexes that extend the eaves to a length almost equal to the diameter of the core. The incline of the roof is gentle and the eaves curve up slightly at their ends. Radiating out beneath the eaves, the orderly alignment of beautifully assembled bracket complexes that one could almost call "flowers in wood" catch the sunlight. This soaring, broadly extended roof and eave construction could only have been made possible by a hidden roof structure housing cantilevers.

For the cantilever, which is sometimes called a typically Japanese invention, pine wood is used, because pine is about 20 percent stronger under bending stress than *hinoki* cypress. In general, the strength of wood weakens against bending, compression, stretching, and shearing stress, in that order. We often hear the phrase "right materials in the right place," but what is even more important is how the parts used in wooden architecture are devised in the most appropriate shape according to the kind of stress they receive. What determines the fundamental shape of a member is always the above-mentioned principle of wood: cantilevers and rainbow tie beams work most effectively against the stress of bending, pillars and struts against compression, bracket tie beams (*toshihijiki*) and non-penetrating tie beams (*nageshi*) against stretching, and boat-shaped bracket arms against shearing

理が働いている。曲げを有効に活用したのは桔木や虹梁、圧縮は柱や束、引っ張りは通肘木や長押、剪断の対応には舟肘木である。特に、木は繊維と直角方向から集中的に加わる力（剪断力）にいちばん弱いので、舟肘木はそれを大きな面積で受けて力を分散させ、座屈を防ぐ方策である。構造的な対処以外にも、木口、鼻先、表面には丹や胡粉を塗り、干割れ、腐れ、防虫、防水対策として、意匠と一体化させながら、木を長きにわたって持たせる手法が考えられてきた。

地震と版築

日本の自然現象のなかで、雨とともに建築に大きな影響をおよぼしてきたのが地震である。この不可避の破壊力に対して、どのような対策が取られてきたのであろうか。

奈良時代には、すでに大陸からもたらされた礎石式が導入されていたにもかかわらず、伊勢神宮をはじめ、内裏や貴族の邸宅では、古来の掘立式で建物が築かれていた。では、掘立式が礎石式とくらべて未熟で原始的な工法かというと、決してそうではない。これは地震や台風の際、建物に加わる水平力に強く、むしろ日本の自然条件には合ったやり方といえる。

掘立式といっても、地中に穴を掘り、土に柱を挿して埋めるだけではない。そこには必ず根固めという作業がある。1.5mほど地面を掘って地固めをし、地中に石や木の板を据えて柱を立て、柱の周囲に石を入れて埋めていく。この方法は鉄道線路の割石と同様、石の角が互いに力を相殺しつつ分散させる。掘立式はまわりが固められているため、柱の位置が固定されるので、その点で石の上に立つ礎石式よりも地震や台風には有利といえる。

一方、法隆寺では地山まで土をはぎ取り、その上に版築をして地盤を固め、途中で礎石を置き、さらに版築を重ねて礎石のまわりを固め、柱を立てている。版築とは、まず割石を敷き詰め、その上に石灰を混ぜた粘土と小砂利をつき固めて10cmから15cm厚の層にし、さらに砂を敷いて同じ作業を繰り返して1mから2mほど重ねた地業である。中国から伝わったといわれるが、日本では古墳の基礎固めにおいてすでに使用が確認されており、さらに法隆寺以降、時代が下ってからも寺院建設時の地盤強化に必要な基礎だった。これは地盤整備・改良というだけでなく、建物の下に免震層をつくり、地震の水平力の揺れに共振しない仕組みである。今でいう免震構造に近い。この版築地盤が、地震対策に有効であることを先人たちはよく知っていたのであろう。

舟肘木。春日大社若宮神社、拝舎
A boat-shaped bracket arm, Kasuga Taisha Wakamiya Shrine

正倉院正倉の礎石
Foundation stones, Shosoin Repository

伊勢神宮、内宮・外幣殿の掘立柱
Buried posts of the Geheiden, Inner shrine, Ise Jingu

stress. Wood is particularly weak against force concentrated in a direction perpendicular to the fiber of the wood (shearing force), so boat-shaped bracket arms provide a broad surface to receive and distribute load, thereby preventing bending or breakage. The technology developed to assure long life in buildings also included methods other than those relating to structure. In combination with the design, the cut ends of wood, nosings, and surfaces were coated with vermillion paint or *gofun* white pigment as methods to control splitting, rot, insect infestation, and keep out moisture.

Earthquakes and Packed-Earth Podiums

Other than rain, the natural phenomenon that has had the greatest impact on Japanese architecture is earthquakes. How did early architecture deal with this powerful and unpredictable threat?

In the Nara period, although the foundation-stone method had already been introduced from the continent, many important buildings, including Ise Jingu shrine, the imperial palace, and the residences of aristocrats were built using the ancient method of burying the posts directly in the ground (*hottate-shiki*) that goes back to Jomon times. One might think this earthfast post method somehow undeveloped or primitive, yet that is hardly the case. A method strong against horizontal forces such as brought by earthquakes and typhoon winds, it was admirably suited to natural conditions in Japan.

The post-in-ground method is not just a matter of digging a hole, inserting a post and then filling in the hole. It involves a whole process of consolidation of the foot around the post. A firm footing is first consolidated at a depth of about 1.5 meters, the post erected on a foundation stone or a thick wooden slab within the hole, and then stones added to fill in the hole. This method, as with the trackbed used in laying railways, makes use of the sharp edges of stones working against each other to prevent shifting of the footing. Since the ground around the posts in the post-in-ground method is well packed, the posts are stronger against earthquakes and typhoons than if erected on foundation stones.

At Horyuji, however, a different way of consolidating the foundations has been used known as the packed-earth (*hanchiku*) method. The earth is first dug out down to bedrock and then the foundations consolidated with successive layers of fill pounded into place. The foundation stones are set into this base and the earth around them firmly packed. The pillars of the buildings are erected on a consolidated foundation podium.

The packed-earth foundation podium is made by spreading a layer of crushed rock in a pit and consolidating the rock by adding clay mixed with limestone and gravel and pounding in with a tamper (*tako*) in a layer 10 to 15 centimeters deep. This process is repeated to form a firm foundation between one and two meters deep with the upper part and side parts surrounded by stone slabs. It is often said that this method was introduced from China, but study of Japan's ancient *kofun* tumuli has confirmed that it was practiced in Japan from even before that. From the time of Horyuji on down, this was the necessary base for consolidating the earth when building temples. The packed-earth method is used not only to provide firm foundations for the building but to create what is now called a base-isolated layer under the building, a device for absorbing the horizontal forces of earthquakes and dispersing swaying set in motion by the earth's tremors. It is quite similar to seismic isolation structures used today. The people of ancient times seem to have known that the *hanchiku*-prepared foundation was effective against earthquakes.

円柱がつくる祈りの空間

　本書で取り上げている建築をひとことで括るとすれば、円柱文化の建築ということになる。そこは木太い円柱で構成された、祈りの建築空間である。円柱文化の建築は、有史から鎌倉時代あたりで転換期を迎え、鎌倉を境に室町以降は角柱の文化へと移行する。

　祈りの建築空間には、主従がある。主となる神や仏のための空間と、従となる人間のための空間である。あるいは、ルイス・カーン(1901-1974)の言葉を借りれば、仕えられる空間と、仕える空間である。古代の寺院では、堂は全面的に仏のための建物で、いわば仏の住まうところと見なされた。そこには人間が入る余地はほとんどつくられておらず、仏に仕える人間は、堂の外側やその周囲で祈りを捧げるものとされた。ここに空間の序列化が生まれる。当然、内側は主体となる神・仏の空間、外側は客体となる人間の空間となるが、外側の従の空間をつくるとき、「庇」という独特な方法を用いて内部空間が拡張された。

　庇の空間にはいくつかの形がある。古代の仏堂は、唐招提寺金堂で見られるように、柱を二重にめぐらせて立て、中心部分(身舎)とその周囲に取りつく部分(庇)で構成された。また、三佛寺投入堂のように、庇を周囲や前後に差し掛けて空間を拡張する形があり、さらに中心部分(身舎)と庇を一連の屋根でつなげたものに、嚴島神社の両流造や宇治上神社の拝殿がある。また、裳階と呼ばれる差し掛け屋根のついた囲いを外周に取りつける例は、法隆寺金堂や五重塔においてすでに見られ、平等院鳳凰堂や東大寺金堂はその代表例である。正堂に対する礼堂、内陣に対する外陣という形もある。室生寺金堂、東大寺法華堂、東大寺二月堂に見られる。

　主従空間の関係は、建築の構成要素についても明確に分けられ、日本建築をつくる際の法則性をつくりだしてきた。柱の形状や太い細い、天井や床の高低差やその形式(たとえば、格天井や化粧屋根裏、板床や土間床)によって、空間の主従の境界が明示される。そのとき、神や仏を直接取り囲む空間には、必ず円柱が使われる。円柱とは、聖なる空間を形づくる正式な柱である。日本では、円柱をつくるのは丸太の四つ割りから八角、十六角と、斧や手斧で斫ったり、槍鉋で削ったりする工程を経て円にするため、手間をかけてつくらなければならない。つくる過程からも、円柱は特別な柱の形であり、それが立つことで形成される空間は特別な場所となる。

　また、法隆寺の金堂や五重塔の裳階には角柱が使われているが、これは裳階が人間の用に資する従の空間であるためで、機能面からは、

東大寺法華堂・正堂
Image Hall (*shodo*), Todaiji Hokkedo Hall

法界寺阿弥陀堂
Amida Hall, Hokaiji

宇治上神社拝殿
Worship hall, Ujigami Shrine

The Columns of Religious Spaces

It might be possible to sum up the buildings presented in this book as the architecture of a "round-column" culture. They are all structures built for the purpose of prayer and religious devotion built using thick wooden columns. This round-column culture already existed in Japan at the beginning of recorded history and came to a turning point around the time of the Kamakura period; from the Muromachi period onward, architecture shifted to a culture of square posts.

Religious architectural space is structured on a leader-follower principle. It consists of specific spaces for the divine (the deity enshrined) and specific spaces for the human beings who worship and serve the divine. Louis Kahn (1901–1974) described this relationship as "served and servant space." In the ancient temples, the halls are structures built entirely for native or Buddhist deities and viewed as their abodes. Almost no space was set aside for humans in their design. Those serving the deities were left to offer prayers from outside in the surrounding space. This led to the ranking of spaces. The inside was naturally set aside as the space for the deity and outside was available for the people who were the visitors or servants. But in creating that outside space of service, Japanese temples adopted the distinctive method of expanding the inside space by adding aisles (*hisashi*).

The buildings presented here exemplify a number of forms of aisle space. Ancient temple and shrine halls, as we can see in the Toshodaiji Kondo, were basically made by erecting columns in two concentric layouts, one for the central core or *moya*, and the other forming an aisle or enclosure encircling the core. Another type, which is seen in the Nageiredo hall at Sanbutsuji temple, was attached around or in front or back of the core as an expansion of the space. There are also examples where the *hisashi* and the core area are covered by a continuous roof, as seen in the *nagarezukuri* flowing roof at Itsukushima Shrine and the worship hall of Ujigami Shrine. Examples where a pent roof enclosure called a *mokoshi* is attached around the circumference of the core are seen in the Horyuji Kondo and Five-story Pagoda, and the Phoenix Hall at Byodoin and the Todaiji Kondo are leading examples as well. There are also configurations consisting of an image hall (*shodo*) and worship hall (*raido*) or of an inner sanctuary (*naijin*) and outer sanctuary (*gejin*). These can be seen in the Murouji Kondo, Todaiji Hokkedo, and Todaiji Nigatsudo halls.

The leader-follower or served-servant relationship is clearly demarcated by the structural elements of the architecture and has formed the rules for building in Japanese architecture. The layout of the pillars and use of thick or thin posts, the height of ceilings and floors and their styles (for example, coffered ceiling vs. visible roof structure; board floor vs. pounded earthen floor) clearly signal the boundaries of served and servant. In these buildings, the pillars surrounding the space directly enclosing the deity or deities are invariably round. Round pillars are the formal element for creating sacred space. In Japan, round pillars are made by first splitting a log into four. The four pieces are then shaped with an adze to eight sides and then sixteen sides and finally rounded off using a spear plane. This involves a great deal of precise and painstaking labor. So in terms of the process by which they are made as well, circular pillars are a very special class of pillar, and erecting them establishes a special place.

The pillars of the *mokoshi* pent-roof enclosures of the Horyuji Kondo and Five-story Pagoda are square in section, and this is because the enclosed space is the "servant" space set aside for human use. Square posts are used also for parts of a building that help to protect it or ventilate it or bring in light,

建物を保護したり、風や光を入れたり、外観の均衡を図る目的でつけられた付加物であるからである。さらに平安時代に入ると、裳階や庇に面取りした角柱が使われるようになる。三佛寺投入堂のところでも述べたように（p. 154参照）、面取り柱は、もともとは円柱を略した仕上げであり、時代が下がるにつれてその初源的なあり方は消えていき、面取り幅は小さくなる。材幅に対して、平安時代1/5前後、鎌倉時代1/6〜1/8、室町時代1/8〜1/10、桃山時代1/10〜1/12、江戸時代1/12以上がその目安である。平等院鳳凰堂（平安時代）の裳階が1/5.7、宇治上神社拝殿（鎌倉時代）が1/7.25、銀閣寺東求堂同仁斎（室町時代）が1/10、園城寺光浄院（桃山時代）の縁側の柱が1/11となる。概して、面取りが大きければ大きいほどざっくりとした大らかな印象となり、小さくなればなるほど繊細できっちりした感じになる。この小さなディテールの寸法には、その時代らしさを反映するプロポーション感覚が表わされており、逆にいえば、その時代らしさをつくるのが面取り寸法なのである。

　神や仏の境界を形づくる円柱空間は永遠性を求める聖域であり、それは時代を経ても大切に守られてきた。一方で、その周囲をめぐる人間のための空間は、様々な形をもって付加され、変化し、多様な空間の形式、差異化を図るディテールを生みだしていった。神と人間との関係を空間において序列化し、秩序を形成していく過程は、日本建築の空間発展史そのものといえるだろう。

銀閣寺・東求堂同仁斎の柱と内法・長押
Detail of the Dojinsai study, Togudo hall, Ginkakuji

or that are designed to give the building balance when seen from outside. When we come to the Heian period, we find pillars of the *mokoshi* or verandas that have been chamfered. As mentioned in the chapter on the Nageiredo of Sanbutsuji temple (see p.155), chamfered pillars are those for which the process of making a circular pillar has been abbreviated, but as the times moved on, the original meaning of chamfering gradually faded, and the chamfered sides grew smaller and smaller. Looking at the extent of the chamfering, in the Heian period the width of the beveling was around one-fifth the width of the post, and decreased to one-sixth to one-eighth in the Kamukura period, to one-eighth to one-tenth in the Muromachi period, one-tenth to one-twelfth in the Momoyama period, and to a very small one-twelfth or even smaller in the Edo period. The proportion of the bevel of the *mokoshi* posts of the Byodoin Phoenix Hall (1053) is 1/5.7, of the Ujigami Shrine worship hall (thirteenth century) 1/7.25, the Dojinsai study of the Togudo hall at Ginkakuji temple (1485) is 1/10, and the veranda posts of Onjoji (Miidera) temple's Kojoin (1601) are 1/11. Overall, the larger the chamfering the rougher the look, while the smaller beveling makes the pillars look neater and finer. The measurements of this small detail of the architecture are an expression of the sense of proportions of the times; in fact, chamfering was a detail that became one of the hallmarks of each era.

The space demarcated for the divine by round pillars is the sanctuary of the sought-after eternity, and its sanctity has been faithfully preserved throughout the ages. The surrounding space for the use of humans, meanwhile, has been attached in all sorts of ways, has been altered, assumed diverse styles and shapes, and has given birth to various distinguishing details. It is interesting to note that the history of the development of space in Japanese architecture is essentially one following the ranking of relations between human beings and the divine and in the process of establishing order in such relations.

［凡例］
- 本書の建物名（和文）については、国指定の文化財の場合、おおむね国の指定名称に従った。
- 時代区分は文化庁編集・発行『国宝・重要文化財建造物目録』（2012年）に準じ、以下の通りとした。
    飛鳥時代（593年－709年・和銅2年）
    奈良時代（710年・和銅3年－793年・延暦12年）
    平安時代（794年・延暦13年－1184年・元暦元年）
    鎌倉時代（1185年・文治元年－1332年・元弘2年／正慶元年）
    室町時代（1333年・元弘3年／正慶2年－1572年・元亀3年）
    桃山時代（1573年・天正元年－1614年・慶長19年）
    江戸時代（1615年・元和元年－1867年・慶応3年）
- 建立年代については、おもに文化庁編集・発行『国宝・重要文化財建造物目録』（2012年）に準じたが、一部近年の調査により年代が判明したものについてはそれを参考にした。
- 図面については、おもに文化庁所蔵図面、修理工事報告書を基本とした。古建築の計画尺度は尺寸であるため、図面の寸法は尺（曲尺・約30.3cm）で表わし、適宜メートルを併記した。スケールバーには曲尺とメートルの縮尺を両方示した。なお、説明の便宜上、法隆寺金堂・五重塔の図面は高麗尺で、唐招提寺金堂の図面は唐尺で表わした。
- 巻末にまとめた掲載建造物の規模形式については、おおむね文化庁編集・発行『国宝・重要文化財建造物目録』（2012年）に従った。

［Notes］
- Historical periods follow the dates given in *Kokuho juyo bunkazai kenzobutsu mokuroku* (Catalogue of National Treasure- and Important Cultural Property-designated Structures), edited by the Agency for Cultural Affairs and published in 2012:
    Asuka period (593–709)
    Nara period (710–793)
    Heian period (794–1184)
    Kamakura period (1185–1332)
    Muromachi period (1333–1572)
    Momoyama period (1573–1614)
    Edo period (1615–1867)
- Construction periods are generally according to the above catalogue (2012), but in some cases reflect newly determined periods of construction due to recent survey findings.
- The drawings in this volume are mainly from the collection of the Agency for Cultural Affairs and reports of repair projects. The traditional units of length for ancient buildings are *shaku* and *sun* (one-tenth of *shaku*), and so the measurements in the drawings are given in *shaku* (*kanejaku*: approx. 30.3 cm); metric measurements are added where deemed appropriate. The scale bars are shown both in meters and in *kanejaku*. The commentaries on the drawings for the Horyuji temple Kondo and Five-story Pagoda, however, cite the *komajaku* (Korean *shaku*) and for the Toshodaiji temple Kondo cite the *toujaku* (Tang Chinese *shaku*).

伊勢神宮

建立年代　2013年造替
所在地　　三重県伊勢市

Ise Jingu Shrine

Completed: Renewed 2013
Location: Ise, Mie prefecture

時代背景

　伊勢神宮は正式には「神宮」といい、皇大神宮（内宮）と豊受大神宮（外宮）を中心とする別宮、摂社、末社、所管社を含めた125社の総称である。内宮は天照大御神を、外宮は豊受大御神を祀る。天照大御神は日（太陽）にたとえられる神であり、皇室の御祖神とされ、豊受大御神は天照大御神の食事をつかさどる神であり、日本人の主食である米をはじめとする衣食住、ひいては産業の恵みを授ける神とされる。

　内宮は伊勢湾に注ぐ五十鈴川の右岸に位置し、その背後に広がる神路山および島路山と呼ばれる山々を宮域とする。外宮は高倉山の北麓、内宮より西北約5キロの地点に位置する。神宮の創祀は今から2,000年以上さかのぼると伝えられるが、社殿を含めて現在のような祭祀形式が確立する時期は、7世紀後半の天武・持統朝の頃と考えられている。平安時代後期に編纂された『太神宮諸雑事記』に、690（持統天皇4）年には内宮の遷宮が、692（同6）年には外宮の遷宮が記録され、一般にこれを式年遷宮の初回と数える。式年遷宮とは、一定の期年で新殿を設営し、そこにご神体を遷す祭儀である。

　神宮の式年は20年ごとと定められており、1,300年以上にわたって連綿と営まれてきた。室町から戦国動乱期（15世紀-16世紀）に中絶期間を経たが、2013（平成25）年で第62回を迎えている。神殿に隣接して同じ広さの宮地が用意されており、式年ごとにかわるがわる一方の敷地を用いて、まったく同じ姿形で建てかえられる。造替は内宮・外宮の正殿をはじめとする社殿、五重（外宮は四重）の垣、門、さらには別宮以下の諸社、鳥居、宇治橋にいたるまで順次行われる。

　正殿は唯一神明造と呼ばれる神宮独特の形式で、柱は根元を地中に埋めこむ掘立柱とする。材はすべてヒノキである。構造柱のほかに、正殿の中央、床下に掘立式で心御柱が立つ。平面規模は正面3間・側面2間、切妻造、萱葺、平入り、棟木の上には堅魚木を並べ、破風の先端が延びて交差する千木がそびえる。

　ヒノキの用材は、古代から13世紀末までは背後の宮域を御杣山（神宮の用材を採る山林）としたが、鎌倉時代末には良材が不足し、以降はおもに木曾のヒノキが用いられている。大正時代からは200年計画で古代の御杣山の復元が図られ、五十鈴川上流の山で植樹と手入れが行われている。第62回式年遷宮では、御造営用材全量の23％が約700年ぶりに神宮の宮域林から供給された。

特徴と見どころ

　場の力、形の力、素材の力。さらに、それを保つ人の力。伊勢神宮の神さびる佇まいは、これらの力が不可分なかたちで作用し合って生起する。場の力を喚起するのは、様々な触媒である。神域へと導く古杉繁る参道。苔むす岩。奥の山々から湧き出でて海へとつながる川の流れ。千年の森。悠久の時間の感覚と、循環・再生を繰り返す自然のもつ生命力の連想が、日本の神の観念と重なり合う。

　杉木立のなか、社殿は素木のヒノキと萱葺という一見素朴な材料でつくられ、環境との調和を見せる。一方で、この素朴さの趣はまた、洗練とも共存する。素材の精を活かしたかたちで、質感の美しさが引き出されている。幾何学的で力強い唯一神明造は、起源を古代の高倉に見る説もあるが、その単純明快な形は抽象性を帯び、神殿建築として結晶している。四重・五重の垣や様々な結界は、禁忌や畏れの感覚を触発し、そこから見え隠れする奥の気配が、神の存在を予感させる。

　20年ごとの式年遷宮は、まるで生き物が新陳代謝するように、社殿に若々しい生命力を吹きこみ、その形を半永久的に保存し、伝えてきた。長い時間軸のなかで、20年を節目にして人と素材を育てる。そして、材木は山から伐り出すだけではなく、旧社殿の用材を削り直して再生し、巧みに再利用してその命を使い切るのである。造替ごとに代から代へと伝授され、受け継がれてきた思想、情報、技術は膨大なものであり、計り知れないほど貴重なものである。

内宮・月讀宮
Tsukiyomi-no-miya, Inner shrine

Historical Background

Ise Jingu shrine—also known as Ise Grand Shrine—refers to a complex of 125 associated, auxiliary, and subordinate shrines centered on the Kotai Jingu (Naiku, the Inner Shrine) and Toyouke Daijingu (Geku, the Outer Shrine). The Inner Shrine venerates the sun goddess Amaterasu Omikami, considered the divine ancestor of the Imperial family. The Outer Shrine enshrines Toyouke no Omikami, the goddess who provides meals to Amaterasu and grants the blessings of food (such as rice, the staple of the Japanese diet), clothing, and shelter and, by extension, industry in general.

The Inner Shrine is located on the right bank of the Isuzu River, which flows into Ise Bay, against the backdrop of Mt. Kamiji and Mt. Shimaji. The Outer Shrine is located about five kilometers northwest of the Inner Shrine and at the northern foot of Mt. Takakura. The origins of Ise Grand Shrine are said to date back more than 2,000 years but the current format of rituals related to its shrine buildings is thought to have been established in the late seventh century during the time of Emperor Tenmu (d. 686) and Empress Jito (645–702). The *Daijingu shozojiki* (Records of Ise Grand Shrine) compiled in the late Heian period documents a *sengu* for the Inner Shrine in 690 and for the Outer Shrine in 692; these are generally counted as the first *shikinen sengu* (the ritual transfer, at regular intervals, of deities to newly constructed shrine buildings).

At Ise Jingu the transfer interval is set at 20 years and the *shikinen sengu* tradition has continued for more than 1,300 years. There was a break during the fifteenth and sixteenth centuries, but 2013 marked the 62nd renewal. Two adjacent sacred spaces that share the same dimensions lie side by side; at each interval the old building is removed and replaced with an identical new on the neighboring plot. The structures that are replaced in turn over time include the main sanctuaries and other buildings of the Inner and Outer Shrines, their layered fences and gates, the buildings and *torii* gates of the subordinate shrines, and even the Ujibashi bridge.

Exhibiting the *yuiitsu shinmei-zukuri* style unique to Ise Grand Shrine, the main sanctuaries are built with pillars sunk into the ground at their base. All the timber used is *hinoki* cypress. In addition to structural pillars, each main sanctuary has a central *shin-no-mihashira* pillar embedded in the ground beneath the floor. Each main sanctuary is three bays wide and two bays deep, entered on its non-gable side, and has a gabled roof covered in thatch. *Katsuogi* billets line the roof ridge and the bargeboards extend beyond the ridge to rise as forked *chigi* finials.

From ancient times through the late thirteenth century, the *hinoki* cypress used in construction was harvested from the sacred Misomayama timberlands behind the shrine precincts. Since the early fourteenth century, when it became difficult to secure material of adequate quality there, *hinoki* from the Kiso area (Nagano prefecture) has been used. A 200-year project to restore the Misomayama timberlands was launched in the early twentieth century, and planting and maintenance has continued in the mountains at the upper reaches of the Isuzu River. At the 62nd *shikinen sengu* renewal in 2013, 23 percent of the cypress used in the construction was supplied from the Misomayama timberlands, the first time its timber was used in some 700 years.

Characteristics and Highlights

The magnificent atmosphere of the Ise Jingu shrine is the result of the interaction of powerful spaces, strong forms, robust materials, and of the piety of the people who maintain it. The power of the space is catalyzed by a number of features: the approach to the shrine precincts lined with lush, ancient Japanese cedar, the mossy rocks, the current of a river that flows from deep in the mountains and connects with the sea, the thousand-year-old forest. Associations with a sense of the eternal and the vitality of a natural world continually cycling and renewed overlap with Japan's concept of the divine.

Standing among towering cedars, the shrine buildings constructed of plain *hinoki* cypress and thatch—seemingly such simple materials—are in harmony with their environment. At the same time, the simplicity goes hand in hand with refinement. Giving life to the spirit of the materials draws out the beauty of their texture. Geometrically powerful, the *yuiitsu shinmei-zukuri* style may, according to one theory, have originated in the raised storehouses of ancient times, but the plain, clear shapes, bordering on the abstract, have crystalized in the distinctive style of shrine architecture. The four- to five-layered fences and various other types of boundaries evoke a sense of the taboo and of awe, while fleeting glimpses of what lies behind them inspire awareness of the presence of the divine.

Rebuilding every 20 years breathes a youthful vitality into the shrine buildings—as if they were living things reborn—and preserves and conveys their form semi-permanently. Over a great span of time, 20 years is an appropriate juncture for the cultivation of both people and materials. New lumber is not only harvested from the mountains but lumber from the old shrine buildings is re-planed and revived and lives on through skillful reuse. The philosophy, knowledge, and techniques passed down from generation to generation with each rebuilding are immeasurably vast and precious.

内宮・風日祈宮の切妻屋根。萱葺きのエッジを直角ではなく、鋭角に刈りこんだ切れの
よいディテール。萱という素朴な素材への洗練された扱い。8本の鞭掛けは、角材から
円錐形に削り出したシンボリックな形態で、その影が棟持柱に映りこむ

The gabled roof of the Kazahinomi-no-miya sanctuary at the Inner Shrine. The trimming of the thatch at the gable to an acute rather than a right angle is a detail that imparts refinement to a material that is essentially very simple. The shadows of the eight, symbolically shaped *muchikake* pins under the peak of the roof—timbers square in section but tapered toward the tips—are reflected on the ridge-bearing post.

遷宮されたばかりの内宮の別宮・風日祈宮を古殿池から見る。別宮も正殿の唯一神明造であるが、規模や細部が異なる。古殿池では旧殿解体後も中央に立つ心御柱はそのままに置かれ、小さな切妻屋根の心御柱覆屋がかけられる

The just-rebuilt Kazahinomi-no-miya sanctuary at the Inner Shrine, seen from the empty site of its previous incarnation. Such associated sanctuaries are built in the same *yuiitsu shinmei-zukuri* style as the main sanctuaries, but differ in scale and in detail. The small, gable-roofed structure seen in the foreground is the enclosure for the *shin-no-mihashira* pillar which is left standing after the dismantling of the old shrine.

内宮・荒祭宮の屋根と棟飾り。棟上には6本の堅魚木が載り、妻側では破風の先端を延ばした千木が交差する。堅魚木の起源は、藁や萱を縄で屋根の棟に結わえつけたその結び目を覆い、雨による傷みを防ぐものである。のちには豪族、さらには天皇の住居のみに許される権威の象徴となり、やがて伊勢神宮をはじめとする神明造などの社殿に装飾的に用いられるようになった

The roof and ridge ornaments of the Aramatsuri-no-miya sanctuary at the Inner Shrine. Six *katsuogi* billets lie along the top of the ridge and the elongated bargeboards at the gable ends rise to form forked finials called *chigi*. The billets originate in protective covers for knots in the rope with which straw or thatch was tied to the ridge. They later became symbols of authority permitted only on the residences of powerful families, and were eventually limited to use by the emperor. Ultimately *katsuogi* came to be used decoratively in *shinmei-zukuri* and some other styles of shrine buildings.

内宮・荒祭宮。ヒノキの削り立ての肌は匂い立つような美しさ。柱は芯持ち材が使われており、瑞垣には上質な中杢材が使われている。白い玉石は宮川の川原で採取されたもので、式年遷宮の際、この敷石までも新たにされる

The Aramatsuri-no-miya sanctuary at the Inner Shrine. The beauty of the freshly planed surfaces of the cypress has an almost fragrant beauty. The pillars are made from logs with the central core while the *mizugaki* inner fence uses flat-cut (*nakamoku*) boards. Collected from the Miyagawa river riverbed, even the white pebbles are replaced on the occasion of each *shikinen sengu*.

内宮・荒祭宮。外側には、長短の円柱を交互に立てた外玉垣がめぐらされ、その内側は、縦板を密に並べた瑞垣で囲われる。奥まるにつれ、神域の禁忌の感覚が強められる。地面では敷石の色を変え、外側は黒みを帯びた「清石」が、内側には「御白石」が敷かれている

Aramatsuri-no-miya sanctuary at the Inner Shrine. The building is surrounded by an inner fence (*mizugaki*) made of closely spaced vertical boards and an outer fence (*tonotamagaki*) made of alternating short and long cylindrical posts. Deeper spaces are invested with a more powerful sense of the sacred and the taboo. The color of the stones covering the ground also varies, with darker *kiyoishi* stones on the perimeter and lighter *oshiraishi* stones on the inside.

(上)内宮・外幣殿。東の妻側にあたる朝の光。古神宝類を収める

(Above) Geheiden outer treasury at the Inner Shrine, with the morning sun striking its east gable end. The Geheiden stores the ancient sacred treasures.

(右)内宮・外幣殿の棟持柱と柱。掘立式で地中に埋めこむ。礎石工法に比べて掘立式は地震や台風の水平力に強い。桁と梁は柱のなかで「渡りあご」で接合され、やはり水平力に対処した工法。その仕口やクサビの木口には胡粉を塗る。棟持柱は垂直ではなく内転びに立つ

(Right) Gable-end post at the Geheiden outer treasury of the Inner Shrine. The posts are buried directly in the ground, a method more robust against the horizontal forces of earthquakes and typhoons than if placed on foundation stones. Longitudinal and transverse beams connect to the posts using *watariago* cogged joints, again a method to address horizontal forces. Rather than standing perfectly straight, the gable-end posts lean slightly inward.

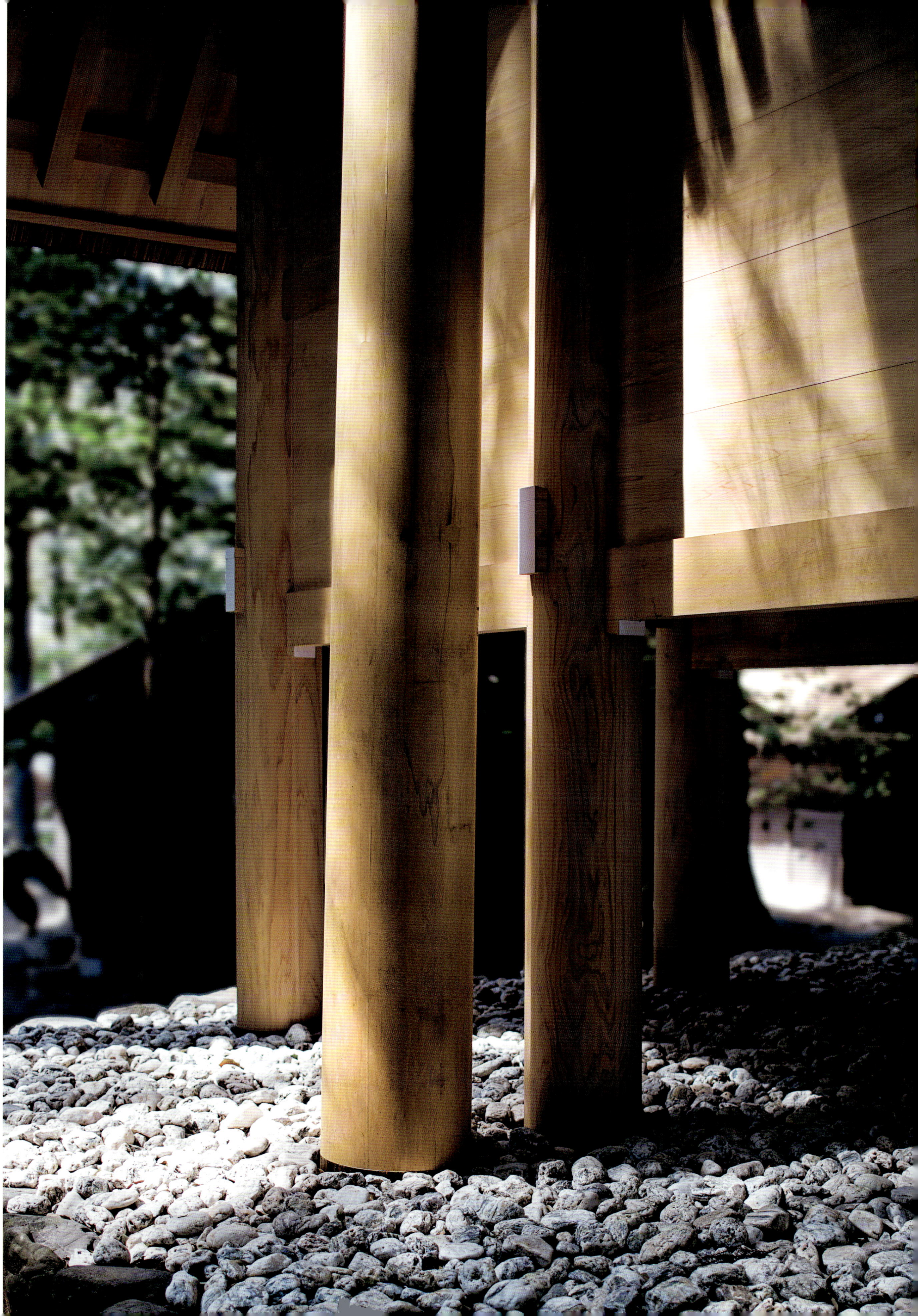

内宮・荒祭宮と古殿池。隣り合わせで東西に二つの敷地が用意されており、20年ごとに
交互に建てかえられる。次の式年遷宮ではふたたび同じ位置に心御柱が立てられ、神の
座として更新される

The Aramatsuri-no-miya sanctuary at the Inner Shrine and its previous site. Every twenty years the sanctuary is rebuilt, its location alternating between two adjacent sites aligned east-to-west. During the next *sengu* transfer, a fresh *shin-no-mihashira* pillar is placed in the same position on the old site to serve as a new seat for the deity.

内宮・忌火屋殿。諸祭典の際、神の御饌を用意する火をおこし、調理する建物。ここでは
屋根と瑞垣のみを新造する。新旧の素材を並置させた佇まいが興味深い。すべてではなく、
傷みやすい部分のみ交換し、更新するのも式年遷宮の考え方の一環

Imibiyaden hall of sacred fire at the Inner Shrine. This building is where fires are lit to prepare and cook sacred foods for various ceremonies. Here, only the roof and the *mizugaki* inner fence are rebuilt, and the combination of new and old materials creates a fascinating atmosphere. Replacing and renewing only those parts of a shrine building that are prone to deterioration, rather than the entire structure, is also part of the concept of *shikinen sengu*.

（上）内宮・由貴御倉（手前）と御酒殿（奥）。由貴御倉は、古くは御饌祭の供えものなどを納めておく倉。御酒殿は、古くは諸神に供える神酒を醸造したという。式年遷宮したばかりで、ヒノキが初々しく輝く
（下）御酒殿（手前）、由貴御倉（奥）の前には蕃塀と呼ばれる屋根つき衝立状の板塀が立つ。一種の目隠しではあるが、恐れ多いものへの遠慮、日本的な「はばかる」という感覚を形にしたもの

(Top) Yuki no Mikura (foreground) and Misakadono (background) at the Inner Shrine. In ancient times, the Yuki no Mikura was a storehouse for keeping offerings used in the Mikesai ceremony, while the Misakadono was used to brew sake to be offered to the various gods. Just rebuilt, their *hinoki* cypress shines with a youthful freshness.
(Bottom) Roofed, partition-like wooden fences called *banpei* stand before both the Misakadono (foreground) and the Yuki no Mikura (background). A form of screen, they embody the instinct of reserve or deference—in which direct display or access to the power of the divine is avoided.

内宮・由貴御倉のディテール。正殿や別宮をつくるための必要な知識、技術、工法が、このような小規模な社殿にもすべて含まれている。
(上)柱・桁・棟との間の空隙は、木の収縮に対する手立て
(下)屋根板の木裏を雨の当たる上に向けて反りを防ぐ。また、庇板を1枚の幅広板にせず2枚に分けることで、木の収縮による割れに対応する

Details of the Yuki no Mikura at the Inner Shrine. Smaller-scale shrine buildings such as this incorporate the same knowledge, skills, and techniques needed to build the main and associated sanctuaries.
(Top) Gaps between pillars, purlins and ridgepoles are a measure taken to address wood contraction.
(Bottom) Roof boards of the gate are oriented with their inner surfaces facing out, where the rain will strike, to prevent warping. In addition, using two overlapping boards for the eaves rather than one broader board prevents splitting as the wood contracts.

法隆寺 金堂・五重塔・廻廊

国宝
建立年代　7-8世紀初期
所在地　奈良県生駒郡

Horyuji Temple Kondo (Main Hall),
Five-story Pagoda, and Corridors

National Treasures
Completed: 7th–early 8th century
Location: Ikoma district, Nara prefecture

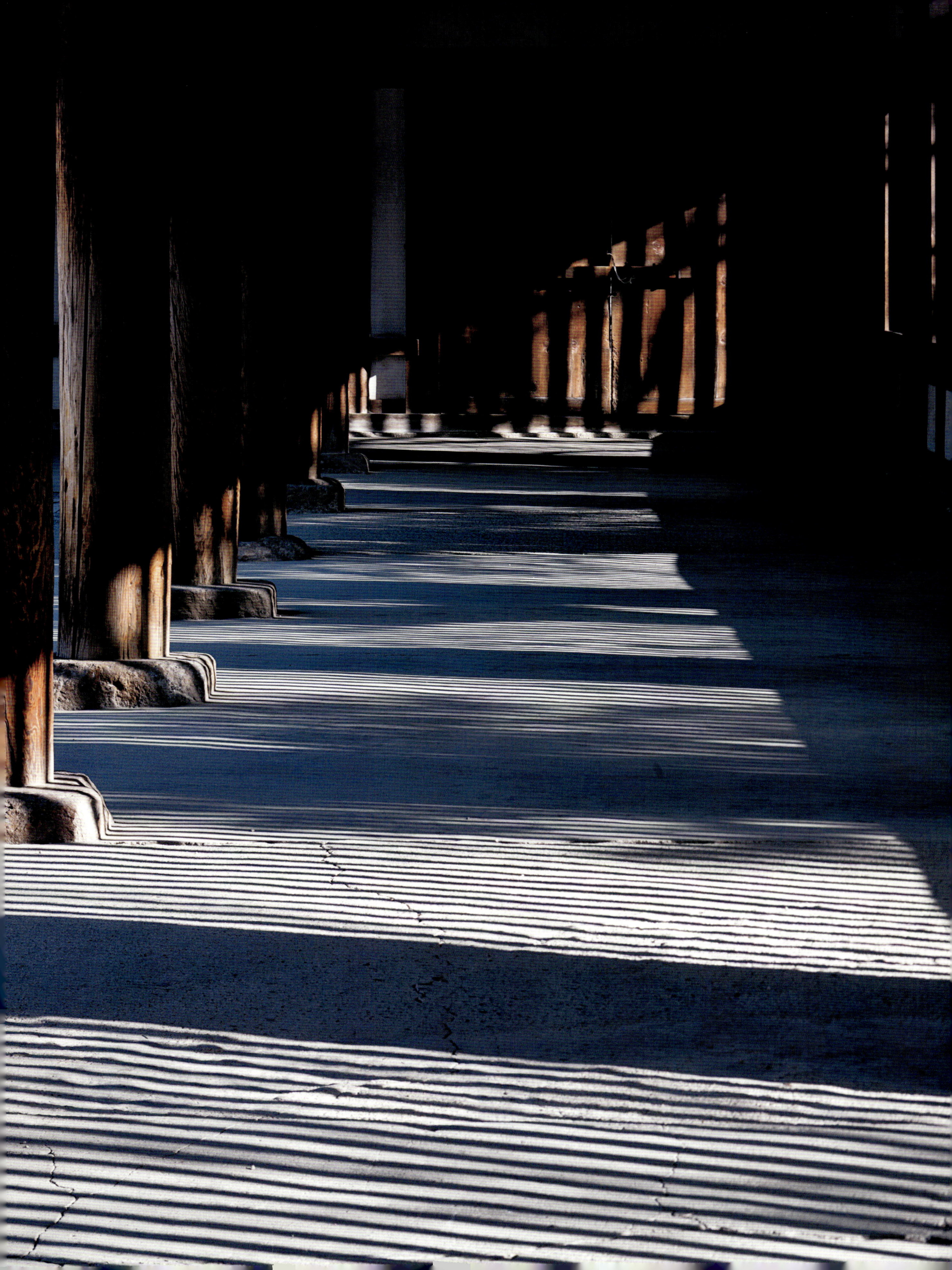

時代背景

　法隆寺の創始は7世紀初頭にさかのぼる。飛鳥様式を今に伝える金堂・五重塔・中門・廻廊などで構成される西院伽藍は、現存する世界最古の木造建築群となる。伽藍はこの西院と、夢殿（739年・国宝）を中心とする東院とに大きく分けられ、境内（約18万7千㎡）は古建築の宝庫で、国宝18件、重要文化財29件を数える。

　6世紀前半、仏教が朝鮮半島を通して日本にもたらされると、その興隆に力を尽くしたのが聖徳太子（574－622）である。601（推古天皇9）年から605（同13）年にかけて、太子は現・東院あたりに斑鳩宮(いかるがのみや)を建てて住み、その西方に斑鳩寺こと法隆寺を建てた。太子の逝去後、643（皇極天皇2）年に太子一族が滅ぼされて斑鳩宮が焼失し、さらに670（天智天皇9）年、『日本書紀』では法隆寺が全焼したと記される。このことから、明治時代半ばより再建説・非再建説論争が繰り広げられてきた。1939（昭和14）年には、西院伽藍の中門より南東の境内地で発掘調査が行われ、塔と金堂とが南北に並ぶ伽藍跡（若草伽藍）が確認された。これを機に、若草伽藍を創建法隆寺とし、西院は670年の火災後から遅くとも711（和銅4）年頃までの間に再建されたとする見方がほぼ定説となっている。

　一方で、いまだ謎が残る部分も多い。太子一族の滅亡後、巨費を投じた西院伽藍の建立は一体だれの主導によるものだったのか。西院伽藍が若草伽藍とは別の場所の、しかも異なる方位軸で建てられたのはなぜか。これらをはじめとする諸々の問題解明には、考古学、建築史学、美術史学、文献史学など、様々な方面から研究が積み重ねられている。

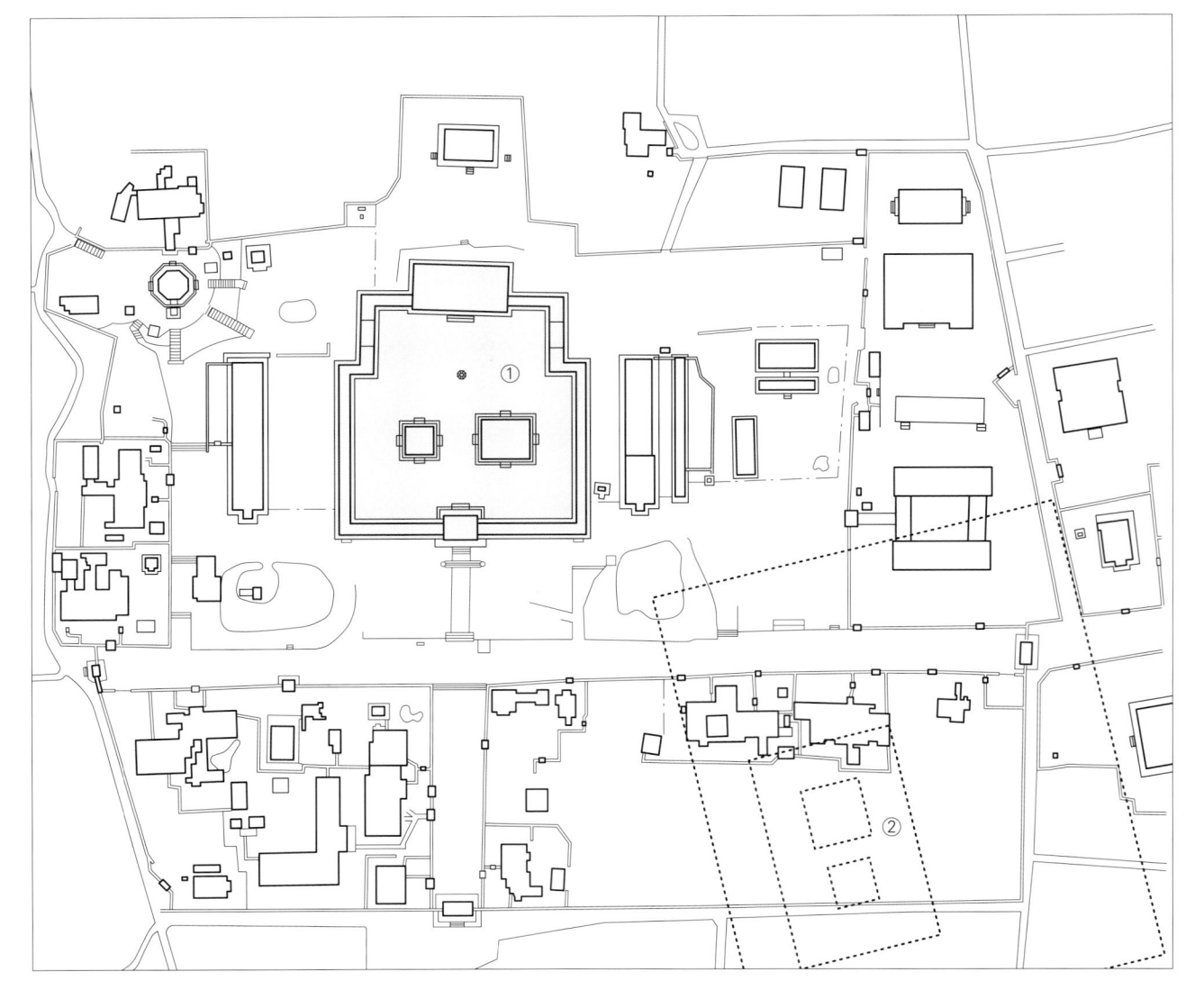

① 西院伽藍主要部
　Western Precinct (Sai-in Garan)

② 若草伽藍
　Wakakusa Garan

西院伽藍・配置図　Site plan of the Western Precinct

Historical Background

The founding of Horyuji temple dates back to the early seventh century. The Asuka-style buildings in the Western Precinct (Sai-in Garan), including the Kondo (the main hall of the temple), the Five-story Pagoda, the inner or central gate (*chumon*), and the corridors (*kairo*), are the oldest extant wooden buildings in the world. Covering roughly 187,000 square meters and broadly divided between the Western Precinct and the Eastern Precinct (To-in Garan), centered on the Yumedono hall (739; National Treasure), the entire temple complex is a treasure trove of ancient architecture containing 18 National Treasures and 29 Important Cultural Properties.

The propagation of Buddhism in Japan after its introduction via the Korean peninsula in the first half of the sixth century was led by the figure known as Prince Shotoku (574–622). Between 601 and 605, he built and lived in the Ikaruga Palace in what is now the Eastern Precinct, and also built Ikarugadera temple (Horyuji) west of the palace. In 643, after the prince's death, his son and heir was attacked by the powerful Soga family and forced to commit suicide. The Ikaruga Palace was burned down and Prince Shotoku's family line came to an end. According to the *Nihon shoki* (Chronicles of Japan), Horyuji, too, was lost to fire in 670. From the end of the nineteenth century the question of whether or not the temple was a reconstruction was much debated. A 1939 archaeological excavation on the temple grounds at a site southeast of the *chumon* gate uncovered the remains of a temple precinct called the Wakakusa Garan that included a pagoda and *kondo* main hall aligned on a north-south axis. As a result, it has been generally accepted that the Wakakusa Garan was the original Horyuji and that the buildings of the Western Precinct were a reconstruction built after the fire of 670 but no later than 711.

Nevertheless, many questions remain unanswered. After the demise of Prince Shotoku's family, who led the enormously expensive project of constructing the Western Precinct? Why was the temple rebuilt in a different location than the Wakakusa Garan, and on a different axis of orientation? In an effort to resolve puzzles such as these, a great deal of research has been accumulated in a variety of fields including history, archaeology, architectural history, and art history.

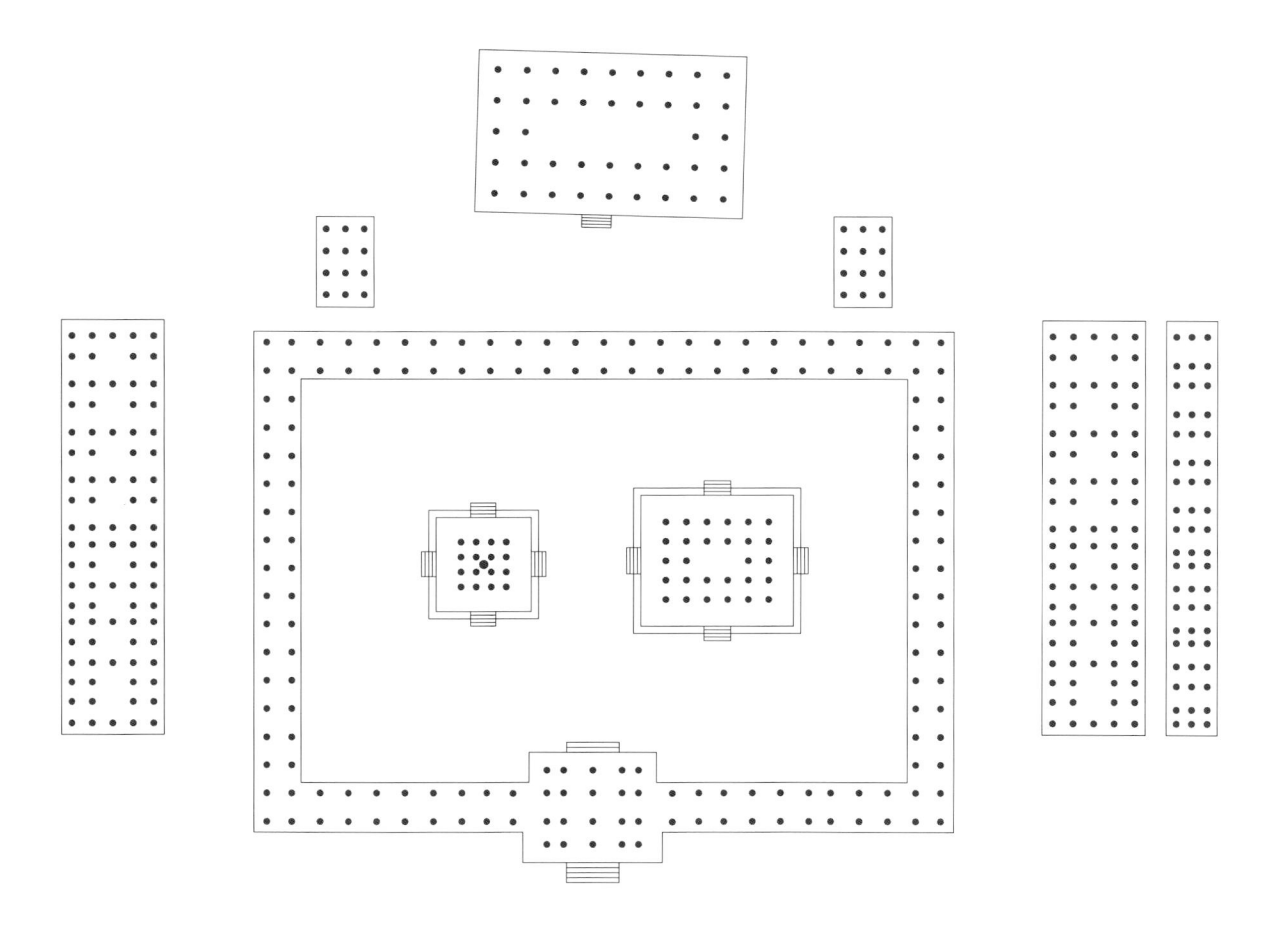

西院伽藍・復元配置図[*2]　Original site plan of the Western Precinct

特徴と見どころ

　6世紀末から8世紀までの仏教寺院の伽藍は、仏舎利を納める塔、本尊を安置する金堂、聖域としての結界をつくる廻廊、その基点となる中門が不可欠の要素であった。法隆寺西院では、東に金堂、西に五重塔が並び立つ「一塔一金堂」の非対称形の配置とし、その四周を廻廊がめぐる古代寺院特有の伽藍構成を今に伝える。現在は北側のほぼ中央に大講堂（990年・国宝）、その東西に鐘楼（11世紀初頭・国宝）と経蔵（8世紀・国宝）が廻廊に取りつくが、これは大講堂再建にともなう拡張で、もとは金堂と五重塔で北側を閉じ、両建物のみが廻廊で囲われた聖域性の強い空間が形づくられていた。

　西院伽藍の中枢部の造営には高麗尺*が使用され、この3/4尺（7寸5分高麗尺）の倍数を基準単位に計画されている。部材についても、肘木、通肘木、雲斗、尾垂木、束、桁、垂木の割りつけなどは7寸5分×6寸（高麗尺）で規格化されており、全体に洗練された統一感がある。さらに塔の初重と五重の軒幅は$\sqrt{2}:1$とし、塔の高さを金堂の高さのほぼ2倍に取り、金堂中心と塔中心間との距離をほぼ塔の高さとするなど、建物単体のみならず、各建物間の均衡が比例により関連づけられ、全体計画が整えられている。

　柱は太く、胴張りをもつのが特徴で、深い軒は雲斗雲肘木と呼ばれる組物が支持する。また、高欄に配された卍崩し組子や人字形割束も、西院伽藍、および、太子一族とゆかりの深い法起寺三重塔（684年頃－706年・国宝）にしか見られない独特の造形である。

　金堂・五重塔・中門の軒は一重で、反りのない角垂木を平行に配する。一方、西院伽藍の次に古い遺構で、白鳳様式（7世紀後半－8世紀初頭）を伝える薬師寺東塔（730年・国宝）をはじめ、奈良時代の遺構は二軒の平行垂木で、円形断面の地垂木と角形断面の飛檐垂木を標準とする。また、軒を支える構造についても、西院伽藍では肘木と斗を一体化した雲斗雲肘木が用いられ、隅方向の支持では、それを45度方向にのみ長く延ばし出す形を取るのに対し、奈良時代以降では肘木と斗を別木で組み合わせた三手先組物で、軒の隅では三方に斗栱を出して支持する。法隆寺焼失の記録から薬師寺東塔の完成までの間は60年しかないが、両者の形式や技法の隔たりは、系統の異なる東アジア仏教建築の影響が、国内外での社会情勢や交流を背景に、日本で併存する状況にあったことを示唆する。

　天平以降の建築に馴れた目で法隆寺に立ち返り、金堂や五重塔を見ると、明快な構造システムや力みなぎる装飾、意匠に新鮮な驚きを覚える。屋根荷重が直接地垂木に伝えられ、それを一木から造り出された雲斗雲肘木が受けとめ、太い柱へと力が伝えられる。そこには、もっとも簡潔な力の流れが見て取れる。これは樹齢1,000年以上のヒノキの大径良材があったからこそ採用できた構造システムであり、このようなヒノキ材が軸組から細部まで適切に使われているからこそ、1,300年以上の歳月を耐え抜いてこられたのである。

　東アジアからもたらされた仏教建築の技術や文化を、日本の風土のなかでどのように受容し、展開したか。それを考える上で、西院伽藍はつねに起点となるものである。

* 1尺約35.6cmとなるが、法隆寺西院の場合、建物ごとに基準尺長が若干異なり、金堂は約35.9cm、五重塔は約35.6cm、中堂は約35.2cmとなる。

南大門から西院伽藍を見る
View from the great south gate toward the Western Precinct

Characteristics and Highlights

From the late sixth century through the eighth century, the essential elements of a Buddhist temple complex were a pagoda containing a relic of the Buddha, a *kondo* main hall housing the principal Buddhist image, the corridors defining the boundaries of the sacred space, and a *chumon* gate from which the corridors extended. Horyuji's Western Precinct preserves the composition typical of such ancient temples in its asymmetrical "one pagoda, one hall" arrangement with the Kondo hall on the east and the Five-story Pagoda on the west, enclosed by corridors on four sides. Today the enclosure also incorporates the Daikodo lecture hall (990; National Treasure) roughly centered to the north with a bell tower (*shoro*, early eleventh century; National Treasure) and sutra repository (*kyozo*, eighth century; National Treasure,) to its east and west. This is the result, however, of an expansion of the enclosure undertaken during the rebuilding of the lecture hall; originally, the north side of the enclosure closed behind the Kondo and pagoda to create a powerfully sacred space that surrounded these two structures alone.

The core buildings of the Western Precinct were designed using the *komajaku* (Korean *shaku*) measure, with the standard unit being multiples of 3/4 *shaku*.* Structural members such as *hijiki* bracket arms, *toshihijiki* bracket tie beams, *kumoto* cloud-shaped bearing blocks, *odaruki* tail rafters, *tsuka* short supports, and *keta* purlins were all standardized at 7-*sun* 5-*bu* (3/4 *shaku*) x 6-*sun* (3/5 *shaku*), giving the whole an unified look. Furthermore, the project as a whole was carefully planned, not only for each individual building but also in the proportional relationships that guided the balance between the buildings. For example, the width of the pagoda's first-story and fifth-story eaves is set to an exacting calculation ($\sqrt{2}:1$), the pagoda is roughly twice the height of the Kondo hall, and the horizontal distance between the center of the pagoda and the center of the hall is about equivalent to the height of the pagoda. The stout columns exhibit the entasis characteristic of Horyuji while the deep eaves are supported by brackets called *kumoto kumohijiki* (cloud-shaped bearing blocks/bracket arms). Decorative flourishes on the balustrades such as mullions incorporating simplified swastika patterns and splay-legged *warizuka* struts are unusual features found only in the Western Precinct and on the three-story pagoda (ca. 684–706; National Treasure) at Hokiji, a temple with close ties to the family of Prince Shotoku.

The Kondo, Five-story Pagoda, and *chumon* gate all have single-layer eaves that use straight, squared rafters arranged in parallel. Meanwhile, the standard practice in the next-oldest structure after the Horyuji Western Precinct—the Hakuho-style Eastern Pagoda (730; National Treasure) at Yakushiji temple—and other structures from the Nara period (eighth century) was to use double-layer eaves with parallel rafters, with the *jidaruki* base rafters round in section and the *hiendaruki* flying rafters square in section. Buildings in the Horyuji Western Precinct also use *kumoto kumohijiki*—integrating the functions of the bearing block and bracket arms—in the structure supporting the eaves, turning them 45 degrees and extending them further out at the corners, while buildings of the Nara period and later used sets of three-stepped *mitesaki* bracket complexes that extended out in three directions at the corners. Only sixty years separate the date when records indicate Horyuji was destroyed by fire and the completion of the Eastern Pagoda at Yakushiji, but such disparities in style and technique suggest that different lineages of East Asian Buddhist architecture coexisted in Japan at the time against a backdrop of complex domestic and international social conditions and exchange.

When we go back to Horyuji after becoming accustomed to seeing architecture dating from the eighth century and onward and look again at its Kondo and Five-story Pagoda, we are struck anew by the clarity of its structural system and the power of its ornamentation and design. The roof load is conveyed directly through the *jidaruki* base rafters to the robust *kumoto kumohijiki*, each carved from a single piece of timber, and then passed on to the thick pillars—a concise and easily visualized flow of forces. Adoption of such a system was only possible because of the availability of large diameter, high-quality *hinoki* cypress trees that were a thousand or more years old. The appropriate use of such material for both framing and details is what has enabled the structure to survive for more than 1,300 years. When considering how the techniques and culture of Buddhist architecture brought from East Asia were adopted and developed in Japanese conditions and culture, Horyuji's Western Precinct is invariably the point of departure.

*The length of one *shaku* is different for each building in the Western Precinct: Kondo 35.9 cm, Five-story Pagoda 35.6 cm, Chumon 35.2 cm.

金堂と五重塔が東西に並び立ち、そのまわりを廻廊がめぐって聖域をつくる。主要建物を廻廊で囲むのは古代寺院特有の形式で、当時からの廻廊を今に伝えるのは法隆寺のみである。五重塔の高さを金堂の高さの2倍とするなど、各建物間の均衡が比例により関連づけられ、寸法上の計画性をもって全体伽藍が整えられている

The Kondo and Five-story Pagoda are aligned on an east-west axis and surrounded by semi-enclosed corridors delineating the temple's sacred space. Although a feature of all the ancient temples, the corridors at Horyuji are the only ones dating from that distant past. The balance of the buildings follows proportional relationships and the measurements of the entire complex are carefully planned.

金堂南側正面。一重の角垂木を平行に並べる。上重の屋根は壁から垂木鼻先までが4.17m、軒桁から垂木鼻先までが2.3mあり、きわめて長い。通肘木を4段重ねて雲斗雲肘木間を強固につなげる。隅では45度のみに雲斗雲肘木を組む。龍の彫り物の支柱は17世紀末の後補だが、軒の垂下防止のため、以前から支柱などの補強策が取られていたという

South façade of the Kondo. The rafters of the upper roof extend 4.17 meters beyond the exterior walls and 2.3 meters from the purlins. Four layers of *toshihijiki* bracket tie beams secure the cloud-shaped bearing blocks/bracket arms, which at the corners are placed at a 45-degree angle. The carved dragon vertical supports are a late-seventeenth-century addition, but some form of reinforcement was probably used to prevent sagging of the eaves even before then.

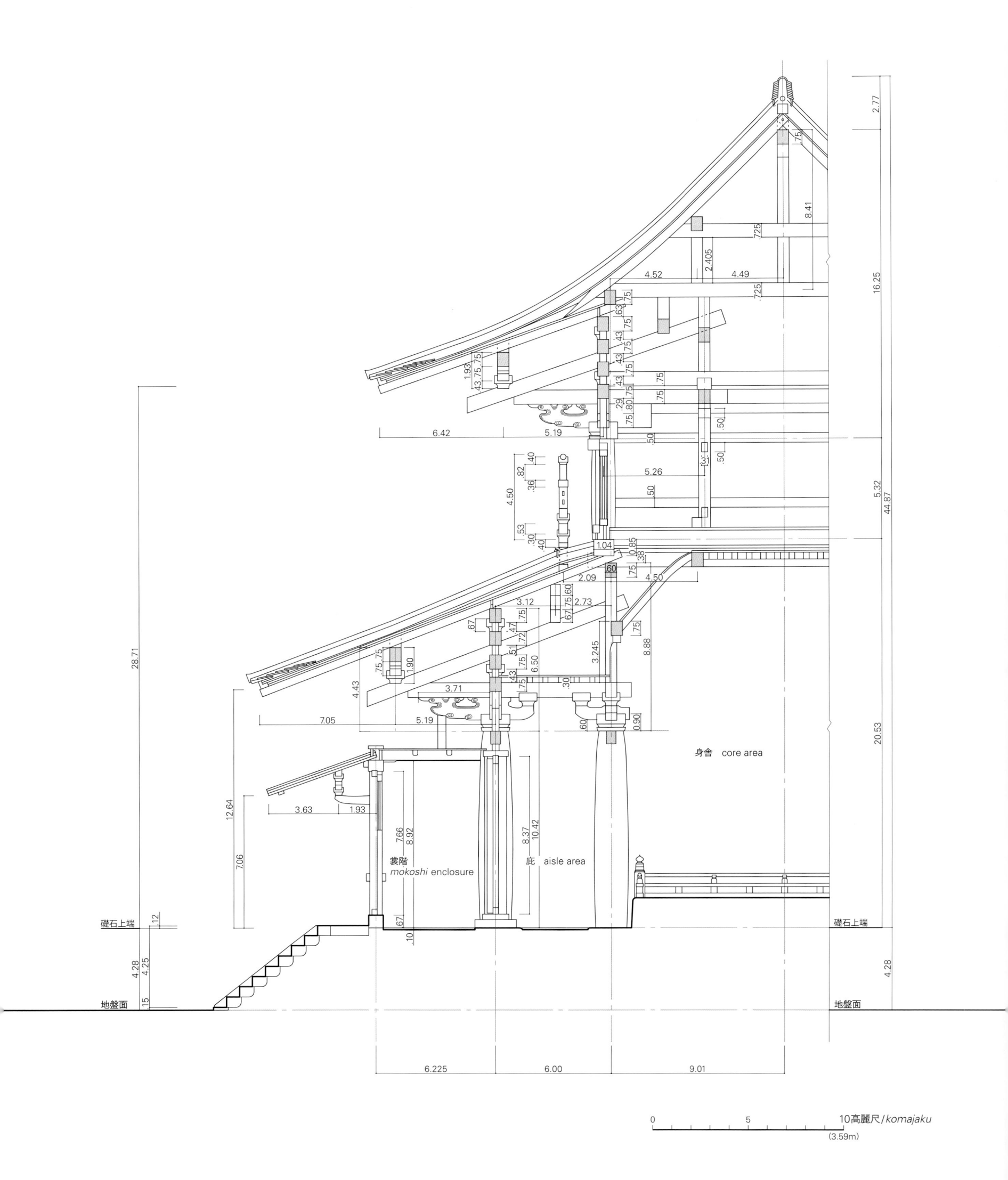

金堂・矩計図。西院伽藍の中枢部の造営には高麗尺（金堂1尺35.9cm）が使用され、この3/4尺（7寸5分）の倍数を基準単位に計画されている。垂木割りと天井割りも高麗尺7寸5分を規準とする。金堂の部材についても、肘木、通肘木、雲斗、尾垂木、束、桁、棟木は7寸5分（26.9cm）×6寸（21.5cm）で同一断面形状にし、規格化している（グレー部分）。野屋根をつくる屋根裏構造ではなく、屋根の荷重そのものを垂木で受ける。柱には胴張りがあり、下から1/3あたりがもっとも太く、最大径は60cm〜66cmある

Sectional detail drawing of Kondo. *Komajaku* (Korean *shaku*) were used in the construction of the core buildings of the Western Precinct (Kondo; 1 *shaku* = 35.9 cm). Note the standardization of the measurements of *hijiki* bracket arms, *toshihijiki* bracket tie beams, *kumoto* cloud-shaped bearing blocks, *odaruki* tail rafters, *tsuka* short supports, *keta* beams, and the *munagi* ridgepole at a uniform cross-section of 7-*sun* 5-*bu* (3/4 *shaku*) × 6-*sun* (3/5 *shaku*) (indicated in gray). Unlike for the *noyane* hidden roofs that were adopted from the Heian period onward, the rafters bear the roof load directly.

金堂・西面。高欄の卍崩し組子と人字型割束は、法隆寺系寺院のみに見られる装飾。下層には裳階（庇状の構造物）をめぐらすが、これは堂本体の計画より遅れて付加された。裳階は、扉以外は全面を連子窓とし、光と風をなかに入れ、内部柱の足元などを風雨から保護する

Kondo, west side. The simplified swastika latticework and splay-legged *warizuka* struts in the balustrade above the lower tiled roof are a feature only of temples affiliated with Horyuji. The *mokoshi* enclosure (with board roof) is believed to be a later addition. The lattices of the *mokoshi* allow light and air to flow inside while protecting the base of the interior columns from wind and rain.

初重の雲斗雲肘木は尾垂木を受け、その上に斗と肘木を載せて軒桁を支える。軒桁は垂木を支え、垂木は瓦の荷重を受ける。瓦は上重・初重ともおよそ13,000枚、各60t。尾垂木には反りがなく、軒桁断面は角形。雲斗雲肘木に水紋が入るのは金堂のみで、五重塔・中門にはない

Cloud-shaped bearing blocks/bracket arms receive the *odaruki* tail rafters and support the lower roof. Bearing blocks and bracket arms set onto the tail rafters undergird the eave purlins, which in turn support the rafters that carry the roof-tile load. The lower and upper roofs each carry around 13,000 tiles weighing 60 tons. In contrast to those in the pagoda and gate, the Kondo cloud-shaped bracket arms are carved with ripple designs.

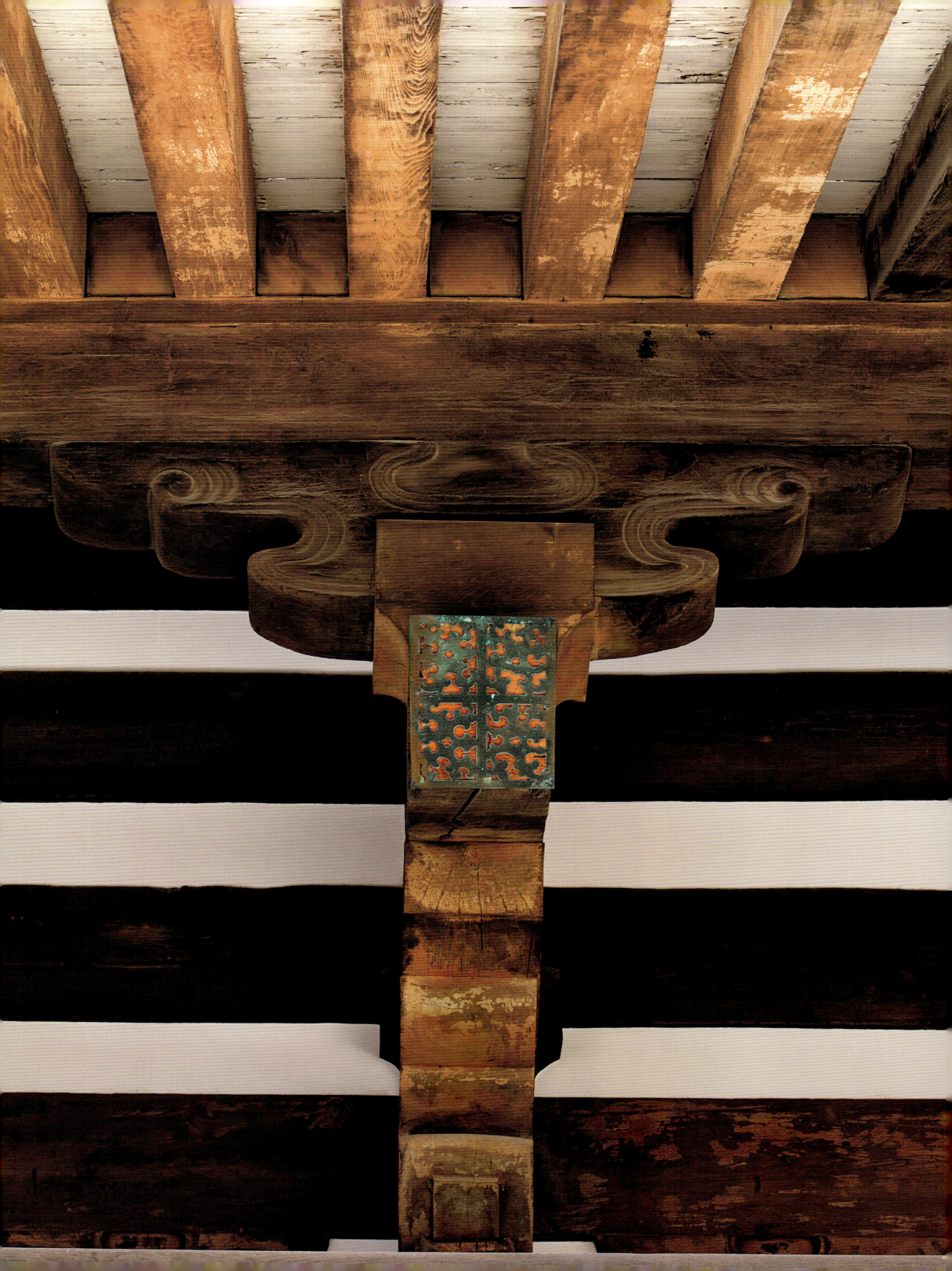

(左)通肘木で固定された雲斗雲肘木。尾垂木の木口は透かし彫りの飾り金具がつく。木は剪断力に弱いが、荷重を肘木で受けて力を分散し、下へと伝える。構造材である肘木を装飾的要素にする

(Left) Cloud-shaped bearing blocks/bracket arms are secured by *toshihijiki* bracket tie beams. The ends of the *odaruki* tail rafters are fitted with decorative metal openwork. Wood is weak against shearing forces but *hijiki* bracket arms receive the load over wider dimensions and disperse it to prevent buckling. A decorative touch has been added to the bracket arms' structural role.

(上)金堂初重隅の雲斗雲肘木。一木づくりで、引張りと圧縮が交差する真ん中には応力がかからず、そこを雲形に繰り抜いて装飾を施している。全体に木部には赤色の丹土、垂木先端に黄土、軒裏に白土が塗られていた。色彩がかすかに残る

(Avobe) Cloud-shaped bearing blocks/bracket arms at a corner of the Kondo's lower roof. The bearing blocks and bracket arm are a single piece of wood, with decorative cloud-shaped hollows at their centers where tensile and compressive forces intersect and stress does not concentrate. The building used to be painted with red *nitsuchi* pigment, yellow *odo* on the rafter ends, and white *hakudo* on the underside of the eaves. Faint traces are visible even now.

初重・裳階。角柱から長い挿肘木を出し、軒を支える。挿肘木の先端はぎりぎりまで細く削った曲線で、軽快な連続感がある。軒裏には白土塗りが残る

Kondo *mokoshi* enclosure. Long bracket arms set into the square columns extend to support the eaves. The slender proportions of the bracket arms create a pleasing rhythm. Traces of white *hakudo* pigment remain on the underside of the eaves.

金堂・裳階扉。幅1m、高さ2.7m、厚み8.4cm。ヒノキの一枚板で中杢材が使われており、少なくとも直径1.3mはある大木から採られた板である。連子は別材ではなく、一枚板から刳り貫いている

Kondo *mokoshi* door. Each door is made of a single cypress board drawn from an off-center part of the tree, which must have been a massive tree at least 1.3 meters in diameter. The door's slats are cut from the solid board rather than inserted as separate pieces. The door's dimensions are width 1 meter, height 2.7 meters, thickness 8.4 centimeters.

中門から廻廊を見る。ヒノキの胴張り柱が力強く連続する

Corridor seen from the Chumon (inner gate). Entasis accentuates the powerful rhythm of the cypress columns.

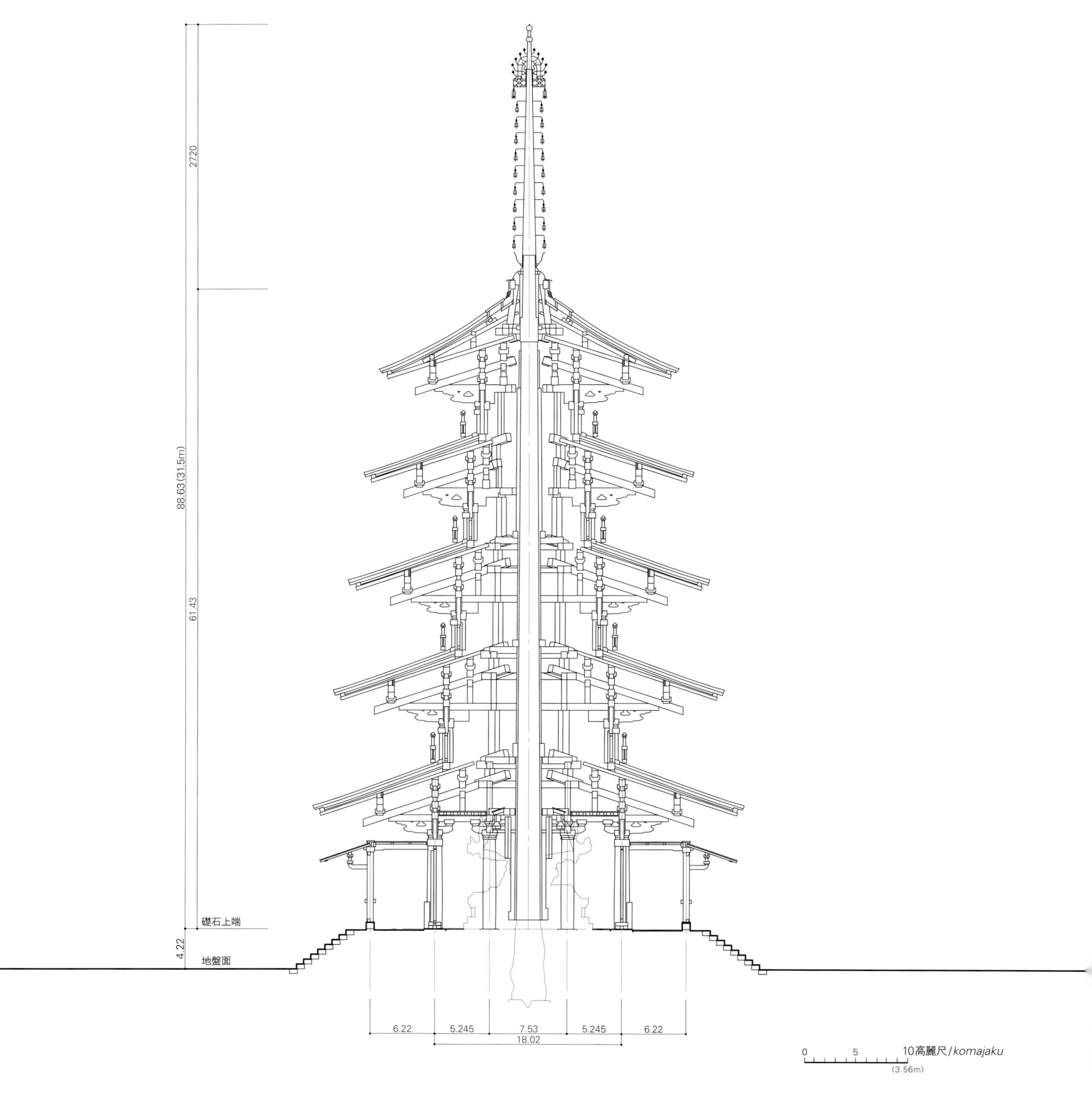

五重塔・断面図。年輪年代調査により、心柱の伐採は594年頃と推定されている。当初足元は掘立てとなり、基壇上面から約3m下に心礎が据えられていた。その上端の中央に舎利奉納孔があって、ここにガラス製舎利容器が納められていたという。地震の際、心柱は建物全体の揺れとは逆方向に振動し、地震力を相殺する

Section of Five-story Pagoda. Research indicates that the timber for the central *shinbashira* pillar was felled around 594. Originally its base was sunk to a central footing about 3 meters below the top of the platform. At the center of the footing was a hollow containing a glass reliquary. During earthquakes, the central pillar swings in the opposite direction from that of the rest of the building, offsetting the seismic force of the quake.

大きく張り出す軒が伸びやかに連なる。ゆるやかな軒先の反りは穏やかな佇まいをつくる。塔の高さは、基壇上から相輪まで31.5m。全体の見え方を重視した比例で、軒幅は五重(10.4m)に対して初重が約√2倍(14.7m)となる。金堂と同じ二重基壇で、側面の凝灰岩にマンガンを多く含む黒土の塗り跡があり、当初は黒い基壇上に立っていたのかもしれない。金堂と釣り合いを取り、初重に裳階を付加している

The layers of overhanging eaves, constructed with an unerring sense of proportion, form a picture of peace and equilibrium. The Pagoda is 31.5 meters from the top of its podium to the tip of the finial. Matching the Kondo, it has a two-stepped podium. Traces of a pigment suggest that the pagoda may originally have stood on a black podium. The *mokoshi* enclosure to the first story was added to maintain the balance with the Kondo.

五重塔・四重、隅の雲斗雲肘木と軒裏。五重塔では、各重の隅に加えて、四重・五重は雲斗雲肘木と力肘木を一木からつくりだす。各重四方の軒先には青銅製の風鐸が吊り下げられ、耳を澄ませば、風とともにかすかに古代の音を響かせる

The corner of the fourth story. The cloud-shaped bearing blocks/bracket arms and *chikarahijiki*, an extension of an interior tie beam, are made of a single piece at the corners of the first through third stories as well as throughout the fourth and fifth stories. Bronze bells hanging from the corners on each story ring faintly in the wind, echoing the sound of antiquity.

五重塔・相輪。下から九輪、水煙、竜車、宝珠。九輪の下には雷祓いの鎌が立てられている。塔への落雷は、鎌倉時代に三重目に落雷した記録が残るのみである

Five-story Pagoda finial. The "nine rings" (*kurin*) are topped with the "water flame" (*suien*), "dragon vehicle" (*ryusha*), and "sacred gem" (*hoju*). Sickles beneath the nine rings serve as talismans for warding off lightning. The only record of lightning striking the Five-story Pagoda was a strike to the third story that occurred during the Kamakura period.

五重塔、裳階と初重の軒裏。裳階の屋根は、板を交互に張り合わせた大和葺。金堂とは違い、五重塔の方は水返しがついており、ディテールの進歩がある

Mokoshi pent roof enclosure and underside of the pagoda first-story eaves. The roof of the *mokoshi* is made with alternating upper and lower planks. The pagoda *yamato-buki* roof of the *mokoshi*, unlike that of the Kondo, is more advanced in its interlocking structure and other details.

五重塔から西の廻廊を見る。平安時代中期から廻廊の折れ曲がり部分（右）を北へ延長した。廻廊の外には西円堂（鎌倉時代・国宝）の屋根が見える

West Corridor beyond the pagoda. From the middle Heian period the shape of the enclosure (far right) was changed, extending it to the north. The roof of the Saiendo (West Octagonal Hall; Kamakura period, National Treasure) is visible behind the corridor.

西廻廊。外周は大きな連子窓を取る。頭貫と内法長押の間に
スリットを開けた美しい構成

West Corridor. Large *renjimado* latticed windows line the outer side. The slit between the *kashiranuki* head-penetrating tie beams and the *uchinori nageshi* non-penetrating tie beams over the windows creates a beautiful composition.

正倉院 正倉

国宝
建立年代　8世紀（奈良時代）
所在地　　奈良県奈良市

Shosoin Repository

National Treasure
Completed: 8th century
Location: Nara, Nara prefecture

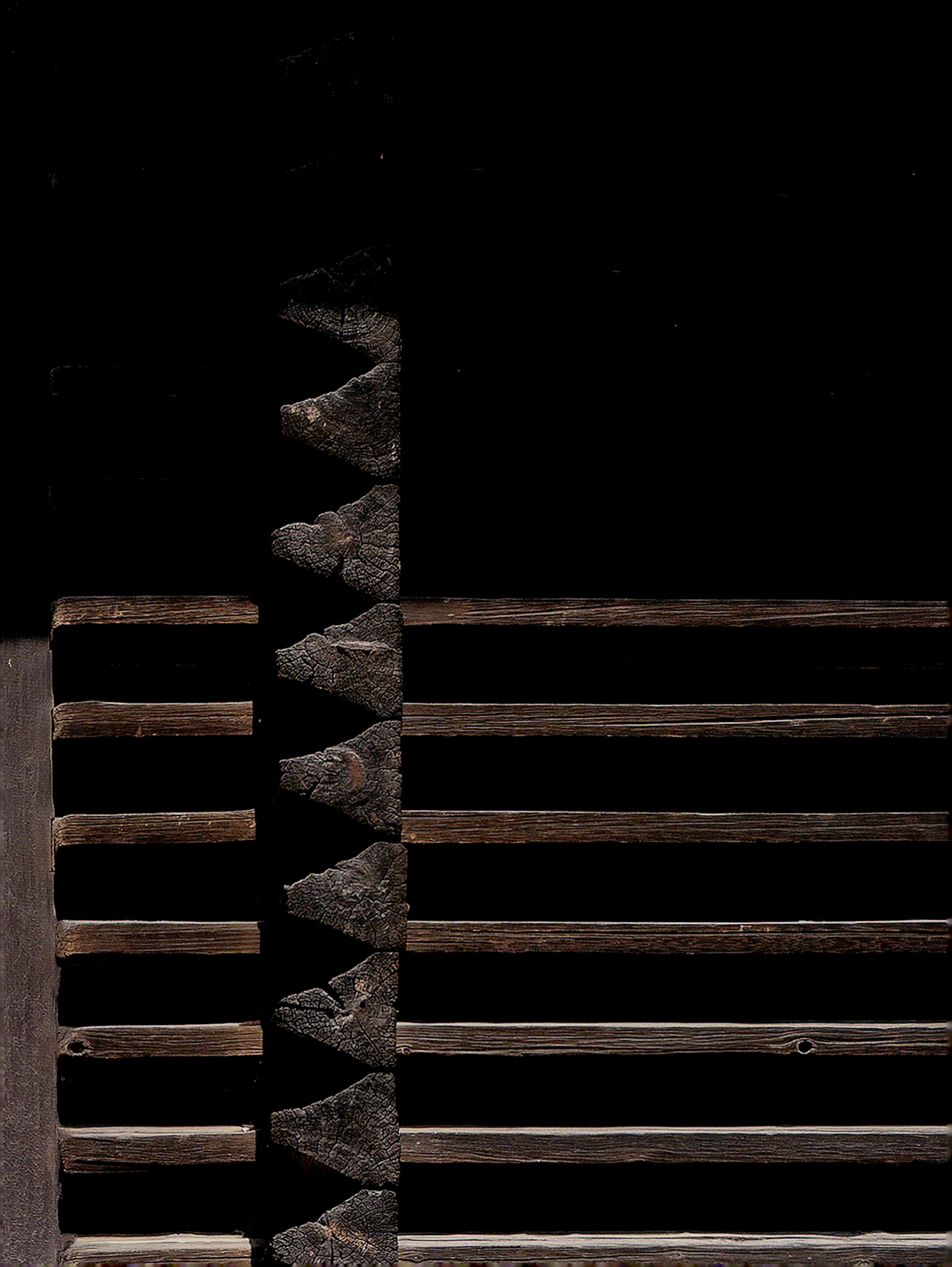

時代背景

　正倉院は、1,200年以上にわたり東大寺に由縁ある品々を保管してきた宝蔵である。正倉という言葉は、もともとは一般名詞で、律令国家（7世紀後半-10世紀初頭）における中央・地方の政庁や寺院の主要な倉のことを指した。正倉の設置された一画を正倉院と呼んだが、現存するのはこの倉のみで、東大寺大仏殿の北西約300mに位置する。明確な建造年代は不明だが、8世紀半ばまでには建設されていたと考えられている。東大寺を襲った2度の兵火により、正倉院に近隣する僧房、講堂、大仏殿など、主要建物は灰燼に帰するが、この倉は火難を逃れ、東大寺創建当初の数少ない遺構の一つとして今日に伝わる。

　日本における校倉は、大陸からの影響で7世紀後半にはすでにあったらしく、正倉院のほかに奈良時代の遺構として4棟（東大寺1棟・手向山神社1棟・唐招提寺2棟）があるが、すべて単倉である。正倉院が特別なのは、奈良時代第一の大寺であった東大寺の正倉にふさわしい、類例を見ない規模にある。

　巨大な高床式倉庫で、間口33m、奥行9.4m、総高14m、床下高さ2.7m、北倉・中倉・南倉の三倉で構成され、全体を瓦葺・寄棟造の屋根で覆った一棟三倉の形式を取る。北倉と南倉は略三角形の校木を20段（桁行）から20段半（梁行）井桁に組み重ねた校倉造で、中倉は正面・背面に厚板を嵌めた板倉造となっている。

　正倉院宝物の起こりは、東大寺を創建した聖武天皇（701-756）の死去にともない、后である光明皇后（701-760）が、756（天平勝宝8）年、天皇遺愛の品々を東大寺本尊・盧舎那仏（大仏）に奉献したことに始まる。収蔵品は多岐にわたり、その大部分が奈良時代の文物で、9,000点余りを今に遺す。長年の間、朝廷の監督のもとで東大寺が管理してきたが、1875（明治8）年以降は政府の直轄となり、現在宮内庁の所管である。

特徴と見どころ

　計り知れないほど貴重な財宝を守り、永遠にそれを保存しようと考えたとき、古代の人々が選んだのは、高床式の校倉造という形の倉庫だった。当時のほかのどんな形態の倉よりも風、雨、地震、火、虫や鳥獣害に対して高い防御力を発揮すると考えられ、「守る」ということに特化した形が校倉である。

　校倉造は、一辺一本で組み上げていく校木の長さに限度があるため、建物の大きさは限られてくる。単倉の場合は規模が小さいため、校木の壁体による組積造で構造は成り立つが、長大な正倉院の場合、柱立ての軸組構造と校倉の長所である耐力壁との組み合わせによってつくられている点が興味深い。実際に正倉院では、屋根荷重などの鉛直荷重を内部に立てた柱で受け、床下に並ぶ礎石上の40本の束柱が積載荷重を均等に受ける。一方、大風や地震といった壁面が受ける力に対して、校倉の壁は厚みがあることから、面外剛性が強い。つまり、垂直の力は柱で、水平の力は壁で受け、建物にかかる応力を明快に分離した構造になっている。その結果得られた強度こそが、1,200年以上も立ちつづけ、宝物を守ってきたこの巨大建築の本領であろう。

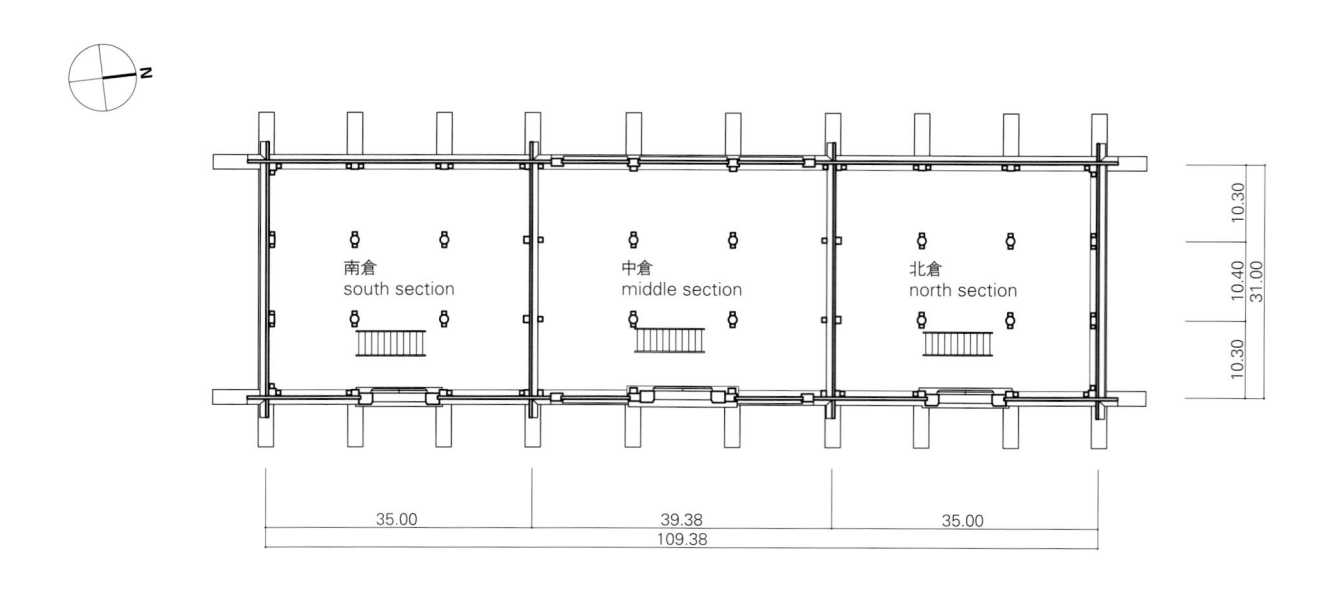

平面図　Floor plan

Historical Background

Shosoin is a treasure house that has stored items related to Todaiji temple for more than 1,200 years. The word *shoso* was originally a common noun that referred to important storehouses at government offices and temples both in the capital and in outlying regions under the *ritsuryo* system of administration (second half of the seventh century to the beginning of the tenth century). The areas where such storehouses stood were called *shosoin*, and Todaiji temple's is the only *shoso* that remains today. It is located about 300 meters northwest of the Todaiji Kondo (Great Buddha Hall). Although its precise date of construction is unknown, the Shosoin repository is believed to have been completed by no later than the middle of the eighth century. Two armed assaults on Todaiji reduced major adjacent structures such as the temple's residential quarters, lecture hall, and Great Buddha Hall to ashes. Having escaped the flames, Shosoin is one of the few structures that remain from the period when Todaiji was first established.

Storehouses made under the influence of continental culture with log walls in the *azekura* style are said to have existed in Japan as early as the late seventh century. In addition to the Shosoin repository, other remaining *azekura* storehouses in the Nara period include one at Todaiji, one at Tamukeyama Shrine, and two at Toshodaiji temple, but all are small-scale structures consisting of only a single storage area. What makes the Shosoin repository special is its extraordinary scale, befitting its position at the largest temple complex of the Nara period.

A massive raised-floor storehouse, the Shosoin repository measures 33 meters wide, 9.4 meters deep, and 14 meters high, with the floor raised 2.7 meters above ground. The building is composed of a north section, central section, and south section, all of which share a hipped roof covered with tiles. The north and south sections are built in the *azekura* style with timbers roughly triangular in cross section stacked 20 high at the front and back, 20.5 high on the sides, and interlocked at the corners. The center section is built in the *itakura* style with thick planks set flush on the front- and rear-facing sides.

The Shosoin was built to house the treasures of Emperor Shomu (701–756), the founder of Todaiji, which were donated by Empress Komyo (701–760) upon her husband's death in 756 as offerings to the Vairocana Buddha, the temple's principal image. The varied collection includes over 9,000 items, most of which are cultural artifacts from the eighth-century Nara period.

For centuries the Shosoin was maintained by Todaiji under the supervision of the Imperial Court. In 1875 it was placed under the direct control of the government and is currently under the jurisdiction of the Imperial Household Agency.

Characteristics and Highlights

When seeking to protect priceless treasures and preserve them for eternity, the ancients chose to use raised-floor storehouses. For purposes of protection, nothing could beat the specialized *azekura* style storehouse for safeguarding against damage from wind, rain, earthquakes, fire, and insect or animal pests.

The *azekura* style's reliance on stacking single timbers on each side necessarily places limits on the size of the building. For small-scale single-section storehouses the timbers can simply be stacked to form the walls; what is of interest in the longer and larger Shosoin storehouse is how post-and-beam construction is combined with *azekura* style bearing walls. In fact, the vertical load (the weight of the roof) at the Shosoin is supported by interior pillars, which distribute the load evenly to the 40 short supports that stand on the foundation stones. The thick *azekura* walls, meanwhile, provide high out-of-plane stiffness against the forces of strong winds and earthquakes. In other words, the building's structure clearly separates the stresses applied to it, with vertical forces carried by the pillars and horizontal forces by the walls. The resulting structural strength is surely the defining characteristic of this building, and what has enabled it to remain standing and to protect its treasures for more than twelve centuries.

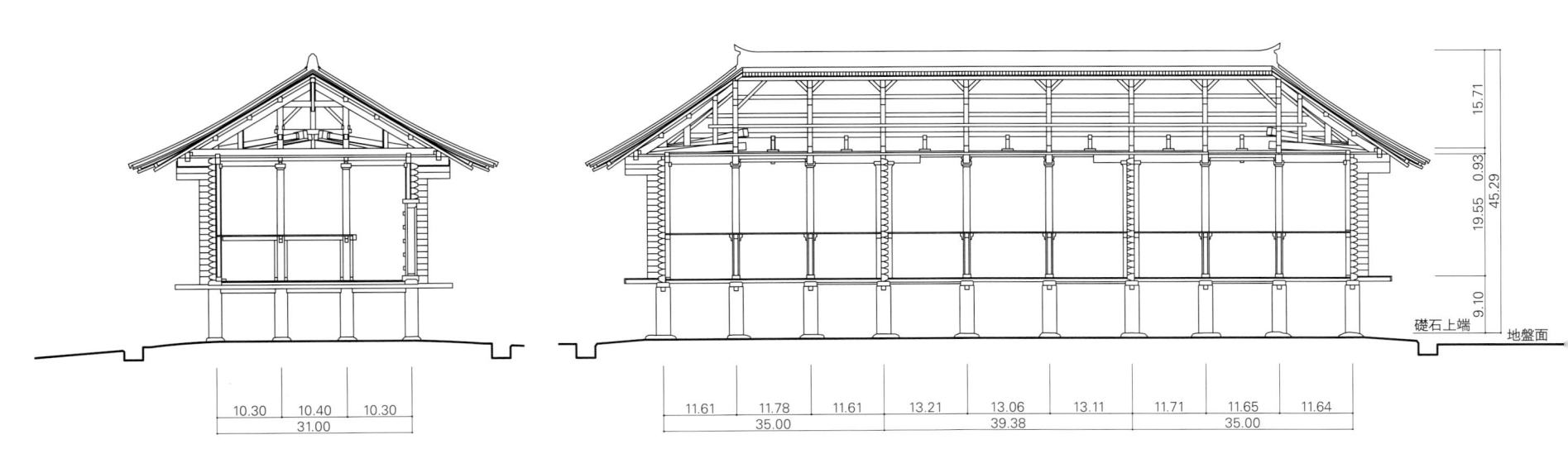

南北断面図　North–south section　　　東西断面図　East–west section

東側正面。東大寺を創始した聖武天皇ゆかりの宝物をおもに収蔵するため、
8世紀後半に建てられた。東大寺創建当時の数少ない建物の一つである。高
床式、三倉からなる一棟三倉形式で、北倉・南倉を校倉、中倉を板倉とする。
間口33m、奥行9.4m、総高14m、床下高さ2.7m

View from east side. One of the few structures to remain from the time of Todaiji's establishment, the Shosoin repository was built in the late eighth century mainly to store treasures related to Emperor Shomu, the founder of Todaiji. Note the north and south sections constructed in the *azekura* "log-cabin" style and the center section in the board-walled *itakura* style.

南西角。略三角形の校木を桁行（左側）20段、梁行（右側）20段半を井桁に組み合わせる。「守る」ことに特化した形

Southwest corner. Timbers roughly triangular in cross section are stacked 20 high along the length of the building (left) and 20.5 high along its width (right), and interlock at the corners, a specialized structural form designed to protect the treasures within.

中倉（左）と北倉（右）の接合部。校木上方3本を長く延ばして舟肘木で軒桁を受けている。二軒繁垂木の上に瓦屋根を載せる

The juncture between the center section (left) and north section (right). Note the extension of the three timbers at the top to accept the eave purlin with a boat-shaped bracket arm. Closely spaced parallel *shigedaruki* rafters for the double-layered eaves support the tiled roof.

自然石の礎石の上に立つ束柱は直径60cm強あり、礎石の形状通りに柱の底面をつくり、
密着させている。地震の際の水平の揺れは、この太い束柱が免震構造として働き、礎石と
の間で地震力を吸収する。柱底面と礎石との間には、薄い鉛板が貼りつけてあり、両者の
密着度を高めるだけでなく、シロアリ対策に有効という

Forty support posts, each measuring just over 60 centimeters in diameter, stand on natural foundation stones arranged in four rows. The bottom of each post has been shaped to fit tightly into the contours of the foundation stone upon which it stands. These thick posts act to dampen horizontal swaying during an earthquake. A thin sheet of lead between the surface of the post and its foundation stone increases the adhesiveness of the fit and effectively inhibits termites.

40本の束柱の上に井桁状に台輪を渡してある。その東西方向に台輪を各約1.8m
片持梁として外へ延ばし、出納の際に仮設的な縁の床を張り出した。内部は2層と屋
根裏部分とに分かれ、柱が立つ。垂直の力は柱で床下の束柱に均等に分散させ、水
平の力は校倉の壁で受けて、建物にかかる応力を明快に分離した構造

A latticed frame is laid out over 40 short support posts. On the east and west sides, the timbers of the frame extend 1.8 meters beyond the exterior walls and were used to support temporary flooring when moving items in or out of the storehouse. The structure clearly separates the stresses applied to it, with interior posts dispersing vertical forces evenly to the support posts beneath the floor and the *azekura* walls accepting horizontal forces.

唐招提寺 金堂

国宝
建立年代　8世紀後半
所在地　　奈良県奈良市

Toshodaiji Temple Kondo (Main Hall)

National Treasure
Completed: Late 8th century
Location: Nara, Nara prefecture

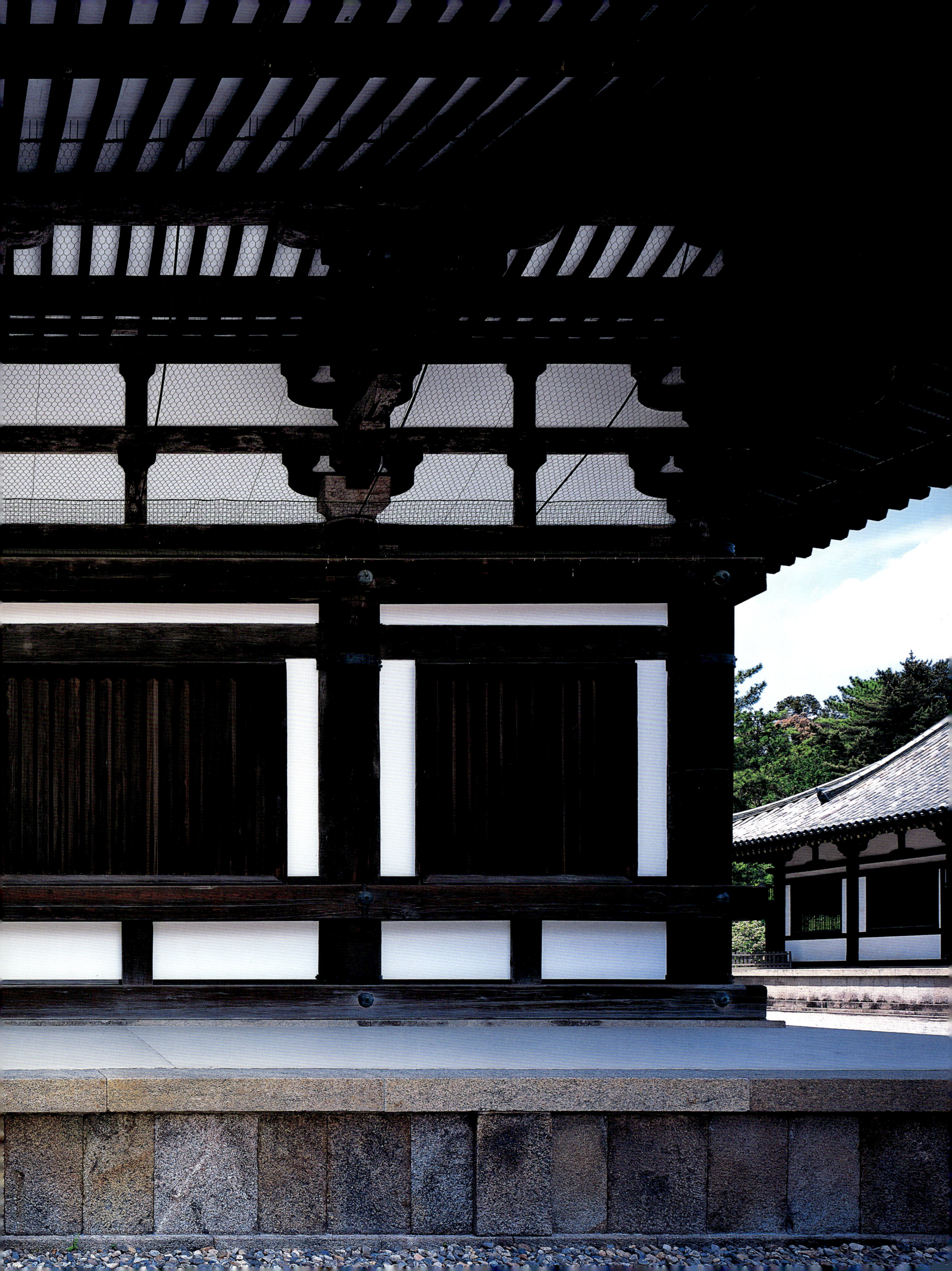

時代背景

　鑑真和上(688-763)が開いた寺として知られる唐招提寺の創立は、759(天平宝字3)年のことである。平城京の右京のなか、薬師寺の北方に位置する。正式な授戒伝律の師として唐より招請された鑑真は、ここを戒律修学の道場とした。伽藍には、奈良時代創立の寺院のなかで唯一、当初からの金堂を遺す。その北側に並んで立つ講堂(国宝)も同時代のものだが、これは平城宮の宮殿建築の一つである朝集殿の移築である。金堂と講堂が南北に並び立ち、講堂の東には経楼(現鼓楼・1240年再建・国宝)、僧房の一部を形成していた東室(現礼堂と東室・鎌倉時代修理再建・重文)、さらにその東側には奈良時代の校倉造りの宝蔵・経蔵(国宝)を備え、天平の雰囲気を今に伝える貴重な伽藍である。近年の調査から、金堂の造営は8世紀後半の可能性が高いと指摘されている。[*3]

　桁行7間、梁行4間の規模をもつ金堂は、正面1間通りを吹放ちの柱列とする。かつてはこの前庇の両側面に廻廊が取りつき、南にあった中門につながって、金堂前面と中門の間に矩形の前庭をつくっていた。金堂の吹放ち柱列は、廻廊の柱列と連続感をもった景観を形づくっていたであろう。

　金堂は元禄、明治、平成に大規模な修理工事を受けた。元禄の修理(1693-1694)では、棟を約2m高めて急勾配にしたため、屋根の量感が増した。また、軸組に貫を加え、長押を太くし、開口部を縮小したため、横材の存在感が強調されることになった。日本建築では、鎌倉時代に構造面で発展があり、中世に古代の建造物が次々と改造・補強されたなかで、この金堂は建立から元禄修理までのおよそ900年間、創建以来の古様を伝える構造形式と姿形を維持してきたことが平成の修理(2000-2009)で指摘されている。純正の奈良時代建築を守り伝えてきたこの金堂は、今も昔も人々が天平文化を考えるときの偉大な指標でありつづけている。

特徴と見どころ

　南大門から金堂を見たときの、堂々とした姿──その周囲にはおおらかな空気感が漂う。この建物をいにしえの仏堂の原形のように感じる印象は、日本人のみならず仏教に由縁ある国々の人々と共有するものではなかろうか。唐からの様式や技法を吸収し、消化して建てられたこの堂は、唐でもあり、日本でもあり、大陸との文化の交差点に立つ建築のように思われる。基壇を築き、その上には礎石が据えられ、太い柱が並び立ち、柱の上部には三手先の斗栱が端正に組み上げられて、軒まわりを格調高く支えている。軒は円形の地垂木と角形の飛檐垂木の二軒(いわゆる「地円飛角」)で、軒先に穏やかな反りをつくって張り拡がる。寄棟造りの瓦屋根の両端には鴟尾が載り、堂の品位を盛り立てている。壁は、戸口以外は四周すべて連子窓とする開放的なつくりである。

　堂へと近づくにつれ、吹放ちとなった列柱の並びの美しさが、その陰影とともに際立ってくる。柱間寸法は、中央間を16尺(29.8cm／唐尺)、その両脇から順次15尺、13尺、11尺と逓減し、中央の優位性を強調しつつ横になだらかな広がりをつくる。かつて廻廊によって形成された金堂の前庭は礼拝・儀式のための空間で、そこから見た金堂の正面性、視覚的効果が十分に意識されている。吹放ちの前庭のなかに入ると、太い柱がつくりだす古代の間合いは1200年以上を経た今も身体に響き、あたかも天平の風が柱間を吹き抜けていくように感じられる。

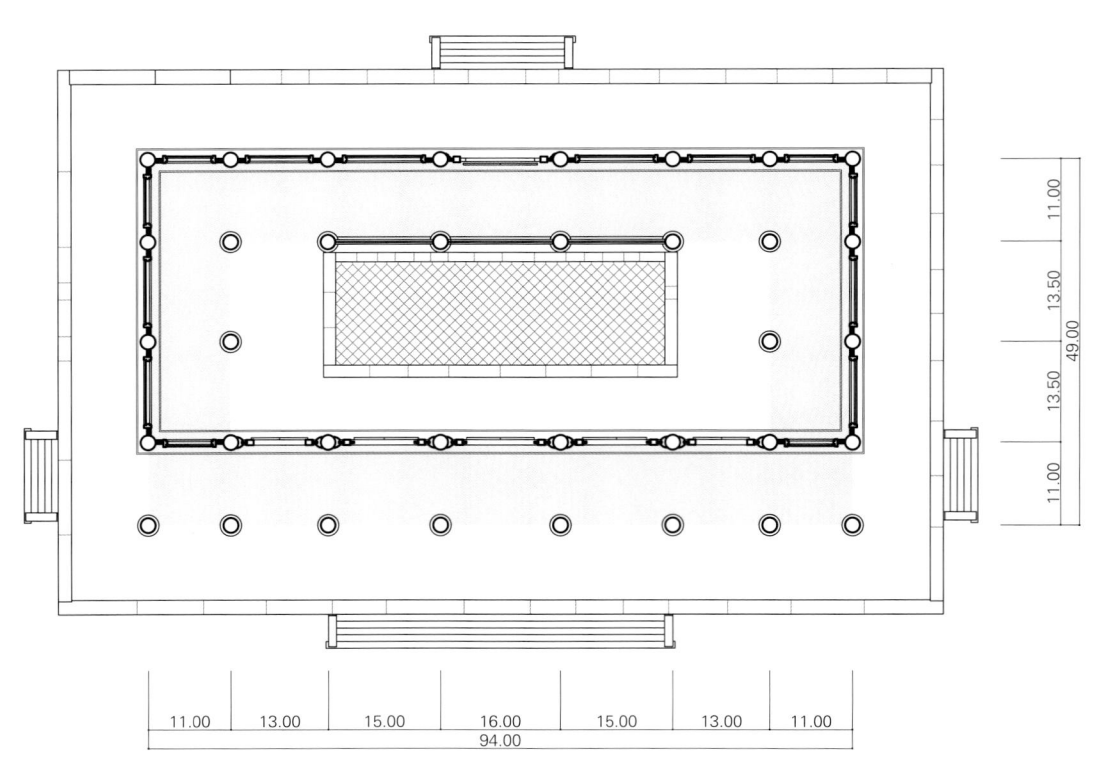

金堂平面図　Floor plan of Kondo (main hall)

Historical Background

Located north of Yakushiji temple in what was the western sector of the Heijo capital, Toshodaiji temple was founded in 759 by the monk Ganjin (Jianzhen; 688–763). Ganjin was invited from Tang dynasty China to formally train and ordain the Buddhist clergy in Japan. Toshodaiji was a privately established center for training in the Buddhist precepts. It is the only temple founded during the Nara period for which the original Kondo main hall still exists. A recent survey has found that the Kondo was likely built in the late eighth century.

The first of the Kondo's four bays is open at the front. At one time, semi-enclosed corridors (*kairo*) attached at both sides connected the Kondo to the *chumon* middle gate to the south of the building, forming a rectangular forecourt. The continuity of the open bay at the front of the hall and the pillars of the corridors must have made a striking scene.

The Kondo underwent large-scale repairs during the Genroku, Meiji, and Heisei eras. The ridge was raised by two meters during the Genroku repairs (1693–1694), making the roof slope steeper and giving it additional mass. During the repairs, *nuki* penetrating tie beams were added to the framework, and the *nageshi* non-penetrating tie beams sandwiching the columns were enlarged, making the openings smaller and emphasizing the horizontal structural members. Japanese architecture developed structurally in the Kamakura period (1185–1332) and many buildings of the ancient period were remodeled and upgraded during medieval times, but this was not the case with the Kondo. During the Heisei repairs (2000–2009), it was revealed that the original form and structure of the Kondo had been maintained for more than 900 years from its completion through the aforementioned Genroku repairs. The Kondo thus embodies the true form of Nara period architecture passed down to our time; it continues to serve as an important standard by which to appreciate the culture of the Tenpyo era.

Characteristics and Highlights

Viewed from the temple's main south gate, the Kondo hall rises majestic and serene in its quiet setting. The sense that this building represents an archetype of ancient Buddhist architecture is surely one that anyone familiar with Buddhism is likely to share. Constructed after Japan had absorbed and digested the styles and technology of the Tang dynasty, it is both Chinese and Japanese, a monument to the intersection of the two cultures. A platform was built, foundation stones put in place, and large columns erected upon them. Trim and strong, the three-stepped bracket complexes (*mitesaki tokyo*) elegantly support the eaves. Buttressed by a system of round *jidaruki* base rafters and square *hiendaruki* flying rafters, the eaves sweep out gently. *Shibi* ornaments resembling the tail of an animal grace the ends of the tiled roof ridge, adding elegance and dignity to the hall. Except for the door openings, the walls on all four sides of the building are fitted with latticed windows, leaving the building very open.

The awesome beauty of the front row of columns, and the interplay of light and shadow among them, intensifies as one approaches the hall. The columns of the central bay are spaced 16 *shaku* apart (1 *shaku* = 29.8 centimeters). This distance decreases incrementally in the outer bays (to 15 *shaku*, 13 *shaku*, and 11 *shaku*), bringing out the dominance of the center and the fluid expansion of the open bays on either side. The forecourt originally formed by the semi-enclosed corridors was used as a space for worship and ceremony, and the design of the front of the Kondo reflects an awareness of the importance of frontality and the visual effect of the hall as seen from the forecourt. Standing under the open eaves at the front of the hall where one can palpably feel its ancient proportions, one can imagine the Tenpyo-era winds that must have blown through these columns 1,200 years ago.

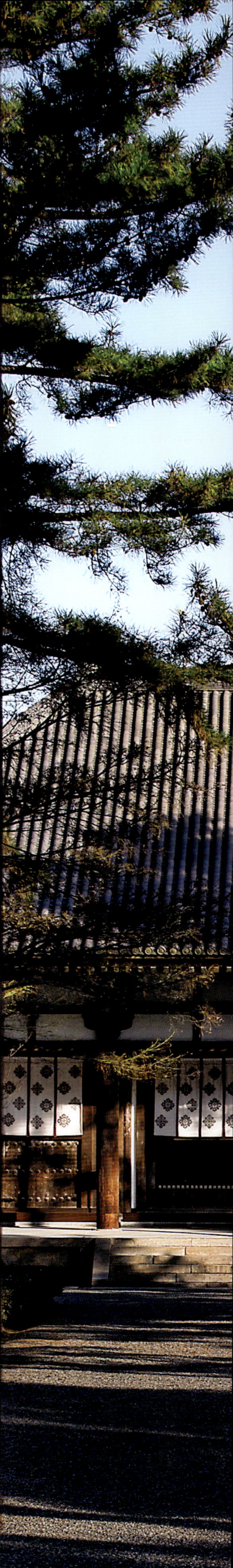

The Kondo in the morning. This is the only *kondo* main hall remaining from the eighth-century (Tenpyo era). Corridors connected to the sides of the Kondo once created an enclosed forecourt.

南東角の基壇と柱。白い粘土と褐色の粘土を厚さ10cm前後でつき重ねた版築土層を基壇とし、花崗岩（創建当初は凝灰岩）の石板で囲う。何層にも重ねた版築は免震構造となる

Southeast podium corner and column. The core of the platform is packed earth made of 10-centimeter-thick alternating layers of white and brown clay. The platform was surrounded by tuff when it was built, and is now enclosed by granite slabs. The many layers of packed earth have a seismic isolation effect.

正面1間通りを吹放ちとした列柱と石階。太さ60cm前後、長さ5m前後のヒノキの円柱8本が悠々と立ち並び、古代の間合いをつくりだす。丹土の赤い塗料がかすかに残る。石階は木津川沿いの加茂で採れた花崗岩で、黒雲母と鉄分の錆が斑状に入り、深みのある質感をもつ

Stone steps and outer row of columns at the front. The eight cypress columns, each roughly 60 centimeters in diameter and 5 meters tall, stand in serene testament to an ancient sense of spacing. Faint traces of red pigment remain. The granite of the steps was quarried at Kamo, along the Kizugawa river in southern Kyoto; the deep tone of the stone comes from black biotite iron mottling.

南西角の連子窓と板蟇股。前庇は礼拝のための空間で、格子状の軒天井を張る

Southwest corner slatted windows and solid board frog-leg strut. The portico, a space for worship, has a latticed ceiling.

吹放ちの柱を頭貫のみで連結し、身舎柱とは虹梁でつなぐ。柱上は三手先斗栱で軒を支える。唐の様式を採り入れた三手先斗栱として、薬師寺東塔に次ぐ古例の一つであり、最上格の建物に使われる組物である

The columns are fastened together with head-penetrating tie beams and connected to the core columns with rainbow beams (koryo). Three-stepped bracket complexes above the columns support the eaves. This is among the oldest examples of three-stepped bracket complexes, which incorporate the style of Tang dynasty China and were used for buildings of the highest status.

東面妻側。扉以外の柱間にはすべて連子窓が入る。二段に重なる間斗束、
三手先斗栱、白壁の余白の組み合わせが明快。大きな寄棟造の屋根が載り、
頂部に鴟尾を掲げる。反りをもつ深い軒の美しさ

East side. The bays between columns are all fitted with slatted windows. The arrangement of double-stacked struts and three-stepped bracket complexes stands out distinctly against the white plaster walls. The *shibi* roof ornaments highlight the sweeping lines of the great hipped roof.

新薬師寺 本堂

国宝
建立年代　8世紀
所在地　　奈良県奈良市

Shin Yakushiji Temple Hondo (Main Hall)

National Treasure
Completed: 8th century
Location: Nara, Nara prefecture

勾配のゆるい屋根を広げ、立ち居を低くし、天平建築の穏やかな佇まいを伝える。水平材は柱頂部の頭貫と扉上の内法長押のみで、簡素な白壁の存在感が引き立つ。白壁の縦横比はほぼ1：√2で整えられている

With its broad, gently sloping roof and low profile, this main hall conveys the unassuming lines of Tenpyo era architecture. The only visible horizontal members are the head-penetrating tie beams at the top of the pillars and the non-penetrating tie beams above the doors, accentuating the simplicity of the white walls. The ratio of width to height in the white walls is approximately that of 1 to the square root of 2.

時代背景

　奈良時代、都がおもに平城京にあった710（和銅3）年から794（延暦13）年の平安遷都までの間をとくに天平時代と呼び、中国・盛唐期の文化・思想の影響を受けて、建築、彫刻、絵画、工芸など、あらゆる芸術分野で高度な修練と発展があった。天平文化を推進し、支えたのが聖武天皇と光明皇后であり、また、2人が血筋を引く藤原氏一族であった。

　新薬師寺は、光明皇后が聖武天皇の病気平癒を祈願して建立し、創建年は747（天平19）年とされる。当初の中心堂宇は現本堂の位置より西方約150mにあり、金堂、東西両塔、講堂、僧房、食堂などを備えた大規模な寺院であった。主要伽藍地からはずれて立つ現本堂も当初からの遺構だが、もともと金堂として建てられたものではなく、本来の堂名はわかっていない。平安時代中期の962（応和2）年に大風で金堂ほか諸堂が倒れて中心伽藍を失ったのち、現本堂を中心にして、おもに鎌倉時代に堂宇が整えられた。旧中心伽藍に関しては近年発掘調査が行われ、旧金堂とみられる大型基壇建物跡が見つかっている。[*4] 旧金堂は2m近くの高い基壇を持ち、正面60m以上の類例のない大きさの建物とされ、伝えられてきたように、7軀の七仏薬師如来像を安置した正面9間の仏殿であったことが裏付けられた。

　現本堂の内部では中央に円形の須弥壇を構え、本尊・薬師如来座像（奈良時代末－平安時代初期・国宝）を中央に安置し、そのまわりを日本最古の十二神将立像（奈良時代・国宝・1軀補作）が円陣に取り巻く。鎌倉時代の1310（延慶3）年には本堂の前に礼堂がつくられたが、明治の解体修理（1896-1898年）では礼堂を取り、簡潔な姿に復元・修理されている。

特徴と見どころ

　もっとも素朴なかたちで、天平建築の姿を今に遺すのがこの堂である。勾配のゆるい屋根を広げ、立ち居を低くした佇まいはじつにゆったりとして穏やかである。壁面は扉と漆喰壁だけで構成され、窓はなく、横材は扉の上に打たれた内法長押と柱間をつなげる頭貫のみで、きわめて簡明である。壁面と屋根の量感の釣り合いがよく、均整の取れた外観がつくりだされている。

　内部は化粧屋根裏で、柱と梁、桁、扠首（棟木を支えるための合掌形の斜材）による簡潔な架構が一目で見渡せ、明快な力の流れが視覚にそのまま伝わってくる。架構と一体化した開放感あふれる空間は現代に通じる感覚があり、何度訪れても新鮮さを失わない堂である。

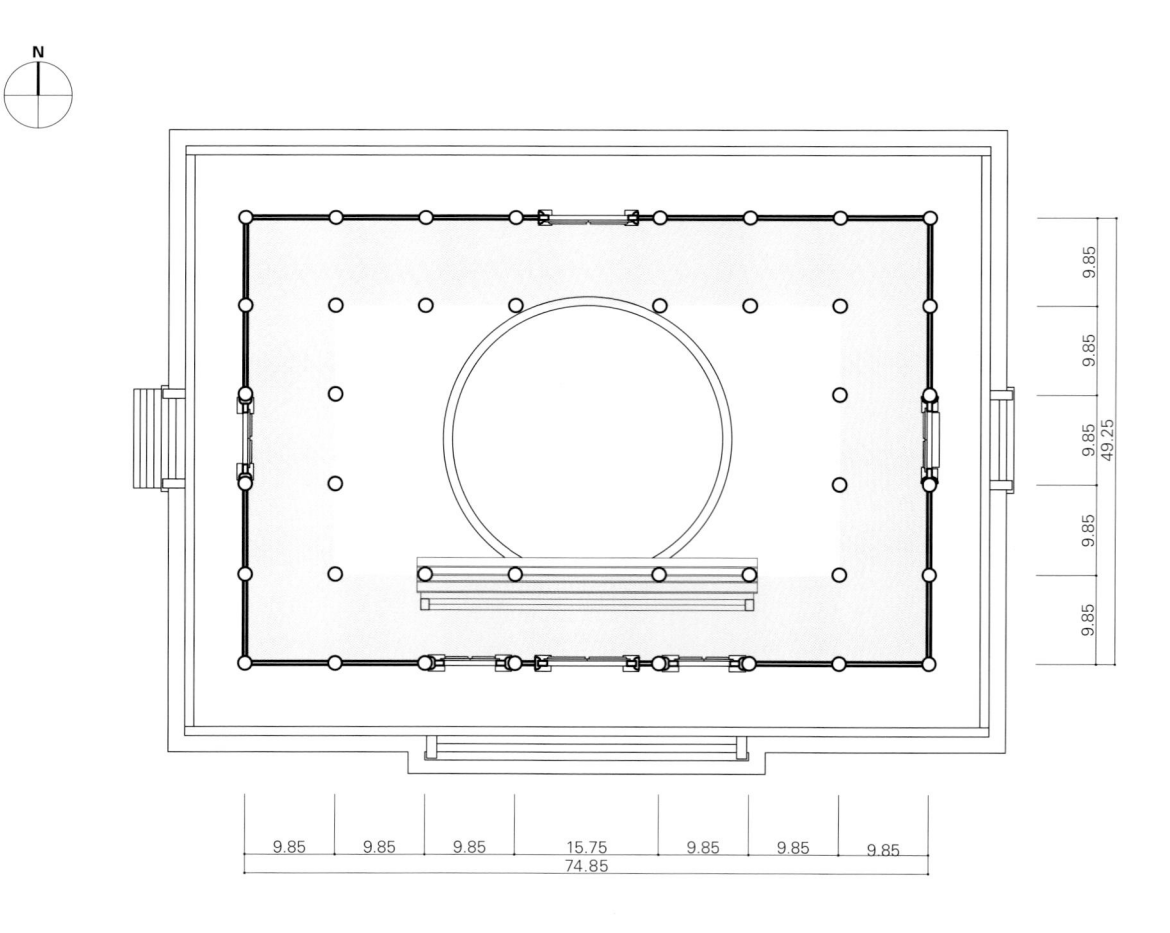

本堂平面図　Floor plan of Hondo (main hall)

Historical Background

The Tenpyo period, which extends from 710 to 794 during which the capital was located mainly in Nara (at the Heijo palace), coincided with the height of the Tang dynasty in China. The influx of Tang culture set in motion advances in technology and developments in architecture, sculpture, painting, and all the arts and crafts. The great promoters of Tenpyo culture were Emperor Shomu and Empress Komyo as well as the powerful Fujiwara family to which they were related.

According to widely accepted accounts, Empress Komyo had Shin Yakushiji temple built in 747 as an act of devotion when Emperor Shomu was suffering from illness. Originally centered 150 meters to the west of where the Hondo (Main Hall) now stands, the large complex included a *kondo* (golden or main hall), east and west pagodas, a lecture hall, priests' living quarters, and a refectory. The *kondo* and other primary structures of the original complex were destroyed by a typhoon in 962 (mid-Heian period). In the Kamakura period, the main buildings were rebuilt centered on the current Hondo, whose original function, some distance from the original complex, is unknown.

The current Hondo houses a circular *shumidan* altar at its center upon which rests the temple's principal image, a seated statue of Yakushi Nyorai (Buddha of Medicine; National Treasure dated to late Nara to early Heian period), surrounded by the standing statues of the Twelve Heavenly Generals, Japan's oldest statues of their kind (Nara period, National Treasures, one image supplemented). In 1310, during the Kamakura period, a worship hall was added in front of the Hondo, but during dismantling and repair work done in 1896–1898, the worship hall was removed and the Hondo was returned to its original, simpler form.

Characteristics and Highlights

Today this building allows us to appreciate the attractions of Tenpyo architecture in their simplest form. The low building with its extended, gently sloping roof has an atmosphere of calm and unassertive tranquility. Its walls consist only of doors and plaster surfaces. Without windows, the exterior is simple and distinct, with *uchinori nageshi* (non-penetrating beams) above the doors and *kashiranuki* (head penetrating tie beams) the only horizontal members. The exquisite balance between the walls and the roof mass gives the building its fine sense of proportion.

On the interior, the simple structure of columns, beams, purlins, and *sasu* (the diagonal members that support the ridge beam) is visible at a glance. The space is integrated with the structure, giving an open feel that speaks to a modern sensibility with a freshness that never seems to fade no matter how many times one may visit.

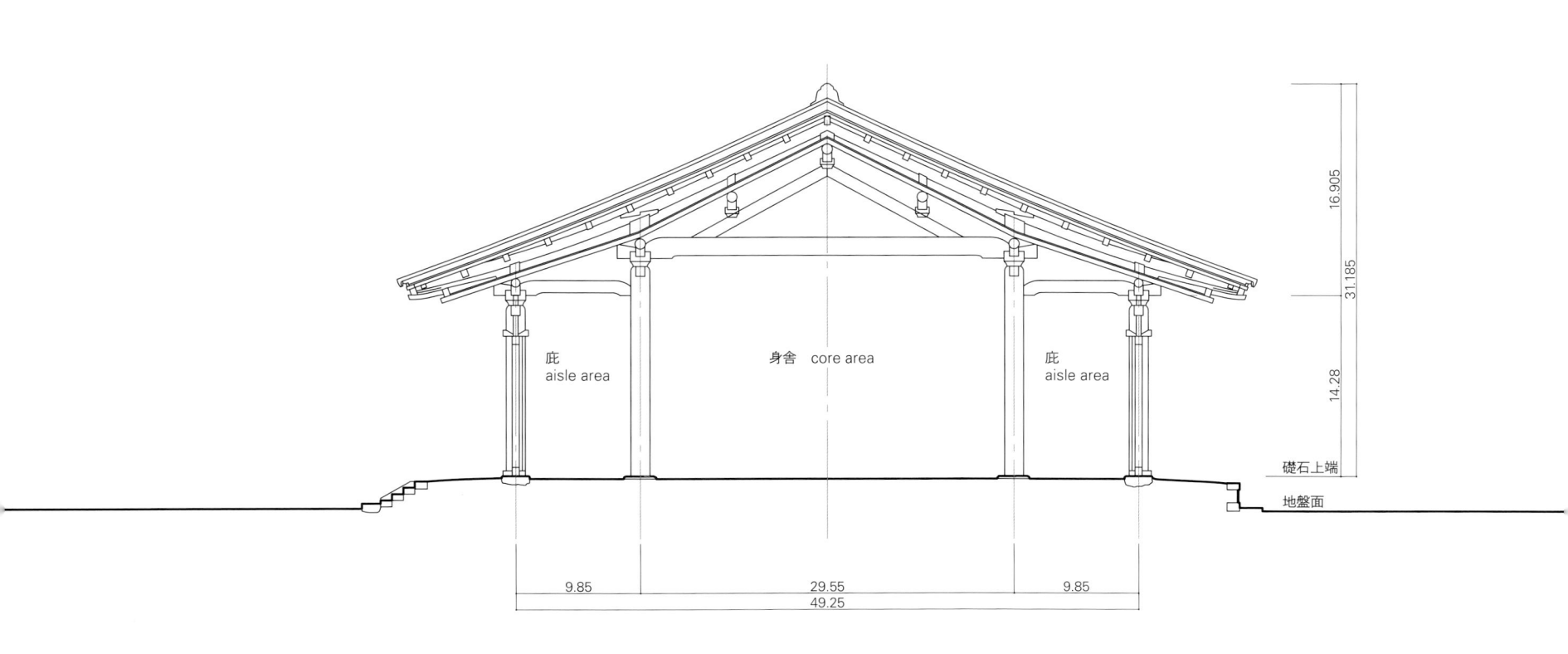

本堂・南北断面図　North–south section of Hondo (main hall)

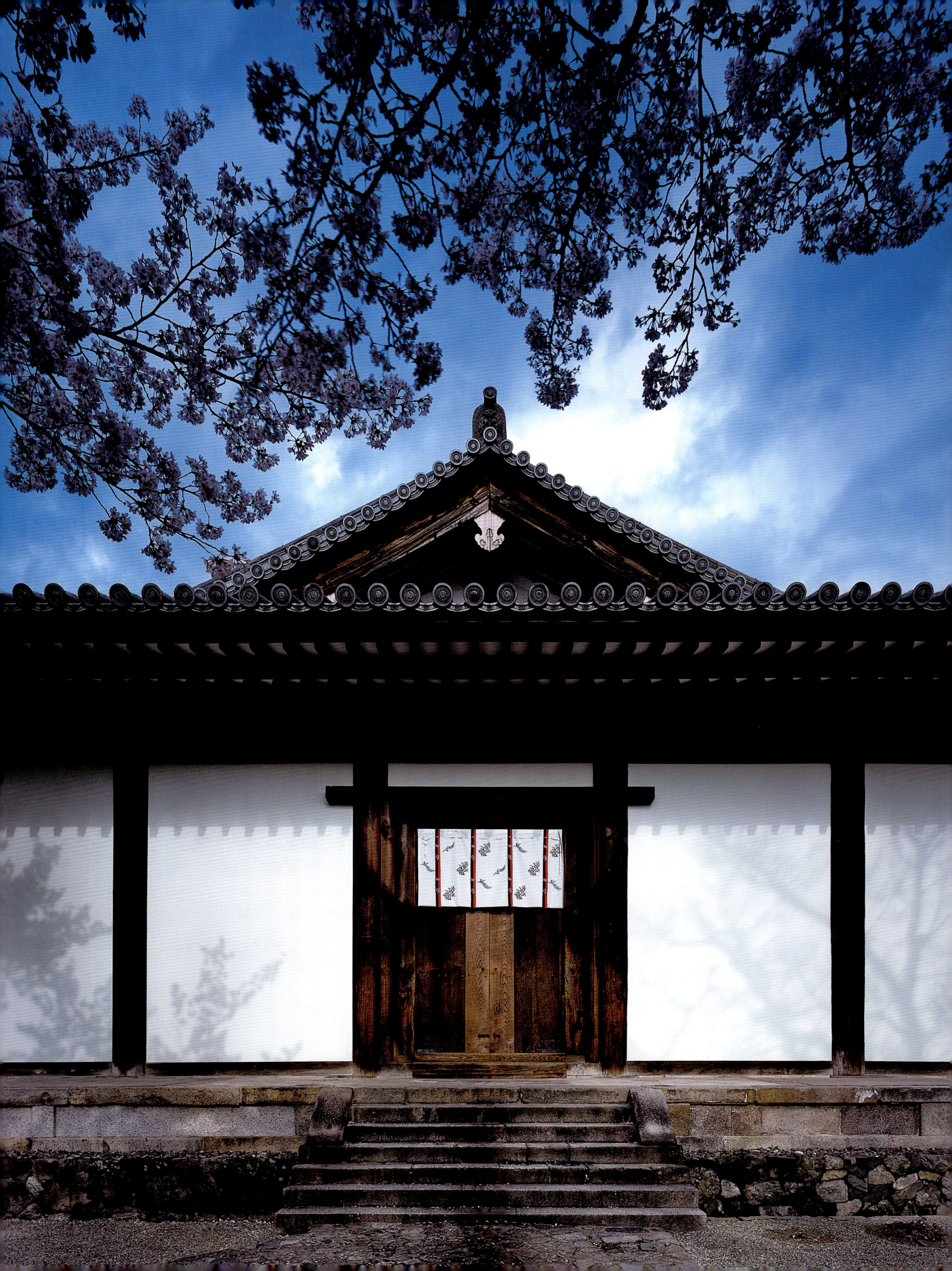

妻側西面。鬼瓦は13世紀のもの。軒裏の垂木は二軒で、地垂木（下）が円形断面、飛檐垂木（上）が角形。大斗の上に肘木を載せ、直接桁を受ける簡素で軽快な軒裏

West gable end. The roof's *onigawara* ridge-end tiles date to the thirteenth century. The underside of the eaves incorporate double rafters, with the lower base rafters round in cross-section and the upper flying rafters squared. The structure of the underside of the eaves is simple and light, with the wall purlin supported by a bearing block and bracket arm pair.

本尊薬師如来坐像を須弥壇中央に安置し、そのまわりを日本最古の十二神将立像が円陣に取り巻く。化粧屋根裏による開放感ある空間。伸びやかな垂木と白い天井板との対比が明快で美しい

The principal image, a seated statue of Yakushi Nyorai (Buddha of Medicine), rests on a central altar circled by Japan's oldest statues of the Twelve Heavenly Generals. The underside of the roof is exposed, opening up the space. The long, dark rafters stretching over the white ceiling boards make for a striking contrast.

堂の中心には円形の須弥壇が据えられている。大梁上に立つ
叉首が連続し、力の流れを明快に表現する

The circular altar occupies the center of the building. Above, the series of diagonal braces show clearly the transmission of weight to the primary rainbow beams.

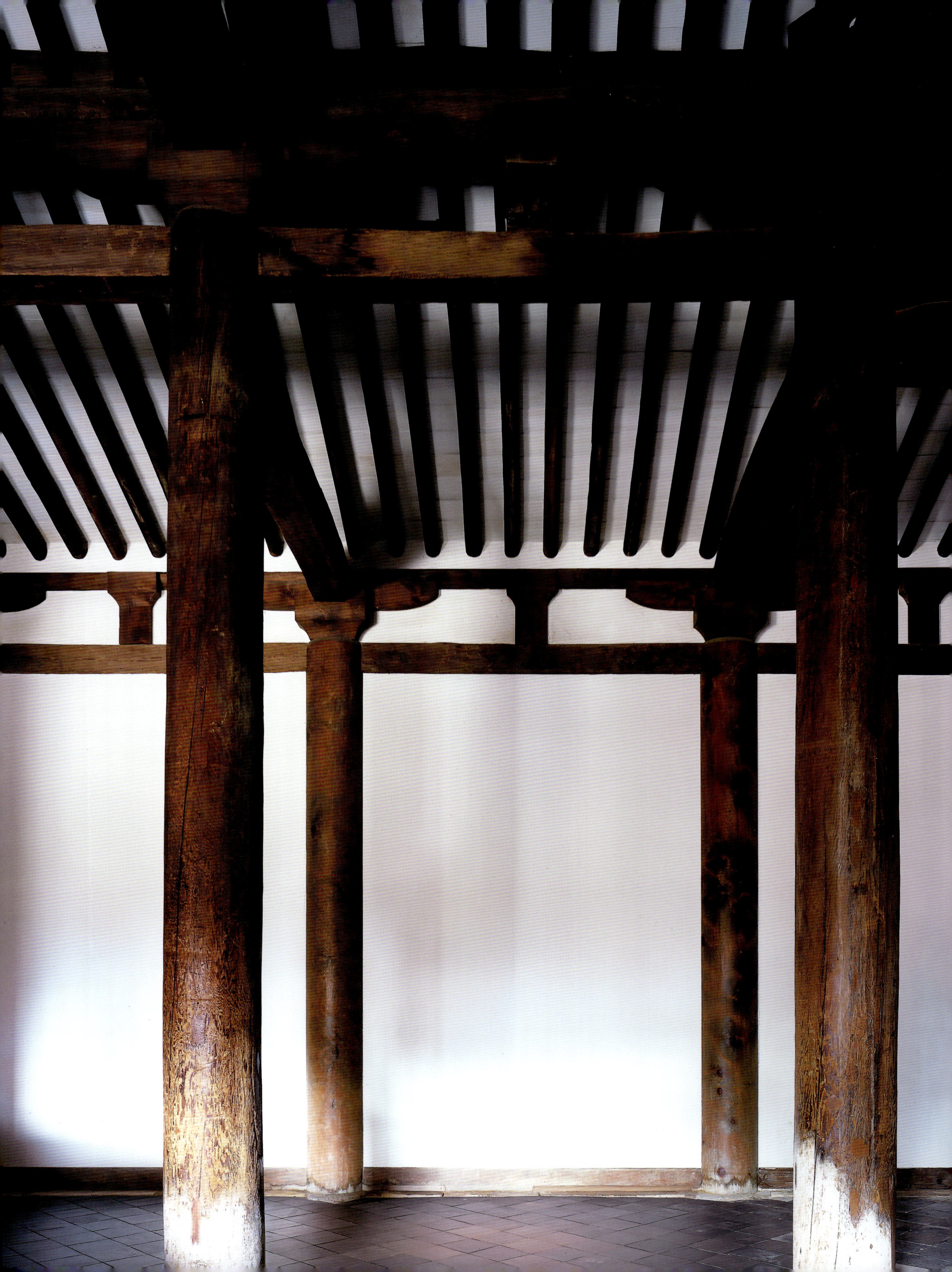

身舎と虹梁でつなげられた庇空間は、天井勾配を変えることで空間に主従の関係をつくる

The angle in the ceiling marks the hierarchy of building core and surrounding aisles.

元興寺 極楽坊禅室

国宝
建立年代　1200年前後
所在地　　奈良県奈良市

Gangoji Temple Gokurakubo Zenshitsu Hall

National Treasure
Completed: c. 1200
Location: Nara, Nara prefecture

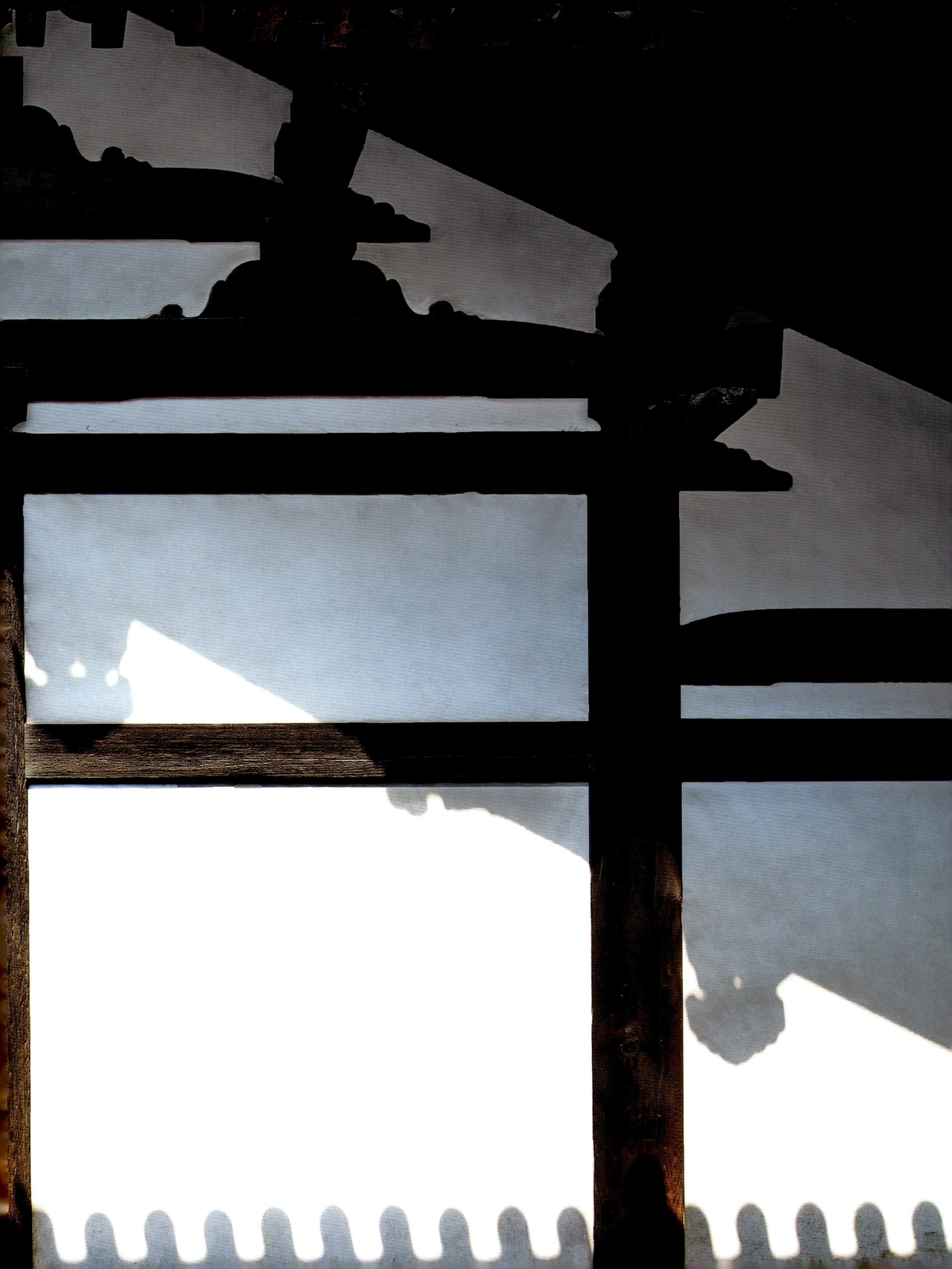

時代背景

　元興寺の前身は日本で最初の本格的な仏教寺院・法興寺（飛鳥寺）で、596（推古4）年、大臣を務めた蘇我馬子（-626）が飛鳥の地に建立した。この寺が平城京の遷都にともない、718（養老2）年に興福寺の南に移転し、寺名を改めて元興寺とされた。寺域15町の大伽藍を有したが、都が平安京に移されると徐々に衰微し、時を経て大部分の堂宇を失った。

　天平時代に建てられた僧房の一部を活かし、鎌倉時代初期の1200年前後に修造・再建されたのが禅室である。この建物は今も東西約30mにおよぶ伸びやかな外観が印象的だが、もともとこの場所には、12房をもつ大規模な僧房（東室南階大房）が立っていた。その長さは約86mにもおよぶ長大なものであったという。鎌倉時代初頭にはそのうちの8房が残っており、途中を馬道として、東3房を曼荼羅堂に、西4房分をそのまま改修して禅室とした。曼荼羅堂は現在禅室と隣接する極楽坊本堂（国宝）で、1244年に改造・再建されて現在にいたる。一方、禅室の部材はほとんどが鎌倉期のものであることから再建と見なされるものの、小屋組には奈良時代やそれ以前の古材も再利用されていることがわかっている。屋根高や側柱高、軒の出についても旧僧房に倣うが、これはもともとひとつながりであった旧僧房の東側半分がまだ立っていたため、天平以来のその建物との調和を意図して建てられたためである。

　禅室の再建は僧重源（1121-1206）の東大寺再興の時期と重なり、大仏様の影響が構造や細部に見られる。天平時代の僧房の佇まいを今に伝える数少ない遺構であり、その形姿を大切に守りつつ、大仏様によって再生され、その後、時代時代の用を満たしてきた建物である。

特徴と見どころ

　天平時代にここで起臥した僧侶の生活を思い描いてみる。いにしえに大伽藍を誇った元興寺の痕跡を一断片残すにすぎない建物ではあるが、禅室にはそんな想像力を掻き立てるに十分な佇まいがある。伽藍を象徴する塔や金堂のような表向きの建造物とは違って、この建物は美しさを求めてつくられたわけではない。だが、そういった建物だけがもつ素朴な心地よさ、清々しさを漂わせている。

　基壇をもたず、柱や束は自然石の礎石上に立つ。長い縁と切妻屋根がつくりだす水平線は低く、親しみやすい。屋根瓦には、元興寺の前身である飛鳥寺で使われていた瓦が今も一部に使われており、焼成ムラのある色合いは屋根全体の印象に豊かな質感を与えている。軒は簡潔に一軒の角垂木で、木口には大仏様らしく鼻隠し板を打つ。組物は平三斗に挿肘木を併用したもので、腕木だけで軒を支えるかたちとなり、簡にして要を得た構造である。

　部屋の一単位は天平時代以来の「3間1房」の形式を踏襲する。円柱の立つ1間を角柱2本で3等分し、真ん中に扉、左右に連子窓を組み合わせる。その単位がつくりだす僧房らしい規律性と連続感が、爽やかなリズムを刻んでいる。

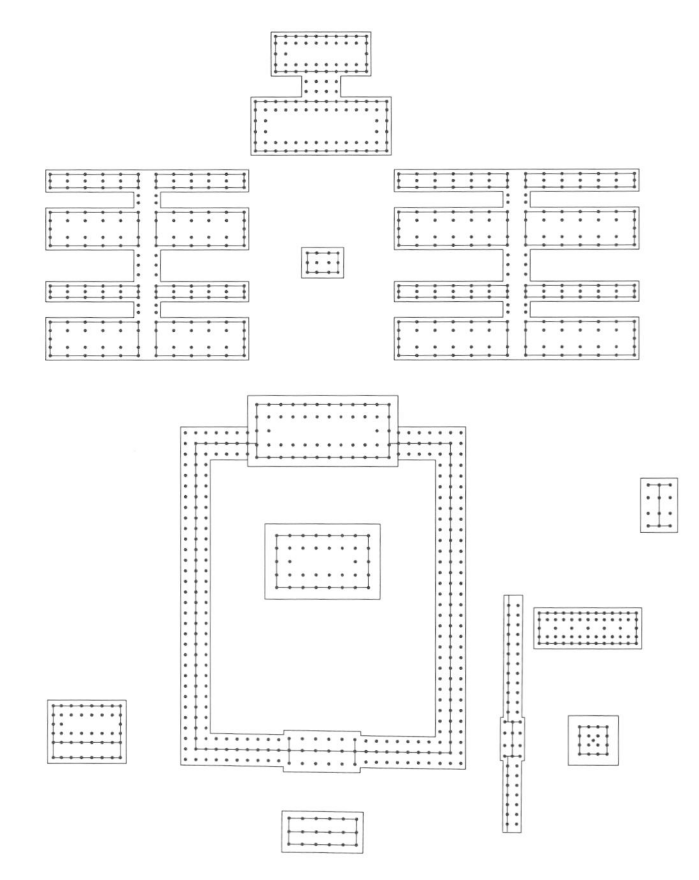

伽藍復元図 [*5]　Original site plan

Historical Background

The precursor of what is now Gangoji was Hokoji (Asukadera), Japan's first Buddhist temple, founded in Asuka (southern part of present-day Nara prefecture) in 596 by the powerful minister Soga no Umako (d. 626). Following the transfer of the capital to Heijokyo (northern part of present-day Nara prefecture) in 710, the temple was moved to the south of Kofukuji temple in 718 and its name changed to Gangoji. The once-massive temple complex gradually declined following the subsequent transfer of the capital to Heiankyo (Kyoto) in 794, and most of its buildings were lost with the ravages of time.

The Zenshitsu hall was rebuilt around the year 1200 at the start of the Kamakura period, making use of part of priests' quarters originally built during the Tenpyo era (eighth century). Today roughly 30 meters east-to-west, the hall's long exterior is impressive, but the structure that once stood on the site stretched for 86 meters and had twelve residential cells. From the eight of these cells that remained at the beginning of the Kamakura period, three on the east were turned into a Mandala-do hall, four on the west were repaired and converted into the Zenshitsu hall, and a passageway (*medo*) was opened between them. The Mandala-do hall was rebuilt in 1244 as the Gokurakubo main hall (National Treasure) now adjoining the Zenshitsu. The Zenshitsu is considered a reconstruction because nearly all of its structural members date to the Kamakura period, but the roof frame is also known to reuse older materials dating to the Nara period and earlier. The height of the roof, the height of the *gawabashira* perimeter pillars, and the depth of the eaves are modeled on the former priests' quarters, whose Tenpyo-era eastern half was still standing at the time the Zenshitsu, designed to harmonize with that older structure, was built.

The rebuilding of the Zenshitsu was contemporary with Chogen's rebuilding of Todaiji temple, and the influence of the Daibutsuyo style can be seen in both its structure and details. The building is one of the few examples to retain the style of Tenpyo-era priests' quarters to the present day, its appearance having been carefully maintained even as it was reborn in the Daibutsuyo style and used for various purposes from one period to the next.

Characteristics and Highlights

Although the Zenshitsu represents but a fraction of Gangoji's once magnificent temple complex, it is more than enough to stimulate our imagination when we attempt to picture the communal lives of the priests here during the Tenpyo era. Unlike the official buildings that symbolized the complex, such as its pagoda or main hall, the priests' quarters were not built with the pursuit of beauty as the primary guiding principle, and yet they exhibit a simple, comfortable, freshness all their own.

Rather than resting on a stone podium, the building's pillars and short supports stand on natural foundation stones. The long eaves of the gabled roof have a low, inviting horizontality while color variations (caused by firing irregularities) in the roof tiles, some of which were previously used at Asukadera, Gangoji's predecessor, enriches the visual texture of the roof. The squared rafter ends of the simple, single eaves are covered with fascia boards, as is typical of the Daibutsuyo style.

Individual rooms followed the *sanken ichibo* (one cell three bays) format used in the Tenpyo era. The front of the cell between two rounded pillars is divided into three bays using two squared pillars, flanked by slatted *renji* windows on either side. The sense of order and continuity—so appropriate to priests' quarters—that results from the use of such units also sets up a fine structural rhythm.

極楽坊本堂（手前）と禅室
Gokurakubo main hall (foreground) and Zenshitsu

禅室(手前)と極楽坊本堂(奥)を背面(北側)から見る。禅室はもと天平時代の僧房。
奥の本堂西側の屋根には、元興寺の前身である飛鳥寺(596年)で使われていた瓦
が葺かれている。禅室の北面は南面と扉や窓の形が異なり、北面は開口が小さい

North façade of the Zenshitsu (foreground) and the Gokurakubo main hall (background). Visible on the roof of the main hall are roof tiles previously used at Asukadera (596), Gangoji's predecessor temple. The shape of the doors and windows differs on the Zenshitsu's north and south faces; the openings are smaller on the north.

南面。屋内に廊下はなく、縁側が動線となる。軸組みは地貫、内法貫、頭貫。柱間には、桟唐戸、その左右に連子窓。内側には障子が入る

South façade. There are no hallways in the interior so the veranda acts as the connecting passageway. The framework includes penetrating tie beams above the floor, above the doors, and at the top of the pillars.

連子窓を内部から見る。内法の高さは2.1m（約7尺）。もとは畳敷きではなく、板敷であった

Renjimado slatted windows seen from the interior. From the threshold to the head jamb measures 2.1 meters. Now covered with tatami, the interior was originally floored with boards.

南東隅。随所に大仏様のディテールが採用されている。頭貫の木鼻には大仏様の繰形がつき、柱に肘木を直接挿しこむ挿肘木が使われ、大斗で繰形つきの実肘木を受けて軒桁を支えている。軒は一軒、直線の角垂木

Southeast corner. Molding characteristic of the Daibutsuyō style can be seen on the nosings of the head penetrating tie beams and the *sanehijiki* purlin-bearing bracket arms. The eaves are single-layered with straight, squared rafters.

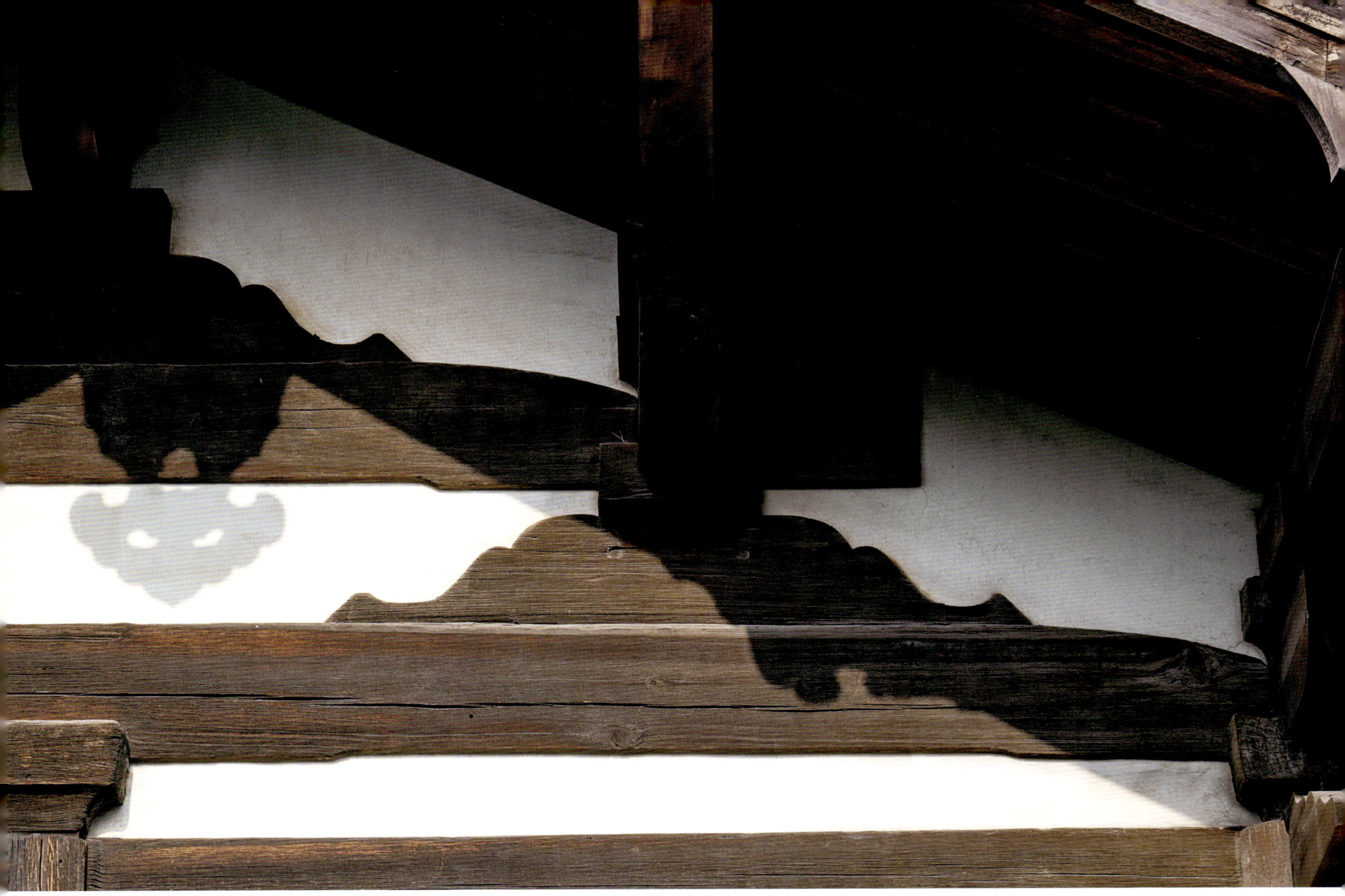

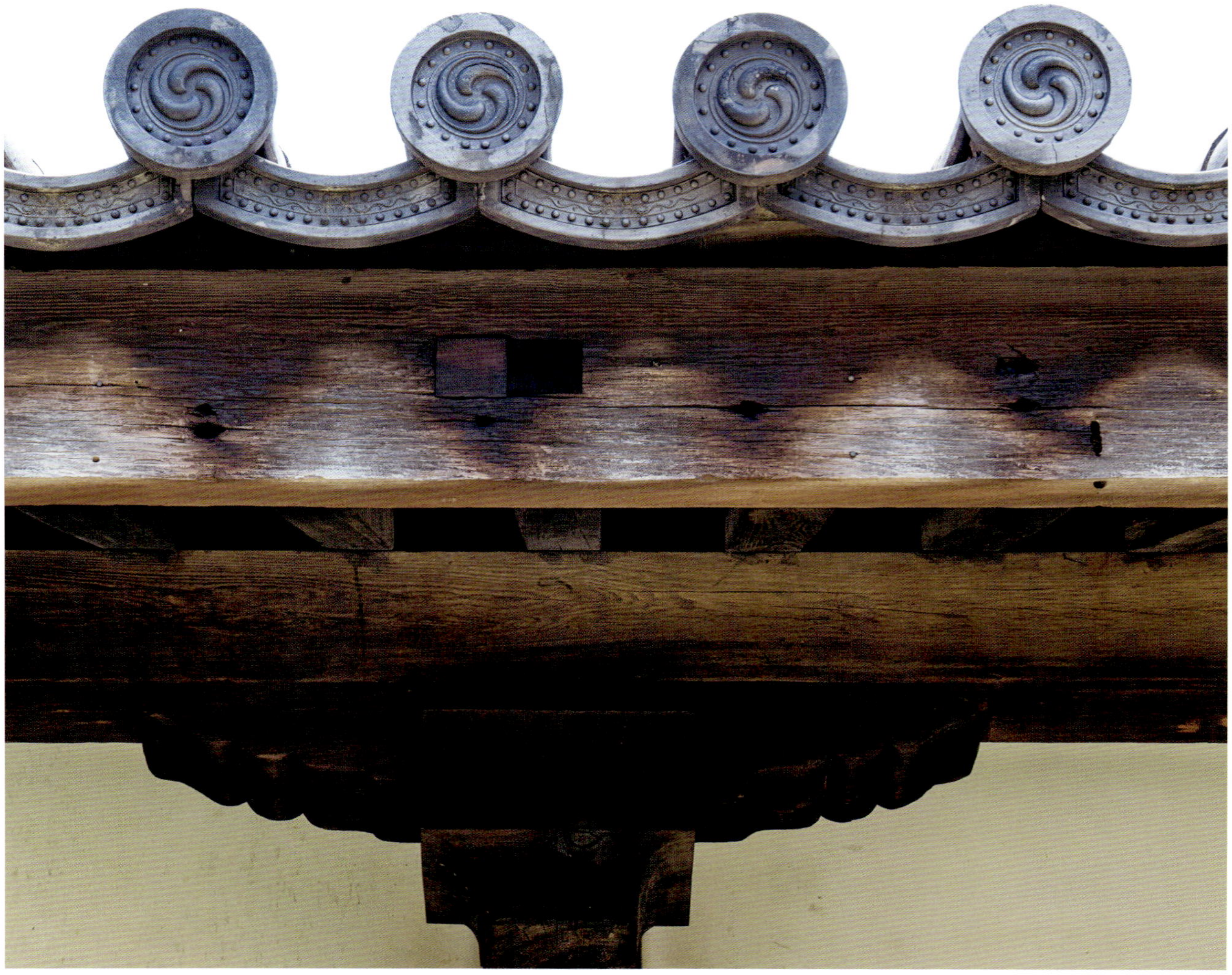

(左上) 西側の妻飾り。二重虹梁蟇股。猪の目懸魚の影が映りこむ
(左下) 垂木の木鼻には、大仏様の特徴である鼻隠し板がつく

(Top left) Gable pediment embellishment incorporating double *koryo* rainbow beams and *kaerumata* frog-leg struts. The shadow cast by the *inome gegyo* boar's-eye gable pendant is visible at left.
(Bottom left) The rafter ends are covered with fascia boards as is typical of the Daibutsuyo style.

(上) 挿肘木で軒桁を支える素朴にして簡潔なディテール

(Above) Supporting the *nokigeta* eave purlins with *sashihijiki* bracket arms inserted into the shaft of the pillars is a simple, concise detail.

室生寺 五重塔・金堂・灌頂堂

国宝
建立年代　五重塔：800年頃　金堂：9世紀　灌頂堂：1308年
所在地　奈良県宇陀市

Murouji Temple Five-story Pagoda, Kondo (Main Hall), and Kanjodo Hall

National Treasures
Completed: Five-story Pagoda, c. 800; Kondo, 9th century; Kanjodo Hall, 1308
Location: Uda, Nara prefecture

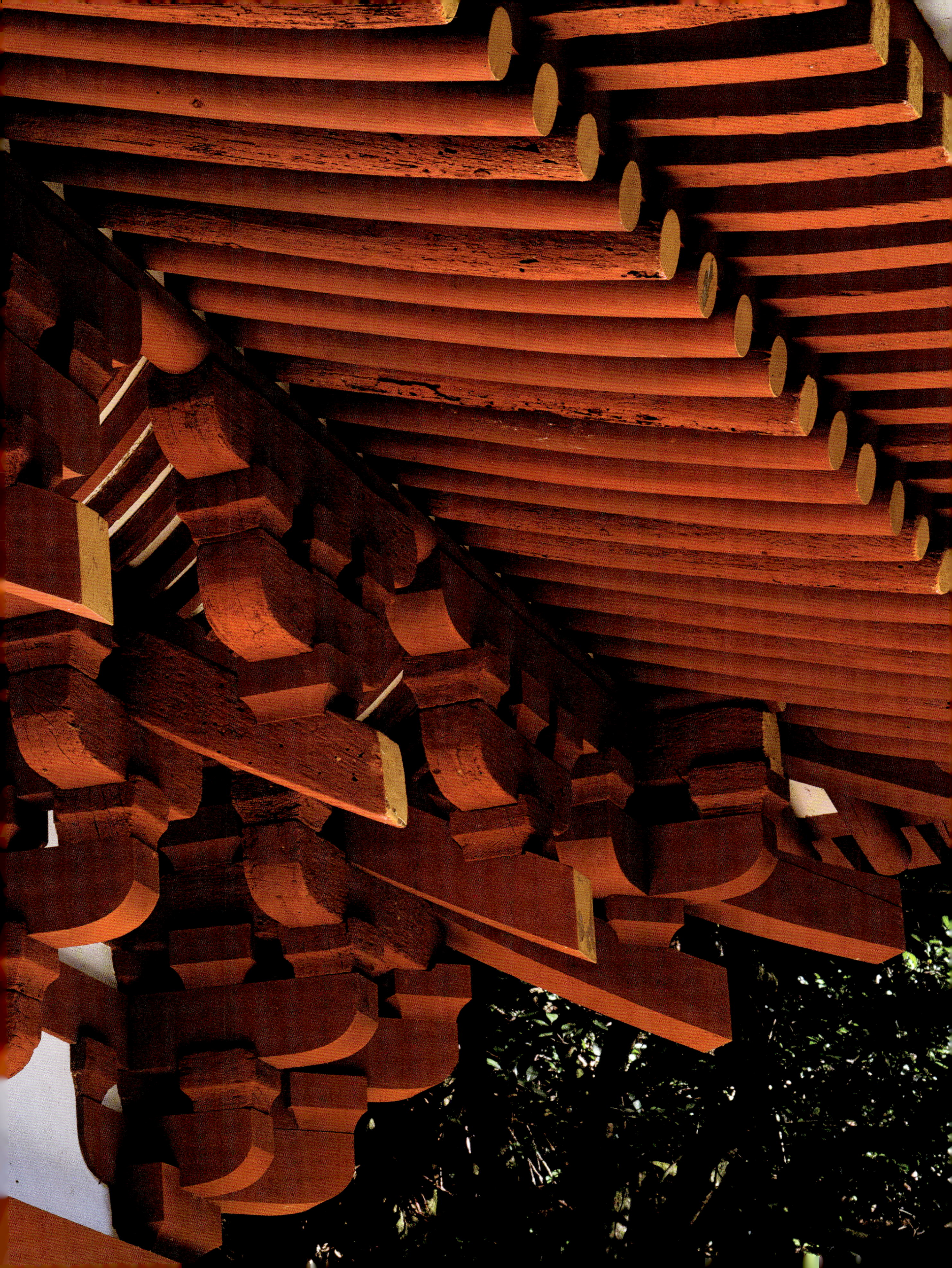

時代背景

　奈良県の東、三重県との県境に近い室生の渓谷を蛇行して流れる室生川の上流をさかのぼると、緑深い杉木立に囲まれたなかに室生寺がある。このあたりは古来、水をつかさどる竜穴神が棲む聖域と伝えられ、独特の山容水態から山林修行の地として知られた場所であった。室生寺の創建年は精確には不明だが、奈良時代末から平安時代初期（8世紀末）とされ、開基は法相宗興福寺の僧・賢璟（714－793）である。このことから寺は興福寺に属する一方で、天台宗、やがて真言宗との関わりが深くなり、1701（元禄14）年には真言宗に編入された。密教的な山岳寺院として伽藍が整備され、山腹を這うようにして堂塔が山深い奥の院まで点在する。平安時代へと移り変わるこの時期、都の平地に伽藍を開く南都仏教のあり方から、山林修行を目的に俗界を離れ、自然の気に満ちた山中に堂宇を築く動きが始まる。時代を同じくして、比叡山に入った最澄（767－822）、高野山に入った空海（774－835）の動向と室生寺の歴史は重なり合う。

　平安時代前期の建物や仏像を今に伝え、堂宇のなかでもっとも古い五重塔は、最近の調査で800年前後の建立とされている。[*6] その後、少し遅れて建てられた金堂の正堂部分は平安前期、興福寺にゆかりある弥勒堂が鎌倉前期、灌頂堂とも呼ばれる真言系の本堂が鎌倉後期（1308年）、奥の院の弘法大師を祀る御影堂が室町前期の造営である。土地の竜王を守護神とする自然崇拝の信仰を基盤に、南都仏教、真言・天台の両密教が複層的に重なりつつ、そのどれをも共存させながら時間をかけて形成された伽藍である。

特徴と見どころ

　山の精気に身体を浸しつつ、見上げる、上る、立ち止まる、という動作を繰り返しながら、石段に誘われて山の上へ奥へと歩を進める。ここは、垂直に点景と点景を結ぶようにして展開する山地伽藍である。まず、長い石段（鎧坂）上に徐々に姿を現す古色をまとった金堂に出迎えられる。寄棟造の屋根は柿葺きで、周囲の樹木と調和した佇まいを見せている。堂は南に向き、すぐうしろに山を抱え、斜面の狭小な土地に立つため、正面の礼堂部分は懸造になっている。そこには縁がめぐらされ、内部には西側面へまわって入堂する形式である。平安初期におけるこの堂の建立時は、3間×1間の身舎に1間の庇をめぐらせた堂であったが（現正堂部分）、江戸前期の1672（寛文12）年に懸造となった礼堂がつくられ、屋根は入母屋から寄棟に変更された。礼堂部分の屋根は正堂から縋破風を見せて滑らかに葺き下ろされ、その曲線が優美な印象をつくる。

　金堂の西側にまわり、さらに石段を上ると、鎌倉後期創建の灌頂堂（本堂）が姿を現す。真言宗において授戒の法式を行うための堂で、灌頂堂としては最古の遺構である。外部・内部ともに大仏様の影響が見え、また、反りの強い入母屋造の大屋根が載る。

　灌頂堂の西側、石段を上ると、緑のなかに浮かび上がるようにして立つのが五重塔である。塔の立地は山あいを縫うようにして光が射しこむ特別な地で、春分・秋分の前後には、1日に2度、塔は朝日と西日を浴びる。伽藍がまだ整備される前、杉の原生林が生い茂る山中に選定された塔の立地は、ほかにはない光が射す特別な場所である。

　屋根は建立から700年間ほどは板葺で、室町時代頃に柿葺、その後、江戸時代中期以降から檜皮葺となり、周囲の緑に柔らかく融けこむような佇まいができあがった。塔の総高は基壇を除いて16.1m。屋外に立つ五重塔としてはもっとも小さい。軒の勾配がゆるく、その出は深く、老杉が高々とそびえるなかに伸びやかな水平線を描いている。

奥の院へ導く参道
Approach to the innermost sanctuary

Historical Background

Murouji temple stands in a deep cedar forest in the upper reaches of the river that winds through the Murou ravine at the border of Nara and Mie prefectures. Since ancient times, this area was known as the dwelling place of the dragon god who presides over the water supply. Marked by the distinctive natural beauty of its mountains and streams, it was also popular as a training ground of Buddhist ascetics.

The exact date of the founding and completion of Murouji temple is unknown, but it is believed to have been founded by the priest Kenkei (714–793) of the Hosso sect Kofukuji temple at the end of the eighth century, around the end of the Nara period and the beginning of the Heian period. While belonging to Kofukuji, the temple had close associations with the Tendai sect and later with the Shingon sect until it was finally admitted into the Shingon sect in 1701. The complex is arranged in the esoteric Buddhist mountain temple style, stretching up the mountainside with its buildings scattered along a path rising high up the forested incline. During the transitional era between the Nara period, when the great temples built on the Nara plain were ascendant, and the Heian period, when major new temples were established in Kyoto, a movement began among those seeking ascetic training to separate themselves from the secular world and build Buddhist temple buildings in the mountains surrounded by nature. The early history of Murouji temple overlaps with the period when Saicho (767–822) moved the center of his activities to Mt. Hiei and Kukai (774–835) went to Mt. Koya.

The temple faithfully transmits to our time the architecture and statuary of the early part of the Heian period. The five-story pagoda, the oldest of the buildings, has recently been determined to have been built around 800. The inner shrine of the Kondo main hall of the temple was built a short time later in the early Heian period. The Mirokudo, with its strong links to Kofukuji, was built in the early Kamakura period. The Kanjodo hall, related to the Shingon sect, was built at the end of the Kamakura period (1308). The Mieido, the innermost sanctuary where Kobo Daishi (Kukai) is enshrined, was constructed in the early Muromachi period. Murouji's temple complex evolved over a long expanse of time, originating in the ancient nature worship centered around reverence for the dragon god and incorporating layers of Nara Buddhism and Tendai and Shingon esotericism. These layers have long coexisted in the same space.

Characteristics and Highlights

Enveloped in the spirit and energy of the forest, the visitor is carried upward by ancient stone steps—climbing, gazing upward, climbing, pausing—over and over. At this mountain temple the settings of each structure are connected vertically. First is the Kondo main hall, its time-weathered form gradually coming into view up the long flight of stone steps known as Yoroizaka ("armored slope"). With its thin wooden shingles (*kokerabuki*), the hipped roof appears to be a part of the surrounding trees. Tucked into the mountain slope on a small site facing south, the building has a *raido* worship hall section constructed in the *kakezukuri* overhang style. When the Kondo was originally constructed in the early Heian period, its 3-bays-by-1-bay *moya* core was surrounded by 1-bay-deep eaves (the current *shodo* inner shrine section) but in 1672 during the middle Edo period, the *kakezukuri* style worship hall was added and the roof was changed from the *irimoya* hip-and-gable to a *yosemune* hipped roof. The roof of the worship hall continues unbroken from the main roof, revealing the *sugaruhafu* bargeboards whose curve gives the building its graceful elegance.

Up the stone steps to the west of the Kondo, we next come to the Kanjodo hall built towards the end of the Kamakura period. The hall was used to perform the initiation ritual involving the sprinkling of holy water on the head as practiced in the Shingon sect, and it is considered to be the oldest extant example of its kind. Both the interior and exterior of the building show the influence of the Daibutsuyo style.

Ahead, as we climb the stone steps on the west side of the Kanjodo, the five-story pagoda appears, as if floating against its backdrop in the greenery. The pagoda is located in the contour of the mountain in just such a way that it catches the rays of the sun. Around the spring and autumn equinox, the pagoda is lit up by both morning and evening sunlight. The site, which was the very first to be selected in the virgin forest as the pagoda was erected before the rest of complex was built, is indeed a very special place unlike anywhere else within the temple grounds.

For the first 700 years of its life, the pagoda was roofed in *itabuki* (board) shingles; then around the Muromachi period, it was reroofed with *kokerabuki* thin wooden shingles. The roofing was changed again in the middle Edo period to *hiwadabuki* cypress-bark shingles, creating the current look that merges seamlessly into the surrounding trees. The pagoda measures 16.1 meters above the podium. It is the smallest open-air built, five-story pagoda known today. The lively horizontal lines of its deep, gently sloped eaves contrast with the verticality of the tall old-growth cedar forest.

五重塔は800年頃の建立。老杉の木立のなか、春の西日を浴びて石段上に優美な姿を浮かび上がらせる。軒の出は各重ほぼ同じで、軒の勾配もゆるく、伸びやかな水平線を描く

The five-story pagoda was built around the year 800. Bathed in the light of the setting sun in spring, it stands against a backdrop of ancient cedars at the top of the stone steps. The gentle lines of the low-pitched eaves, nearly the same length on each story, exalt its graceful proportions.

下が柿葺、上が檜皮葺の二重の軒付けとなり、厚みがある。これは屋根の葺材が板葺（創建—室町時代頃）から柿葺（室町—江戸中期）、さらに檜皮葺（江戸中期—現在）へと変遷してきた経緯があるためである。裏甲と下軒付け（柿板軒付け）を合わせて白塗りしており、庇の厚みが特徴的である

The thick edges of the eaves are made with cypress bark above and thin wooden shingles below. This reflects the transition in roofing materials over time from wood shingles to thin wooden shingles and then to cypress bark. The white paint on the eaves filler (*urago*) and lower eave edges brings out their lines distinctly.

緑の中、赤の対比が鮮やかに映える。三手先斗栱は各重同じ大きさで、上重へ行くほど詰めて並べられている。二重垂木で、下の地垂木が円、上の飛檐垂木が角の「地円飛角」。典型的な天平様式の流れにある

The three-stepped bracket complexes are the same size on each story but come closer together with each ascending level. The double-layered eaves are made in the *jien hikaku* style with a lower layer of base rafters round in section and an upper layer of flying rafters square in section, a classic example eighth-century Tenpyo era style.

金堂の礼堂部分にかかる孫庇が搥破風を見せて滑らかに葺き下ろされ、優美な曲線をつくる。
この部分は江戸時代、1672（寛文12）年の改築による

The *magobisashi* roof extension over the worship hall portion of the Kondo forms a graceful curve, revealing the *sugaruhafu* extended bargeboards. This portion of the building was added in 1672.

朝一番の光を浴びる金堂。建立は平安時代前期。背後には斜面が迫り、山の精気のただなかに佇む。屋根は柿葺で周囲の樹木と調和する

The Kondo in the first light of morning. Erected in the ninth century, it stands in the midst of the forest's vitality, the mountain slope close at the rear. Its roof of wooden *kokerabuki* shingles blends in well with the surroundings.

金堂、南向きの正面。礼堂部分は斜面に拡張して建てられ、縁をまわす。
当初材にはヒノキではなく、土地のスギが使われていた

South façade of the Kondo. The worship hall portion is built out over the slope as an extension and surrounded by a veranda. Rather than cypress, local cedar was used for the principal structural members.

西側から見た金堂の寄棟造の屋根。柔らかな芽吹きの樹木のなかに現れ出る
伸びやかな線。古色をまといつつも、屋根の品格が際立つ

The hipped end of the Kondo as seen from the west. Sloping gently among the budding trees, the lines of the roof embody antiquity with outstanding elegance.

灌頂堂の軒裏。鎌倉時代の1308年に建立。垂木は反りをつけた二重角垂木。二手先斗栱は二手目を尾垂木で持ち出し、軒支輪をつける。扉は桟唐戸、内法貫をめぐらせて木鼻には繰形をつけるなど、大仏様・禅宗様の影響が見える

The underside of the eaves of the Kanjodo hall. Built in 1308 during the Kamakura period, the building incorporates curved, double-layered rafters. The upper level of the *futatesaki* two-stepped bracket complexes projects out over the *odaruki* tail rafters and incorporates *nokishirin* convex struts. The *sankarado* paneled entrance doors topped with *uchinorinuki* penetrating tie beams, as well as incised nosings, show the influence of the Daibutsuyo and Zenshuyo styles.

灌頂堂の西の妻側。虹梁太瓶束式の妻飾りは大仏様の意匠の影響が強い。太瓶束上の肘木にも繰形がつく

West gable end of the Kanjodo hall. The embellished gable pediment with curved transverse beam and bottle strut shows the influence of Daibutsuyo style design. The bracket arms above the bottle strut are also incised.

灌頂堂の入母屋造、檜皮葺の屋根。山の中腹にあって、
急勾配の大屋根の存在感が引き立つ

The hip-and-gable of the Kanjōdō hall is roofed with cypress bark. In its mountainside location, the steep pitch of the massive roof leaves a powerful impression.

醍醐寺 五重塔

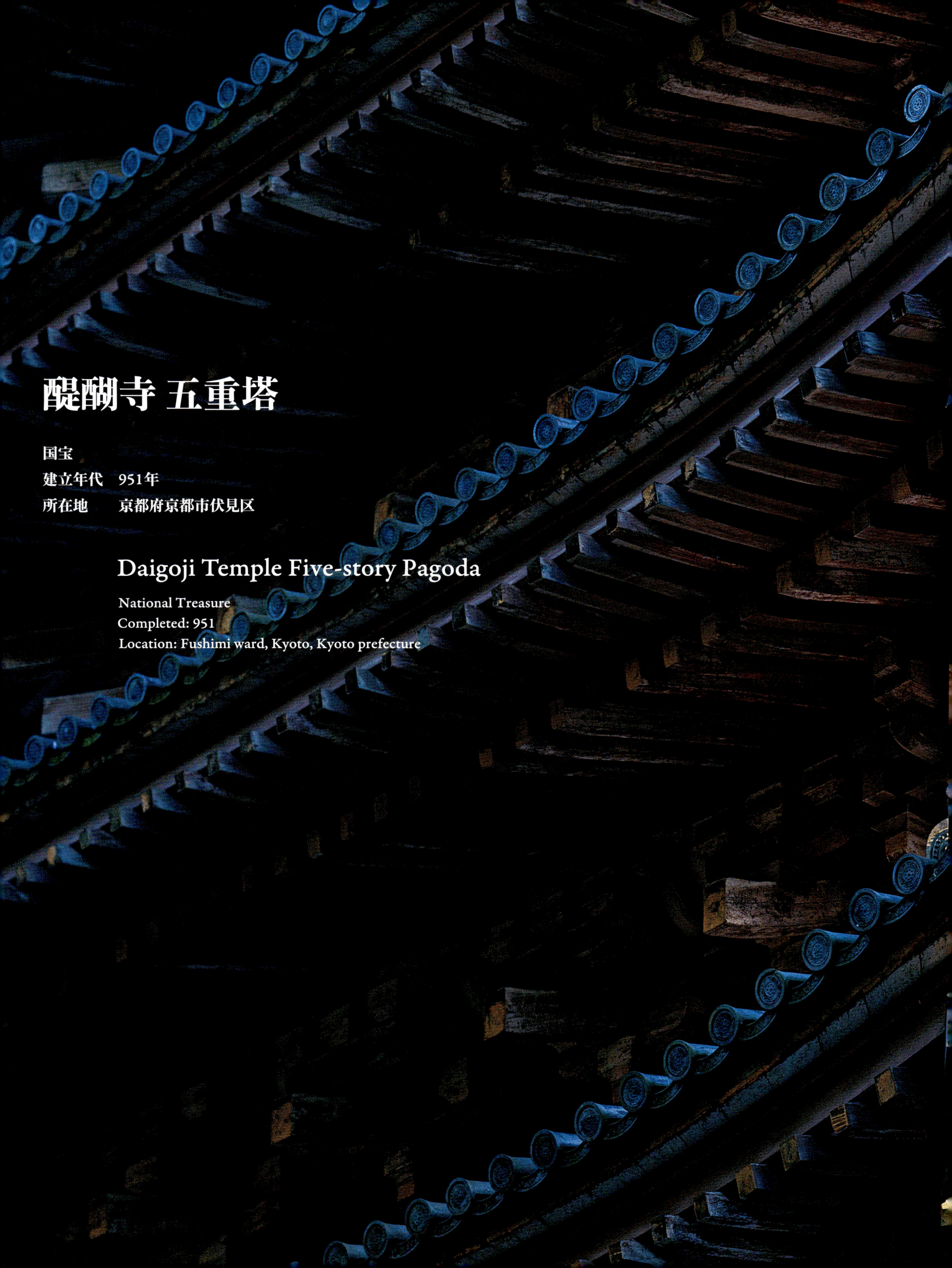

国宝
建立年代　951年
所在地　　京都府京都市伏見区

Daigoji Temple Five-story Pagoda

National Treasure
Completed: 951
Location: Fushimi ward, Kyoto, Kyoto prefecture

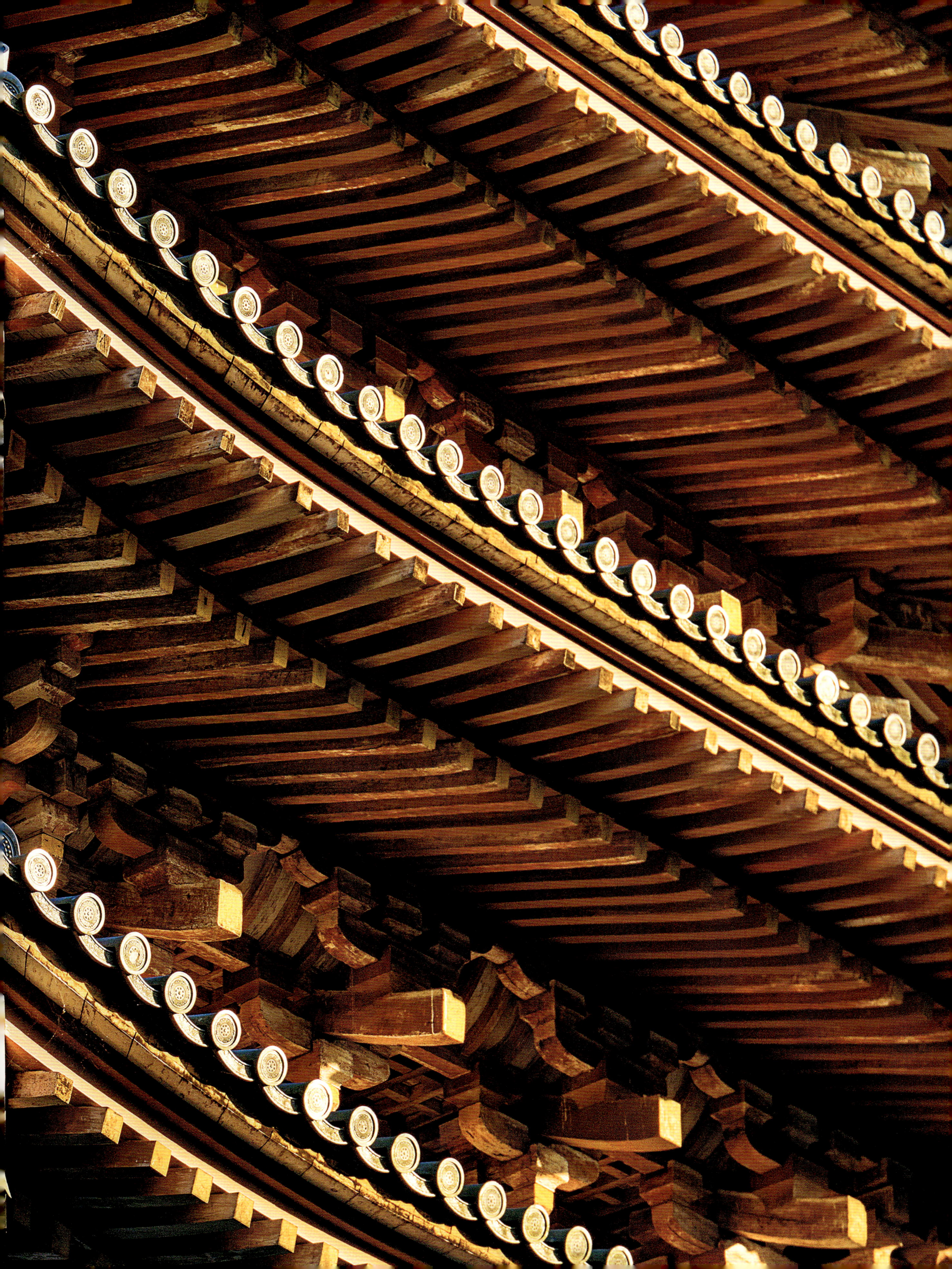

時代背景

　平安京へ遷都が行われ(794年)、新たな時代が到来すると、天皇が後押ししたのは最澄、空海が起こした密教であった。醍醐寺は真言宗醍醐派の総本山で、標高450mほどの醍醐山の頂から西側の山麓にかけて伽藍が広がる。真言宗の開祖・空海の孫弟子にあたる聖宝(832-909)が、874(貞観16)年、醍醐山上に堂を建てたことから寺の歴史は始まる。907(延喜7)年には、鎮護国家を託された山上密教寺院として醍醐天皇(885-930)の御願寺となり、山上の上醍醐の伽藍が築かれ、その後、伽藍整備は山のふもとの下醍醐にもおよんだ。

　下醍醐の境内に立つ五重塔は、930(延長8)年に逝去した醍醐天皇の冥福を祈るため、皇子の朱雀天皇(923-952)が御願・起工し、弟の村上天皇(926-967)の御代となった951(天暦5)年に竣工、翌年に塔供養が行われた。かつての下醍醐の境内は、南から北へ南大門、中門、金堂、講堂が軸線上に並び、中門と金堂間には廻廊が取りついていた。五重塔は廻廊の外、金堂から見て斜め前方の南東の位置関係で建てられており、伝統的な奈良式の伽藍配置とほぼ同じ形式を踏襲していた。

　しかし、塔の初重内部には両界曼荼羅の諸尊をはじめ、真言宗を広めた祖師の御影が心柱の覆い板や四天柱、壁面などに描かれている(951年・国宝)。6世紀の仏教伝来以来、仏舎利を奉安する目的で建てられてきた塔婆は、密教の時代となってその意味が更新される。本塔は、伝統的な塔の形は引き継ぎながらも、密教の曼荼羅の世界、および真言の教義を表わすための塔として位置づけられている。

　都からほどよく離れた地に立つ醍醐寺も、室町時代に洛中を火の海にした応仁・文明の乱(1467-1477)の災禍と無縁ではなく、1470(文明2)年に兵火にかかり、下醍醐の堂宇のほぼ全部を失った。そのなかで稀有にしてこの塔は難を逃れ、創建時から遺る唯一の建造物として、また、京都府下における最古の木造建築として今に伝えられている。

特徴と見どころ

　木割が太く、全体に力がみなぎり、安定感のある塔である。江戸時代末までに屋外に建てられた現存する五重塔の内4番目に高く、塔の総高は約38m、そのなかで相輪部分が約13mあり、全体の1/3を占めているのが特徴となる。九輪もたっぷりとして大きく、塔身と相輪の二つの要素が堂々とした均整美をつくりだしている。

　上重へ逓減する割合はゆるやかで、当初、屋根は板葺であったと考えられている。軒は角垂木による二軒で、前時代からの大陸様式を写した「地円飛角」(地垂木の断面を円形、飛檐垂木を角形)の軒は、この塔が建てられた時代にはすでに古様になっていたのかもしれない。一方、100年後に建てられた平等院鳳凰堂(1053年)の垂木は地円飛角を採用しているものの、その洗練された三手先斗栱とくらべると、本塔は隅の斗栱の収まりが古式で、いまだ進化途上にあったと推定されている。だが、寸法的にも視覚的にも、整理統一される一歩手前の力強さを残したディテールこそが、この塔の魅力でもある。

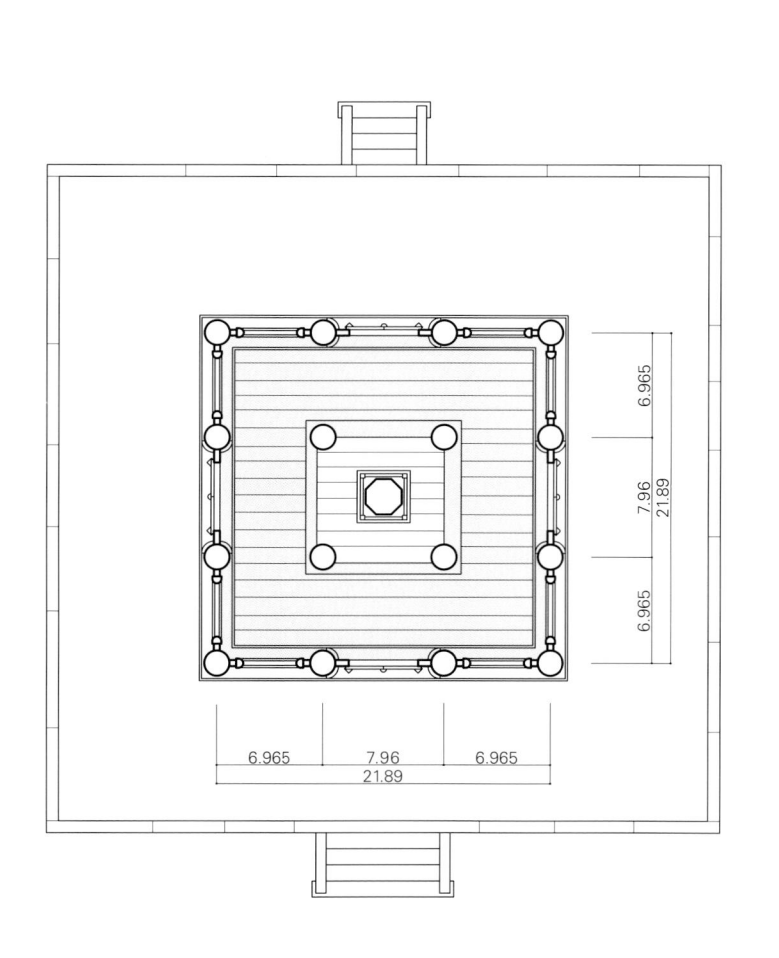

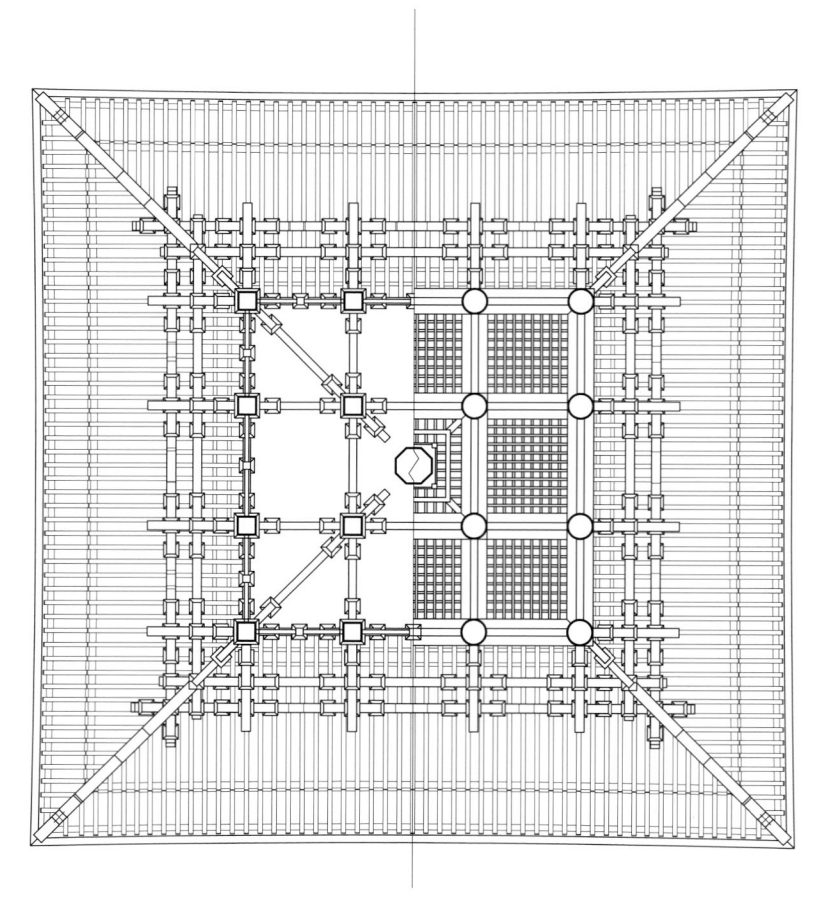

初重平面図　Floor plan of the first story

初重見上図　Ceiling plan of the first story

0　10　20尺/shaku
(6.06m)

Historical Background

In 794, after the capital was moved from Nara to Heian (present-day Kyoto), ushering in a new era, the emperor backed the Esoteric Buddhism of the great priests Saicho and Kukai, who respectively founded the Tendai and Shingon schools of Buddhism.

The history of Daigoji temple, which became the headquarters of the Daigo sect of the Shingon school, began with a hall built on the top of Mt. Daigo in 874 by Shobo (832–909), who had trained under a disciple of Kukai. Its precincts extend from the western foothills of Mt. Daigo to its summit at about 450 meters. In 907, as one of the esoteric mountain temples having been charged with the protection of the state, under the reign of Emperor Daigo (r. 897–930), Daigoji was made an imperial temple, and the buildings of the upper precinct (Kami-Daigo) were first constructed, followed by those of the lower precinct (Shimo-Daigo).

The Five-story Pagoda, which stands in the Shimo-Daigo complex, was planned to pray for the repose of the soul of Emperor Daigo, who died in 930. Completed in 951, it was consecrated the following year. At one time the Shimo-Daigo complex consisted, on an axis extending from south to north, of the Nandaimon gate, a *chumon* middle gate, the Kondo main hall, and a lecture hall, and the middle gate and main hall were connected by encircling corridors on the east and west. Following the style roughly the same as the temple complexes of the Nara period, the pagoda stood on a diagonal to the southeast of the Kondo outside the corridor.

The purpose of pagodas built since the introduction of Buddhism to Japan in the sixth century had been to enshrine relics of Shakyamuni Buddha. This example, however, shows a revision of that purpose for the era of esoteric Buddhism, and the four *shitenbashira* pillars, walls, and the wooden panels covering the *shinbashira* central pillar are painted with portraits of the "eight patriarchs" of the Shingon school and images of the Mandala of the Two Realms (951; National Treasure). While passing on the traditional form of the pagoda, the pagoda represented the world of the mandala and expressed the teachings of esoteric Buddhism.

Although located some distance from the capital itself, even Daigoji did not escape the turmoil and fires of the Onin War (1467–1477) which destroyed so much of the city, and in 1470 soldiers set fire to the buildings of the Shimo-Daigo complex, burning most of them to the ground. Miraculously escaping the flames, the pagoda survives in its original form, the oldest extant wooden structure within Kyoto prefecture.

Characteristics and Highlights

Of the five-story pagodas surviving from the Edo period and before, the Daigoji pagoda is the fourth tallest. Built with extremely robust members, it radiates strength and stability. One feature of this pagoda is that the finial accounts for 13 of the structure's 38-meter height, or nearly a third of the whole, and is equipped with nine ample-sized rings, creating together with the body of the building a magnificent, well-proportioned appearance.

The decrease in size of the roofs of the upper stories is slight, and it is believed that they were originally covered with wooden-slat shingles. The double eaves of each story are composed of square-base and square-flying rafters. By the time this pagoda was built, the use of the *jien hikaku* system (combing circular base rafters and square flying rafters), which emulated the continental style of earlier times, was probably already considered an older style. While the rafters of the Byodoin Hall built 100 years later (1053) follow the *jien hikaku* style, when we compare the three-stepped bracket complexes of the later building with the pagoda, we can see that the joinery of the pagoda was not as tidy and was still developing. The attraction of the pagoda, however, lies in a certain freedom and spontaneity of details just before they would become completely standardized in dimensions and appearance.

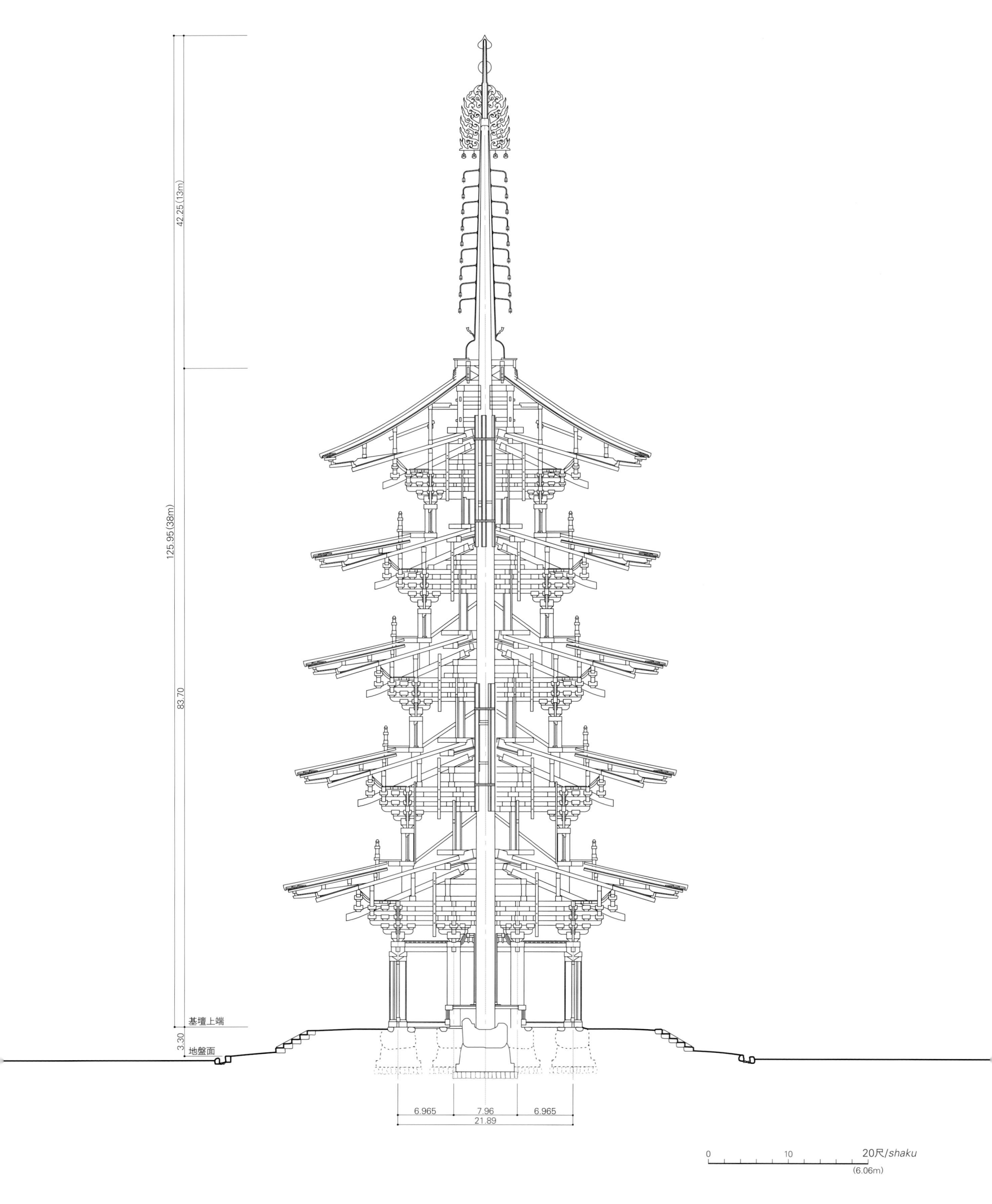

断面図。三手先を構成している肘木と尾垂木は内部まで貫通し、上層からの荷重がかかることで、てこの原理が働き、軒の垂下を防ぐ

Section. Utilizing the principle of leverage, the bracket arms and tail rafters that form the three-stepped bracket complexes penetrate to the interior, where the load of the upper stories prevents the eaves from drooping.

平安中期の951年に竣工。京都府下における最古の木造建築の遺構。総高約38mのうち相輪は約13mで全体の1/3を占め、塔身と相輪が力強い均衡感をもつ。逓減率（初重塔身に対する五重塔身の割合）は0.61。安定感をもちつつ空へと伸びやかに上昇する

Completed in 951, the pagoda is the oldest wooden structure in Kyoto prefecture. The body of the pagoda and its finial exhibit a powerful equilibrium, with the 13-meter finial representing one-third of the building's total 38-meter height. The ratio of the body of the pagoda at its fifth story to that at its first story is 0.61, creating a sense of stability even as the structure reaches to the sky.

軒裏、斗栱と垂木。組物とは、深い軒をつくるため、垂木を支える
軒桁を外側へ持ち出すためのものである。地垂木も飛檐垂木も
角形断面。木口は黄土で塗られている

Underside of the eaves, including a bracket complex and rafters. Bracket complexes enable the construction of deep eaves by projecting outward the eave purlins that support the rafters. Both base rafters and flying rafters are squared in section. The ends of wooden members are painted yellow with ocher.

西面。太陽が落ちる頃、夕日が真っ直ぐに上重を照らすひととき、
木部に塗られていた丹の赤色が浮かび上がる

West face. Direct rays of the setting sun on the upper stories of the pagoda bring out the vermillion painted on the wood.

三徳山三佛寺 奥院（投入堂）

国宝
建立年代　11世紀後半—12世紀
所在地　　鳥取県東伯郡三朝町

Mitokusan Sanbutsuji Temple Okunoin (Nageiredo Hall)

National Treasure
Completed: Second half of 11th–12th century
Location: Misasa, Tohaku district, Tottori prefecture

投入堂は三徳山の標高520m地点、ほぼ北面し、切り立つ岩壁の窪みのなかに組みこまれている。上部は岩が張り出し、天蓋のように堂を覆う。急勾配の斜面に長さの違う柱を立てた懸造となっている

Nageiredo hall stands in the hollow of a sheer cliff on Mt. Mitoku at an altitude of 520 meters. The hall is an example of the *kakezukuri* overhang style. The projecting cliff above the building covers it like a canopy. Each supporting pillar that reaches to the steep rock face below is a different length.

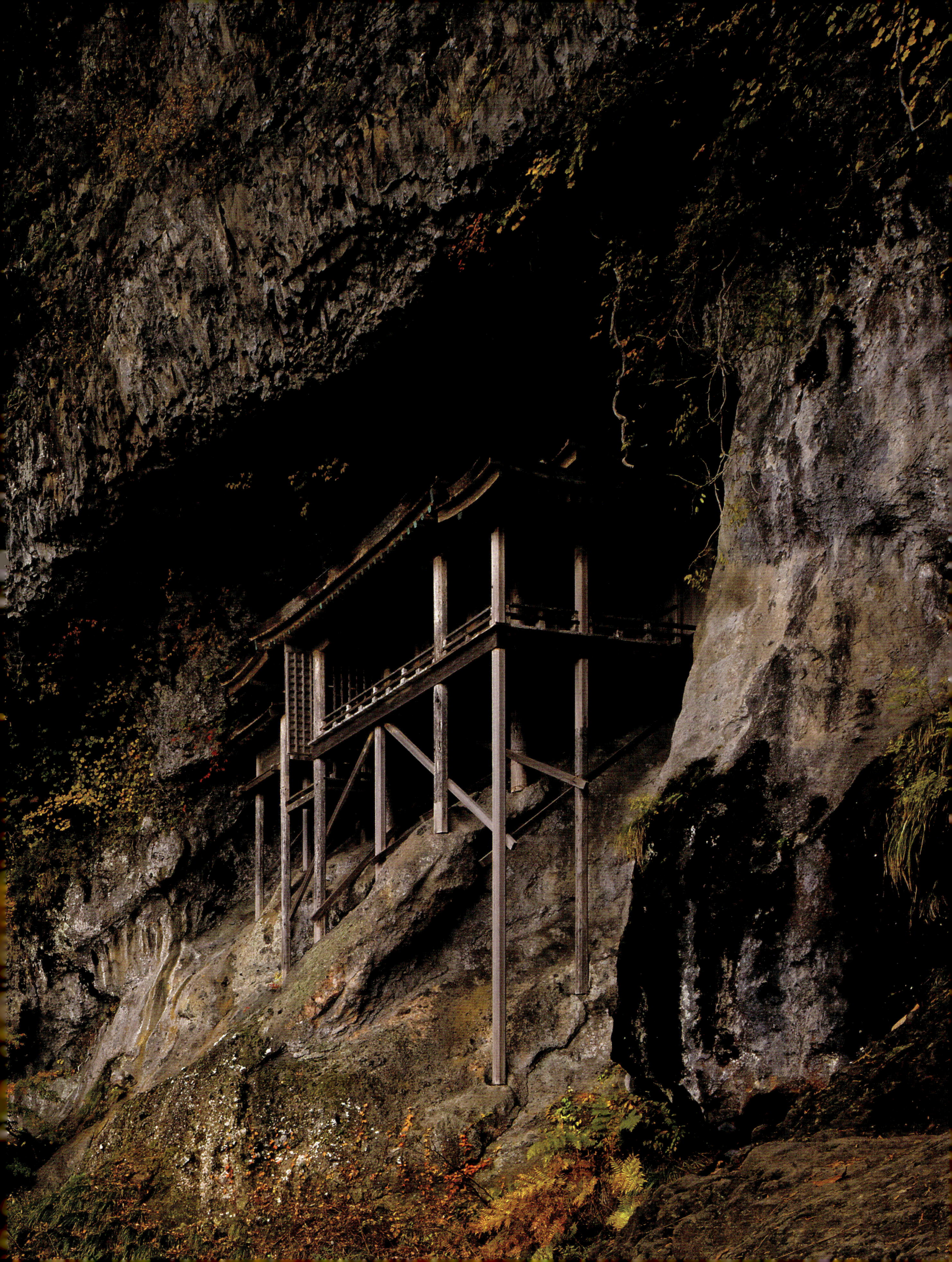

時代背景

　三佛寺は鳥取県の中央部、三徳山（標高890m）の北斜面に伽藍をもつ山岳寺院である。706（慶雲3）年、修験道の開祖・役小角がこの地に蔵王権現を祀ったことを起源とし、最澄の直弟子・円仁（794－864）を寺の開基とする。修験道は、仏教伝来以前からあった土着の神々への信仰や山への自然崇拝が、仏教、とくに天台・真言の密教における山中での修行と結びついて生まれた日本独特の宗教である。深山幽谷に分け入り、厳しい修行を積み、加持祈祷を行い、霊験を体得することを目的とする。平安時代中頃から盛んになったと考えられている。

　三佛寺の伽藍は山麓の本堂や坊と、中腹の奥院からなる。現在、奥院には平安から江戸初期にかけて建立された堂が数棟、山中に散在する。なかでも投入堂（もとは蔵王堂または蔵王殿と称されていた）は、急峻な山道を分け入った最奥に位置し、標高520m地点、切り立つ岩壁の窪みのなかに収められ、懸造で立っている。手前の堂を投入堂、格子で仕切られた奥の部分を愛染堂と呼ぶ。堂の建立年については確実な史料を欠くが、平安時代後期と考えられている。2006（平成18）年に行われた塗装調査では、堂が赤色と白色とで彩色されていたことが確認されている。[7] かつては岩壁を背景に鮮やかな色彩が際立ち、人の知恵と手をかけてつくった建造物として、自然との対比を強く印象づけるものであっただろう。

特徴と見どころ

　投入堂が位置する断崖は谷間の最上部にあり、硬質な安山岩と軟弱な凝灰角礫岩の境界に当たる。堂がすっぽりと収まる岩壁の凹部は最初から多少なりとも陥没していたのであろうが、堂を建てるために、もろい岩質の凝灰角礫岩の地層部分をさらに掘りこむことで場所を確保したのであろう。また、外気の気温変化にくらべて岩のなかの地温の振幅は安定しており、見た目の厳しさとは裏腹に、かなりよい環境を保てる立地といえる。なぜここなのか、を考えるとき、このような建設の諸条件は当然ながら考慮に入れて計画されたはずである。

　古代的な木太さをもった身舎柱の円柱約30cm（約1尺）に対し、庇まわりの部材（柱・垂木・肘木・桁）は大きく面取りされている。庇柱では1/6前後の大面取りである。そのため外側の部材が細身に見え、全体は軽やかな印象となる。面取りは平安時代から見られる技法で、時代が下るほど面取りが小さくなる。まだ台鉋は開発されておらず、槍鉋で円柱をつくりだしていくしかなかった時代、面取り柱にするというのは、本尊を祀る身舎の円柱に対して、あくまで略したかたちの木づくりとなる。投入堂はこのような初源的な面取りのあり方を見て取れる数少ない遺構である。

　この堂は、身舎・庇部分・愛染堂の三つの構成要素に分けられるが、庇部分の建築年代に差があることが指摘されている。[8] 今後の調査を俟つかたちだが、屋根や庇の変則的な納まりからも、増改築を経つつ現在の形となったことはまず間違いない。異なる構成要素を屋根や縁で束ねて統合することにより、むしろ全体のデザイン密度を高めるあり方は日本建築の特質であるが、投入堂ではその手法が絶妙なバランス感覚をもって十全に発揮されている。

三佛寺納経堂（鎌倉時代・重要文化財）
Sanbutsuji Nokyodo (Kamakura period; Important Cultural Property)

Historical Background

Sanbutsuji is a mountain temple whose complex of buildings is located on the north slope of 890-meter-high Mt. Mitoku in central Tottori prefecture. The temple's origins date back to 706 when En no Ozuno (En no Gyoja), the founder of Shugendo mountain asceticism, established a place to enshrine the deity Zao Gongen on the site, while the temple itself was founded by Ennin (794–864), a direct disciple of Saicho, founder of the Tendai school of Buddhism. Shugendo, with its roots in indigenous beliefs and practice of nature worship going back before the introduction of Buddhism, later became closely linked to esoteric Tendai and Shingon Buddhism. Practitioners sought to experience the divine by entering the deep mountains and dark valleys, engaging in religious austerities, and performing rituals and prayers.

The temple complex at Sanbutsuji includes the main hall and priests' residences at the base of the mountain and the inner sanctuary (Okunoin complex) midway up. The inner sanctuary today consists of a number of buildings constructed between the Heian and early Edo periods and scattered along the mountainside. Among them, the Nageiredo hall is located at the deepest part of the mountain at an elevation of 520 meters and accessible only by a precipitous trail. Built in the *kakezukuri* overhang style, it stands in a hollow of the rock cliff. The near section is the Nageiredo, while the far section, separated from it by latticework, is known as the Aizendo. Although no documents pinpoint the date of construction, it is believed to date to the second half of Heian period. An investigation in 2006 of vestiges of pigment confirmed that the building was once painted red and white. Set against the rock wall, the strikingly colored structure must have left a powerful impression—as a product of human ingenuity and craft—in its contrast with nature.

Characteristics and Highlights

The cliff on which Nageiredo is located sits at the highest point of the valley at the boundary between hard andesite above and soft tuff breccia below. The hollow in the cliff containing the hall may have been somewhat concave to begin with but space to construct the building was probably secured by digging away further at the brittle tuff breccia stratum.

While the cylindrical *moyabashira* core pillars (approximately 30 centimeters in diameter) suggest the solidity of ancient times, structural members used around the eaves (pillars, rafters, bracket arms, and purlins) are all deeply chamfered. For the *hisashibashira* eave pillars, the beveling extends to roughly one-sixth of the diameter of the pillars. This makes the outer members look thinner than they actually are, imbuing the whole with a sense of lightness. Chamfering techniques can be seen as far back as the Heian period, but growing more shallow over time. At a time when the *daiganna* block plane had yet to be invented and the *yariganna* "spear plane" was used to shape cylindrical pillars, chamfering pillars was seen as a rough form of carpentry relative to proper cylindrical pillars. The Nageiredo is one of the few places where such early chamfering can be seen.

The building is made up of three constituent parts—the core, the eaves, and the Aizendo—but there are indications that the eaves and the Aizendo were built at different times. Further investigation is needed, but the irregular fit of the roofs and eaves unmistakably suggests that the building's current form is the result of a series of additions and reconstructions. Elevating the design density of the whole by tying together and integrating disparate structures through the use of roofs and railings is a characteristic of Japanese architecture and a technique fully realized in the exquisite sense of balance achieved in the Nageiredo.

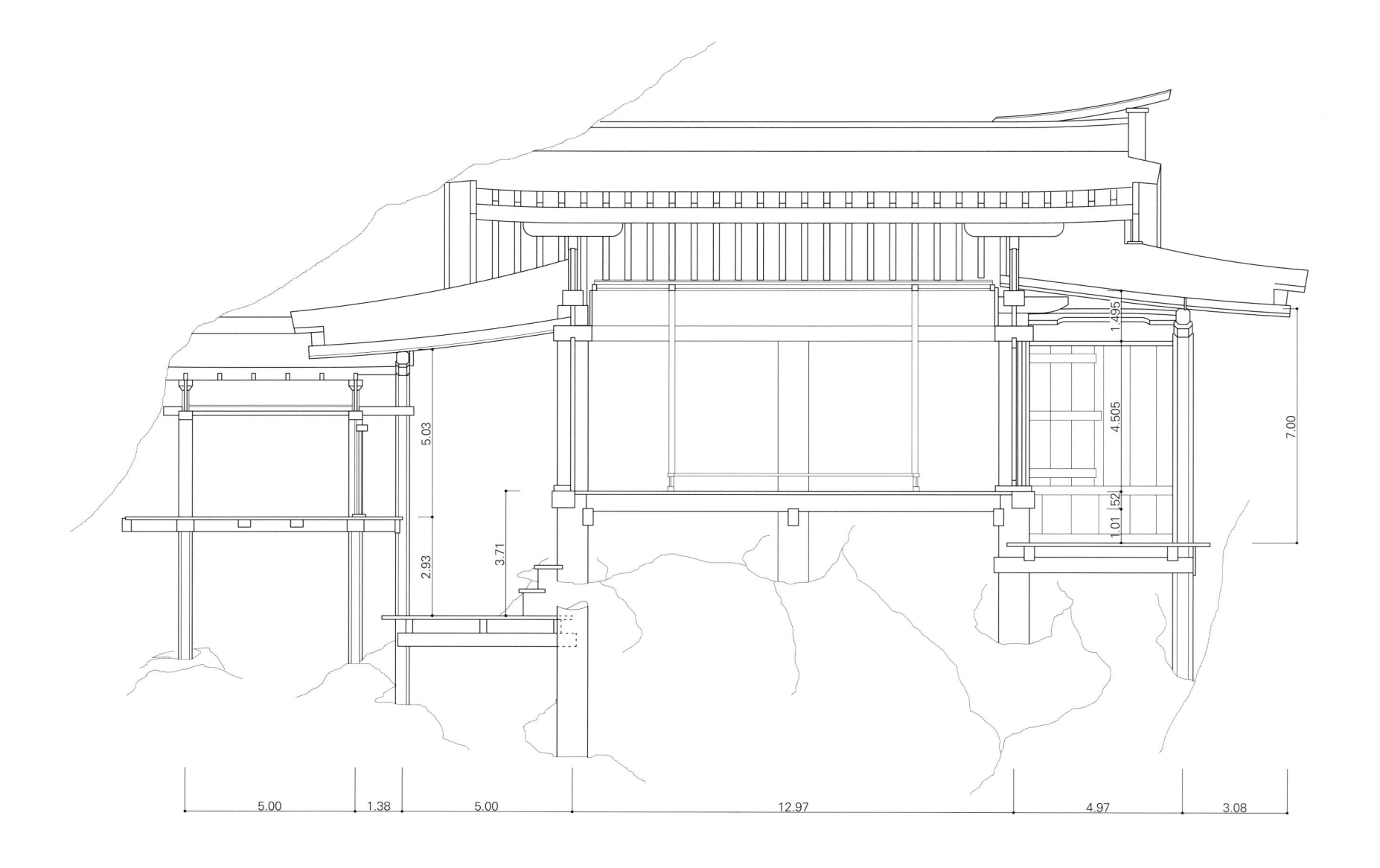

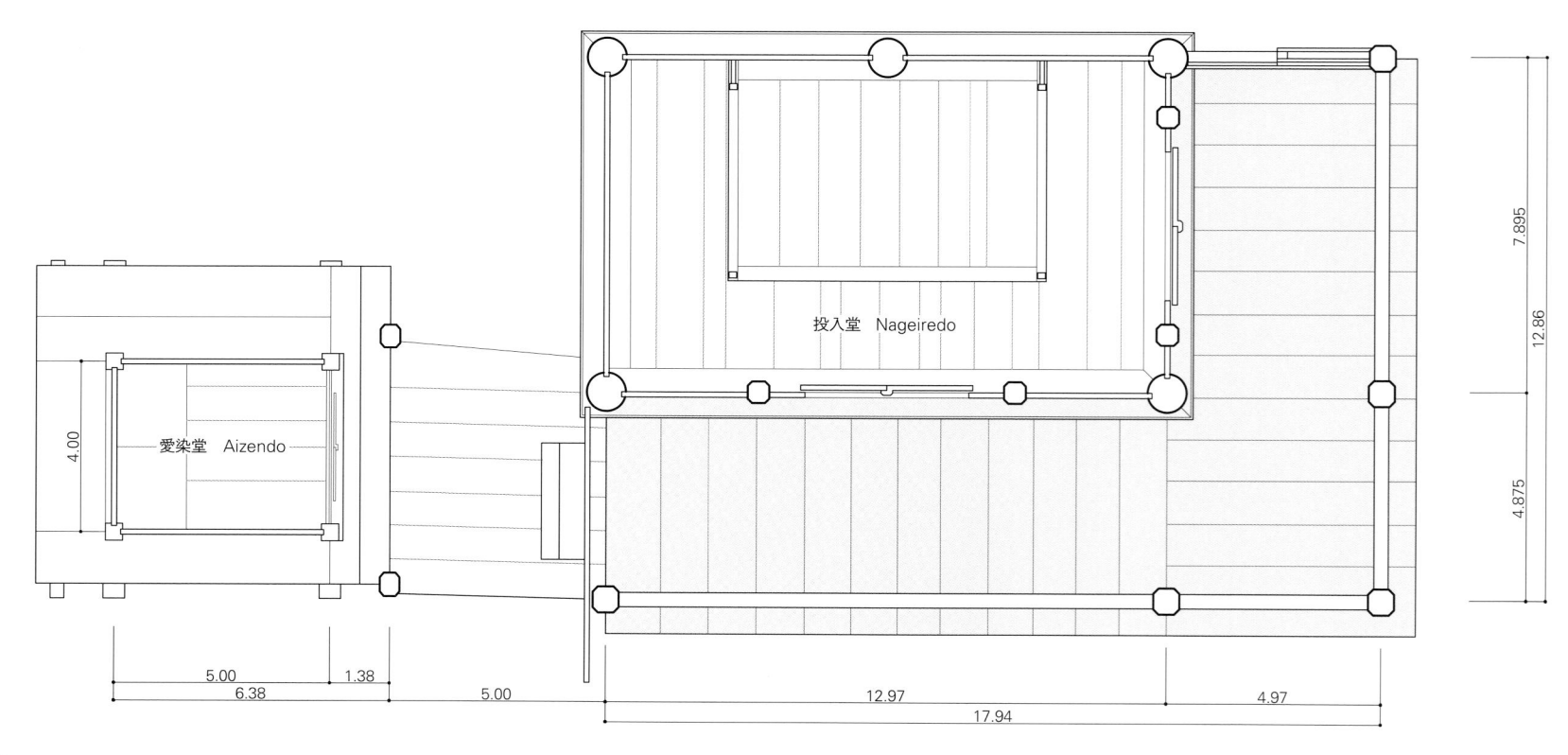

(上)断面図。(下)平面図。桁行1間(背面2間)×梁行1間の身舎、そのまわりに鉤の手にめぐる庇空間、さらに格子で仕切られた愛染堂の三要素で構成される。愛染堂と投入堂を連絡する床は1.1m下がっており、隣接する両堂の間に隔たりがある

(Top) Section. (Bottom) Floor plan.
The building is made up of three elements: the core (Nageiredo) that measures one bay wide (two bays at the rear) and one bay deep; the eaves that surround the core on two sides; and the Aizendo hall, separated from the rest by a lattice partition. The floor connecting the Nageiredo with the Aizendo drops 1.1 meters, forming a gap between the two adjacent structures.

(右)投入堂の身舎は径30cm(約1尺)の円柱で構成されるが、その外側の庇柱は大面取りの角柱(18.9cm角／6.2寸角)で、その面取幅は36mm(1.2寸)から、柱によっては91mm(3寸)もある。そのために全体の印象は細身に見える。投入堂は床下から肘木まで通し柱で、身舎の木太い円柱が床下の右奥に見える

(Right) The core of the Nageiredo is built using cylindrical columns with a diameter of 30 centimeters but the surrounding aisle uses posts square in section that measure 18.9 cm and have chamfers ranging in width from 36 millimeters to as much as 91 millimeters. As a result, the building as a whole has a slender appearance. The pillars of the Nageiredo run continuously from under the floor up through to the *hijiki* bracket arms; one of the core's thick cylindrical columns can be seen in the background at right.

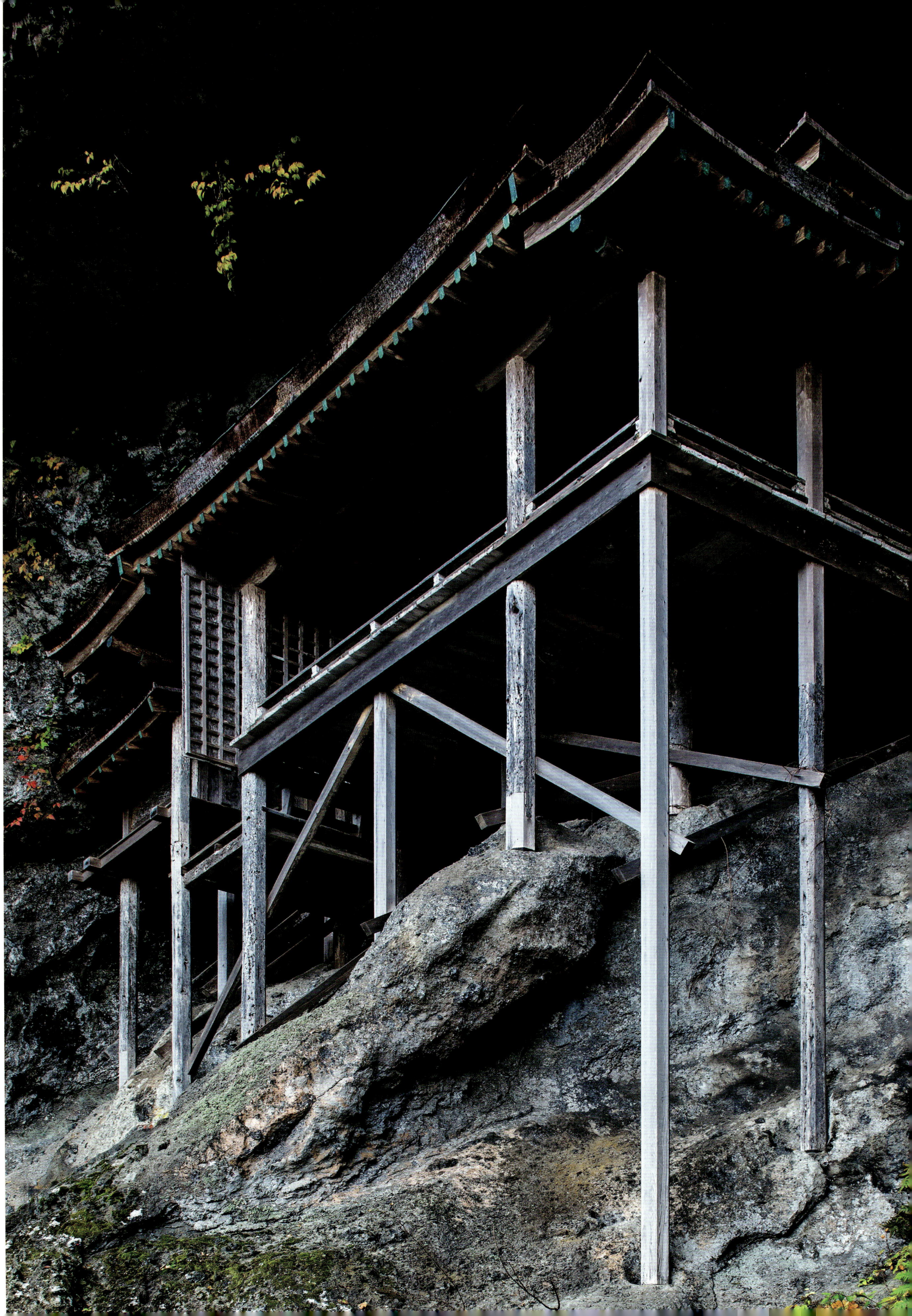

愛染堂と投入堂の複雑な屋根の重なり。柱や扉などには赤が、壁などには白が塗られていたことが調査でわかっている。斜材上部に塗り下地と推測される痕跡が見える

The complex overlapping of the roofs of the Aizendo and Nageiredo. Research has revealed that the pillars and doors were once painted red, and the walls white. Traces of what is believed to be a base coat can be seen toward the top of the diagonal support members.

北西角の屋根と軒裏。身舎の切妻屋根の下に小庇がかけられている。肘木や垂木も大面取りされている。垂木の木口には鍍金された銅製の透かし彫り飾り金具が打たれていた

Roof and eaves at the northwest corner. Eave extensions have been added below the gabled roof that covers the building core. Both *hijiki* bracket arms and *taruki* rafters are chamfered. The ends of the rafters were decorated with openwork fittings made of gilt copper.

平等院 鳳凰堂

国宝
建立年代　1053年
所在地　　京都府宇治市

Byodoin Temple Phoenix Hall

National Treasure
Completed: 1053
Location: Uji, Kyoto prefecture

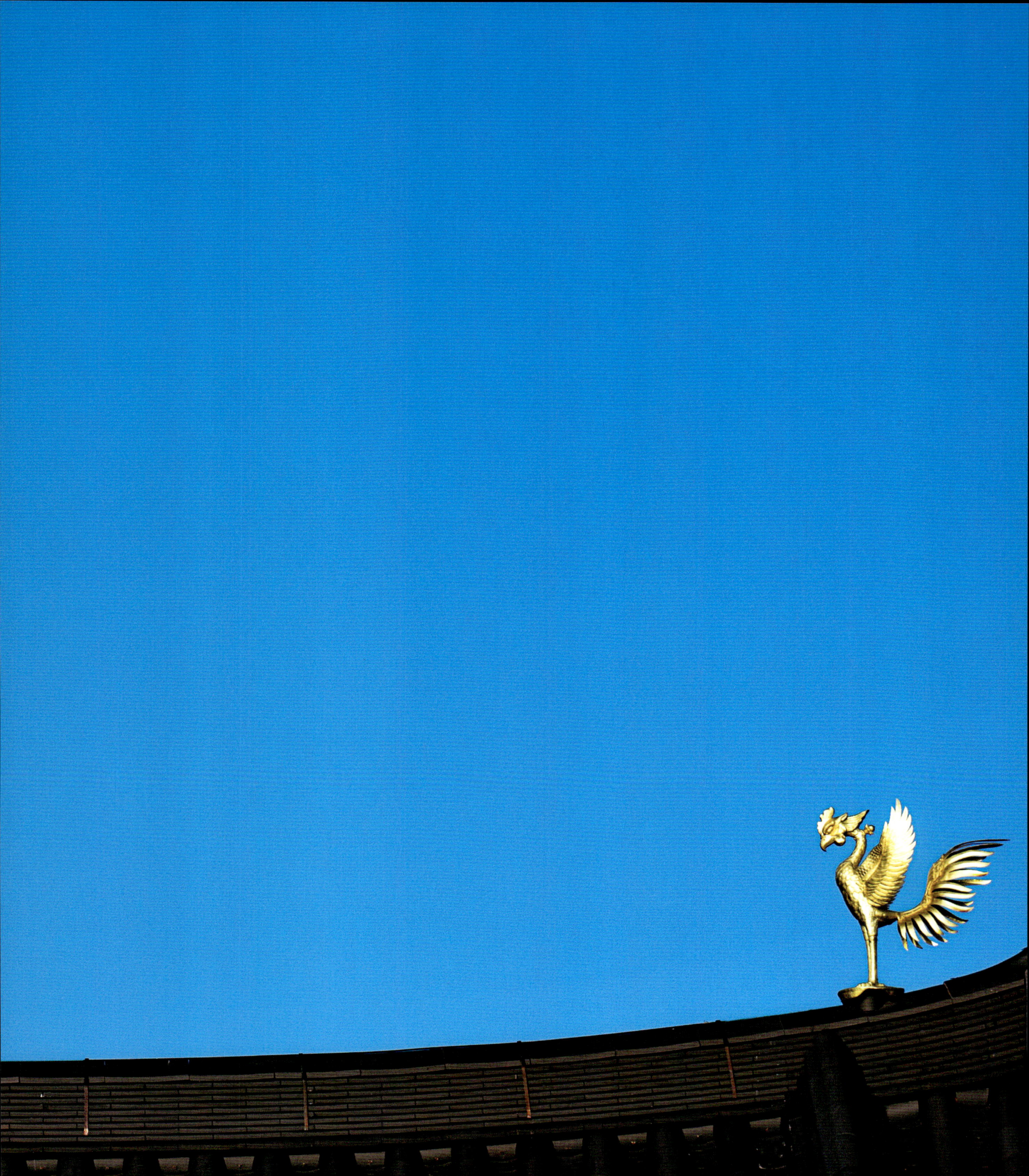

時代背景

　宇治は古くから平安京、南都、近江とつながる交通の要衝の地で、宇治川の豊かな水に恵まれ、東側には山々が広がり、平安時代から貴族の別荘が営まれて、宮廷文化と縁の深い場所である。平等院は宇治川の左岸に位置し、1052（永承7）年、時の最高権力者である関白・藤原頼通（992－1074）が創建した。頼通はこの地を父・藤原道長（966－1027）より譲り受けたが、もともとは9世紀末に嵯峨天皇の皇子・源融（822－895）が別邸を設けた地を道長が手に入れ、それを頼通が引き継ぎ、寺院としたものである。

　鳳凰堂は1053（天喜元）年に建立された阿弥陀堂で、本尊・阿弥陀如来坐像（定朝作・1053年・国宝）を安置する中堂、左右の翼廊、尾廊の4棟からなる一構えの建物である。阿字池の中島に立ち、東に向く。かつては宇治川と平等院とを隔てる堤防はなく、鳳凰堂から池越しに宇治川の流れが、対岸には山々が見渡せて、東側の眺望は開けていたようである。鳳凰堂のほかに、平等院には大日如来を本尊とする本堂や法華堂など、草創期から徐々に密教寺院が備える建造物も並行して建てられ、伽藍が整備されていった。その後、鎌倉から室町時代への移行期にあたる1336（建武3）年の兵火や、度重なる火災などにより、鳳凰堂を除く創建以来の堂宇の大半を失った。

　鳳凰堂は平安中期から極楽往生を願って盛んとなった浄土信仰を受け、阿弥陀如来の住む西方浄土に見立てて築かれた苑池を中心に建物が配置されている。阿弥陀堂にあたる中堂は、正面3間、側面2間の主要部に、通常の仏堂であればその外周に庇をめぐらせるところを、直接裳階（差し掛け屋根）を主要部に取りつけたつくりになっている。この特殊な立面は、庇をなくして池越しからも本尊を拝めるように配慮したもので、裳階の中央間を一段高く切り上げて正面性を強調し、その奥の格子に開けられた華鬘形の窓からは阿弥陀如来像を拝顔できるようになっている。中堂に取りつく左右の翼廊は楼造で、廊が池に向かって曲折する部分はさらに楼閣を構えて3層となる。仏典が説く浄土の有りさまを絵画化した「浄土変相図」には、鳳凰堂に類似する廻廊や楼閣が描かれており、その着想への影響が指摘されている。

　この世に極楽浄土を現出させるべく、庭園と建築、内部の彫刻・工芸・絵画において、平安の貴族文化における粋を凝集し、創意と贅を尽くした総合的な浄土教芸術の完成形を今に伝える。

特徴と見どころ

　水という舞台装置に光（太陽の角度）を掛け合わせて建物の設計に取りこみ、華麗で幻想的な景をつくりだすことで、極楽浄土のイメージを喚起する。鳳凰堂が示す明快なコンセプト、構想力、巧みな建築表現は、1,000年近くを経た今も新鮮さを失わず、その美しさはわれわれを触発し、平安の世に引きもどす力を蓄えている。

　鳳凰堂の姿を幻影のように映しだす阿字池と、眼前の宇治川の流れによる池と川の二重化された水のイメージとともに、そこには水の向こうにある「彼岸」が暗示されている。対岸の山から昇る朝日は正面から鳳凰堂を照らすが、とくに春分・秋分の彼岸には中堂真向かいから日が昇り、中央格子の華鬘形の窓には、神々しく輝いた阿弥陀如来像のお顔が現れる。一方、夕日は中堂の背後に落ち、格調高く反り上がった屋根、鳳凰、調和美を誇る堂全体のシルエットを浮かび上がらせる。西側の裳階の両壁面は、創建期の設計では連子窓となっていたことがわかっており、背後から連子を通して堂内に夕日を射し入れて、西方浄土からの阿弥陀来迎を彷彿させるひとときすら計算されていたのかもしれない。

　頼通は天体の運行と天然の景を取りこみ、大きな構想力をもって理想郷の現出を試みた。その美意識は、堂宇の配置から建物細部の寸法にいたるまで充溢し、隅々まで反映されている。

Historical Background

From ancient times, Uji occupied an important position on the roads linking Kyoto to the north, Nara to the south, and Omi to the east. Favored by the abundant waters of the Uji river and backed by mountains on the east, the area became the location of aristocratic villas beginning in the Heian period and developed close ties to the culture of the court. Byodoin temple was built on the left bank of the Uji river in 1052. The land was originally the site of a villa constructed by Minamoto no Toru (822–895), son of Emperor Saga, at the end of the ninth century, and later acquired by Fujiwara no Michinaga (966–1027). It was Michinaga's son, Fujiwara no Yorimichi (992–1074)—chief advisor to the emperor and one of the most powerful figures of the day—who, after inheriting the land, built the temple there.

The Phoenix Hall (Hoodo) is an Amida hall constructed in 1053 and made up of four conjoined structures: a central hall enshrining the temple's principal image, a seated Amida Buddha (sculpted by Jocho, 1053, National Treasure); wing corridors to its left and right; and a tail corridor behind. It faces east on an island in the middle of a pond called Aji-ike. In the days when no embankment separated Byodoin temple from the Uji river, the unobstructed view to the east would likely have made it possible to look across the pond from the Phoenix Hall and see both the flow of the Uji river and the mountains on its far side.

In the temple's early days, Byodoin was a large complex containing, in addition to the Phoenix Hall, esoteric Buddhist buildings such as a main hall (*hondo*) that enshrined Dainichi Buddha and a lotus hall (*hokkedo*). The majority of these structures, however, were lost to the ravages of war and several fires in the transition from the Kamakura to the Muromachi period.

The Phoenix Hall reflects the influence of Pure Land Buddhism, which became popular beginning in the middle Heian period. Its positioning at the center of an artificial garden pond reflects the Pure Land image of Amida Buddha's paradise, where the faithful believed they would be reborn after death. It transmits to the present day the essence of the aesthetic taste of Heian aristocratic culture and the heights of creativity and luxury in the Pure Land Buddhist arts as they converged in landscape gardening and architecture and—inside the hall—in sculpture, applied arts, and painting.

Characteristics and Highlights

The building's design incorporates light (the angle of the sun), through its setting on the pond, to create splendid, otherworldly shadows that inspire thoughts of the Pure Land. The Phoenix Hall's clarity of concept, imaginativeness, and deft architectural expression remain no less fresh today after the passage of nearly 1,000 years, with a grace and beauty that has the power to draw us back into the Heian world.

The Phoenix Hall's overlapping images of water—the mirage-like reflection of the building in the surface of the Aji-ike pond and the flow of the Uji river that once passed immediately before it—hint also at the Other Shore (nirvana). Rising over the mountains on the far side of the river (and directly opposite the central hall on the vernal and autumnal equinoxes), the morning sun illuminates the Phoenix Hall from the front, revealing the serene and luminous countenance of Amida Buddha framed by the *keman*-shaped window in the central lattice. The evening sun, by contrast, sets behind the central hall, silhouetting the elegantly upturned rooflines tipped with symbolic phoenix figures, and the exquisitely harmonious outline of the structure as a whole. The walls of the *mokoshi* enclosure on the building's west side are known to have originally been designed with slatted *renji* windows that would have allowed the rays of the setting sun to pour into the hall from behind, perhaps to evoke Amida's descent from the Western Pure Land to welcome the souls of the dead. Yorimichi made the natural landscape and the movements of celestial bodies all part of his grandly imagined manifestation of utopia. His aesthetic pervades and shapes every aspect of the design from the placement of the temple buildings to the size and shape of their architectural details.

春分の朝。鳳凰堂は東向きで建てられており、真東から太陽が昇る春分・
秋分の時季は、正面から朝日で照らされる。空と水との間に、浄土さながらの
美しい建築が立ち上がる

Morning on the vernal equinox. The Phoenix Hall faces east on an island. On the vernal and autumnal equinoxes, this beautiful building appears between sky and water as a vision of the Pure Land.

中堂の入母屋造、裳階の差し掛け屋根、翼廊の切妻造、隅楼の宝形造――それぞれの屋根の勾配、軒の反りが複雑に重なり合いながらも、優美な感覚でまとめあげられている。南側の瓦（左上）は、平安時代のものを葺き直してある

The complex layering of different pitches and upturned eaves. The central hall's *irimoya* hip-and-gable roof, the pent roofs of the *mokoshi* enclosures, the gabled roofs of the wing corridors, and the pyramidal roofs at the corners form a graceful whole. The roof tiles on the south side of the central hall (at upper left), although set in place more recently, date to the Heian period.

身舎の太い円柱を裳階の細い角柱で囲み、全体の見え方に軽快感をつくる。角柱の大面取りが、陰影を刻む。裳階柱の上から1/5あたりに通る飛貫は鎌倉時代の後補。当初、柱を連結するのは頭貫のみで、裳階をより大きな気積の吹放ち空間に見せていただろう

Thinner, squared pillars supporting the *mokoshi* give the whole a sense of lightness. The wide chamfers on the squared pillars create deep shadows. The tie beams penetrating the pillars of the *mokoshi* about one-fifth down from their tops are Kamakura-period additions; the pillars were originally connected only by the head-penetrating tie beams, which must have made the *mokoshi* enclosure seem an even larger, airier space.

中堂の扉、身舎を支える円柱、その周囲をめぐる裳階柱。円柱は60.6cm
(2尺)の太さがある。一方、裳階は角柱25.7cm(8.5寸)角に面取り幅
4.5cm(1.5寸)の大面取りとする。赤色の塗料は、黄土を焼いて赤色に
した丹土が塗られている。当初、扉の表面は朱漆塗りであった

The doors of the central hall, the columns supporting the building core, and the pillars of the *mokoshi* enclosure that surround them. The columns measure 60.6 centimeters in diameter while the squared pillars of the *mokoshi* measure 25.7 centimeters per side with 4.5 centimeter-wide chamfers. The red *nitsuchi* pigment is made from burned ocher. The surfaces of the doors were originally coated with vermillion lacquer.

中堂の南東角。尾垂木や垂木の木口は鍍金された透かし彫りの飾り金具で
きらびやかに荘厳されている。洗練された地円飛角の繁垂木と三手先による
華麗な軒裏空間

Southeast corner of the central hall. The ends of the rafters are decorated with gorgeous gilt openwork metal fittings. The underside of the eaves incorporates three-stepped bracket complexes and refined, closely spaced double rafters.

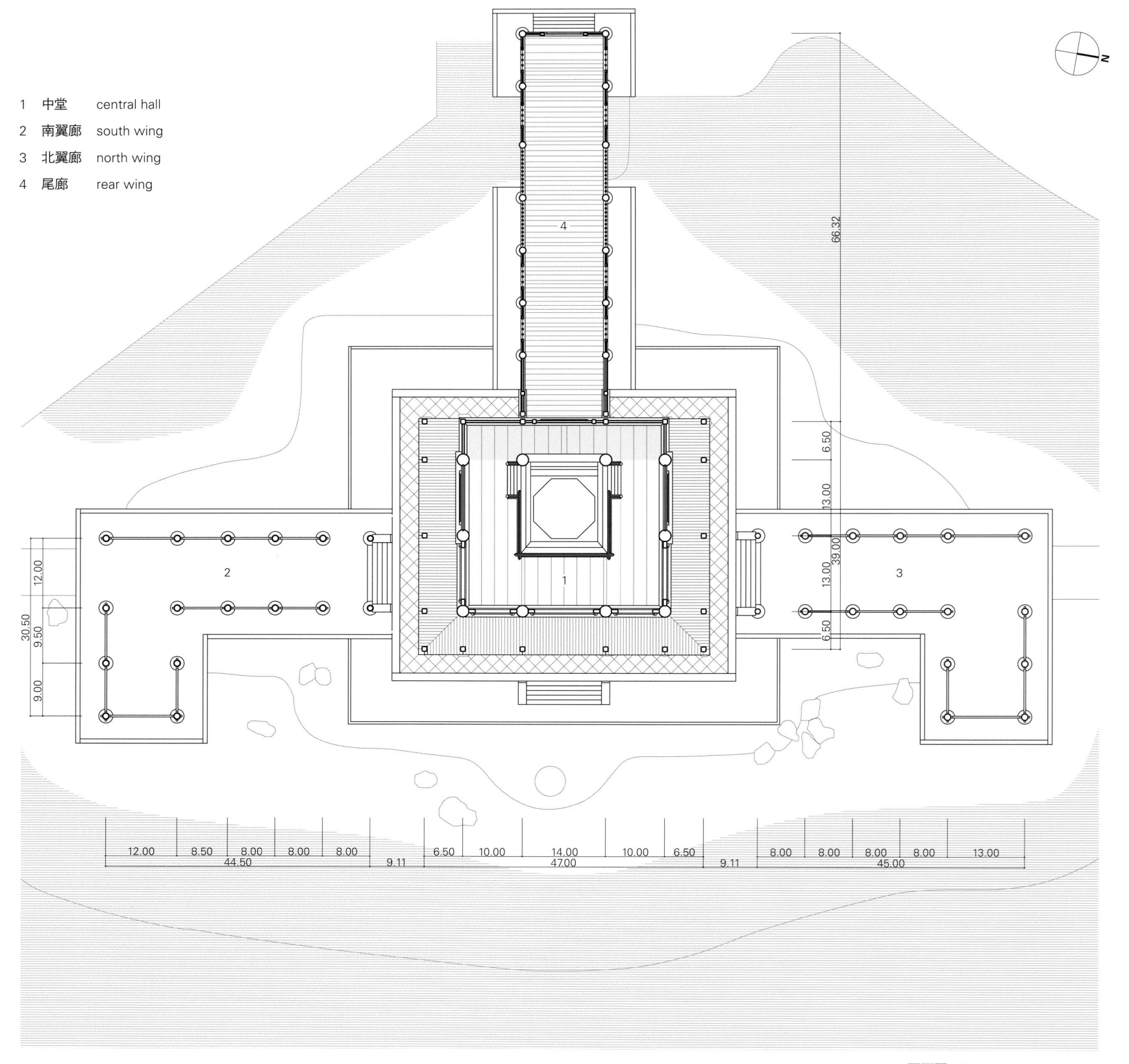

1	中堂	central hall
2	南翼廊	south wing
3	北翼廊	north wing
4	尾廊	rear wing

平面図　Plan

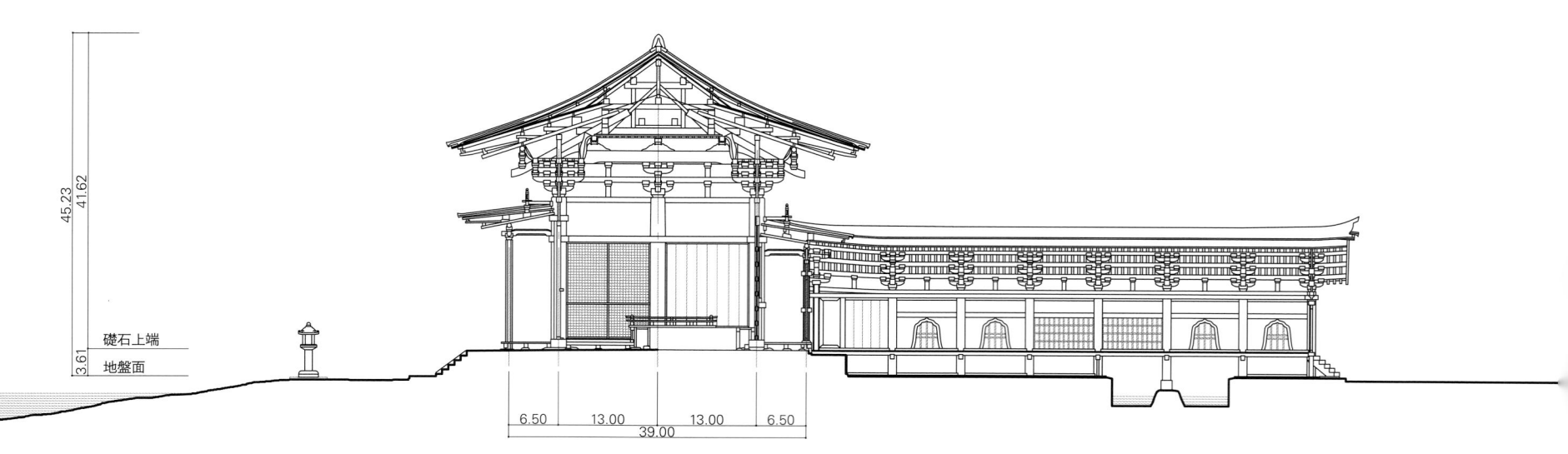

東西断面図　East-west section

0　　10　　20尺/shaku
(6.06m)

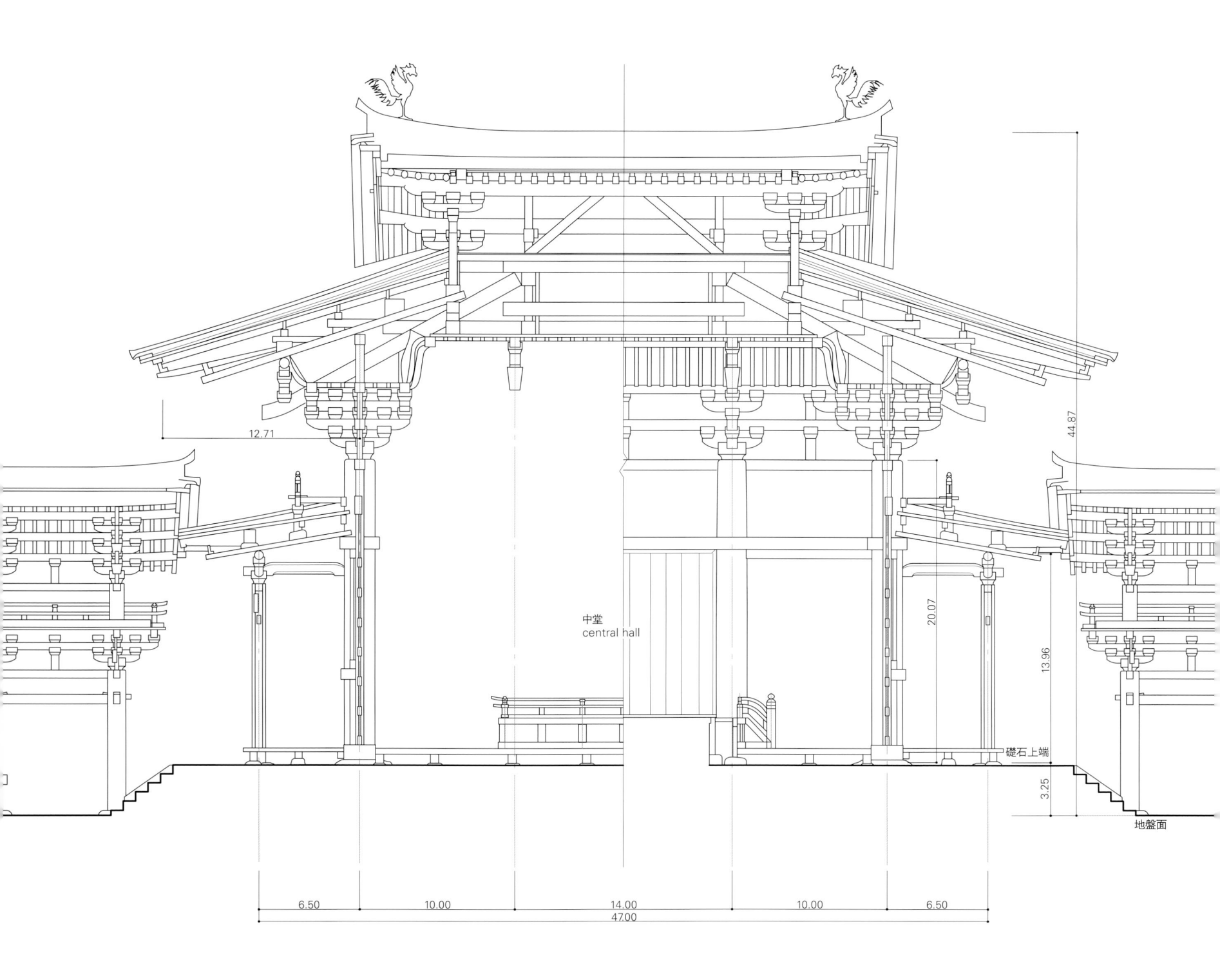

矩計図。柱心より3.85m（12.71尺）出した軒を支える構造は、桔木を入れた構造ではなく、二重の垂木と野垂木によって荷重を分散させ、総持ちする方式が取られている

Sectional detail drawing. Rather than incorporating *hanegi* cantilevers, the structure supporting the eaves—which extend 3.85 meters from the center of their supporting columns—effectively distributes the load using double rafters and hidden rafters.

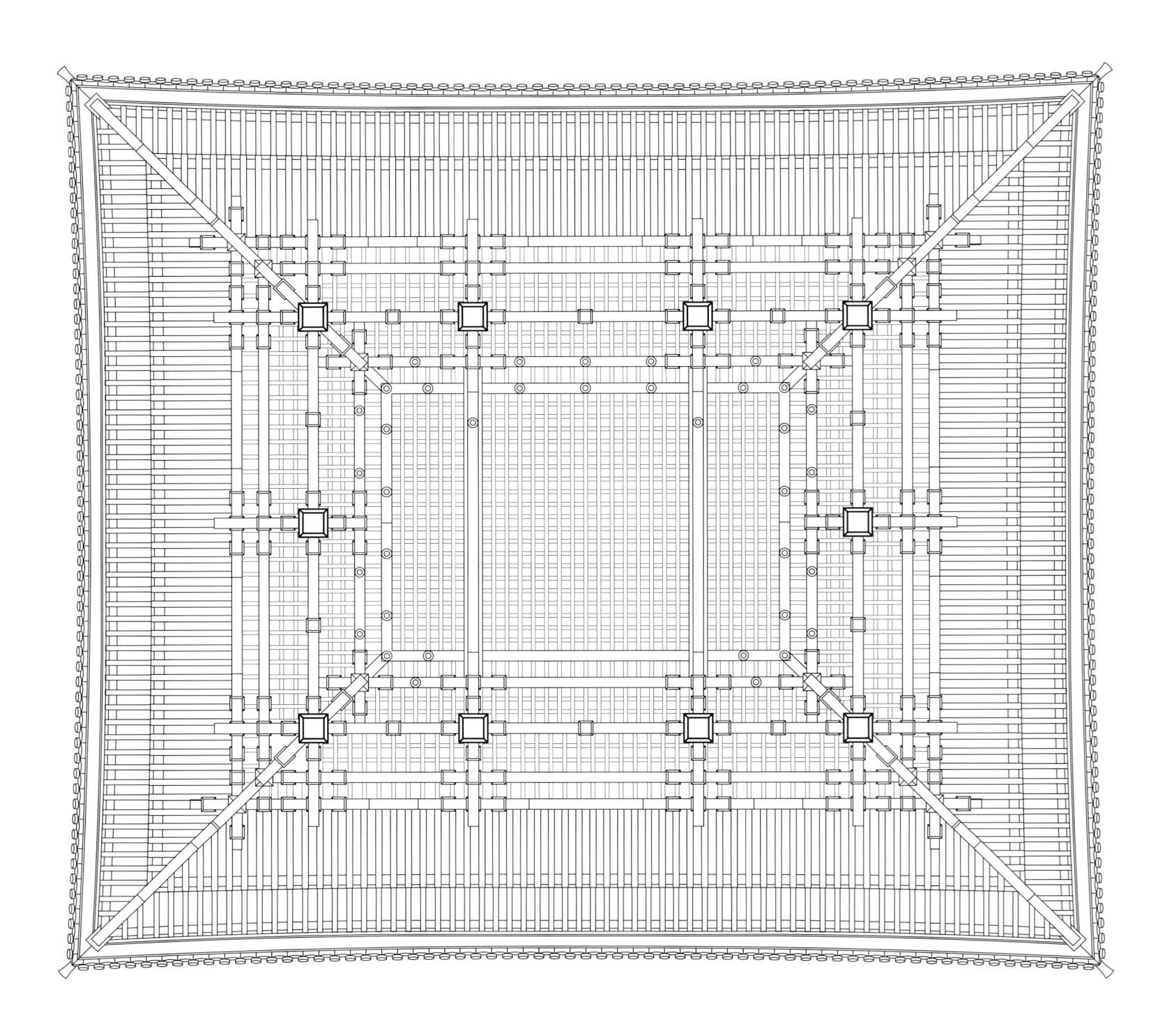

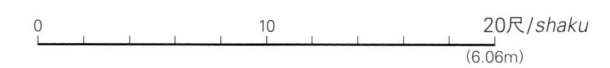

中堂・天井見上図。2本の大梁の上に天井が張られている。大梁の柱間スパンは7.87m。大梁の断面を小さくする工夫がされている

Ceiling plan of central hall. Two principal beams cross a span of 7.87 meters just below the ceiling. Care has been taken to ensure these principal beams appear small in cross-section.

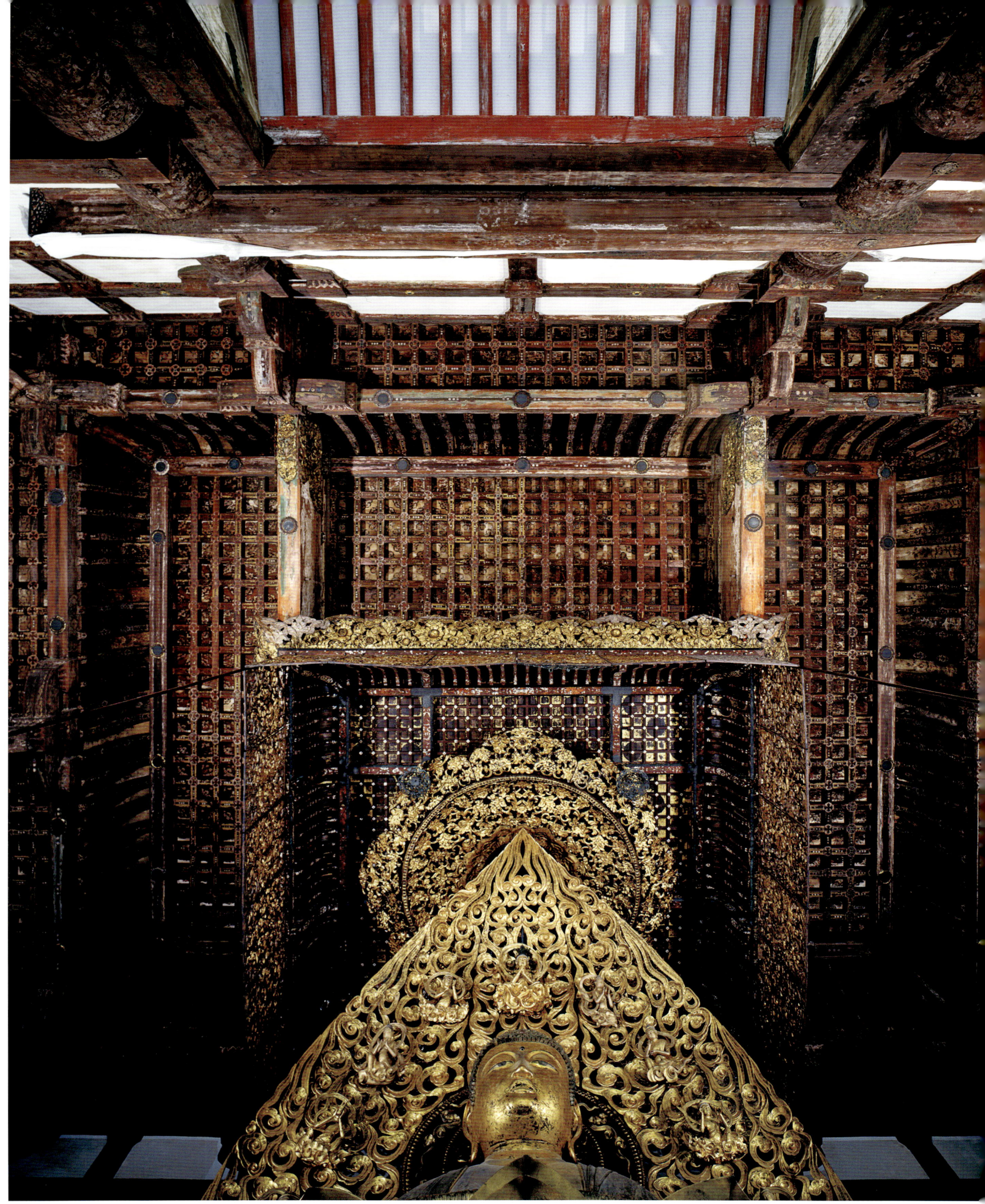

中堂内部、折上小組格天井を見上げる。本尊の阿弥陀如来坐像、天蓋、その周囲は宝相華唐草紋を透かし彫りにした垂板で囲われている。仏像だけでなく、周囲の荘厳にも仏師・定朝が指揮を執ったとされる。往時の輝きと鮮やかな色彩をほぼ失うが、格天井の構成部材にも螺鈿や蒔絵などが施されており、1,000年前のまばゆいばかりの仏堂空間が想像される

Central hall interior, looking up at the coved, coffered and finely latticed ceiling (*oriage kogumi gotenjo*). The principal image (a seated sculpture of Amida Buddha) and canopy are enclosed by *suiban* hanging panels decorated with arabesque openwork carving. The sculptor Jocho is said to have directed not only the production of the principal image but also its magnificent surroundings. Their brilliance and vivid color have been largely lost to the past, but even the structural members of the coffered ceiling are decorated with mother-of-pearl and *makie* gold lacquer work, hinting at the dazzling Buddhist space created here a thousand years ago.

発掘調査にのっとり、平安時代の州浜が復元されている。水際は石が水平に近いかたちで水に入りこんでいき、池と中島とを滑らかに結ぶ

The shoreline recreates that of the Heian period as revealed through archaeological excavations; the stones enter the water nearly level, smoothly connecting island and pond.

春分の朝。裳階中央部の屋根を切り上げており、
華鬘形窓の奥の阿弥陀如来坐像を池越しから
拝することができる

Morning on the vernal equinox. The elevated central roof section of the *mokoshi* enclosure makes it possible to pray to the image of Amida Buddha, seated behind a *keman*-shaped window, from across the pond.

西方浄土を彷彿させる黄昏時の鳳凰堂。軽快な
シルエットが空と水に浮かび上がる

The Phoenix Hall at twilight, so suggestive of the Western
Paradise, with its rhythmical silhouette emerging from the sky
and the water.

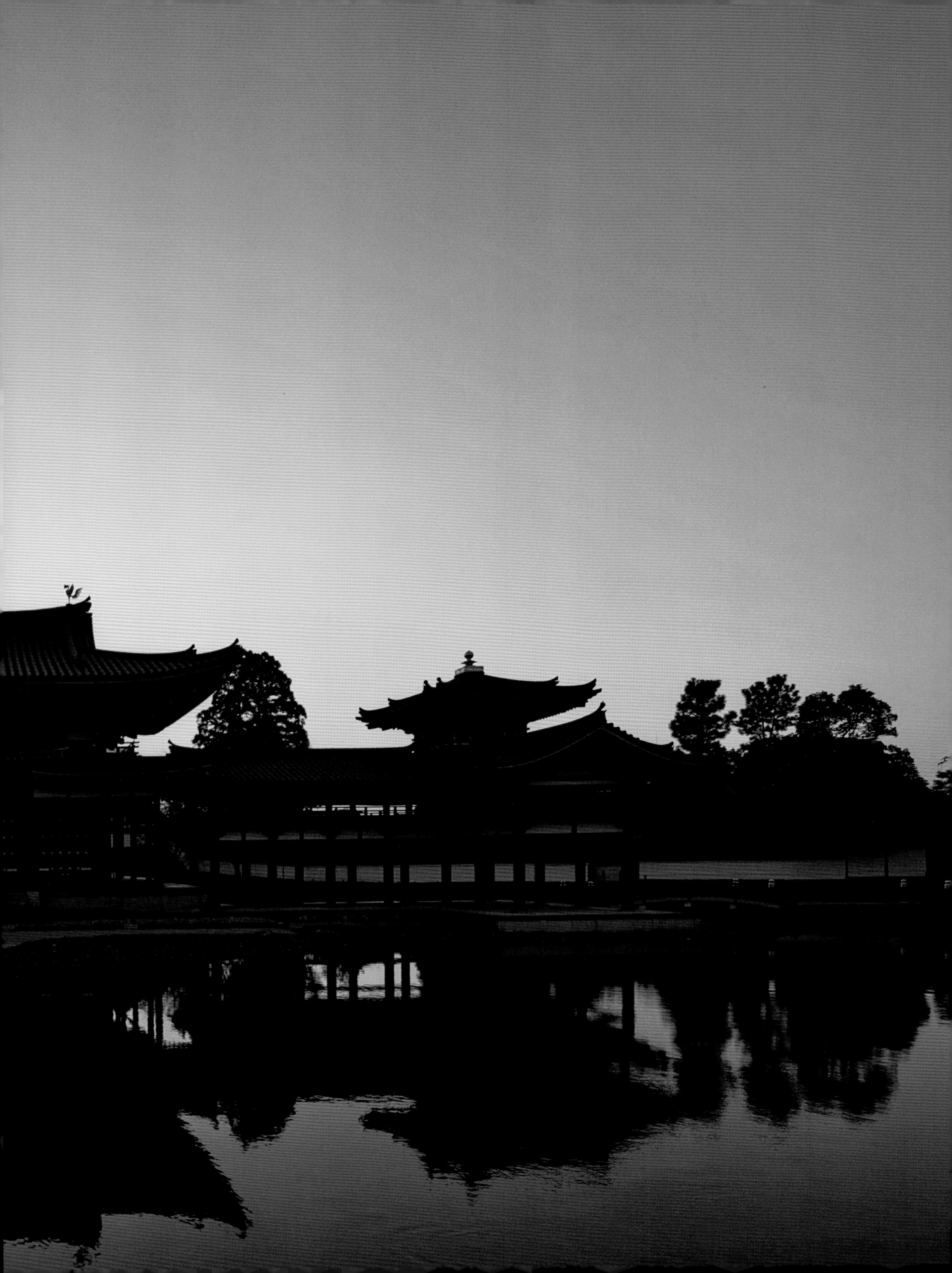

法界寺 阿弥陀堂

国宝
建立年代　1226年頃
所在地　京都府京都市伏見区

Hokaiji Temple Amida Hall

National Treasure
Completed: c. 1226
Location: Fushimi ward, Kyoto, Kyoto prefecture

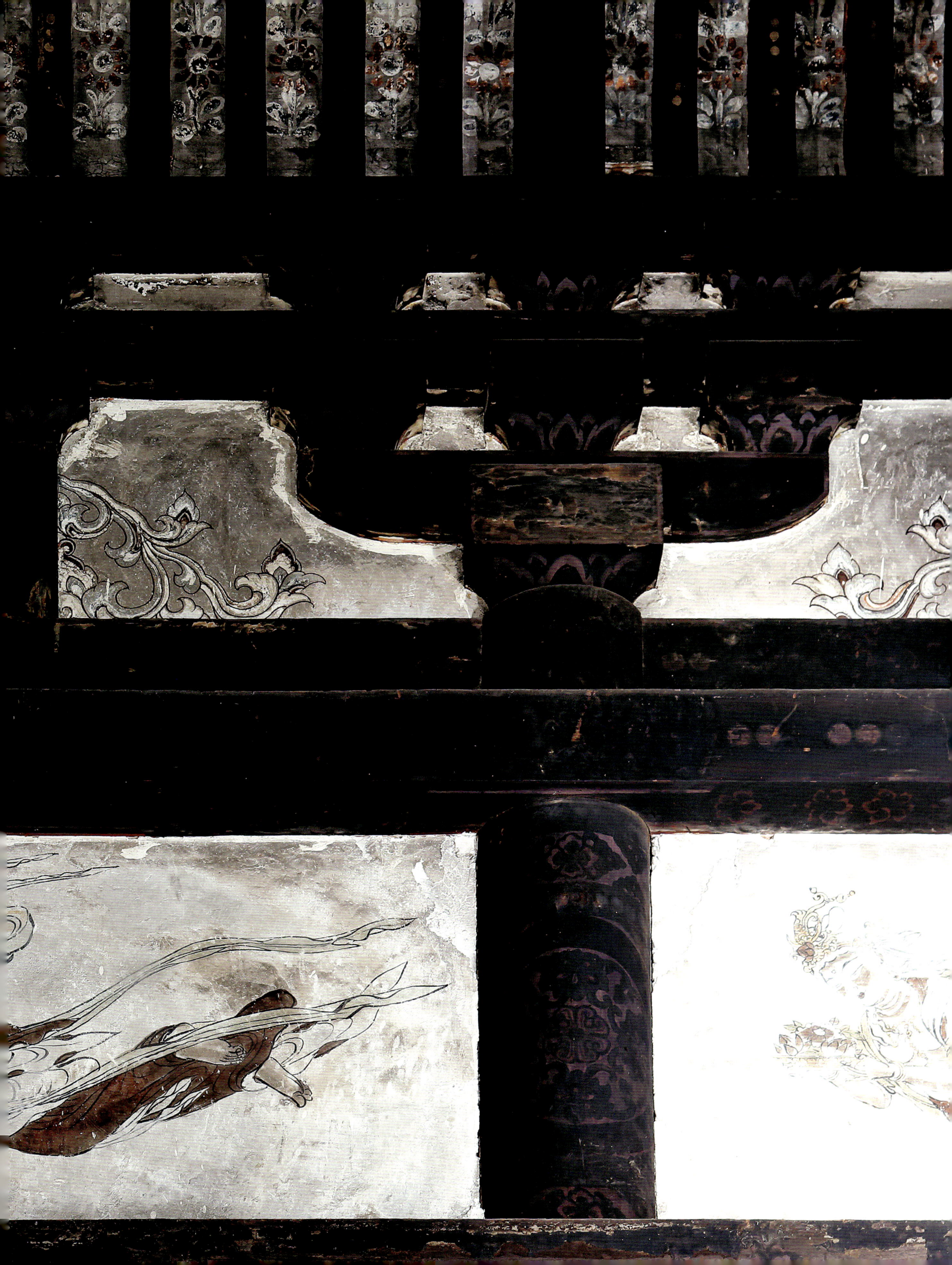

時代背景

　法界寺は京都・山科盆地の南東の日野に位置する。1051（永承6）年、日野資業（988-1070）が薬師堂を建立したことで、日野家の菩提寺として礎が築かれた。日野家は平安時代に朝廷の中枢を占めた藤原氏の血筋を引き、藤原一族のもとで命脈をつないできた貴族である。浄土真宗の開祖・親鸞（1173-1262）、室町幕府の誕生に貢献した醍醐寺座主・賢俊（1299-1357）、足利義政（1436-1490）の妻・日野富子（1440-1496）もこの一族の出である。

　天台宗にゆかりの深い寺として日野資業の子孫が堂宇を整えたが、阿弥陀堂については、平等院鳳凰堂（1053年）の本尊と同じ仏師・定朝（-1057）による阿弥陀像があったという伝えや、1130年頃には計5躯の阿弥陀像を有し、同じ頃には境内近隣も含めて4棟の阿弥陀堂が立っていたことが記録でたどられ、阿弥陀信仰の篤い寺であったことが知られる。しかし、1221（承久3）年、承久の乱の兵火で堂宇の大半を失い、このときに唯一焼失を免れたのが、現在の堂に安置されている阿弥陀如来坐像（平安時代・国宝）と推察されている。その後、唱導の大家として知られた僧・聖覚（1167-1235）により、1226（嘉永2）年頃に再建された阿弥陀堂が現堂と考えられている。

特徴と見どころ

　方形の阿弥陀堂としては最大規模の仏堂で、裳階をつけて立ちの高い外観の均整を図り、内部は大きなボリュームの空間を形づくる。阿弥陀如来坐像は太い四天柱に囲われた須弥壇上に安置されており、来迎壁がないために仏像背後の透けが大きく、空間はいっそう広々と感じられる。四天柱と側柱とは柱筋をそろえていないため、この間をつなぐ虹梁がかけられておらず、かわって細かい間隔の化粧垂木をかけ渡してつないでいるところが大きな特徴である。そのため化粧垂木の下は何も遮るものがなく、天井の白板を背景にして、伸びやかな垂木が中心へと向かう上昇感を高めている。

　四天柱には計64体の尊像の画、長押上の小壁の内外には、飛天や楽器、宝相華などが流麗な線で描かれ、阿弥陀仏を讃えて華やかに周囲を荘厳する。平安時代の浄土教信仰にもとづく貴族的な阿弥陀堂の側面を保持する一方で、この堂がもつ簡潔な方形プランと開放的な広さは、ここが念仏を唱えながら阿弥陀仏のまわりをめぐる行道の空間としての機能をもち、より多くの人々の収容を想定して建てられたことをうかがわせる。庶民に仏法を広めた唱導僧・聖覚が再建に関わったとされるこの堂は、鎌倉初期における仏教の大衆化を受けた阿弥陀堂の新たなあり方をも示唆しており、それは重源の建てた浄土寺浄土堂（1194年）とも通じる部分があるものだろう。

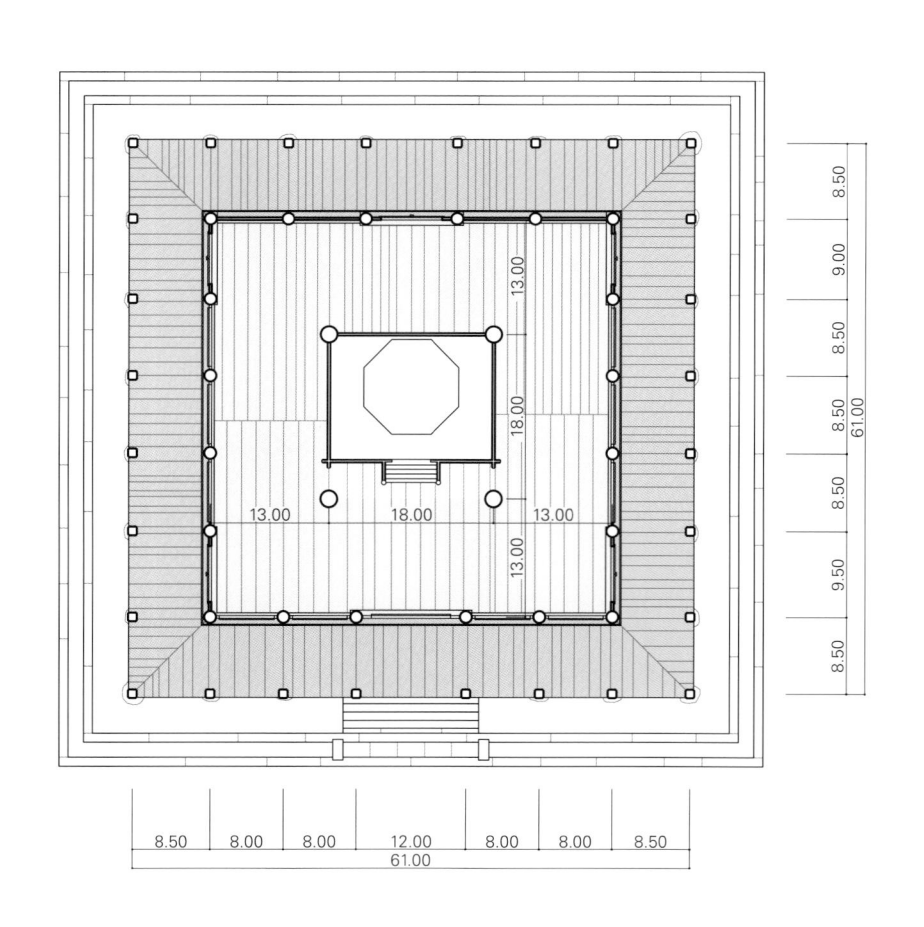

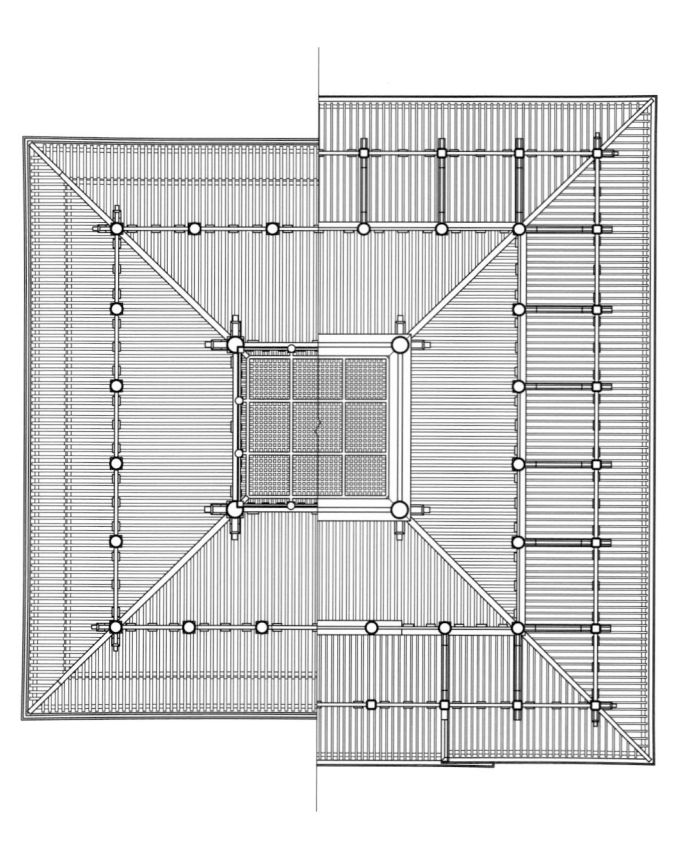

平面図　Floor plan

天井見上図　Ceiling plan

Historical Background

Hokaiji temple is located at the southeast edge of Kyoto's Yamashina basin in Hino. Hino Sukenari (988–1070) erected a Yakushi hall in 1051 that established the foundations for this Hino clan family temple. A descendent line of the Fujiwara, who were at the center of the imperial court during the Heian period, the Hino was an aristocratic family that benefitted from its ties to the Fujiwara. Other notables who came from the Hino clan include Shinran (1173–1262), founder of the Jodo Shinshu sect of Pure Land Buddhism; Kenshun (1299–1357), the chief priest of Daigoji temple who contributed to the birth of the Muromachi shogunate; and Hino Tomiko (1440–1496), wife of Ashikaga Yoshimasa (1436–1490), the eighth Muromachi shogun.

Hino Sukenari's descendants provided the temple with buildings befitting its close ties to the Tendai school, and the temple is known in particular for its devotion to Amida Buddha. Tradition has it, for example, that the Amida hall once held an Amida statue that had been carved by Jocho (d. 1057), sculptor of the principal image enshrined in the Phoenix Hall (1053) at Byodoin Temple, and records indicate that as of around 1130 the temple held a total of five Amida images. Around that time there were a total of four Amida halls located in and near its precincts. Most of the buildings were destroyed by fire during the Jokyu disturbance of 1221; the statue enshrined in the Amida hall today is believed to be the only one to have survived. The hall itself is thought to have been rebuilt by the priest Shokaku (1167–1235), known as a major proselytizer for Buddhism, around 1226.

Characteristics and Highlights

The Amida hall at Hokaiji is one of the largest square Amida halls in existence; the addition of a *mokoshi* enclosure counterbalances the building's height while creating a spacious interior. A seated image of Amida Buddha (Heian period; National Treasure) is enshrined on a *shumidan* altar at the center of four thick *shitenbashira* pillars. The lack of the usual *raigokabe* back wall creates a greater transparency behind the image and increases the expansiveness of the space. One major characteristic is that because the *shitenbashira* pillars and *gawabashira* perimeter pillars are not aligned, they are linked not by *koryo* transverse beams but rather by exposed rafters laid at a narrow pitch. The sense of upward motion is heightened by the fact that nothing obstructs the view of the exposed rafters as they stretch up toward the center against the white boards of the ceiling.

The *shitenbashira* pillars are decorated with paintings of 64 venerated figures while inside and outside of the small walls above the *nageshi* beams that connect the pillars are heavenly beings, musical instruments, and arabesque floral patterns drawn in flowing lines, creating surroundings both lively and sublime to glorify Amida. While the building preserves aspects of an aristocratic Amida hall grounded in the Jodo faith of the Heian period, with its compact square plan and expansive openness it was probably also built to accommodate a larger number of people and to function as a space for circumambulating its Amida image while reciting the *nenbutsu*. Believed to have been rebuilt with the involvement of the great priest Shokaku, who spread Buddhism among the common people, the hall suggests the new form of Amida hall that emerged as the result of the popularization of Buddhism in the early Kamakura period. This is a feature shared with the Amida hall built by Chogen at Jodoji temple (1194).

内部には大きな空間が形成されている。四天柱を立てて内陣をつくり、四方に外陣をつくる。四天柱と側柱との間を化粧垂木でつないでおり、垂木が伸びやかに中心へと向かう。四天柱の小壁には、生き生きとした線で飛天が描かれている

The interior is a vast space formed by *shitenbashira* pillars demarcating the inner sanctuary from the outer sanctum surrounding it on four sides. The pillars around the sanctuary and those around the perimeter (*gawabashira*) are linked by exposed rafters that stretch toward the center. The small wall areas above the *shitenbashira* pillars are decorated with flying celestial beings (*hiten*) in lively lines.

高い折上格天井は空間の上昇感をつくる。本尊の阿弥陀如来坐像は、平安中期の作といわれる。四天柱の柱には金剛界曼荼羅の諸尊が描かれている

The coved and coffered ceiling accentuates the sense of height in the space. The principal image of a seated Amida Buddha is said to have been made in the middle Heian period. The *shitenbashira* pillars depict various Buddhist figures from the Diamond Realm (Vajradhatu) Mandala.

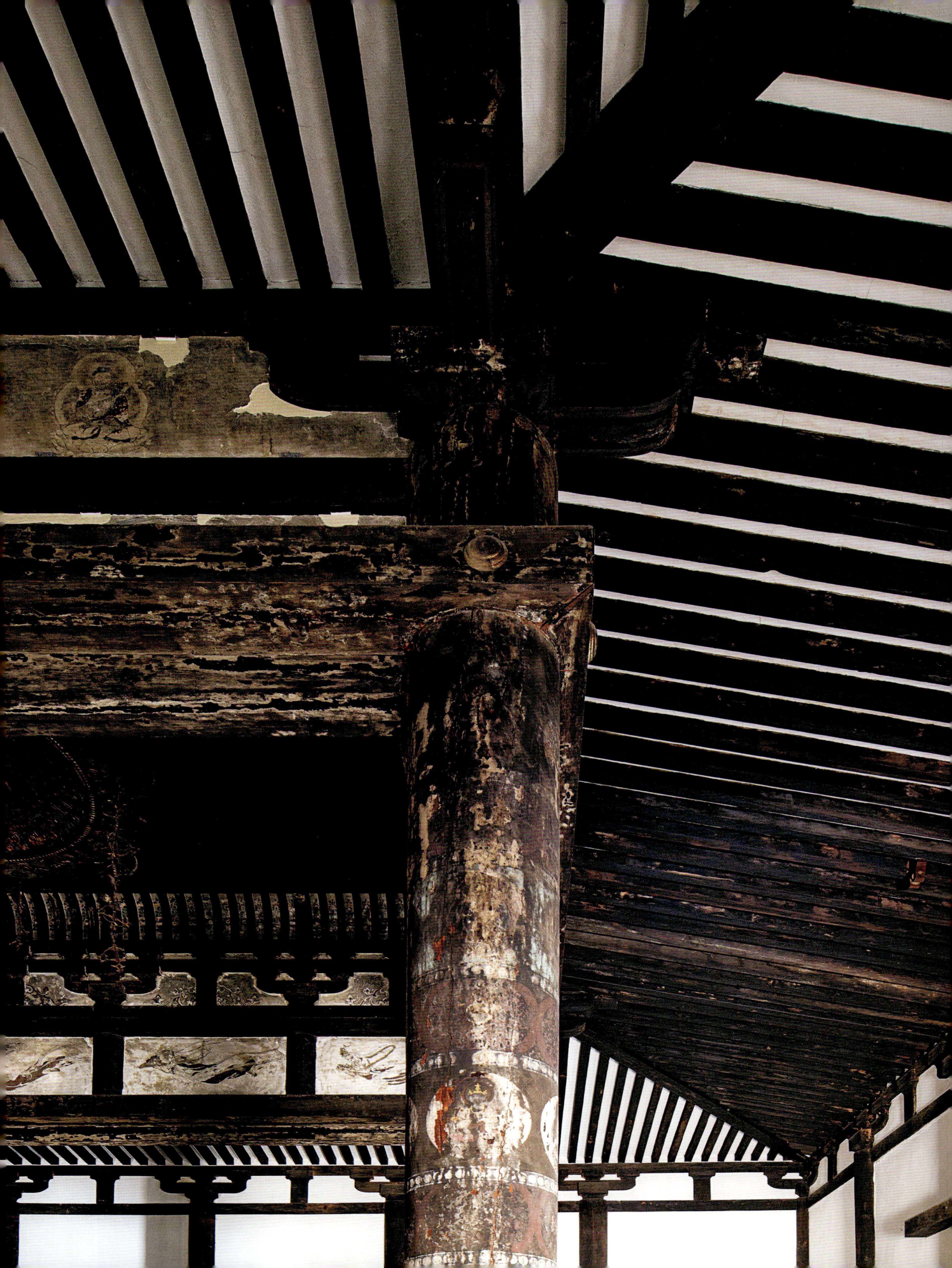

（左）木太い四天柱。径は54.4cm（1尺8寸）

(Left) The *shitenbashira* pillars are thick, measuring 54.5 centimeters in diameter.

（上）天井の南東隅、垂木を見上げる。天井の白板と垂木の黒の対比が現代的。垂木は22.7cm間隔で配されている

(Above) Looking up at the rafters of the southeast corner. The contrast between the black rafters and the white ceiling gives the space a modern feel. The rafters are spaced at intervals of 22.7 centimeters.

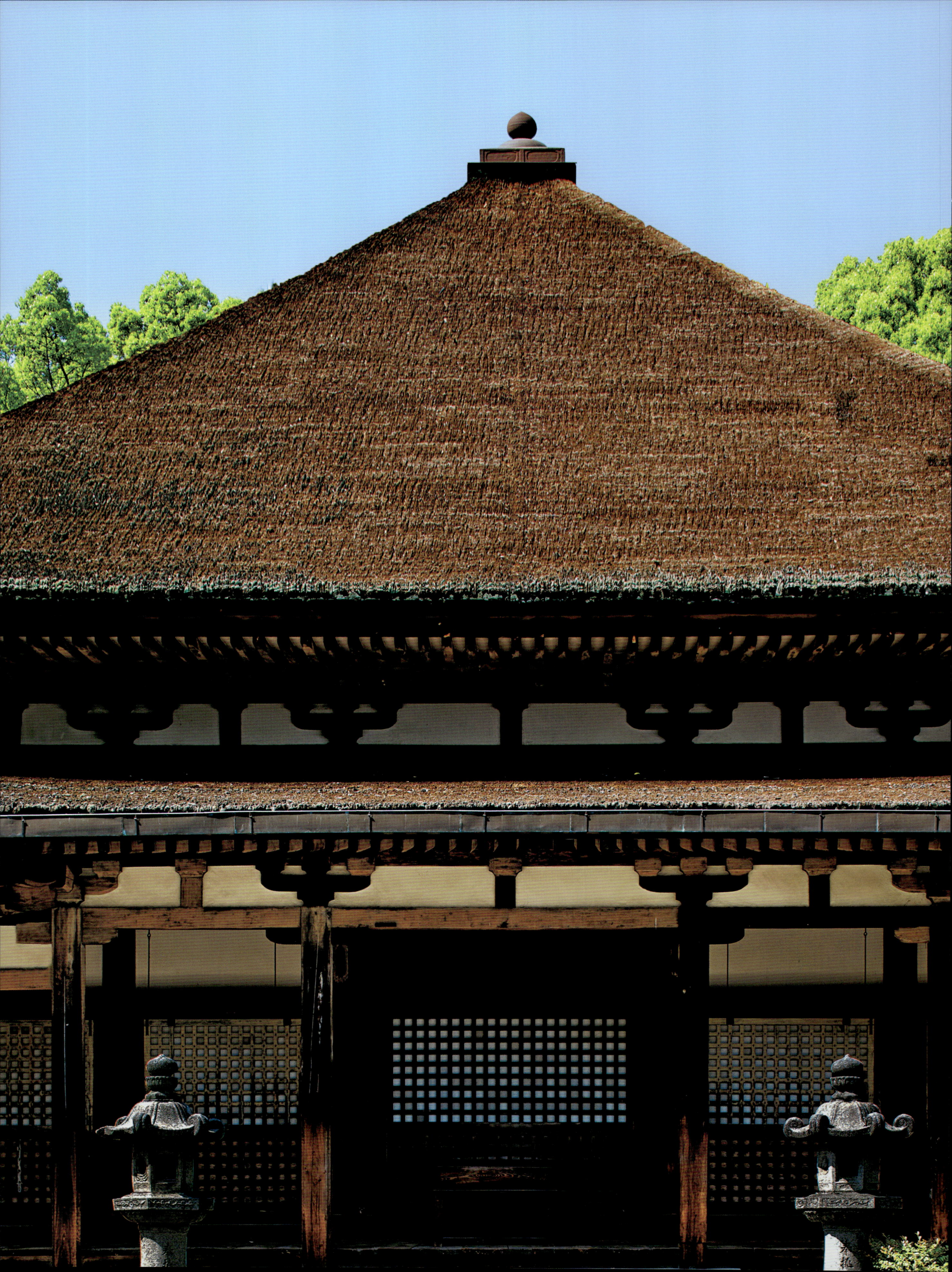

（左）南側正面。宝形造・檜皮葺の大きな屋根がかかり、裳階がつく

(Left) South façade with its *mokoshi* enclosure beneath the great pyramidal roof of cypress bark shingles.

（上）裳階の吹き放たれた列柱と身舎の軒裏。裳階柱は大面取りの角柱。身舎の軒は大きく反り上がる

(Above) A line of pillars supporting the open *mokoshi* enclosure and the eaves extending from the building core. The *mokoshi* pillars are squared and chamfered. The eaves of the building core have a graceful upward sweep.

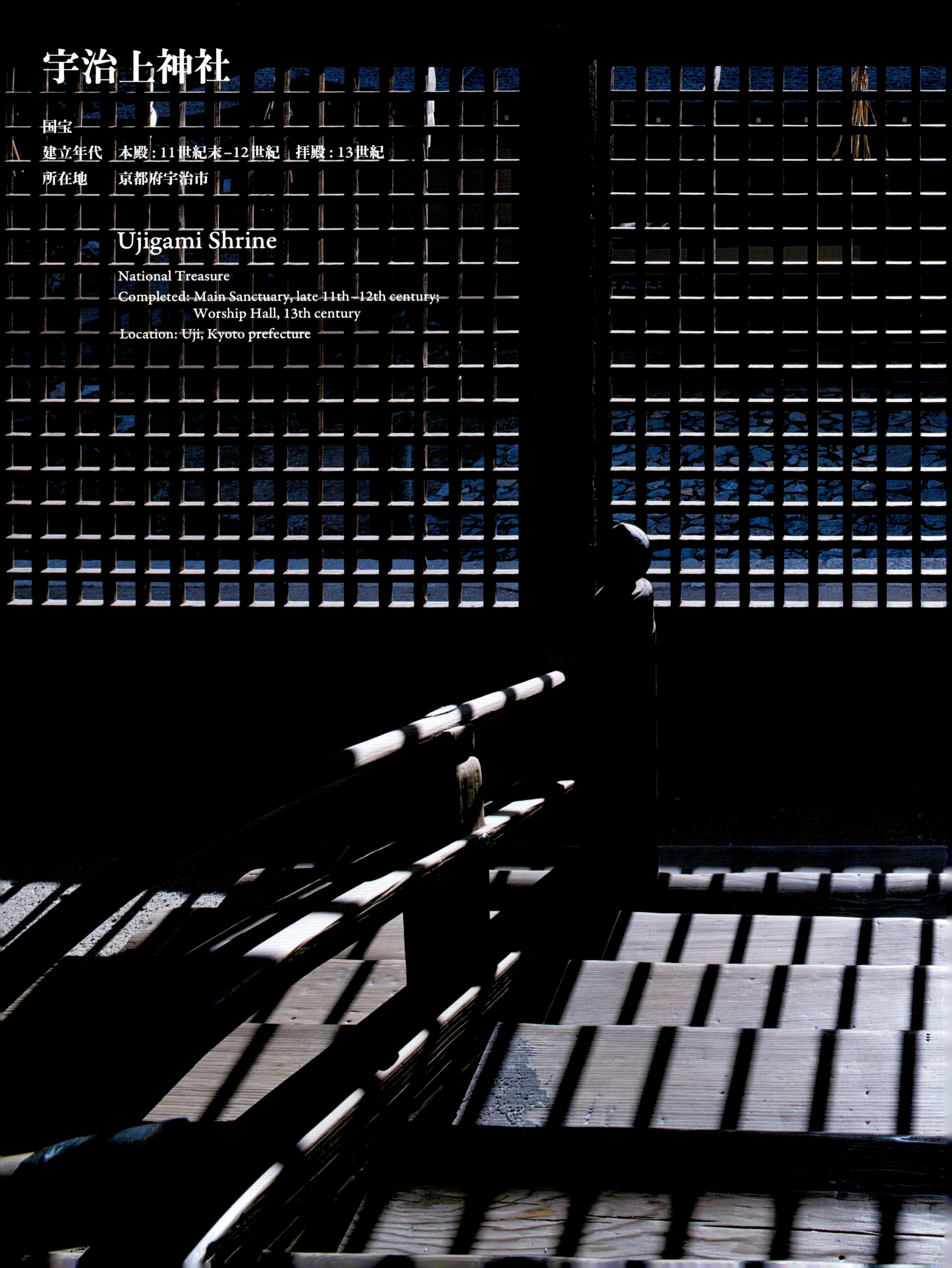

宇治上神社

国宝
建立年代　本殿：11世紀末–12世紀　拝殿：13世紀
所在地　　京都府宇治市

Ujigami Shrine

National Treasure
Completed: Main Sanctuary, late 11th–12th century;
　　　　　　Worship Hall, 13th century
Location: Uji, Kyoto prefecture

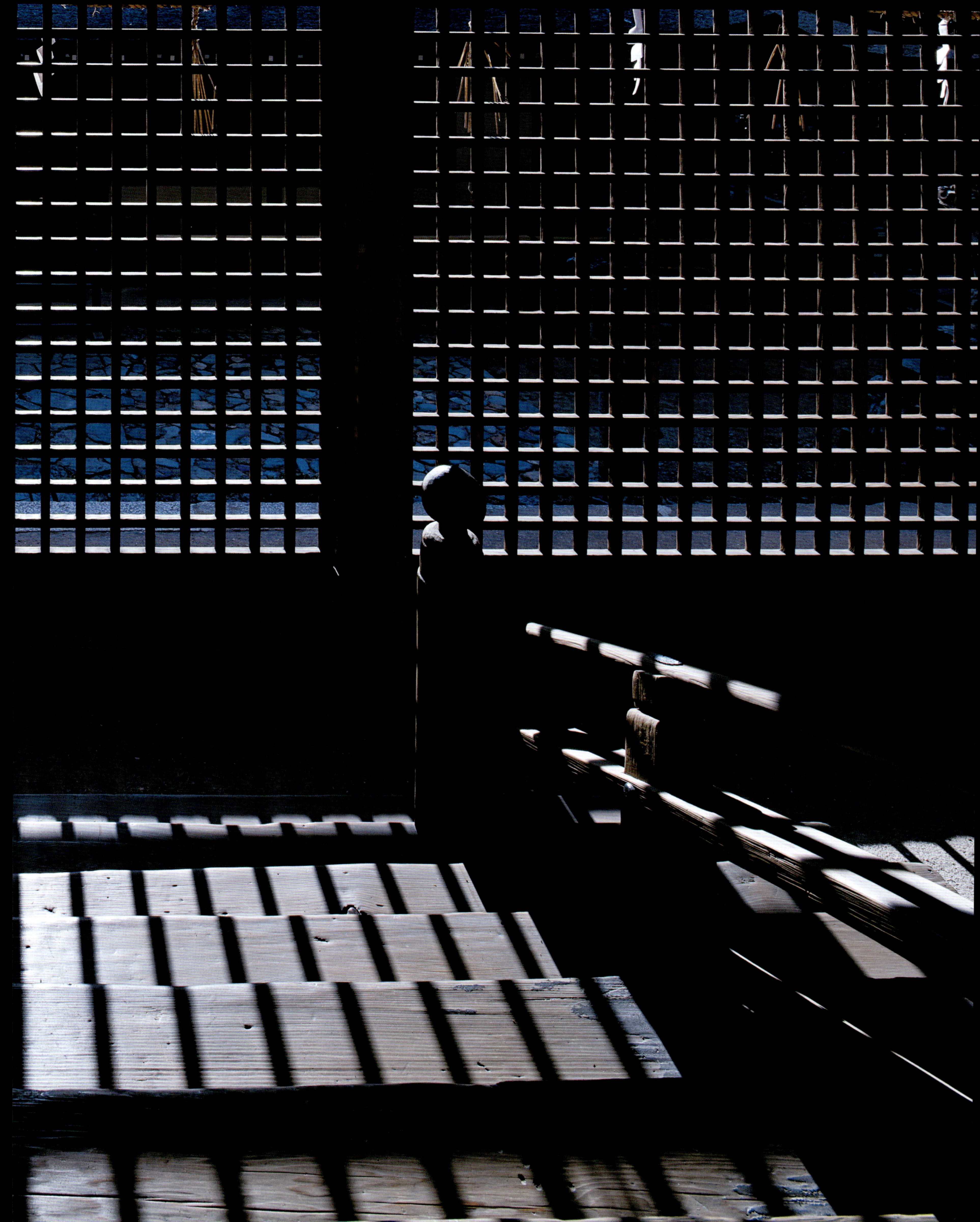

時代背景

　宇治川の右岸、仏徳山のふもとに宇治上神社は位置する。宇治川の流れに向けて南西に建てられ、川を挟んで平等院とは向かいあう位置関係にある。境内から川寄りに下った場所には宇治神社があり、両社で離宮社と呼ばれてきたという。平安時代の記録に、離宮社の名が平等院との関係において現れることから、鳳凰堂（1053年）ができ、貴族がこぞって宇治に参詣するようになって、対岸にある当社も信仰を集め、社殿が整備されていったと考えられている。

　山側の本殿の前に拝殿を配し、境内の本殿脇には春日社（鎌倉時代・重文）をはじめとする摂末社が祀られている。本殿の建立年は不明だが、蟇股の様式や部材の調査から平安時代後期の11世紀後半から12世紀の間とされ、現存する本殿建築として最古の遺構となる。形式は、正面1間・流造の内殿3殿を横に並べ、これに覆屋をかける。応神天皇、菟道稚郎子、仁徳天皇をそれぞれに祀る。左右の2殿は覆屋の側面壁（奥2間）と背面壁、外周の柱、屋根を共有する珍しい形を取る。内殿3殿の平面規模はまちまちで、それが覆屋にも反映され、柱間寸法は不揃いとなる。中央の中殿がいちばん小さく、屋根、壁、柱も覆屋と共有せずに独立している。3殿はそれぞれ建てられた年代が異なるとされ、左殿（向かって右）が11世紀後半、右殿（向かって左）は12世紀初期を下らないと見るのが通説である。内殿と覆屋は一体のものとして計画されたことが構造からわかるが、それ以前は3殿が別個に立っていた可能性も考えられ、成立過程への興味は尽きない。

　拝殿は部材の検討から鎌倉時代前期（13世紀）の建立、その後、14世紀前半に改造を受けたと推定され、現存する最古の拝殿である。拝殿は祈祷をはじめ、祭礼、奉納などの目的で使われる建物である。もともとはご神体を祀る本殿正面の庭で祭祀が執り行われるかたちであったが、やがて祭員の着座する建物が必要とされたことがその起こりとされる。野天で行われていた古来の礼拝形式の影響から、初期の拝殿は土間床であった可能性も指摘されるが、当社の拝殿は床が板張りで、身舎と両庇部分とを分けて3室に仕切る。両脇の室は参籠所や控えの間として使われたのかもしれないが、住宅であれば居室に相当する空間づくりである。檜皮葺の優雅な屋根や、蔀戸、舞良戸の建具からも上流貴族の住宅建築を彷彿させるこの拝殿は、宗教的な使用目的をもった建物が、住宅的手法へと近づく中世建築の特徴を示している。

特徴と見どころ

　本殿は川の向こうに沈む太陽の西日を午後から徐々に受けるが、そのとき、覆屋の格子で濾されて内殿に入射する光の美しさは格別である。赤みを帯びた夕日は、内殿の高欄や木階に格子状の影を投げかけ、内部を神々しい光で荘厳する。格子で割った光を入れることで、光は凝縮され、空間がより上質なものへと昇華するのが感じられる。

　拝殿と本殿との中間にある石敷きの空間は、両殿を緊密に結びつつ、本殿との絶妙な距離感をつくりだしている。蔀戸をすべて開け放ったとき、爽やかに透ける拝殿を通して見る本殿の姿は秀逸で、清らかな空気の流動が目に見えるようである。拝殿の両脇の壁は、構造的に見れば耐震性を確保するためのもので、この壁があるからこそ、身舎の部分は潔く最大限に開放にできる。大きく優美な屋根の下、「開く―閉じる」のバランスが見事である。

本殿覆屋
Outer enclosure of the main sanctuary

Historical Background

Ujigami Shrine is located in the foothills of Mt. Buttoku overlooking the Uji river to the southwest and facing Byodoin temple across the river. This shrine and Uji Shrine, somewhat lower down and closer to the river, were together called the "Rikyusha" or the "villa shrines." Records from the Heian period suggest that the term came about because, after the Phoenix Hall of Byodoin temple was built in 1053, members of the nobility visiting the temple were also attracted to the shrines on the opposite bank, leading to the renovation and addition of shrine buildings.

The date of the construction of the main sanctuary (*honden*) is unclear, but based on the style of the *kaerumata* frog-leg struts and a survey of structural components, it is estimated to have been built between the late eleventh and twelfth centuries, making it the oldest extant example of *honden* architecture. In style, the building incorporates three one-bay-wide inner sanctuaries (*naiden*) with flowing (*nagarezukuri*) roofs, lined up side-by-side within an outer enclosure. These inner sanctuaries are dedicated to Emperor Ojin, Uji no Wakiiratsuko, and Emperor Nintoku. The structure is unusual, with the inner sanctuaries on the sides sharing lateral walls (two bays), rear walls, outer pillars, and roofs with the outer enclosure. The variation in size of each of the three inner sanctuaries is reflected in the irregular spacing of the pillars of the outer enclosure. The three inner sanctuaries are believed to have been built at different times, with the one on the right generally thought to date to the second half of the eleventh century and the one on the left no later than the early twelfth century. Their structure suggests that the inner sanctuaries and outer enclosure were planned as an integrated whole, but the possibility remains that the three inner sanctuaries previously stood independently; the process by which the building came to be as it is today remains something of a mystery.

An analysis of the structural members of the worship hall (*haiden*) indicates that it was erected in the thirteenth century and renovated in the early fourteenth century, making it the oldest *haiden* in existence. A worship hall is used for activities such as prayers, ceremonies, and dedications. Shrine rituals were originally performed in an open space before the main sanctuary enshrining the object of worship, but eventually there came a need for a building where those engaged in the ceremonies could sit. The worship hall at the Ujigami Shrine has wooden floors and rooms to each side that may have been used for solitary prayer or as anterooms. With its elegant roof covered in cypress bark shingles and woodwork such as *shitomido* latticed shutters and *mairado* wooden sliding doors, the worship hall is reminiscent of the residential architecture of the upper aristocracy, displaying the tendency in medieval architecture to apply the methods in dwellings to buildings with religious functions.

Characteristics and Highlights

As the main sanctuary is gradually bathed in the rays of the afternoon sun as it sets on the far side of the river, the light that streams into the inner sanctuaries, filtered through the latticed windows of the outer enclosure, is of extraordinary beauty. The shadows of the lattices cast onto the *koran* balustrades and wooden steps of the inner sanctuaries fill the interior with a heavenly solemnity. One can sense how the use of lattices breaks up yet concentrates the light, transforming the space into something even more elegant.

The stone-paved area between the worship hall and main sanctuary ties the two closely together while also establishing a finely calibrated distance between them. When all of the worship hall's *shitomido* latticed shutters are open, the sanctuary is clearly visible through the transparent structure; the currents of fresh air sweeping the hall seem almost visible. Structurally speaking, the walls on both sides of the worship hall are designed to make the building more earthquake resistant. It is these lateral walls that enable the core of the building to be so graceful and open, with such an exceptional balance of "open and closed" beneath an elegant roof.

左殿・蟇股（平安時代）
A frog-leg strut of the left inner sanctuary (Heian period)

覆屋の格子で濾された西日は、神々しい光に満ちた空間をつくりだす。3社の規模は少しずつ異なる。中殿がもっとも小規模で、左殿・右殿は構造の一部を覆屋と共有する。蟇股は建立年代を推測する重要な手がかりだが、左殿(右奥)のものが最古で、平等院鳳凰堂(1053年)に近い様式とされる

Filtered through façade latticework, the setting sun fills the inner sanctuaries with a heavenly light. Each of the three inner sanctuaries is slightly different in size. Those on the left and right side share parts of their structures with the enclosure. Frog-leg struts can offer important clues for dating when structures were built. The frog-leg strut of the left inner sanctuary (back right) is believed to be the oldest as it is stylistically similar to those of the Phoenix Hall (1053) at Byodoin temple.

冬至の頃。向きが南から西へ30度ほど振れており、午後から徐々に内殿に光が射しこむ。
格子の上部は菱格子とし、二種類の格子の影が映しだされる

Afternoon sun slants into the main sanctuary during the winter solstice, the latticework casting diamond-shaped and square shadows over its steps. The building faces about 30 degrees west of due south.

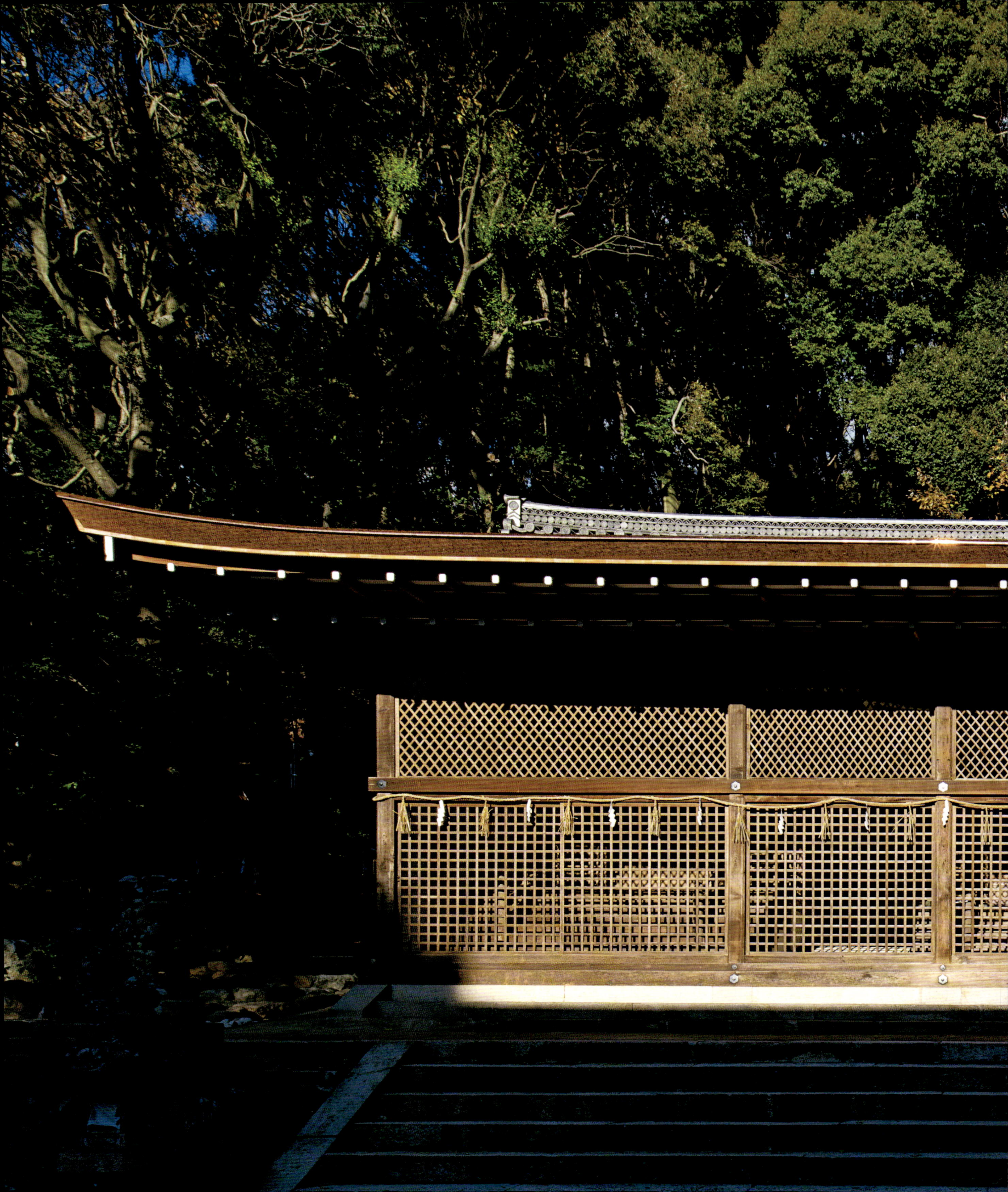

The main sanctuary stands on a slope with its back to the mountain. The presence of the enclosure has contributed greatly to protecting the inner sanctuaries.

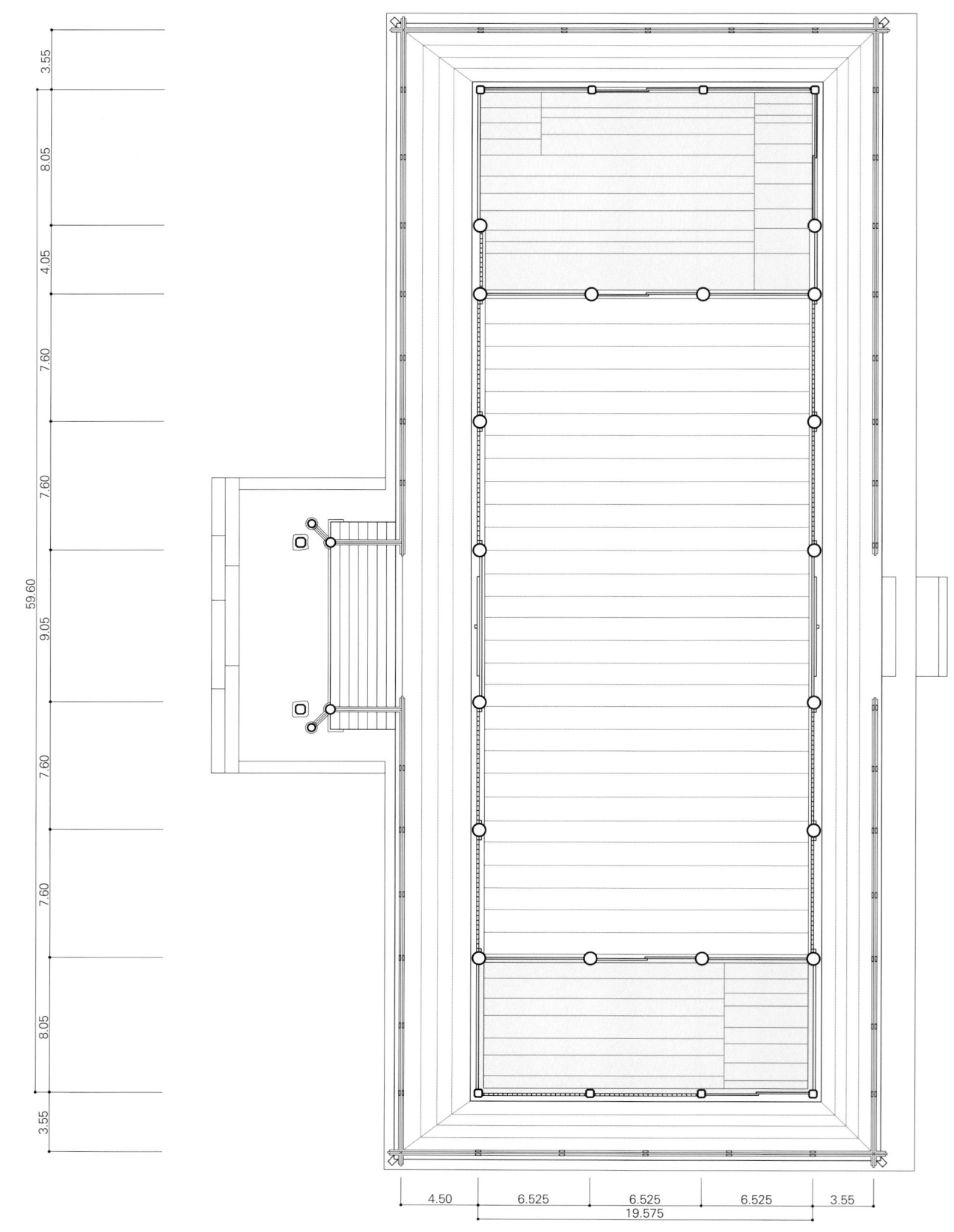

拝殿平面図　Floor plan of the worship hall

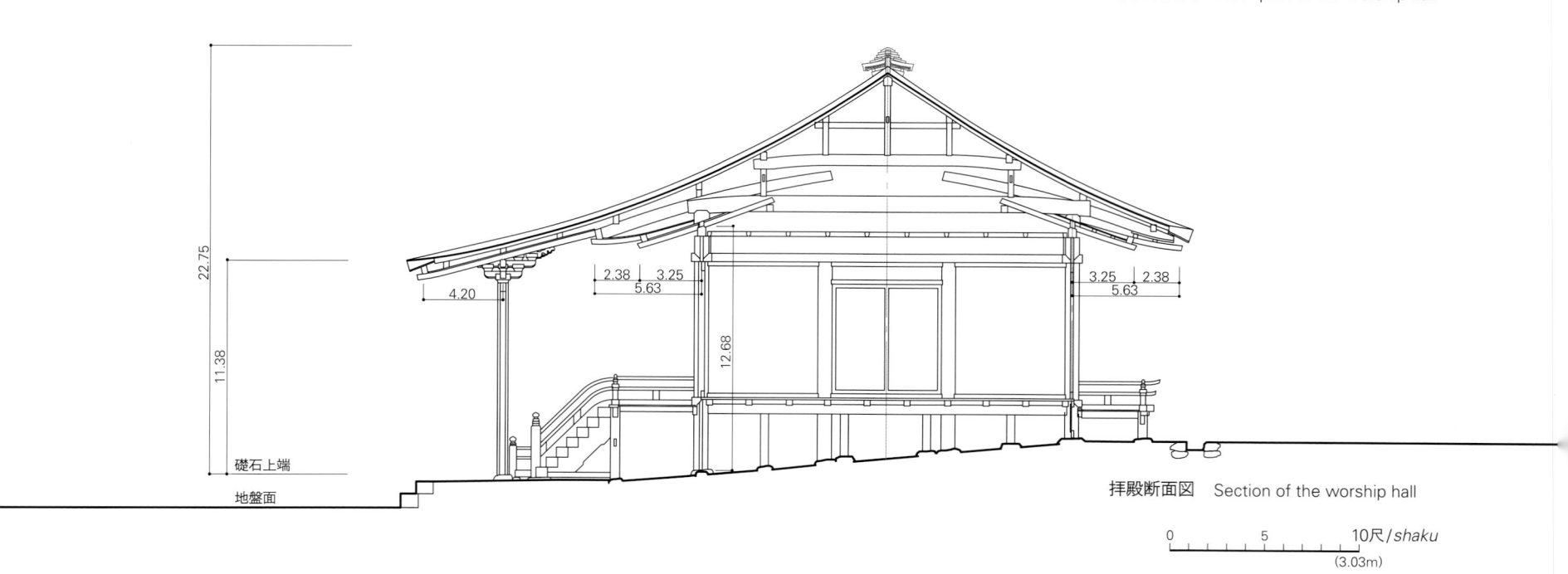

拝殿断面図　Section of the worship hall

0　5　10尺/shaku
(3.03m)

本殿平面図　Floor plan of the main sanctuary

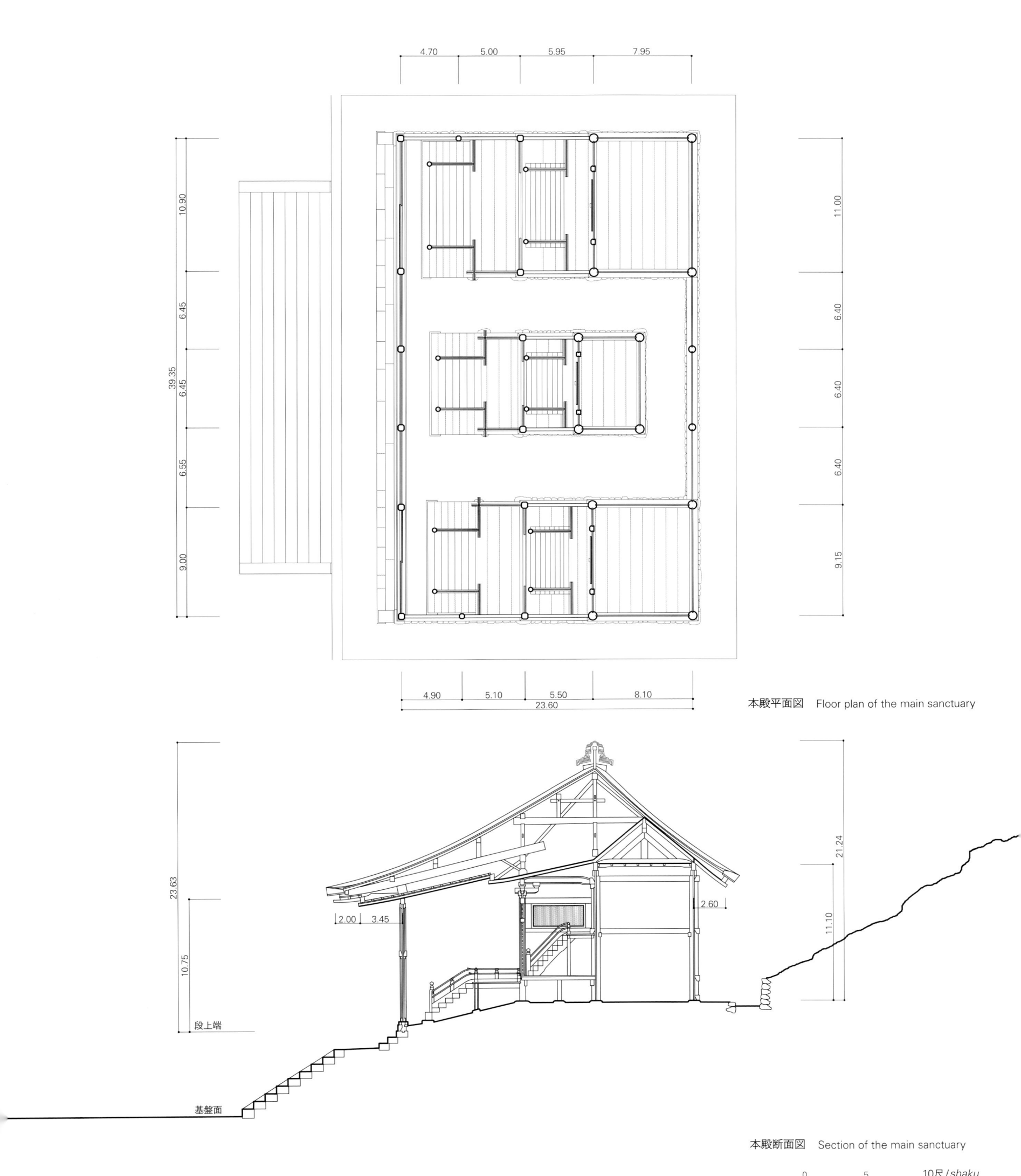

本殿断面図　Section of the main sanctuary

0　　5　　10尺/*shaku*
(3.03m)

本殿・東面妻側。流造の葺き下ろし屋根が伸びやかで優雅。覆屋と内殿（左殿・右殿）は後方2間の構造を共有している。斜面の下方には、石敷きの空間を挟んで拝殿が平行に立つ

East end gable of the main sanctuary. The flowing *nagarezukuri* roof extends elegantly toward the worship hall, oriented parallel to the main sanctuary and separated from it by a space paved with stone.

本殿・東側の屋根。ヒノキ板を柾目に割り、12mm間隔に葺いた
檜皮葺。美しい曲面部の箕甲をつくる技術は最高水準である

East end of the main sanctuary roof. The cypress shingles are overlapped at 12 millimeter intervals. The highest level of skill is required to create the beautiful curve of the *minoko* drooping verge.

拝殿。鎌倉時代の建立。切妻造の屋根の両妻1間に庇1間を付加し、縋破風で連続する。正面には向拝をつける。拝殿の蔀戸を開け放つと、空間は爽やかに透け、本殿へと視線の抜けをつくる。大きな屋根の下の開閉バランスが見事

Worship hall. Built during the Kamakura period, each gabled end incorporates an additional one-bay eave and extended bargeboards. The façade includes a step canopy. When all the latticed shutters of the worship hall are opened the space becomes refreshingly transparent, revealing a view of the main sanctuary behind. The balance of open and closed spaces beneath a massive roof makes a magnificent prospect.

ら本殿を見る。その
遠近感は絶妙であ
じがある。内法長押

Looking toward the main sanctuary from the interior of the worship hall with the latticed shutters—traditional panels that date from the Heian period—raised. The paved area and stone steps between the two buildings create a fine-tuned perspective. The floor is covered with boards, the ceiling is coffered, and the space above the non-penetrating tie beam over the door is narrow in the manner of the *arikabe* style.

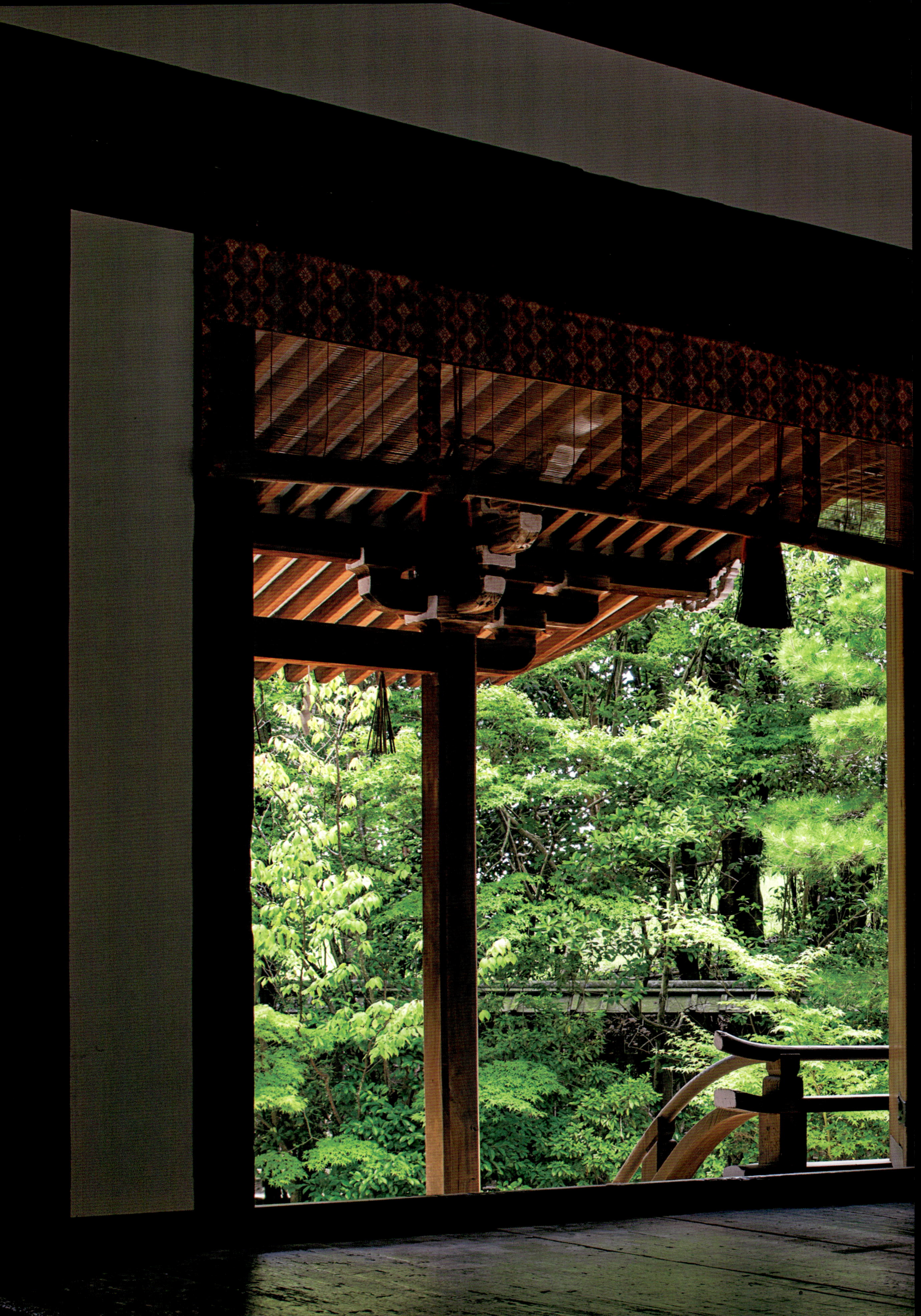

拝殿から境内を見る。蔀戸を開け放つと、外部と内部が融け合う。内法の高さは2.12m（7尺・右2間）で、外へと潔く、大きく開かれる。御簾がかかり、貴族の雅やかな住宅建築を彷彿させる。高欄上部の横木（架木・平桁）端部を撥ね上げ、形に流動感をつくる

Scene of the surroundings from within the worship hall. With the latticed shutters raised, inside and outside merge. The distance from threshold to the head jamb is 2.12 meters (right side), robustly opening the space to the outside. The *misu* bamboo blinds recall the elegant spaces of Heian aristocratic residences. The upturned ends of the balustrades create a sense of motion and flow.

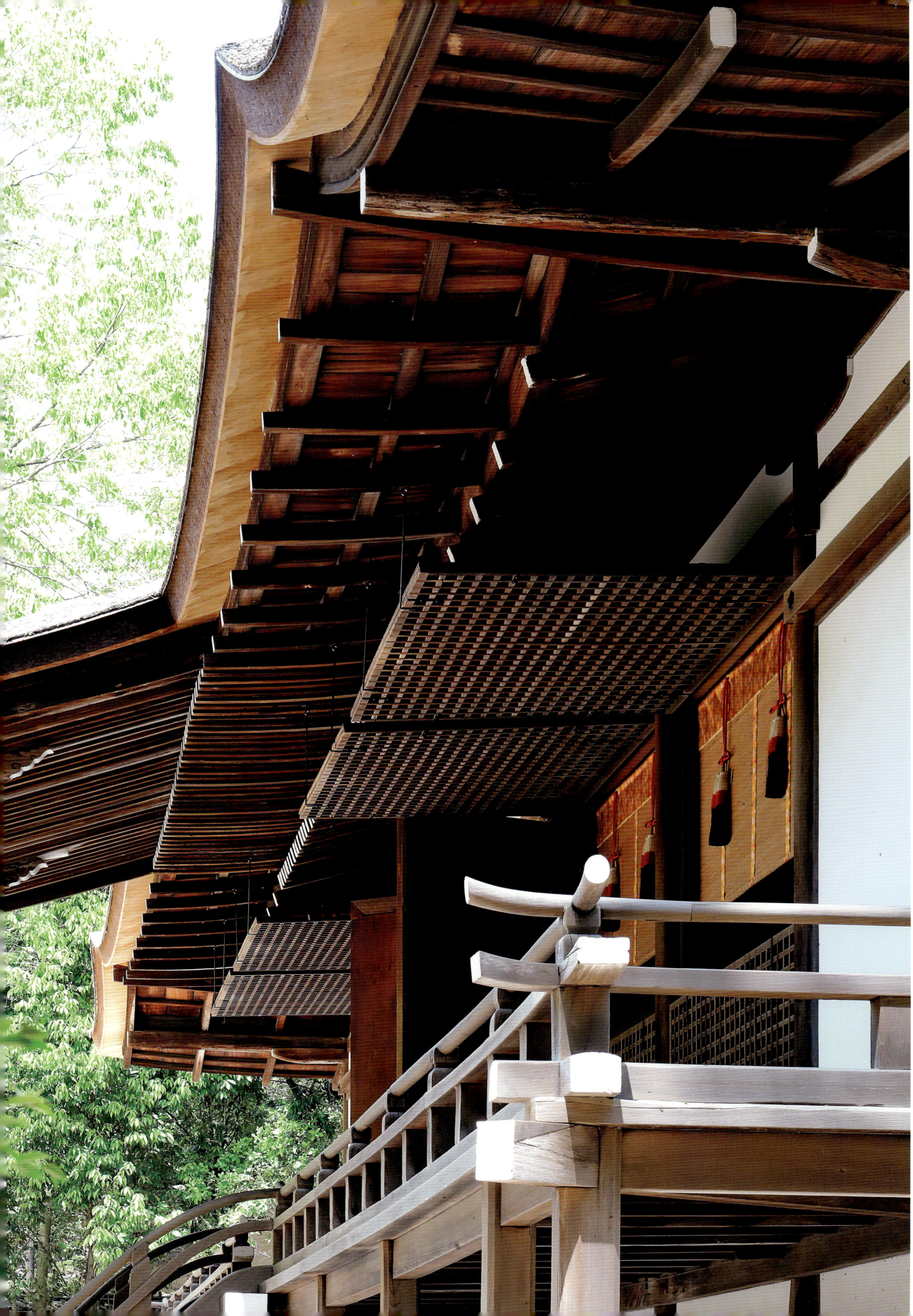

(左)拝殿東側から見た軒裏。下から高欄、御簾と蔀戸、二軒の疎垂木、向拝。飛檐垂木の下面を反り上げ、屋根の反りと呼応させる。向拝を繁垂木としたため、身舎もこの部分のみ繁垂木とする

(Left) The underside of the eaves seen from the east side of the worship hall, showing (from below) the balustrades, the *misu* blinds and *shitomido* latticed shutters, the double-layer of widely spaced *mabaradaruki* rafters, and the step canopy (at left edge). The lower faces of the flying rafters are curved upward to mirror the upturn of the roof. The central section uses closely spaced *shigedaruki* rafters to match those of the step canopy.

(上)両脇は白壁で、内部では仕切られて小部屋となっている。控えの間として機能する「従」の空間で、身舎側は円柱、庇側は角柱とする。開放的な身舎側に対し、耐力壁としても機能する

(Above) The enclosed areas on each side have white exterior walls and interiors that are partitioned into smaller rooms. Subordinate spaces that functioned as anterooms, these are bound by cylindrical columns on the core sides and squared pillars on the aisle sides. In contrast to the open building core, these side areas function as bearing walls.

南西角、庇を支える角柱。柱幅127mm(4.2寸)に対して、面取幅15mm(5分)。舟肘木、垂木も面取りされており、軽やかである

A pillar square in section supporting the eaves at the southwest corner. Such pillars measure 127 millimeters with chamfered edges measuring 15 millimeters. The *funahijiki* boat-shaped bracket arms and rafters are also beveled, giving the structure a sense of lightness.

南側、身舎側には円柱が立つ。横材の木割が細く、繊細で歯切れのよいプロポーション。柱の径210mm(7寸)、それに対して内法の見付け55mm(1.8寸)、上部の長押の見付け102mm(3.4寸)

Core-side circular column on the south face of the building. The measurements used in the building result in narrower horizontal members with crisp, delicate proportions. While the pillar measures 210 millimeters in diameter, the head jamb measures 55 millimeters and the *nageshi* non-penetrating tie beam above it 102 millimeters.

嚴島神社

国宝
建立年代　13世紀前半–17世紀前半
所在地　　広島県廿日市市

Itsukushima Shrine

National Treasure
Completed: First half of 13th–first half of 17th century
Location: Hatsukaichi, Hiroshima prefecture

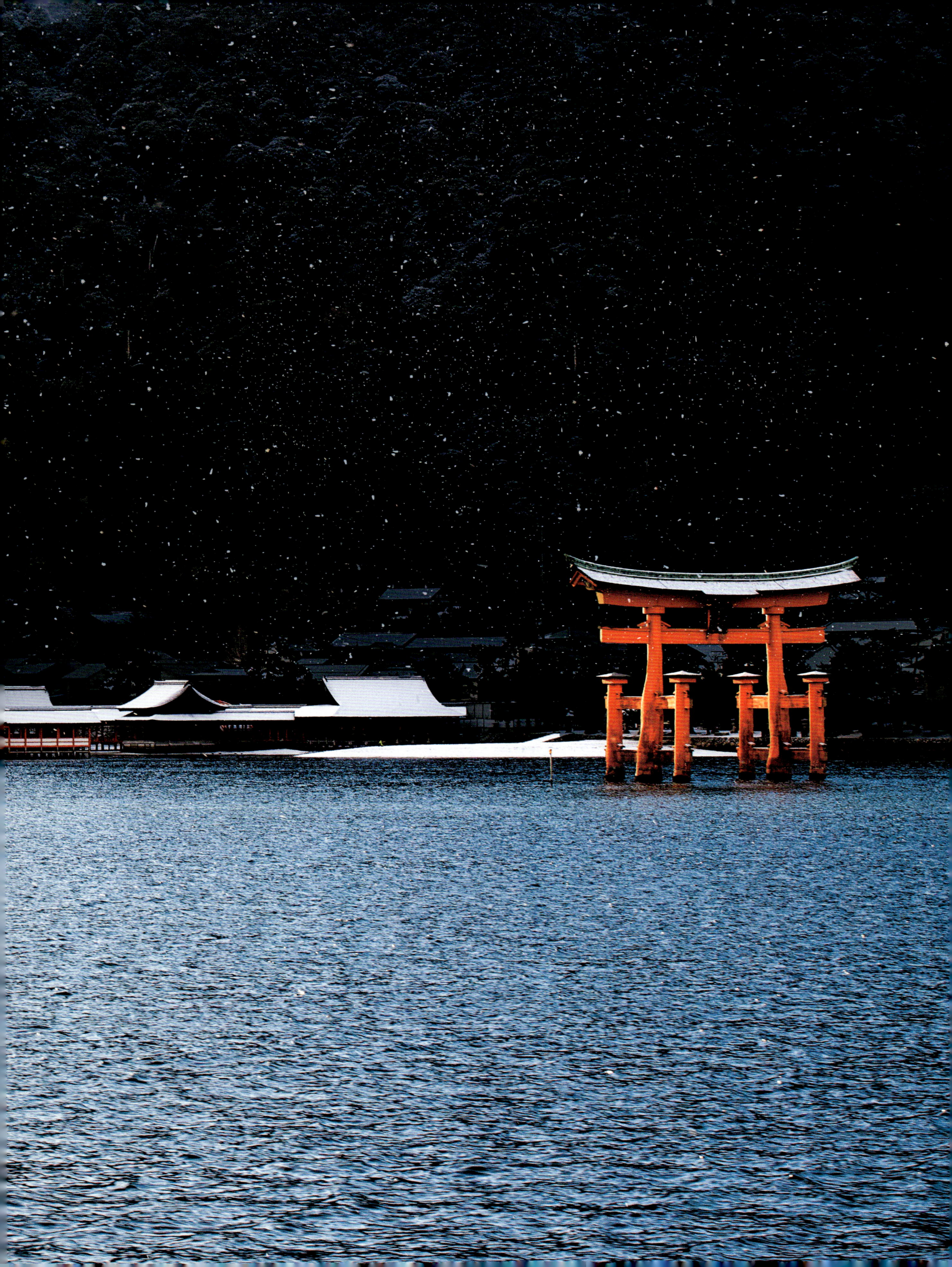

時代背景

　広島湾の西方に位置する厳島(宮島)は周囲30kmほどの小さな島だが、その主峰・弥山(標高535m)への崇拝から島全体が神聖視され、古くから信仰を集めてきた。厳島神社が海浜から海上にかけて建てられ、島上での築造が避けられたのも、島を神の土地とする考えがおおもとにあったと考えられている。神社の創始は593年(推古天皇元年)と伝承され、正史上では9世紀初めに初出する。海上交通の要衝の地にあることから、海の女神とされる宗像三神──市杵島姫、湍津姫、田心姫──を祀る。平安時代の12世紀には、瀬戸内の水軍を治めた平清盛(1118−1181)の信仰を受け、仁安年間(1166−1169)にかけて社殿が整備された。清盛の存命中は後白河法皇(1127−1192)の御幸(1174年)をはじめ皇族・貴族の参詣が盛んとなり、華やかな行事が社殿で執り行われたことから、当初からそれにふさわしい空間構成が整えられていたと考えられる。

　鎌倉時代には2度の火事(1207年・1223年)に遭い、1241(仁治2)年に再建。現在の社殿はこの再興時のものが基調となり、時代とともに改修の手が加えられていったものである。ただし本社本殿については、1571(元亀2)年に建てかえがあり、廻廊については永禄から慶長年間の棟札(1563年−1602年)から、この時代の再建とされる。再建・修造に際しては古様を守る方針が取られ、現社殿の基礎をなす鎌倉時代の造営についても、平安時代の社容が踏襲されていると考えられている。

特徴と見どころ

　社殿の屋根と屋根をつないで連結する。そして、廻廊でひとつながりに束ねる。個々の要素が複雑に絡み合いながら統合され、有機的な建築の姿をつくりだしているのが厳島神社である。しかも、海辺を敷地に、山を背景に、自然と一体化して類例のない建築景観がもたらされている。満潮時には社殿は海上に浮かぶように見え、干潮時には大鳥居までが砂浜の上に立っている。潮の満ち干きとともに刻一刻と変容するその姿は、宇宙のリズムを建築に取りこみ、それを視覚化したものともいえるだろう。

　じつに大きな構想のもとで建てられた建築であるが、その下敷きには、平安時代を通して盛んに造営された寝殿造の住居と庭園、天皇や上皇による離宮の手法があることは指摘されてきたところである。本社も客神社も本殿は両流造と呼ばれるが、身舎の前後に庇を付加したつくりや、庇と庇を檜皮葺で重ねながら、建物と建物とが融け合うように一体となる複雑にして優雅な屋根の連なりは、まさに寝殿造の姿を彷彿させる。さらに、各社や舞台を廊伝いに結ぶ形式や、水辺と陸地とを橋で渡す仕掛け、蔀戸による柱間装置など、寝殿造に共通する建築手法が駆使されている。厳島神社に感じられる王朝的な雰囲気は、このような手法の集積によるものであり、そこでつくられる間合いであろう。廻廊は複雑に折れ曲がり、見る地点によって眺めは変化に富む。歩みを進めるとともに、朱に彩られた透けと重ねの空間が繊細な陰翳と奥行をもって展開する。一方、平舞台に出れば大きく海へと開かれる。ここで繰り広げられる舞いや音楽は、神に奉納されるためにある。宮殿建築とも親近性をもったこの社殿の計画は、山と海の神という畏怖すべき対象を得て、従来にない構想の大きさをもち、祈りのための比類なき美の形を生みだしている。

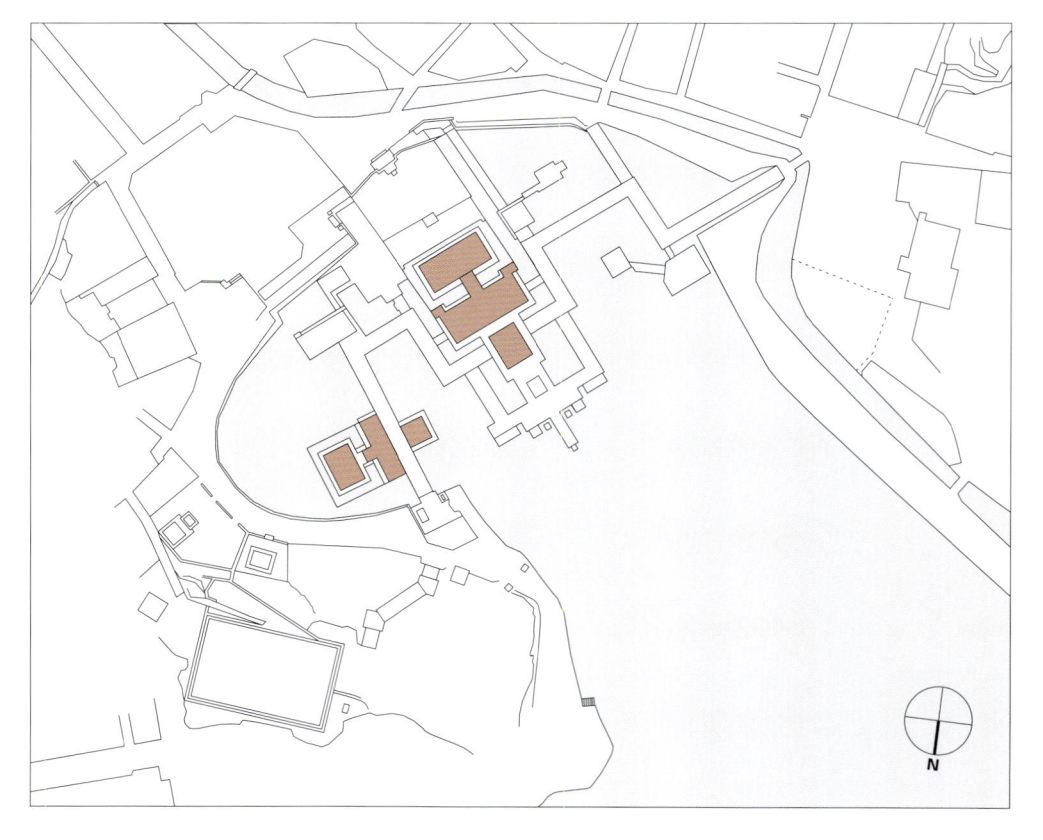

社殿配置図　Site plan

Historical Background

Itsukushima (Miyajima) is a small island, roughly 30 kilometers in circumference, located in the west part of Hiroshima bay. Worship of the island's main peak, Mt. Misen (535 meters), led the entire island to be seen as sacred and made it the object of religious devotion since ancient times. Itsukushima Shrine is built from the shore out over the water, apparently out of reluctance to build on the island itself, which was thought to be a special abode of the gods. Traditionally said to have been established in 593, the shrine is dedicated to the three Munakata goddesses of the sea: Ichikishima-hime, Tagitsu-hime and Tagori-hime. The location was strategic in terms of maritime trade and first appears in official histories in the early ninth century. During the Heian period the shrine received the patronage of Taira no Kiyomori (1118–1181), who had established control over the pirate forces in the Inland Sea, and the shrine buildings were constructed between 1166 and 1169. Many members of the imperial family and aristocracy visited the shrine while Kiyomori was alive—including a visit by the cloistered emperor Go-Shirakawa (1127–1192) in 1174—and many elaborate ceremonies were performed at these buildings, which are thought to have been designed from the outset as suitable venues for such events.

The shrine suffered fires twice during the Kamakura period in 1207 and 1223 and was rebuilt in 1241. This reconstruction forms the base of the current shrine buildings, though they have undergone repairs and modifications over time. The main sanctuary (*honden*) of the main shrine, however, was rebuilt in 1571 and ridge tags (*munafuda*) remaining from 1563 to 1602 suggest that the corridors (*kairo*) were rebuilt at that time. Reconstructions and repairs have been guided by a policy of retaining ancient styles; the Kamakura period reconstructions that form the base of the current shrine buildings are believed to follow their Heian period antecedents.

Characteristics and Highlights

Each roof is connected to the next, and the whole tied together with corridors. The individual elements are integrated in convoluted ways to create the organic architectural forms that characterize Itsukushima Shrine. Built out over the sea with the mountains as a backdrop, the shrine forms an incomparable architectural landscape, merged with its natural surroundings. At high tide the shrine buildings seem to float above the surface of the water and at low tide the sea recedes to a point even beyond the Great Torii (O-torii) Gate. Their forms seem transformed moment by moment with the rising and falling of the tides, incorporating the very rhythms of the cosmos.

Although guided by grandly conceived plans, the shrine is also noted as employing the techniques of the *shinden-zukuri*-style residential architecture popular during the Heian period, as seen in the villas of emperors and retired emperors. The complex also makes full use of *shinden-zukuri* architectural techniques in its corridors for connecting the different shrines and stages, the bridges that connect the waterside structures to the land, and the treatment of space between the pillars and *shitomido* latticed shutters. The corridors turn in one direction and then another, creating a succession of variously changing views. Walking along them reveals spaces of transparency and overlap, colored with vermillion and revealing delicate shadows and perspectives. The Hirabutai, a broad stage at the front of the shrine for performing dance and music dedicated to the gods, opens out onto the sea. With close resemblances to palace architecture, the plan of this shrine dedicated to the gods of the mountains and the sea unfolds on an unprecedented conceptual scale.

満潮時の夕暮れ。本社の方を見る。島の主峰である弥山のふもと、海浜から海上へかけて社殿が立ち並ぶ。一番奥から本社本殿、その手前に平行して拝殿、さらに直交して祓殿が立ち、各社殿は檜皮葺の屋根で滑らかにつながれている

High tide at twilight looking toward the main shrine. The shrine buildings extend out from the shore and over the ocean at the base of Mt. Misen, the island's highest peak. The shrine buildings are all smoothly joined together by roofs shingled with cypress bark: furthest in the background is the main sanctuary, followed by the worship hall and, extending forward and perpendicular to the others, the purification hall (*haraiden*).

東廻廊。家扠首と柱の連続感がつくりだす奥行き。ここは社殿群への東からの導入部となる

East corridor. The succession of diagonal braces and pillars creates a sense of depth in this approach to the cluster of shrine buildings.

摂社客神社・本殿。格子による透けが奥行きをつくる。遮りつつも空間を透かし、奥の
気配を強めている。注連縄、そこから下がる紙垂、両脇の榊によって、結界の感覚は
強められ、ここから先が神域であることを示す

Main sanctuary of the auxiliary Marodo Shrine. The see-through effect of the lattices accentuates the sense of depth: screening while revealing heightens the presence of the inner recesses. The sacred *shimenawa* rope, the paper *shide* streamers hanging from it, and the *sakaki* branches standing on both sides strengthen the sense of a boundary (*kekkai*)—that which lies beyond is sacred.

高舞台あたりから東廻廊を見る。廻廊は幾重にも折れ曲り、
朱に彩られた透けと重ねの空間が展開する

The east corridor seen from the stage. The winding corridors create a vermillion world of see-through and overlapping spaces.

西廻廊と反橋を見る。すべての社殿を廻廊でつなぎ、陸地との間は橋で連結する。水に反射した光が天井に映りこみ、光の揺らぎをつくりだす。床板の間には隙間を空け、高潮で浸水した際、水圧を緩和する

The west corridor and *soribashi* arched bridge. All the shrine buildings are connected by corridors, but bridges link the shrine to land. Light reflected off the surface of the water reflects on the underside of the roof, shimmering with the movement of the waves. Gaps are left between the floorboards to mitigate water pressure when the corridors flood during high tide.

西側から見た廻廊、本社本殿と拝殿の屋根の連なり。右奥には大国神社の
屋根が見える。木々の深い緑で丹塗りの朱が鮮やかに引き立つ

Corridor seen from the west and the roofs of the main sanctuary (center) and worship hall (left). In the background at right is the roof of the Daikoku Shrine. The vermillion of the corridors stands out vividly against the deep green of the trees.

摂社客神社の本殿(手前)と拝殿の屋根。前後の軒を曲線で流れるように延ばした
両流造の屋根が連なる。屋根から妻にかけて滑らかに曲げ下ろした箕甲は、妻側に
深い陰影をつくりだし、そのエッジを特徴ある造形にしている

The roofs of the main sanctuary (foreground) and worship hall at the auxiliary Marodo Shrine. Both are made in the *ryonagarezukuri* style, with both front and back eaves incorporating flowing lines. The smooth curve of the *minoko* drooping verge where the roof meets the gable gives the edge a distinctive shape and forms deep shadows in the gable end.

本社本殿・妻側の庇の深い奥行き。横板壁は胡粉塗り、破風、垂木、柱、長押、組物などは朱塗り、連子窓は緑青を塗った緑。猪の目懸魚は装飾的要素だが、桁と棟木の木口を雨風から守る機能も兼ねている

The deep eaves of the gable end of the main shrine's main sanctuary. The horizontal boards of the exterior wall are painted white; the bargeboards, rafters, pillars, non-penetrating tie beams, and bracket complexes vermillion; and the slatted windows green. The *inome gegyo* boar's-eye gable pendants are decorative elements that also protect the ends of the purlins and ridgepole from wind and rain.

本社本殿、両流造の屋根の妻側。日本建築は柱や梁などを外部にそのまま現す真壁構造である。中央2間が身舎部分、側面各1間が庇部分となる

The gable end of the *ryonagarezukuri* roof at the main shrine's main sanctuary. Japanese architecture typically uses *shinkabe* construction, in which structural members such as pillars and beams are exposed to the exterior. The two bays in the center indicate the core space, and the bays on either side the aisle space.

Kasuga Taisha Auxiliary Wakamiya Shrine

Important Cultural Property
Completed: 17th–19th century
Location: Nara, Nara prefecture

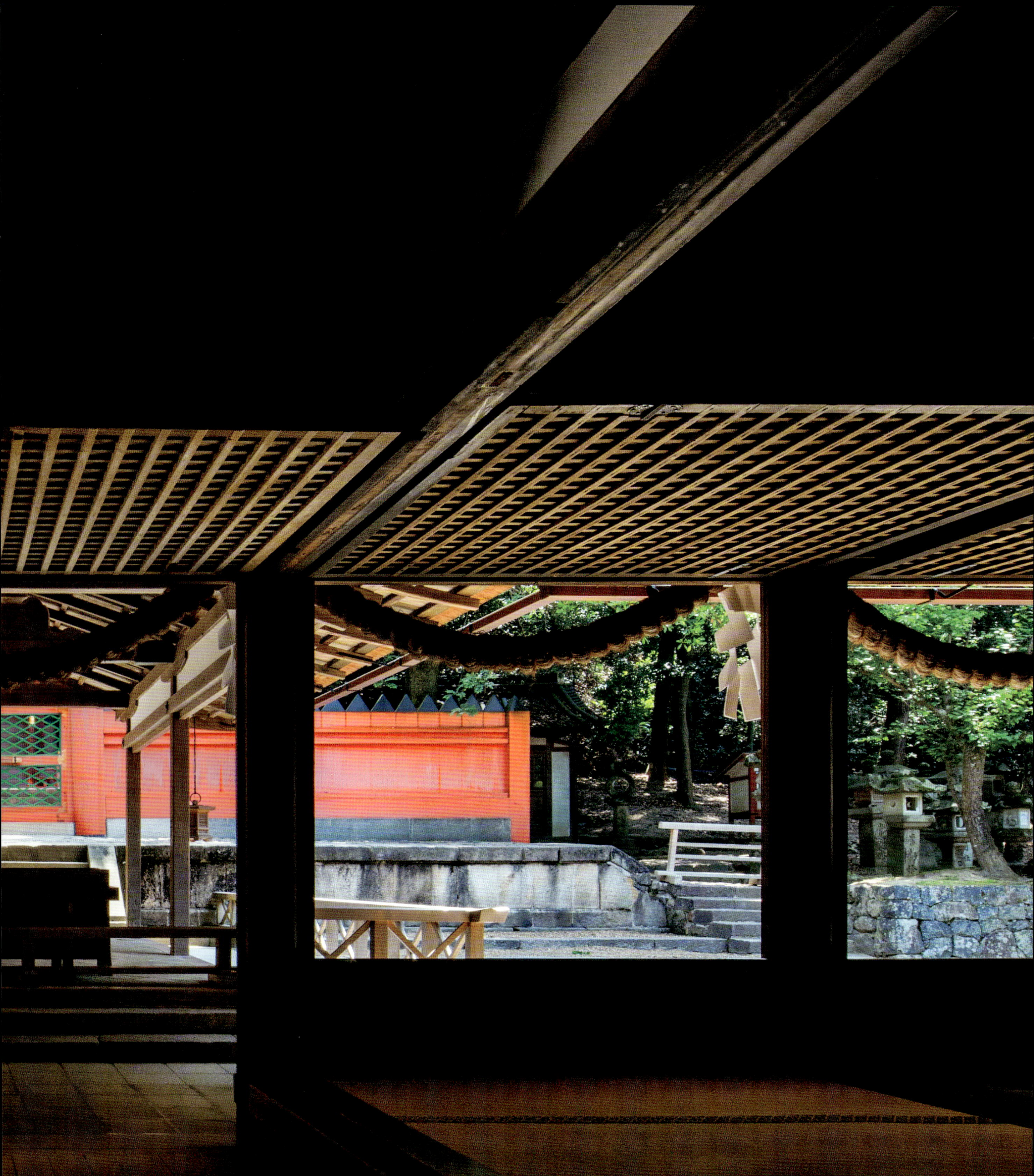

時代背景

　平城京の東端に位置する御蓋山は、古くから神の宿る山として崇拝を集めてきた。この地に春日社を建てたのは、称徳天皇(718-770)の勅命を受けた藤原永手(714-771)とされる。社の創建は平城京遷都後の8世紀、本社本殿の造営は768(神護景雲2)年とする。やはり藤原氏の氏寺である興福寺の東に隣接し、そこから御蓋山にいたる広大な台地が社の神域で、本社や付属社殿が立つ。

　本社の南側に、山を背にして摂社・若宮神社がある。祭神は本社本殿に祀られる四神のうち、藤原氏の祖神である天児屋根命と比売神との御子である天押雲根命である。本殿は1135(保延元)年に関白・藤原忠通(1097-1164)が飢饉や疫病の防御を願って造営した。現建物は1863(文久3)年の造替時のものとなる。忠通は1136年、若宮の祭神に祭礼を奉仕したが、それが今も途切れなくつづけられている「春日若宮おん祭」の始まりで、2015(平成27)年で880回を数えた。これは毎年12月17日の一昼夜のみ、若宮の祭神を本殿から仮殿の御旅所に迎えて神楽などの芸能を奉納し、神へ奉仕する祭である。御旅所は毎年新しく建てられ、祭が終わるとただちに撤去される。

　若宮本殿の前に立つのが細殿および神楽殿の建物で、それに直交して接続する切妻造・吹放ちの建物が拝舎である。細殿・神楽殿の起源は本殿と同時期にさかのぼるが、現建物は1613(慶長18)年の造替による。平安以来、神楽殿では神楽が奉奏され、一方、細殿は古くは「経所」とも呼ばれていたように、おもに興福寺僧侶が儀式の際に着座する部屋となる。

　拝舎は1178(治承2)年の創建、現建物は1863(文久3)年の造替時のものである。石畳が敷かれ、神事の際には神職がここに着座する。1309(延慶2)年頃に成立した絵巻物『春日権現験記』には、現状とほぼ変わらぬ細殿・神楽殿と拝舎が描かれている。*9 ここは平安以来、おん祭をはじめとして有形無形のものが不可分なかたちで保持され、両者の古式が守り継がれてきた場所である。

特徴と見どころ

　ゆるやかに曲がるアプローチから見える石階上の細殿・神楽殿の佇まいは、一度目にしたら忘れられない美しさである。檜皮葺で切妻屋根をかけ、片側の庇を延ばして滑らかに葺き下ろし、優雅な非対称の屋根を見せる。その奥には、吹放ちの拝舎の柱が清らかな透けの空間をつくりだしている。環境を巧みに活かした配置による、絶妙な遠近感である。

　本殿は神社としては珍しく西向きに立ち、西日を受けて神々しく輝く。細殿・神楽殿の身舎柱は円柱、天井は総化粧屋根裏で、本殿側の柱間は10間のうち8間を蔀戸とし、平安王朝風の雰囲気を漂わせる。ここでは祭神へ神楽を捧げるために、蔀戸を内側へ吊り上げて本殿側に向けて空間を全開する。細殿・神楽殿と拝舎両建物の、伸びのある直線的な連続感のなか、舟肘木が刻むアクセントが小気味好い。

　洗練された若宮の社殿と好対照をなすのが、毎年の春日若宮おん祭で建てられる御旅所の行宮である。太い皮付き松丸太の架構に、屋根には青々とした松葉を葺き、原始的な力を秘めた姿である。概して、仮設物であっても形を丁寧に整えるのが日本人の建築的性向である。だが、この御旅所のように、ざっくりとした素朴さのなかに宿る生命感を故意に温存した建物の例はそうそう見当たらず、興味は尽きない。

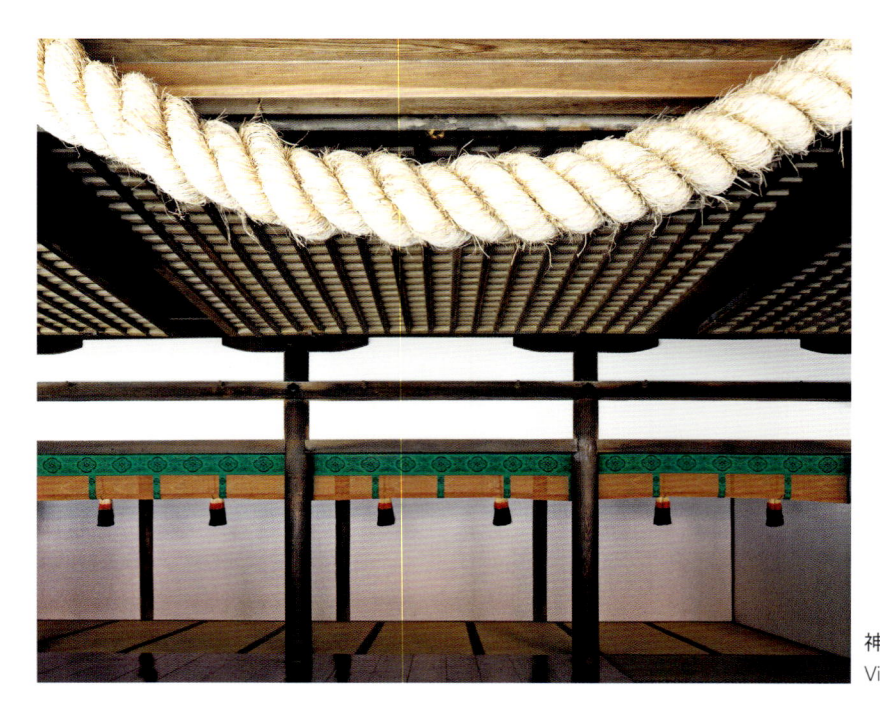

神楽殿を見る
View into the Kaguraden

Historical Background

Located on the eastern edge of Heijokyo (the capital at Nara), Mt. Mikasa was worshipped since ancient times as a mountain abode of the gods. Kasuga Taisha shrine, or Kasuga Grand Shrine, was built in the area by the powerful Fujiwara no Nagate (714–771) at the order of Emperor Shotoku (718–770) during the eighth century after the transfer of the capital to Heijokyo. Shrine lore dates the completion of the main sanctuary to 768. The shrine's main and auxiliary buildings stand in expansive precincts that are adjacent and to the east of Kofukuji, tutelary temple of the Fujiwara clan, and extend all the way to Mt. Mikasa.

To the south of the main shrine, with its back to the mountain, stands an auxiliary edifice called Wakamiya shrine. The deity enshrined there is Ame no Oshikumone no Mikoto, child of Ame no Koyane no Mikoto—ancestral god of the Fujiwara clan—and the goddess Himegami (both counted among the four gods enshrined in the main sanctuary of the main shrine). The Wakamiya shrine sanctuary (*honden*) was originally built in 1135 by the regent Fujiwara no Tadamichi (1097–1164), to ward off famine and plague. The current structure dates to the rebuilding of 1863. Tadamichi held a festival for the deity enshrined at Wakamiya in 1136, beginning the unbroken tradition of the Kasuga Wakamiya On-Matsuri festival, which has just been held for the 880th time in 2015. During this festival, for one day and night only every year on 17 December, the deity of Wakamiya is transferred from the main sanctuary to a temporary dwelling called the *otabisho* and received there with offerings of *kagura* music and dancing. The *otabisho* is rebuilt every year and promptly removed after the festival concludes.

Parallel to the Wakamiya main sanctuary stands the long Hosodono and Kaguraden building and, connected to it at a right angle, the gable-roofed, unenclosed Hainoya worship hall. The origins of the Hosodono and Kaguraden lie in the same period as the main sanctuary, but the current structure dates to the rebuilding of 1613. *Kagura* music and dance has been performed at the Kaguraden since the Heian period, while the Hosodono—as suggested by the fact that in former times it was called a Kyosho ("sutra place")—was primarily used as a room where priests from Kofukuji could perform ceremonies while seated.

The Hainoya worship hall was originally built in 1178; the current structure dates to the rebuilding of 1863. This stone-paved area is where the Shinto priests sit when performing Shinto rites. The *Kasuga gongen kenki* (Legends of Kasuga Shrine), a picture scroll produced in 1309, includes illustrations of the Kaguraden, Hosodono, and Hainoya worship hall that look much as they do today. Since the Heian period, the shrine's traditions both tangible and intangible have been maintained together and handed down faithfully in their ancient forms to the present day.

Characteristics and Highlights

The Hosodono and Kaguraden building seen at the top of the stone steps at the end of the sloping approach makes an unforgettable sight. In elegant asymmetrical lines, the cypress-bark shingled gable slopes gracefully over extended eaves. Beyond it, the pillars of the open worship hall frame a clear, transparent space. This skillful incorporation of the surrounding environment enhances the sense of depth and perspective.

Unusual for a shrine, the main sanctuary faces west and is bathed in the splendid light of the setting sun. The *moyabashira* core pillars of the Hosodono and Kaguraden are cylindrical columns, and eight of the ten bays facing the main sanctuary are fitted with *shitomido* latticed shutters. Although strongly suggestive of the atmosphere of the Heian court, here the shutters open to the inside to extend the space toward the main sanctuary when offering *kagura* performances to the enshrined deity. The *funahijiki* boat-shaped bracket arms pleasingly punctuate the long lines of the Hosodono, Kaguraden, and Hainoya worship hall.

Providing a striking contrast to the refined buildings of the Wakamiya shrine, the *otabisho* built every year for the festival exhibits a rustic fortitude, utilizing a frame of stout, unpeeled pine logs and a roof covered in fresh pine boughs. Generally, the inclination in Japanese architecture is to shape things cleanly and carefully even when building temporary structures, so this is a fascinating and unusual example of a structure that intentionally retains the vitality inherent in the rough and unsophisticated.

本社本殿から南へ100m、ゆるやかなカーブの参道に沿って御間型灯籠が並び立つなか、石階上に細殿・神楽殿の建物が見えてくる

One hundred meters south of the main sanctuary of the main shrine, beyond a gently curving approach lined with Oaigata stone lanterns, the Hosodono and Kaguraden building comes into view at the top of a flight of stone steps.

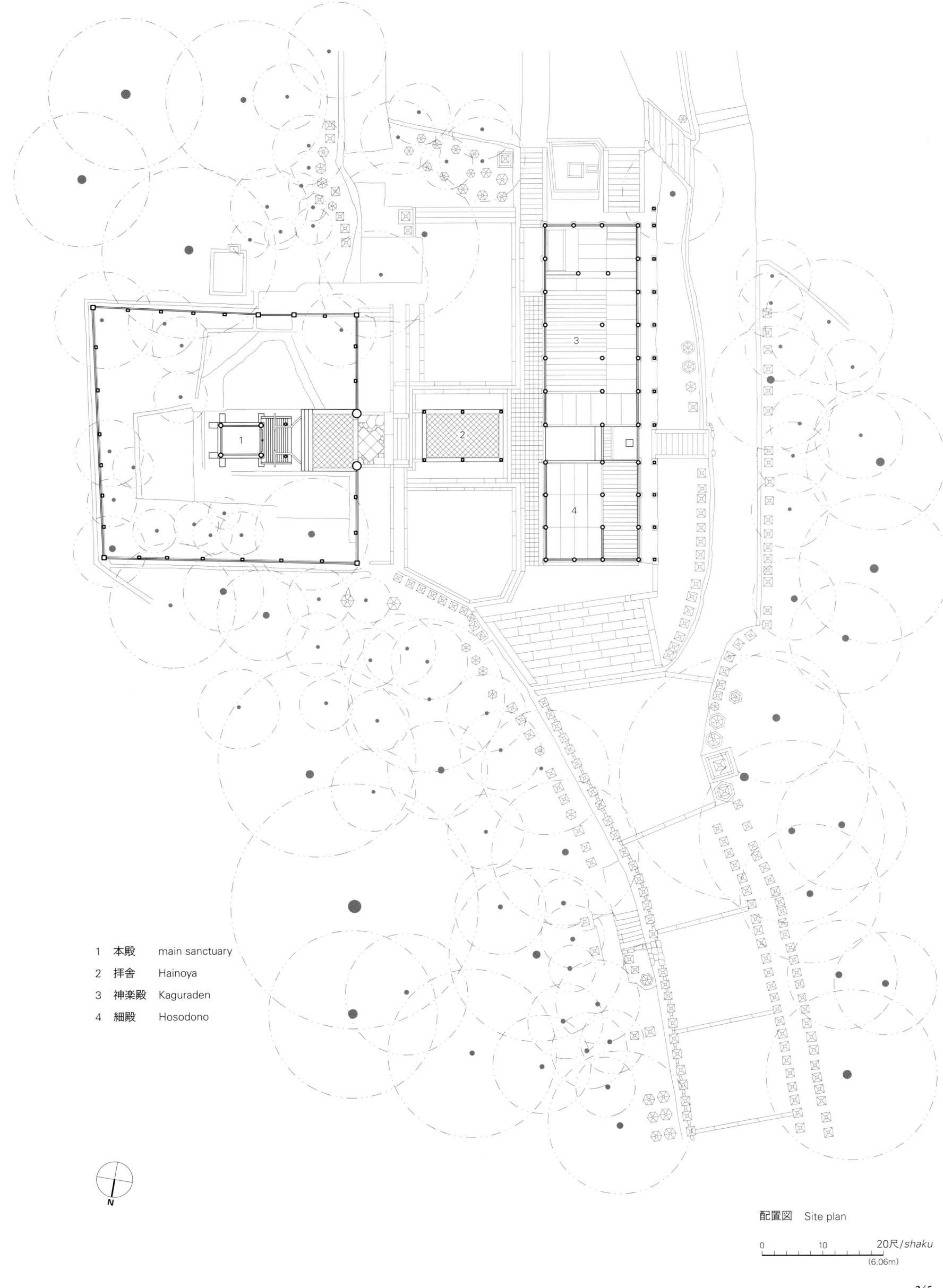

1	本殿	main sanctuary
2	拝舎	Hainoya
3	神楽殿	Kaguraden
4	細殿	Hosodono

配置図　Site plan

細殿・神楽殿の北・妻側。優雅な非対称の流造の屋根。板扉（左）と
舞良戸（右）の内法長押の高さをわずかにずらし、めりはりの効いた
見え方をつくる。奥（左）には直交して拝舎が立つ

The north gable end of the Hosodono and Kaguraden, showing the graceful, asymmetrical *nagarezukuri* flowing roof. The slight variation in the height of the *uchinori nageshi* non-penetrating tie beams over the pair of swing doors (left) and the *mairado* sliding doors (right) gives the building's appearance a sense of rhythm. The Hainoya worship hall, oriented perpendicularly to the building, is visible in the background at left.

（上）若宮本殿と細殿・神楽殿をつなぐ拝舎（中央）。本殿は御蓋山を背に、西向きに立つ。背景には天然記念物のナギの樹林が広がる

(Above) The Hainoya worship hall (center) connects the Hosodono and Kaguraden with the main sanctuary (right). The sanctuary faces west with Mt. Mikasa at its back. A grove of *nagi* trees, designated as a protected plant species, stands in the background.

（右）若宮本殿。春日大社本殿と同形式の春日造。瑞垣は厚板を並べ、上部先端を三角形に尖らせる。各板幅は異なるが、三角形の角度を微妙に変えて頂点の高さをそろえ、全体を調整する。微妙な不均等の感覚が形の強さをつくる

(Right) The main sanctuary of Wakamiya shrine is built in the same *kasugazukuri* style as the main sanctuary of Kasuga Taisha. The *mizugaki* fence is made of thick boards arranged vertically with their upper ends forming into triangles. The width of each board varies but the whole is harmonized by slightly varying the angle of each triangle such that all of their tips are aligned. The subtle sense of imbalance has impact.

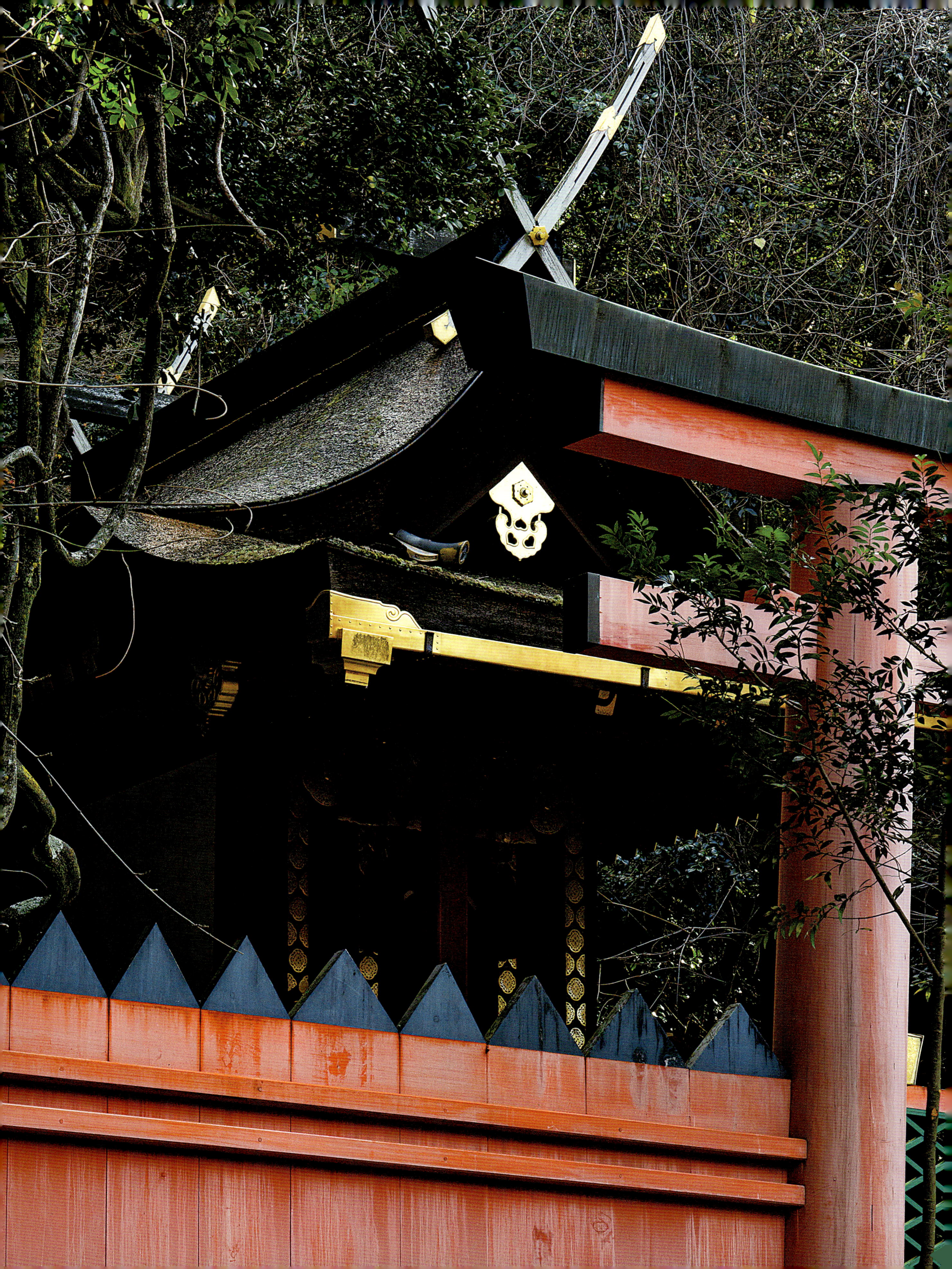

拝舎の柱まわり。横材（内法と長押）の見込み差が深く、歯切れのよいディテール。柱は120mm、面取り幅8mm

Close-up of the pillars of the worship hall. The insert of the horizontal braces between the pillars adds an interesting detail beneath the broad underside of the sturdy *nageshi* tie beam. The pillars measure 120 millimeters square with a chamfer width of 8 millimeters.

拝舎の舟肘木。そのプロポーションは、長押上の細い小壁に合わせて細身で繊細である

Slender *funahijiki* boat-shaped bracket arms at the worship hall, their delicate proportions designed to fit the short wall above the *nageshi* non-penetrating tie beam.

御旅所の行宮、西面。土壁に白漆喰で塗られた鱗紋には、粗さのなかに神秘の力がこもる。皮付きマツ丸太を組み立てた架構に、屋根は垂木の上に竹の木舞を打ち、杉皮を並べ、松葉を葺く。半戸外となる庇空間（右側）が、身舎とほぼ同じ面積であるのが興味深い

West side of the *otabisho* temporary dwelling. In its roughness, the white plaster scale motif on the earthen walls exhibits a mysterious power. Above the frame of unstripped pine logs, bamboo laths attached to rafters are covered with Japanese cedar bark and pine boughs to form the roof. Interestingly, the space under the eaves at the right covers nearly the same area as the building core.

御旅所の行宮はおん祭の際、若宮の神が仮に鎮座する一昼夜限りの社。切妻造に松枝の千木を揚げる。妻入りで向拝がつき、その下の高欄や階段には薦が使われている。素材は違っても、本社本殿や若宮本殿と同じ春日造の構成

The *otabisho* is a temporary dwelling where the deity of Wakamiya shrine resides for one day and one night during the Kasuga Wakamiya On-Matsuri festival. Its gabled roof is topped with forked finials made of pine branches. *Komo* straw mats are used for the balustrades and steps under the step canopy at the entrance on the gabled end. Although the materials differ, the style is the same *kasugazukuri* used in the main sanctuaries of both the main shrine and Wakamiya shrine.

高山寺 石水院

国宝
建立年代　13世紀
所在地　　京都府京都市右京区

Kosanji Temple Sekisui-in

National Treasure
Completed: 13th century
Location: Ukyo ward, Kyoto, Kyoto prefecture

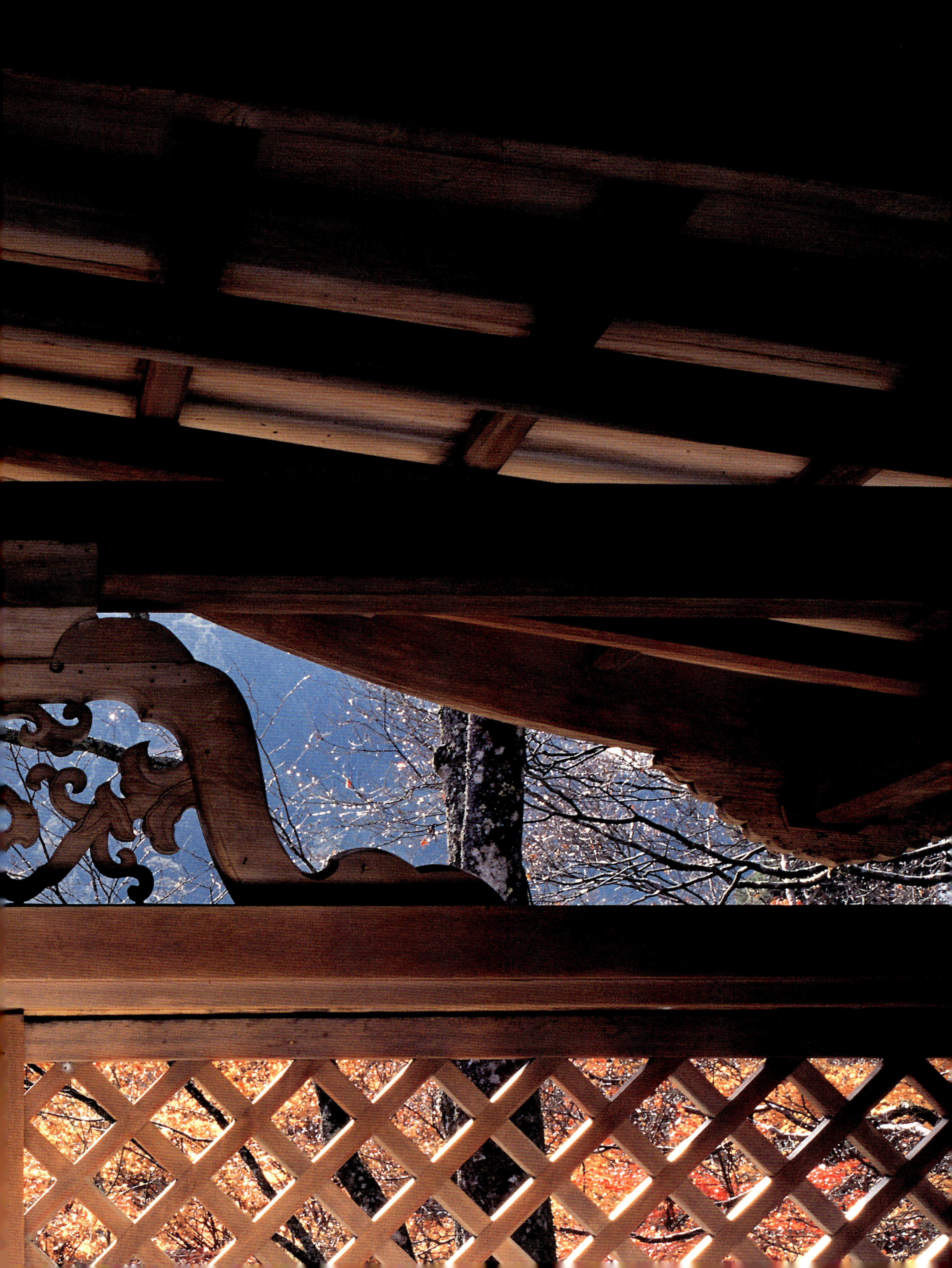

時代背景

　高山寺は京都市の北西、山深い栂尾に位置し、鎌倉時代に活躍した名僧・明恵上人(1173−1232)の寺として知られる。山林修行の寺として、その開創は奈良時代(8世紀)にさかのぼるというが、1206(建永元)年に後鳥羽上皇(1180−1239)よりこの地を下賜された明恵が高山寺と号し、中興した。高山寺は応仁・文明の乱、戦国の世で堂宇が荒れたが、石水院は戦火を逃れ、鎌倉時代の遺材を有する明恵ゆかりの遺構である。

　明恵の住房として1216(建保4)年頃に建立されたというが、その建物自体は1228(安貞2)年の水害で破壊され、谷向かいにあった東経蔵が石水院の名を継ぎ、移築や改造を経て今日のかたちになったとされる。現在地には1889(明治22)年、同寺・金堂の東側から移されたが、このときに床の間を構えた畳敷きの住宅風構成に改められた。

　『高山寺縁起』では、1235(文暦2)年、東経蔵の西面に春日・住吉の両明神の神影が祀られたと記されることから、その建物はたんなる経蔵ではなく、経蔵兼社殿のかたちを取っていたことが示唆される。また、1637(寛永14)年の石水院指図(平面図)によると、蟇股の入る現在の「庇の間」は「落板敷」、その奥は「内陣」と記されていて、庇の間に向けて春日・住吉両明神が祀られている。このことから、庇の間は内陣に対する拝殿の役割を果たす空間であったと考えられている。今も内陣と庇の間との境には神殿構えの板扉が入り、その名残をとどめる。石水院の春日・住吉両明神は早くから貴人の帰依を集めたことから、かなり初期の段階から拝殿空間を備えた建物であったと想定される。庇の間に入る蟇股は、補修部分や後補も含まれるが、鎌倉期の意匠と考えられている。

特徴と見どころ

　石水院は内にいながらにして、自然のただなかに浮遊するかのように感じられる建物である。目の前に広がる風景は、明恵の慈しんだ山々の緑である。そのなかでも板敷(屋久杉)の庇の間は、西面と南面を透けた格子とし、透かし彫りの蟇股を入れ、内と外の空気が融け合うような魅力的な空間をつくりだしている。風は格子で梳かれて爽やかに部屋を通り抜け、まるでその風が目に見えるようである。西面の透格子は半蔀で、上半分を外に撥ね上げればさらに空間は開放されて、内と外との一体感は強まり、自然の気が充満する。蟇股の両肩は伸びやかな曲線を見せ、「水藻形」と呼ばれる透かし彫りは優美でありながらも手が込みすぎず、透きの余白は鎌倉時代のおおらかさを感じさせる。この蟇股によって、片流れの化粧屋根裏は浮かんでいるような軽快感を生み、庇の間には洗練の雰囲気が漂う。

　一方、このように開放的な空間であろうと、直射光は入ってこない。深い庇の裏にバウンドしていったん吸収され、和らげられてからグレー・トーンの光の粒子となり、それがさらに格子で濾されて部屋の奥へと拡散していく。石水院の庇の間は、伝統的な日本の採光方法、光への感性を示す好例でもある。

西面・向拝つきの妻側
West gable with a step canopy

Historical Background

Located in the mountainous Toganoo area in the northwest part of Kyoto, Kosanji is known as the temple of the eminent Kamakura period Priest Myoe (1173–1232). The origins of the temple had been established as far back as the Nara period (eighth century) as a place for practice of religious austerities in the mountains. The site was bestowed upon Myoe in 1206 by cloistered emperor Go-Toba (1180–1239) and Myoe restored the temple as Kosanji. Most of the temple buildings fell to ruin during the period of civil wars that began with the Onin War (1467–1477) and continued through the sixteenth century. Sekisui-in, however, managed to survive the wars as a precious heritage of the Kamakura period linked to Myoe.

Sekisui-in is said to have been built in 1216 as Myoe's residence, but that original structure was destroyed by flood in 1228. The eastern sutra repository on the far side of the valley inherited the Sekisui-in name and eventually took its present form after being moved and renovated over the years. When it was moved from the east side of the temple's main hall (*kondo*) to its current location in 1889, it was remodeled to incorporate residential-style tatami mats and a *tokonoma* alcove.

The *Kosanji engi* (Tales of the Origin of Kosanji Temple) records that in 1235 pictures of the deities Kasuga and Sumiyoshi were venerated on the west face of the eastern sutra repository, suggesting that the building then served not only as a sutra repository but also as a shrine building. A 1637 ground plan of Sekisui-in describes what is now the *hisashi-no-ma* enclosed space with its distinctive *kaerumata* frog-leg struts as having a low wooden floor. The room behind, labeled "inner sanctum" where Kasuga and Sumiyoshi were enshrined, faced the *hisashi-no-ma*. This suggests that the enclosed area served as a worship hall (*haiden*) for the inner sanctum. Traces of this relationship can still be seen in the shrine-like wooden doors at the boundary between the inner sanctum and the *hisashi-no-ma*. Given that the aristocracy embraced Sekisui-in's deities Kasuga and Sumiyoshi at an early date, it is presumed that the worship hall was prepared quite early in the building's life. The frog-leg struts of the *hisashi-no-ma* include sections that have been repaired or added later, but are believed to have been designed during the Kamakura period.

Characteristics and Highlights

Even when inside Sekisui-in, one feels a sense of floating in the midst of nature. The scenery spreading before one's eyes is the same mountain greenery so loved by Myoe. The *hisashi-no-ma*, in particular, with its plank flooring made of *yakusugi* cryptomeria, incorporates openwork frog-leg struts and see-through lattices on the west and south sides to create an appealing space where the atmosphere of inside and outside merges. One can practically see the wind passing refreshingly through the lattices and into the room. The west side is fitted with *hajitomi* lattices whose upper halves can be swung up to the outside to open the building even further, strengthening the sense of unity between inside and out and suffusing the space with natural energy. The "legs" of the frog-leg struts form graceful curves while their *mizumo* (water plant)-style openwork is elegant but understated and the blank in-between spaces suggest the generous scale of the Kamakura period. These frog-leg struts create a sense of lightness, as if the ceiling were floating, and suffuse the enclosure with an atmosphere of refinement.

At the same time, despite being such an open space, the interior is not exposed to direct sunlight. Outside light is absorbed and softened as it rebounds from the underside of the deep eaves, is filtered by the lattices to a gentler quality of light, and diffuses deep inside. The Sekisui-in *hisashi-no-ma* is a good example of a traditional sensitivity to the manipulation of natural light.

南面の縁側
Veranda on the south side

庇の間。南面（奥）は引違戸の上部菱格子、西面は蔀戸とし、さらに内法長押より上部を開放して蟇股を入れた透ける空間。掛込み天井で、大面取り疎垂木、木舞打ち。神殿構えの扉が残る奥の間（左側）には、かつて住吉・春日両明神の神影が祀られており、庇の間はその拝殿として機能した

Hisashi-no-ma enclosed space. The south side (back of photo) is fitted with sliding doors whose upper portions incorporate diamond-shaped latticework while the west side is fitted with *shitomido* latticed shutters. The space in the transoms is fitted with frog-leg struts. The rafters of the sloped ceiling are widely spaced and broadly chamfered. Previously, when paintings of the deities Kasuga and Sumiyoshi were enshrined behind the Shinto sanctuary-like doors to the left, the *hisashi* space functioned as a place for worship.

西側・蟇股と蔀戸のシルエット。蟇股上の桁と天井の間も透かせて、天井は軽やか。庭からの光は深い軒裏に反射して鎮められ、さらに格子で濾されて、和らいだ光となる。直射光を入れない日本的な採光方法の典型である

The frog-leg struts and *shitomido* latticed shutters on the west side in silhouette. The open space above the frog-leg struts gives the ceiling a feeling of lightness. The light from the garden is softened as it reflects against the underside of the deep eaves and

天井板と垂木の間に木舞を挟んで隙間をつくり、部材同士をつけない清潔感のあるディテール。長押（右）と鴨居（左）の成をそろえずに納め、空間を軽快に見せている

Inserting roof laths between the ceiling boards and rafters to create a gap is a refreshing detail that keeps the members from abutting across their length. Note the joint where *kamoi* lintel (left) and *nageshi* non-penetrating tie beam (right) intersect without aligning their heights, giving the space an air of lightness.

柱の面取りと長押のプロポーション。鎌倉時代らしい寸法の面取りが、石水院の空間を特徴づける。柱幅147mmに対して面取り幅19.5mm。長押の成は80mm。舟肘木も面取りされ、軽やかである

Note the proportions of the chamfered pillar and the height of the *nageshi* non-penetrating tie beam. That the *funahijiki* boat-shape bracket arm is also chamfered enhances the sense of lightness. The width of the chamfers is typical of the Kamakura period and a distinguishing feature of the space at Sekisui-in. (Pillar width 147mm; chamfer width 19.5mm; *nageshi* height 80 mm)

石山寺 多宝塔

国宝
建立年代　1194年
所在地　　滋賀県大津市

Ishiyamadera Temple Tahoto (Pagoda)

National Treasure
Completed: 1194
Location: Otsu, Shiga prefecture

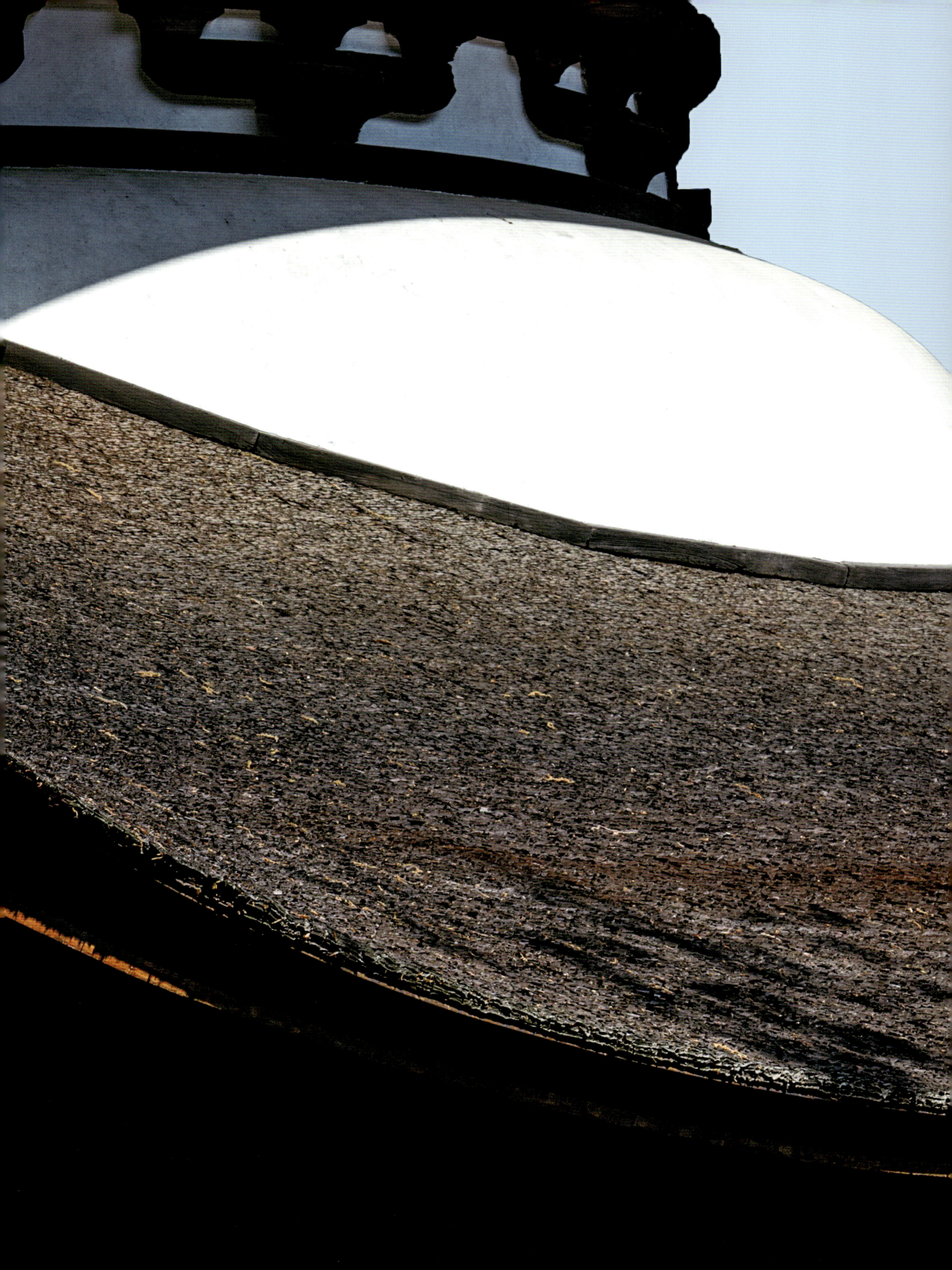

時代背景

　多宝塔は本堂の北東、珪灰石の奇景を前にして見上げるかたちで、伽藍のなかでもいちばん高い位置に立つ。鎌倉時代の初め、1194（建久5）年に源頼朝（1147-1199）からの寄進によって建立され、多宝塔として今に伝えられる最古の塔である。初重内部には四天柱を立て、須弥壇を置いて本尊・大日如来坐像（快慶作・鎌倉初期・重文）を安置し、四天柱には金剛界諸仏、五大明王などが描かれている（鎌倉初期・重文）。

　多宝塔は、平安時代に空海の発案によって始められた日本独自の塔形式である。下重が方形、上重が円形平面の二重塔で、屋根は宝形造、檜皮葺、相輪を持つ。816（弘仁7）年、嵯峨天皇（786-842）から高野山の地を下賜された空海は、山内に金剛峯寺を開き、2基の塔（大塔・西塔）の建設を計画する。この塔計画は空海在世中には実現せず、9世紀後半になって完成したが、大塔は初重が方5間の大塔形式と呼ばれるもので、総間が約24m（80尺）もあったという。一方、石山寺多宝塔の初重は方3間、総間が約5.8m（19.2尺）でほぼ1/4の規模、大塔形式を小型化したものとなる。空海による大塔形式では、内部は円形に配置した12本の柱列を二重に立て、その同心円の内部に四天柱を立てて諸仏を安置し、外陣・中陣・内陣の三つの領域がつくられていた。この原形から、石山寺をはじめとする今に遺された下重方形・上重円形という一見謎めいた多宝塔の形態は、円形平面の軸部に方形の裳階を取りつけた形から発展したものとされ、11世紀初頭には、石山寺と同様の小型化・簡略化された多宝塔形式が広まっていたと考えられている。

特徴と見どころ

　大きな傘の下で大切なものを守る——この塔は、その発想の洗練の極みともいうべき例証である。雨の多い日本では、建物を雨から防御するために大きな屋根をかけ、深い軒をつくるための工夫を重ねて、独自の構造と形を発展させてきた。組物を整え、野屋根をつくり、野垂木と地垂木の間には桔木を入れて軒を支え、地垂木・飛檐垂木を長く外へと延ばして軒を深めるのである。この塔では、円形の軸部に四手先の斗栱を組み、軒を軸部直径とほぼ同じ長さにまで延ばして、繊細な陰影に富んだ深い軒をつくりだしている。

　相輪は全体の1/3、上重の軒高は総高のほぼ1/2を占める。下重の軸部が低く、横に広いため全体に安定感があり、一方で上層の逓減が大きいために引き締まったシルエットをつくりだしている。現存する多宝塔としては最古例となるが、この塔の傑出した美しさは、高野山の創建大塔以来多く建てられてきた多宝塔形式の、一つの到達点として見ることができる。

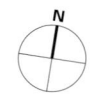

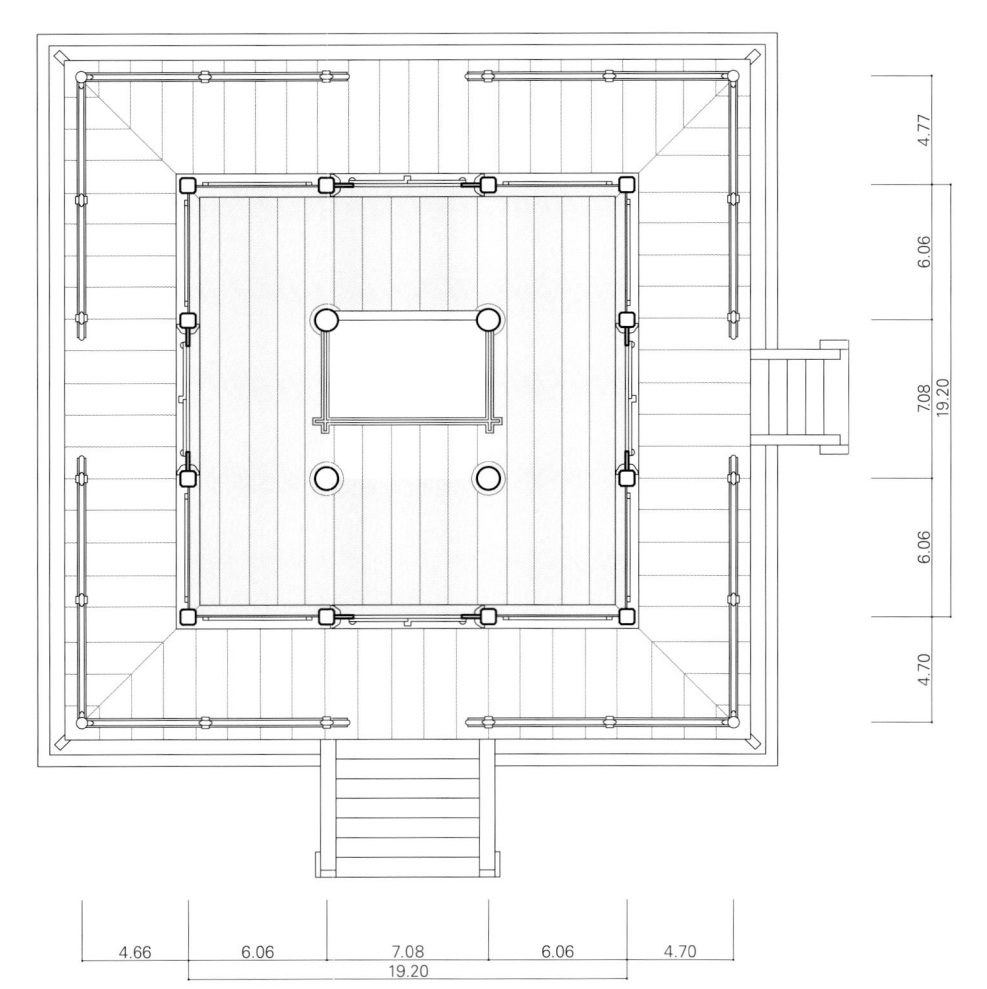

下重平面図　Floor plan of the lower story

上重見上図　Roof plan from below

Historical Background

The two-storied stupa pagoda (*tahoto*) at Ishiyamadera temple stands northeast of the temple's main hall, rising at the highest point of the grounds on the slope above the distinctive wollastonite rock formation. Built in 1194 with a donation from Minamoto no Yoritomo (1147–1199), founder of the Kamakura shogunate, it is the oldest extant example of the *tahoto* pagoda style. The interior of the first story has four round pillars marking the sanctuary for the hall's principal image, a seated statue of Dainichi Buddha (sculpted by Kaikei; early Kamakura period; Important Cultural Property). The pillars are decorated with pictures of Buddhist deities of the Diamond Realm and the five great kings of wisdom (early Kamakura period; Important Cultural Properties).

The *tahoto* is a distinctively Japanese style of pagoda devised by Priest Kukai in the early Heian period. The lower story is square in plan and the upper story circular. The roof is pyramidal (*hogyo-zukuri*), shingled with cypress bark, and topped with a decorative finial. In 816, Emperor Saga (r. 809–823) granted Kukai the land on Mt. Koya where Kongobuji temple was founded. As part of its precincts, Kukai planned the construction of two pagodas. The plan for the pagodas was not realized in Kukai's lifetime; they were constructed in the latter half of the ninth century. One of the original pagodas was quite large; it is said to have been five bays wide for a total width of about 24 meters (80 *shaku*). The Ishiyamadera *tahoto*, at three bays and 5.8 meters (19.2 *shaku*) wide, is one-fourth its size. Kukai's large pagoda was supported by two rings of 12 posts each that formed concentric circles around an inner sanctuary with four posts at its corners, thus forming three realms: an outer sanctuary (*gejin*), a middle sanctuary (*chujin*), and an inner sanctuary (*naijin*) where Buddhist deities were enshrined. The somewhat puzzling design of the *tahoto* with its square lower story and circular upper story is thought to have developed by attaching a square *mokoshi* enclosure to the circular core of that earlier layout. The building of smaller, abbreviated *tahoto* like the one at Ishiyamadera we see today may have been popular in the early eleventh century.

Characteristics and Highlights

The idea of protecting what is treasured and sacred beneath a large, spreading roof reached perhaps the height of refinement in the *tahoto*. Japan being a country where precipitation is high, temple carpenters devised many innovations in order to build the broad roofs and deep eaves that would protect buildings from rain, creating distinctive structures and shapes in the process. Bracket complexes were put in place, hidden roof structures were assembled, and cantilevers were inserted that utilized leverage to support the eaves, extending them outward using base rafters and flying rafters, or double rafters. In this pagoda, four-stepped bracket complexes surround the circular core section, providing support for eaves stretching out about as long as the diameter of the core, creating rich effects of light and shadow.

The finial accounts for about one third, and the upper story about half, of the height of the building. The lower story is low and broad, giving the whole a sense of stability, while the much smaller upper story gives the building a tight, compact look. This oldest example of an extant *tahoto* stands out for its beauty, suggesting that it may represent the height of the *tahoto*-style pagodas that developed from the large pagoda first built at Mt. Koya.

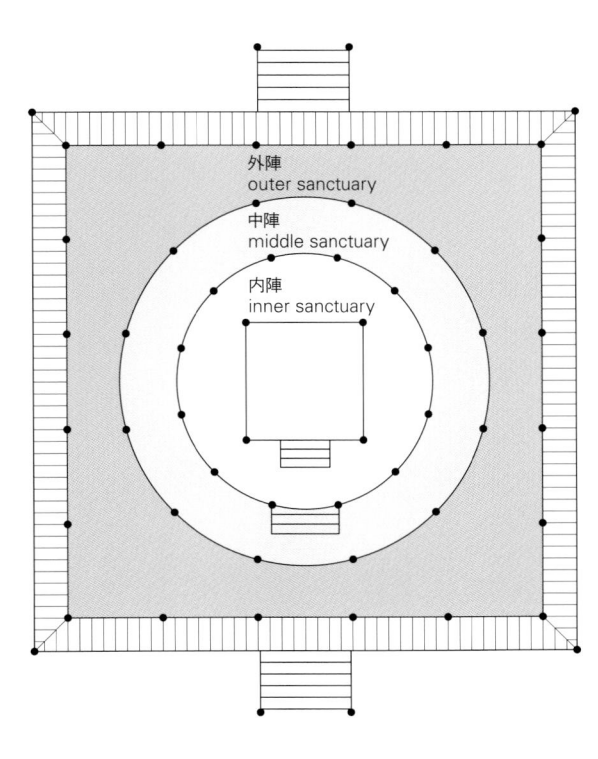

金剛峯寺・大塔図[*10]   Plan diagram of large pagoda in Kongobuji

石山寺珪灰石の背後、南を正面にして立つ。亀腹の白い曲面と檜皮葺・宝形造の美しい屋根、相輪が緑の中に浮かび上がり、洗練された姿を見せる

Rising behind the Ishiyamadera wollastonite rock formation, the Tahoto stands facing south. The refined forms of the pagoda's white plaster dome, cypress-bark-covered pyramidal roof, and finial stand out amid the greenery.

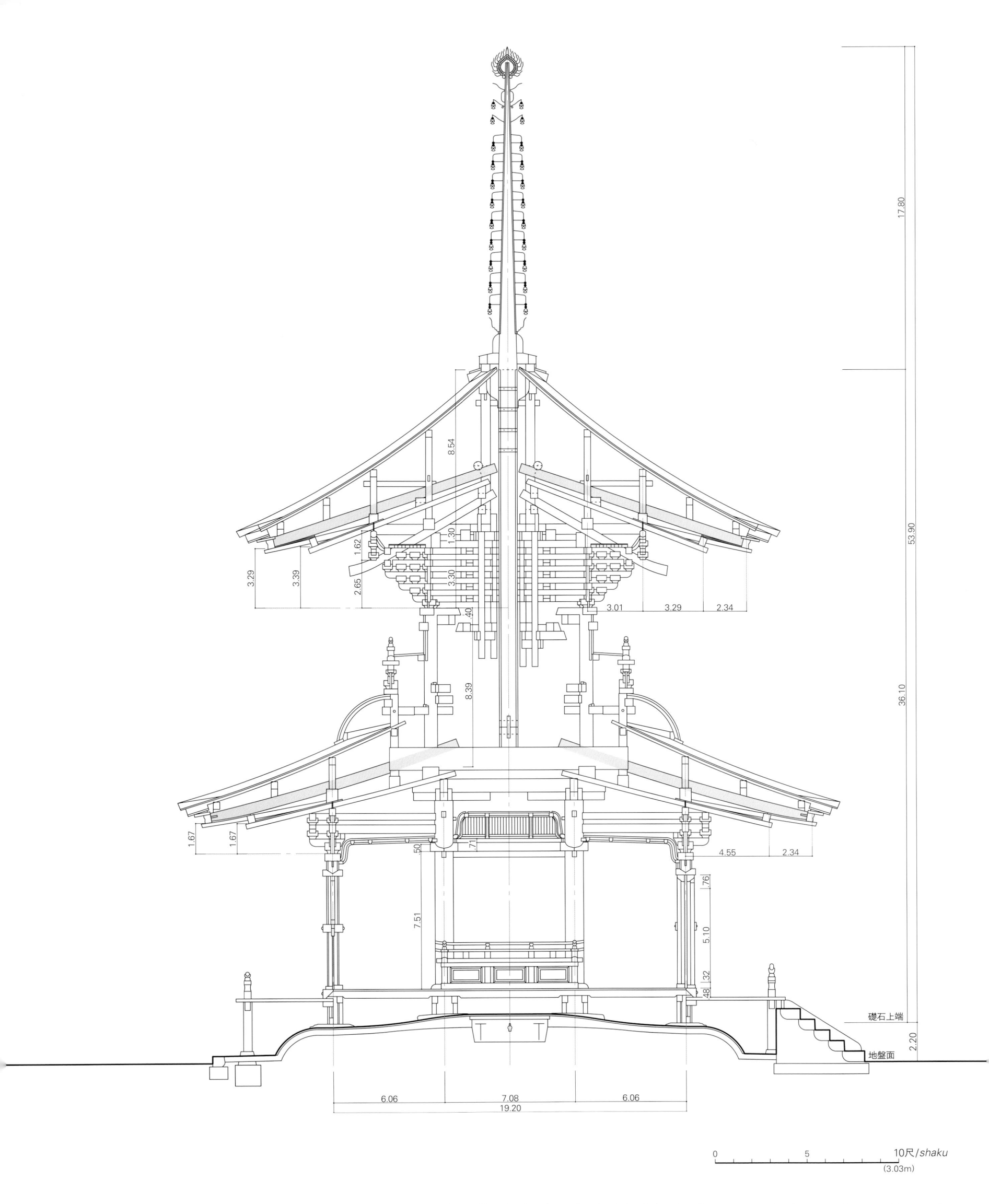

矩計図。四天柱の上に梁を載せ、心柱はその上の大梁から立ち上げる。屋根には桔木が入り、てこの原理で軒を支える一方で、四手先斗栱を組んで地垂木・飛檐垂木を長く延ばし、軒を深めている

Sectional detail drawing. Beams are set in place over the four *shitenbashira* pillars; further above these are the principal beams upon which the central *shinbashira* pillar stands. *Hanegi* cantilevers in the roof structure provide the leverage that supports the eaves. The eaves are lengthened with *yotesaki* four-stepped bracket complexes and extended base and flying rafters.

木造建築の宝石ともいえる美しい姿。均衡の取れたプロポーション、上重の深い軒の出と軽快な軒反り、下重の単純明快さと対比を見せる上重の複雑さ。亀腹の白に反射した光を受けて、繊細な四手先斗栱が鮮やかに浮かび上がる

The beautiful stupa pagoda is a jewel of wooden architecture with finely balanced proportions; the complexity of its upper story—with its exceptionally deep, gracefully upturned eaves—contrasts with the simplicity and clarity of the lower story. Light reflecting off the white plaster dome highlights the delicate *yotesaki* four-stepped bracket complexes above.

深い軒先を支える四手先斗栱と軽やかな反りをもつ二重の垂木。上重の軸部直径約
2.6mに対し、軒をほぼ同じ長さに出す。降水量の多い日本では、いかに深く庇を延ば
して、建物本体を雨から守るかが大きなテーマとなる

Four-stepped bracket complexes support the double rafters, extending the eaves in a gracefully upturned line. The core of the upper story is about 2.6 meters in diameter, roughly matching the depth of the eaves. One of the major challenges for Japanese architecture was how to extend the eaves in order to protect the building proper in a climate of heavy rainfall.

四手先斗栱は扇状に配置されている。亀腹の上に台輪を置き、平三斗の腰組を組み、それを通肘木でつなぎ、その上に木口刻みの板を置いて高欄をまわす

The radiating *yotesaki* four-stepped bracket complexes. Directly above the dome, *daiwa* beams support *hiramitsudo* (three-on-one, non-projecting) bracket complexes. These are connected by *toshihijiki* bracket tie beams, upon which boards are set that support the balustrade.

興福寺 北円堂・東金堂・三重塔

国宝
建立年代　北円堂：1210年　東金堂：1415年　三重塔：12世紀末−13世紀
所在地　　奈良県奈良市

Kofukuji Temple Hokuendo (Northern Octagonal Hall), Tokondo (Eastern Main Hall), and Three-story Pagoda

National Treasures
Completed: Hokuendo, 1210; Tokondo, 1415;
　　　　　　Three-story Pagoda, late 12th–13th century
Location: Nara, Nara prefecture

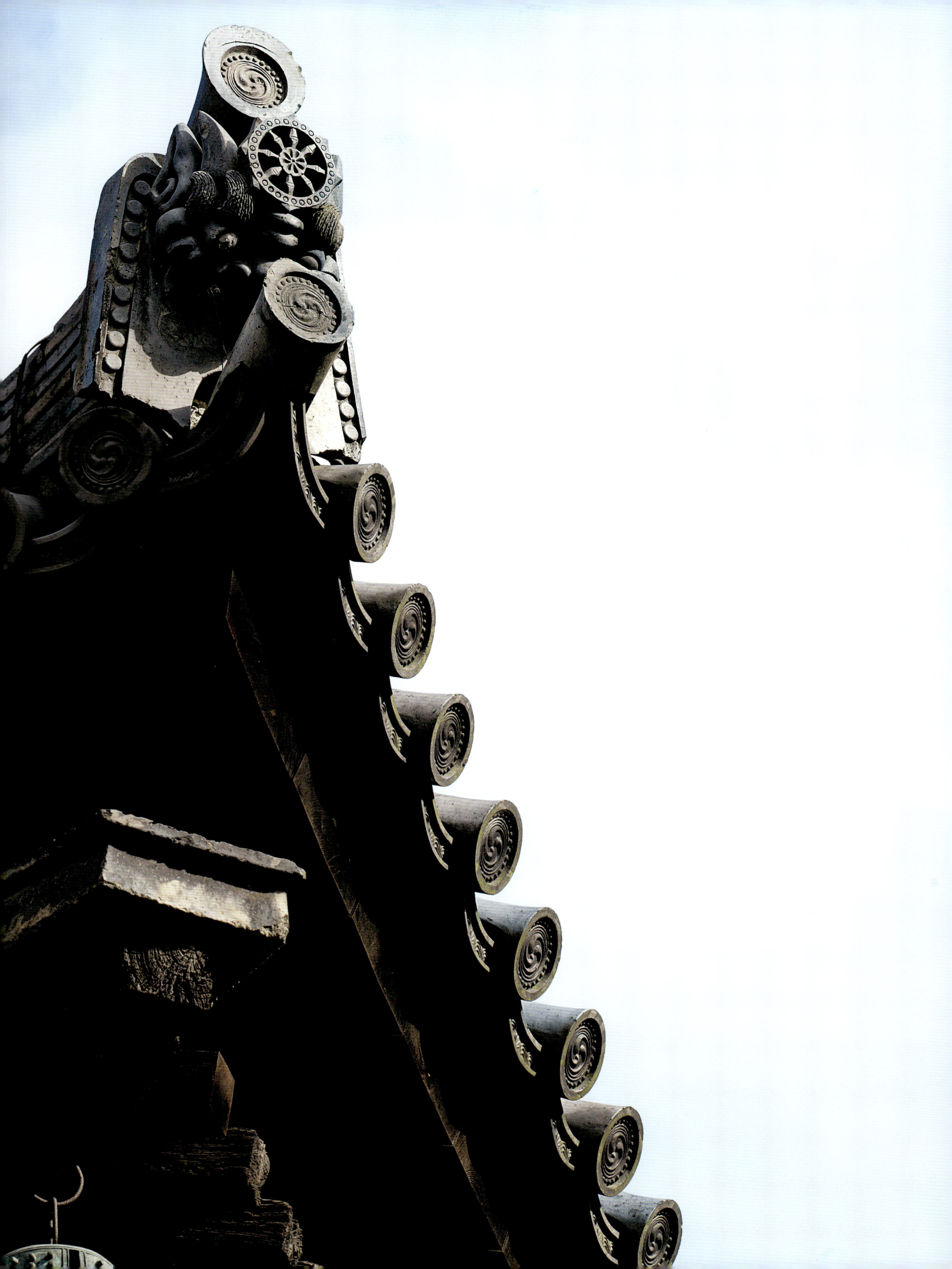

時代背景

　1300有余年の間、度重なる災禍や戦禍に遭いながらも再興されてきたのが興福寺である。御蓋山麓の西に張り出す台地をならした形勝の地に位置し、かつては広大な伽藍を有した。大化改新で功を立て、天智天皇（626－671）の右腕として活躍した藤原氏の祖・中臣（藤原）鎌足（614－669）の子である藤原不比等（659－720）が、710（和銅3）年の平城京遷都とともに、都の東側に隣接する外京の区域に藤原氏の氏寺として伽藍を構想し、建設した。天皇家との姻戚関係により皇室と一体化した藤原氏一族の興福寺は、その氏寺でありつつも特別な存在で、都が京都へ移ってからも中世まで隆盛を誇った。

　創建当時、この寺の中枢部は廻廊で囲まれた中金堂の領域を中央にして、東側に東金堂と五重塔、西側に西金堂が対置され、幾何学的な伽藍美を誇っていた。平家による南都焼討ちでは全堂宇が焼失し、草創期の建造物は残っていないが、奈良時代に起源をもち、今に伝えられるものとして、東金堂（1415年再建・国宝）、五重塔（1426年頃再建・国宝）、北円堂（1210年再建・国宝）がある。また、平安時代に起源をもつものは、大湯屋（室町時代再建・重文）、南円堂（1741年頃再建・重文）、三重塔（12世紀末－13世紀再建・国宝）がある。再建に際しては創建期の伝統形式を守り、復古的な方針に則ってつくられてきたのが大きな特徴である。

特徴と見どころ

　草創期の主要伽藍配置を思い描くのに手がかりとなるのが、この寺のシンボルである五重塔と、その隣に立つ東金堂である。東金堂は726（神亀3）年、聖武天皇によって薬師如来像を本尊に造立され、五重塔は730（天平2）年、光明皇后によって建立された。相接する二つの建物は5度の火災を経て、東金堂は1415（応永22）年、五重塔は1426（応永33）年頃に再建されたものが今に遺る。

　東金堂は室町期再建とはいえ、その姿はきわめて古代風である。奈良時代の礎石上に立ち、規模、形式とも創建時を踏襲する。高い基壇上、丈の高い柱が立ち並ぶ正面は吹放ちとなっており、急勾配の大きな寄棟造の屋根を載せる。正面は庇柱と身舎柱との高低差をつけておらず（p.294参照）、吹放ち庇の下と身舎とは同じ天井高になって、かなり丈高い見え方となるのが特徴である。側面の壁は頭貫のほかには水平材を見せず、このために壁の見え方が単純明快で、漆喰壁の白い面の存在感が引き立ち、おおらかな美しさがある。古代の堂の形式に倣い、内部は仏の占有空間として、そこに人が入る余地はほとんどない。5度の火災に遭いながらも、一貫して創建当初の仏堂のあり方を固守してきた東金堂の形態は、古代からの流れを想起させるものである。

　伽藍の西側に位置する北円堂は、721（養老5）年、寺の開基・藤原不比等の遺徳を偲び、その一周忌に建てられた。2度の火災で焼失し、現在の建物は1210（承元4）年に上棟したもので、寺内に残る最古の建物となる。八角堂は平面が八角の仏堂で、この堂のほかにも、聖徳太子を祀った法隆寺夢殿（739年・国宝）のように個人を記念するために建てられることが多く、モニュメンタルな性格を強く帯びたものである。

　基壇上に立ち、木太く高い柱に、さらに二段積み（平三斗）の組物を載せて丈を高くする。その上には勾配のきつい大きな屋根が載り、頂には華麗な宝珠・水煙を掲げる。軒は珍しい三軒で、華やぎを高めている。八角形の幾何学的な形態が空に鮮やかに浮かび上がり、藤原氏隆盛の基礎を築いた不比等の永遠性を象徴するにふさわしい造形美である。

　鎌倉初期の東大寺再興とほぼ同時期に再建されたこの堂は、側柱の内法長押の裏側に貫を通して構造を強化しており、和様の建築で内法貫が通された現存最古の例である。この貫は柱を立てる際に組みこまれ、表には見えない。近接する東大寺で採用された技術革新に啓発されながらも、伝統的な佇まいを大切にする方針は、すでに鎌倉初期には確としたものであったとわかる。

　興福寺の建物のなかでも異彩を放つのが、三重塔である。主要堂宇よりも5mほど低まった境内の南西端に立つ。木割が細く、優美繊細な塔で、威風堂々としたほかの堂宇とは印象が異なる。崇徳天皇（1119－1164）の中宮・皇嘉門院藤原聖子（1122－1181）の御願により1143（康治2）年に建立されたが焼失し、再建年代は不明だが、様式や内部の装飾文様から鎌倉前期の作とされている。

Historical Background

Over the course of more than 1,300 years, Kofukuji temple has been repeatedly damaged by disaster and war, but always rebuilt. With an excellent location on a plateau stretching west from the base of Mt. Mikasa, Kofukuji was once a vast temple complex. When the capital was moved to Heijokyo (Nara) in 710, Fujiwara no Fuhito (659–720)—the son of Nakatomi (later Fujiwara) no Kamatari (614–669), who was the founder of the Fujiwara clan—conceived and built the temple complex just outside the capital on the east, as the tutelary temple of the Fujiwara clan. Kofukuji enjoyed special prestige due to the Fujiwara family's close relations through marriage with the imperial family; even after the capital was moved to Kyoto, it continued to flourish into the medieval period.

When originally built, Kofukuji boasted a grand geometrical configuration centered on the Chukondo (Central Main Hall) surrounded by a semi-enclosed *kairo* corridor, with the Tokondo and five-story pagoda on the east and the Saikondo (Western Main Hall) on the west. None of the original structures remain, as the entire complex was reduced to ashes during the attack on Nara by the Taira clan in the late twelfth century, but the buildings extant today that originate in the Nara period include the Tokondo (reconstructed in 1415; National Treasure), the five-story pagoda (reconstructed in 1426; National Treasure), and the Hokuendo (reconstructed in 1210; National Treasure). Those with origins in the Heian period include the Bathhouse (reconstructed in the Muromachi period; Important Cultural Property), the Nan'endo (Southern Octagonal Hall; reconstructed in 1741, Important Cultural Property) and the three-story pagoda (late twelfth–thirteenth-century reconstruction; National Treasure). One of the characteristics of this temple is that the reconstructions followed the restoration approach, employing the original styles of the periods when the buildings were first constructed.

Characteristics and Highlights

The five-story pagoda—the symbol of this temple—and the adjacent Tokondo offer clues for imagining the layout of the entire temple complex at the time of its founding. The Tokondo was built by Emperor Shomu in 726 with an image of Yakushi Nyorai (Buddha of Medicine) as its principal deity, while the five-story pagoda was built in 730 by Empress Komyo. These adjacent buildings were destroyed by fire five times. The existing Tokondo was rebuilt in 1415 and the five-story pagoda around 1426.

Although a fifteenth-century reconstruction, the Tokondo has the appearance of a much older building. Standing on Nara period (eighth century) foundations, in both size and style the structure is true to its origins. A row of tall pillars stands upon the high stone podium at the façade, whose first bay forms an unenclosed aisle, and supports a large, steeply pitched hipped roof. Because there is no height difference between the *hisashibashira* pillars at the outside of the aisle and the *moyabashira* pillars where the aisle meets the building core (see p. 294), the ceilings of the unenclosed aisle and the core appear to be the same height, making the building seem exceptionally tall. No horizontal members other than the *kashiranuki* head-penetrating tie beams are visible on the side walls, accentuating the plainness and simplicity of their white plaster surfaces, to quite grand effect. In consistently adhering to the style of the building at the time of the temple's founding despite repeated reconstructions, the form of the Tokondo embodies continuity from ancient times.

The Hokuendo on the west side of the temple complex was built in 721 to honor the memory of founder Fujiwara no Fuhito on the first anniversary of his death. Lost twice to fire, the building as it is today was completed in 1210 and is the oldest of the temple's buildings. Octagonal halls are often built to commemorate individuals—as with the Yumedono (Hall of Dreams) at Horyuji temple dedicated to Prince Shotoku (built 739; National Treasure)—and charged with a strongly monumental character.

The height of the building is accentuated by the tall, thick pillars rising on the stone podium and the double bracket complexes above them. The steeply pitched roof is topped with a splendid finial with sacred gem (*hoju*) and water flame (*suien*) ornaments. The unusual three-layered eaves contribute to the splendor of the structure. The octagon rises to form a striking geometry against the sky, a fittingly eternal symbol of Fuhito, who laid the foundations for the prosperity of the Fujiwara clan.

Conspicuous among the other buildings at Kofukuji is the three-story pagoda, standing at the southwest edge of the precincts in an area five meters lower than that of the principal buildings. A delicate, graceful structure employing slender structural members, it leaves a very different impression than the other more stately and imposing buildings. Built in 1143 at the request of Fujiwara no Kiyoko (Kokamon'in; 1122–1181), consort of Emperor Sutoku (1119–1164), the building was later destroyed by fire; although the date of reconstruction is unclear, the style and the decorative patterns on the interior suggest that it dates to the early Kamakura period.

北円堂。対称性の強いモニュメンタルな姿を見せる。高い基壇上（1.36m）に立ち、四方に石階をつけ、東西南北の各面に扉、残る4面は連子窓とする。扉上の欄間には通気の横連子が入る

Hokuendo (Northern Octagonal Hall). Powerfully symmetrical and monumental in form, the structure stands on a 1.36 meter-high podium and has stone steps and doors on its north, south, east, and west sides. The other four sides are fitted with *renjimado* slatted windows. The transom windows over the doors incorporate horizontal slats for ventilation.

北円堂の軒は地垂木（長六角形断面）と二重の飛檐垂木による三軒で、
軒の出は約3.5mと深い

Hokuendo. The underside of the eaves is triple-layered, with one layer of *jidaruki* base rafters (elongated hexagons in cross section) and two layers of *hiendaruki* flying rafters, and about 3.5 meters deep.

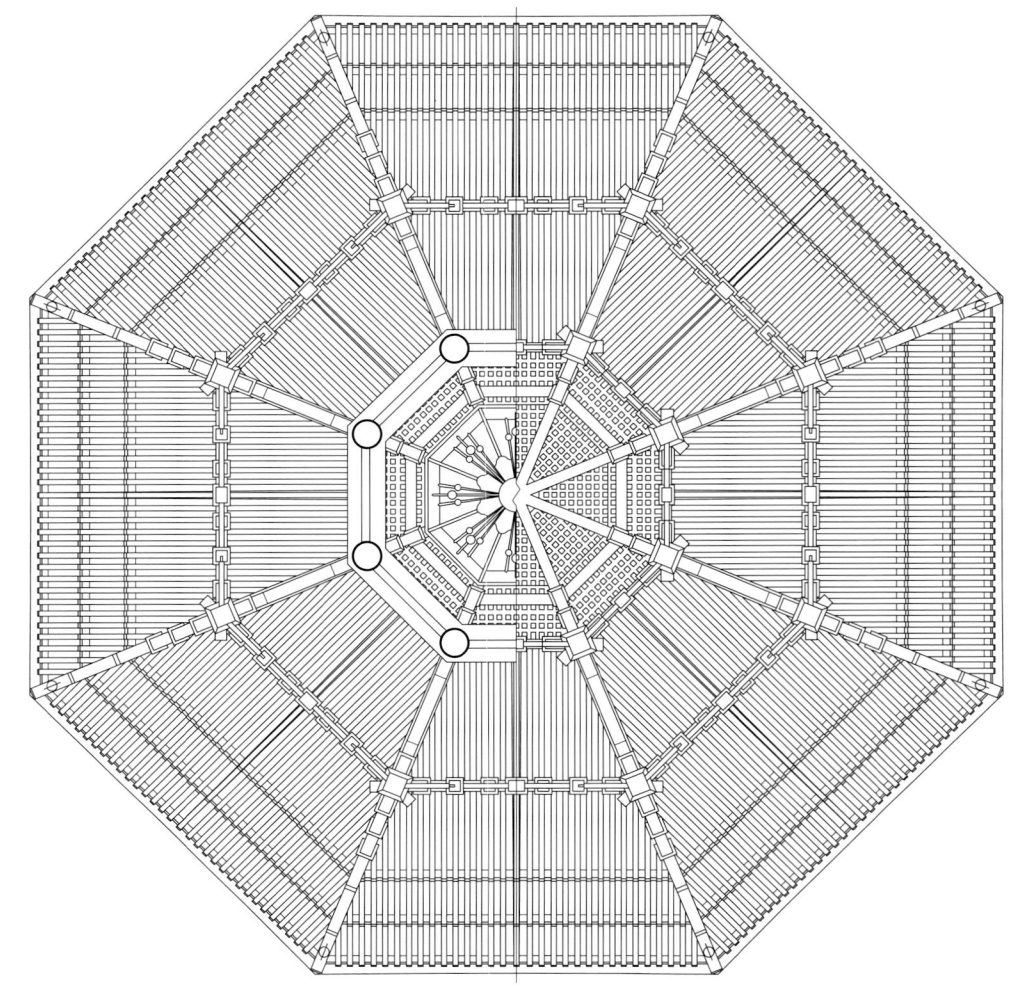

北円堂見上図　Ceiling plan of Hokuendo

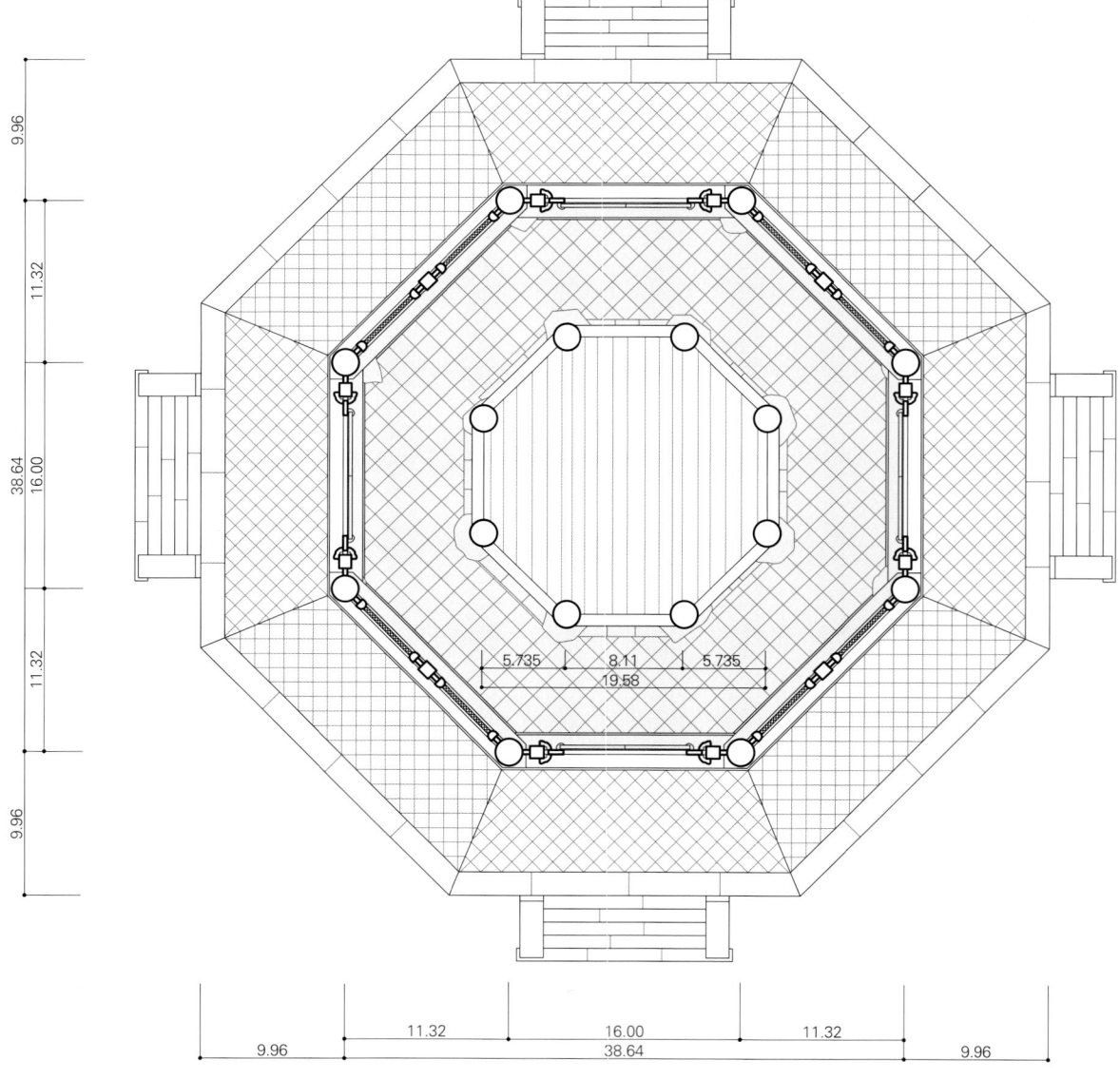

北円堂平面図　Floor plan of Hokuendo

0　　10　　20尺/shaku
(6.06m)

入側柱と側柱は二重の繋虹梁で結ばれている。
上下の虹梁とも側柱側では肘木として斗栱に組
みこまれている(右上)。入側柱径56.4cm、側柱
径53.3cm

The interior pillars and perimeter pillars are connected by double *tsunagikoryo* rainbow beams. Both upper and lower rainbow beams are incorporated into the bracket complexes on the perimeter side as bracket tie beams (upper right).

小壁には木太い平三斗を二段に積み、その上の垂木とともに力強い軒裏を見せる。
垂木の上は板地に胡粉塗の常套ではなく、網代下地に漆喰塗で、白が色褪せずに残る

The small wall sections incorporate two tiers of thick non-projecting bracket complexes that, together with the triple-layered rafters, leave a powerful impression. The vivid white still visible behind the rafters is not the usual *gofun* ground-shell pigment painted on the boards but rather plaster applied to a wickerwork base.

東金堂。勢いよく反り上がる大きな寄棟屋根。基壇上に立ち、前面1間通りは吹放ち
庇で、約5.46mの高い柱が立ち並ぶ。庇柱を身舎柱と同じ高さにそろえ、立ちの高い
威風堂々とした姿を見せる

The Tokondo (Eastern Main Hall), showing the upturned corners of the hipped roof. Standing on a high podium, tall 5.46-meter pillars form an unenclosed, one-bay deep aisle at the building's façade. The alignment of the height of the inside and outside pillars in the aisle enhances the building's impression of lofty dignity.

東金堂の軒先。下から地垂木、飛檜垂木、裏甲、軒瓦。飛檜垂木と裏甲の間が深く、西日を浴びて、光の濃淡をつくりだす

The eaves of the Tokondo showing, from below, *jidaruki* base rafters, *hiendaruki* flying rafters, *urago* eaves filler, and *nokigawara* eaves-end tiles. The deep gap between the flying rafters and the eaves filler creates a powerful contrast of light and shadow in the setting sun.

冬の夕方。正面から西日を受け、垂木の鼻先の影が奥まで映りこむ。右に五重塔の屋根が見える

Evening in winter, with shadows cast by the rafter ends reaching deep beneath the eaves. Visible at the right is the roof of the five-story pagoda.

(上)東金堂内部。二手先斗栱を組み、桁を受け、そこから支輪を立ち上げるとともに虹梁を受ける

(Above) Tokondo interior. The *futatesaki* two-step bracket complexes support purlins from which short, curved *shirin* rise in transitioning to the *koryo* rainbow beams.

(右)内陣とその周囲の外陣。奥深くまで西日が射しこむ

(Right) Looking from the inner sanctuary to the outer sanctuary on its perimeter, with light from the setting sun reaching deep into the interior.

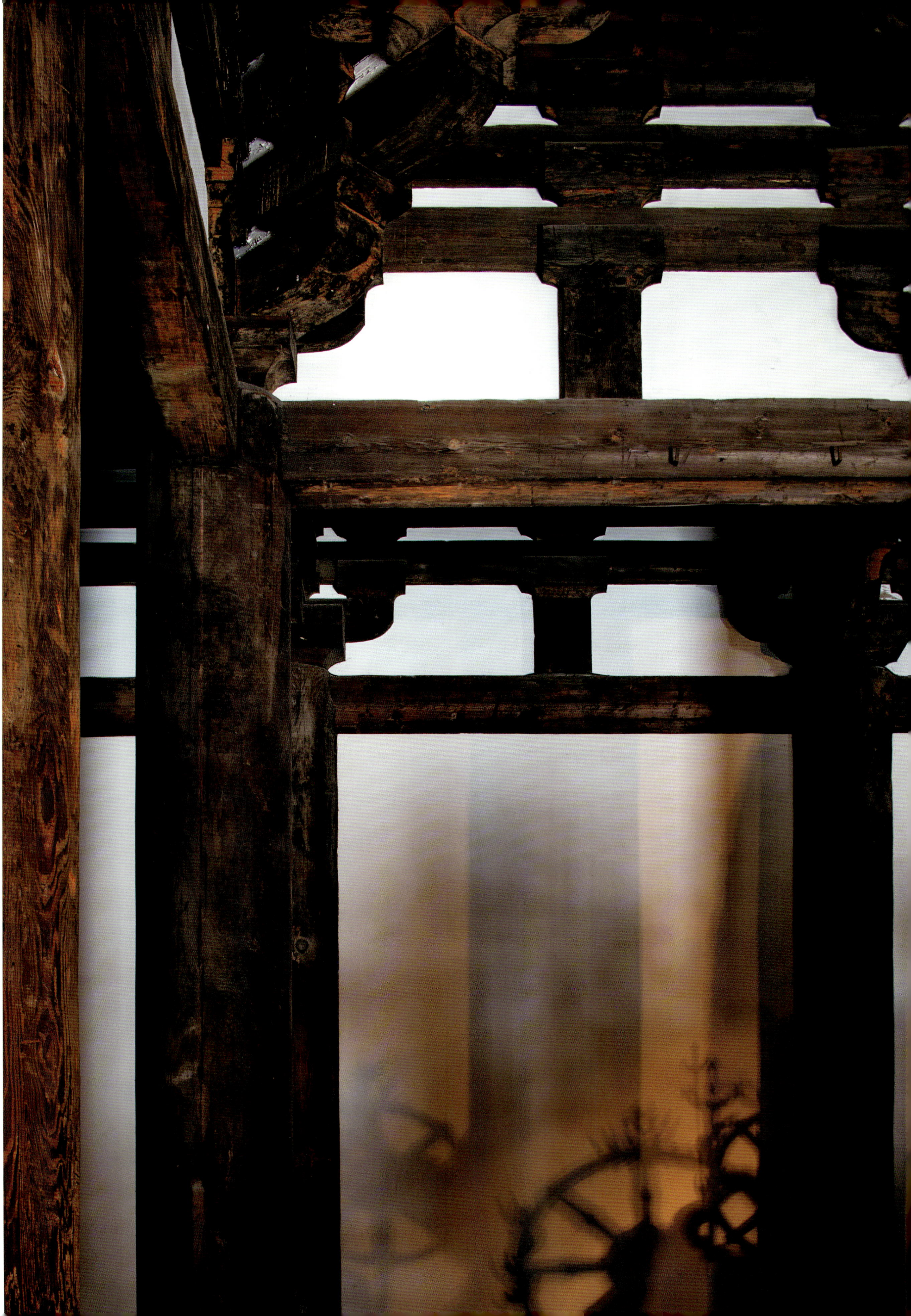

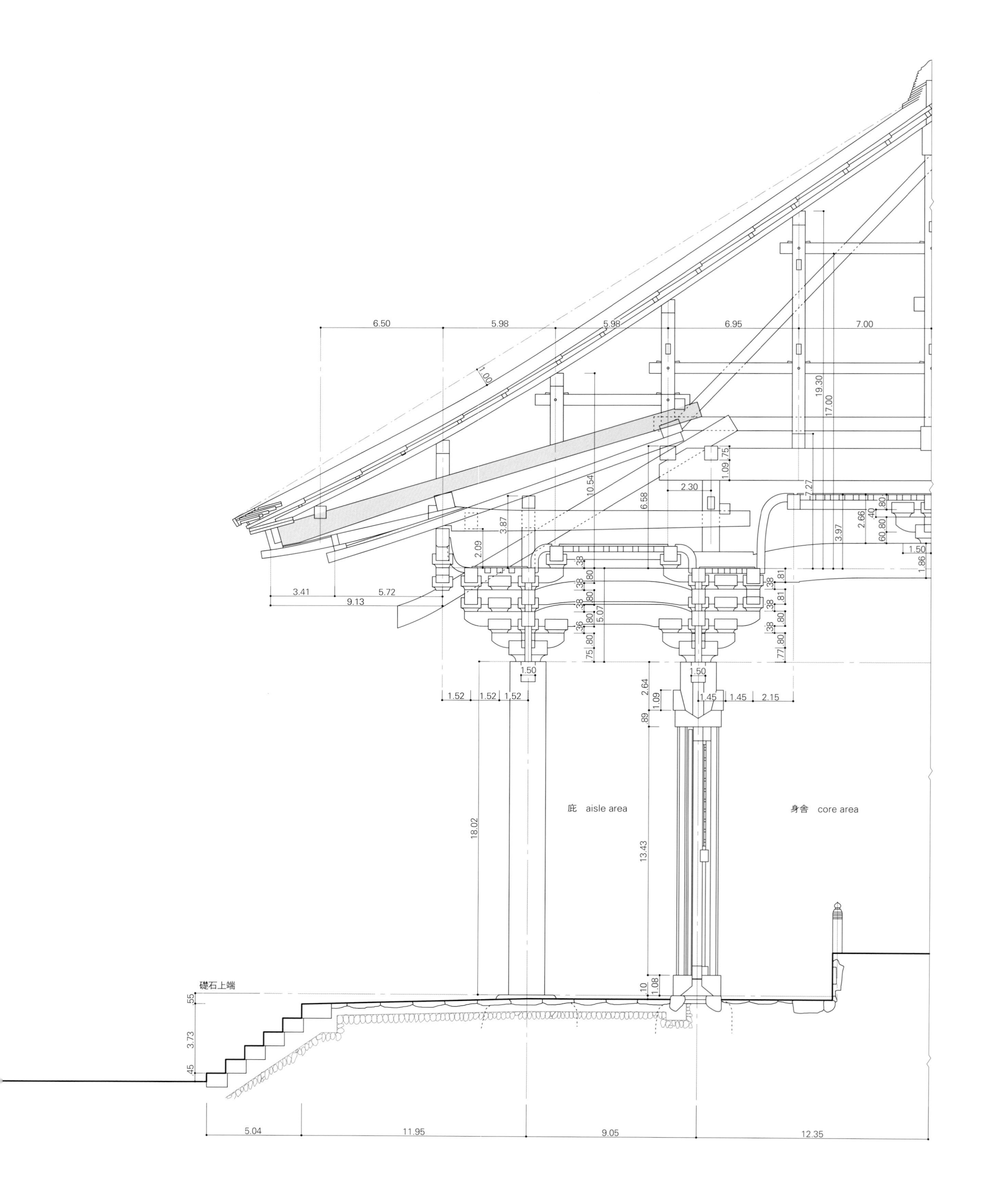

東金堂矩計図　Sectional detail drawing of Tokondo

東金堂・内部。組入天井を張る。約8.2m（27尺）の天井高。8世紀建立の唐招提寺金堂の内部とほぼ同じ構成で、4本の虹梁を渡して身舎を形成する

Interior of the Tokondo. The latticed ceiling is about 8.2 meters high. Although rebuilt in the fifteenth century, the Tokondo is structurally similar to the Tenpyo-style interior of the Kondo main hall at Toshodaiji temple of the eighth century; four *koryo* rainbow tie beams span the ceiling to form the core area.

南・妻側。簡潔で大らかな白壁。吹放ち庇側(左1間)も壁とする。再建に次ぐ再建を経た堂だが、やはりここには天平の間合いがある。白壁の中央2間のプロポーションは、地貫から頭貫まで約1:$\sqrt{2}$。両端間は約1:2で、明快な比例で構成される

Tokondo south end. Trim and stately, the white walls extend to the aisle part at the front of the building (the leftmost bay). Although repeatedly rebuilt, the hall retains its Tenpyo era sense of spacing. The proportions of the two central walls, measured from the *jinuki* beams at their base to their *kashiranuki* head penetrating tie beams, work out to a ratio of one to the square root of two, while the side walls exhibit a ratio of one to two—models of proportional clarity in each case.

三重塔。洗練された美しさを誇る

The refined beauty of the Three-story Pagoda.

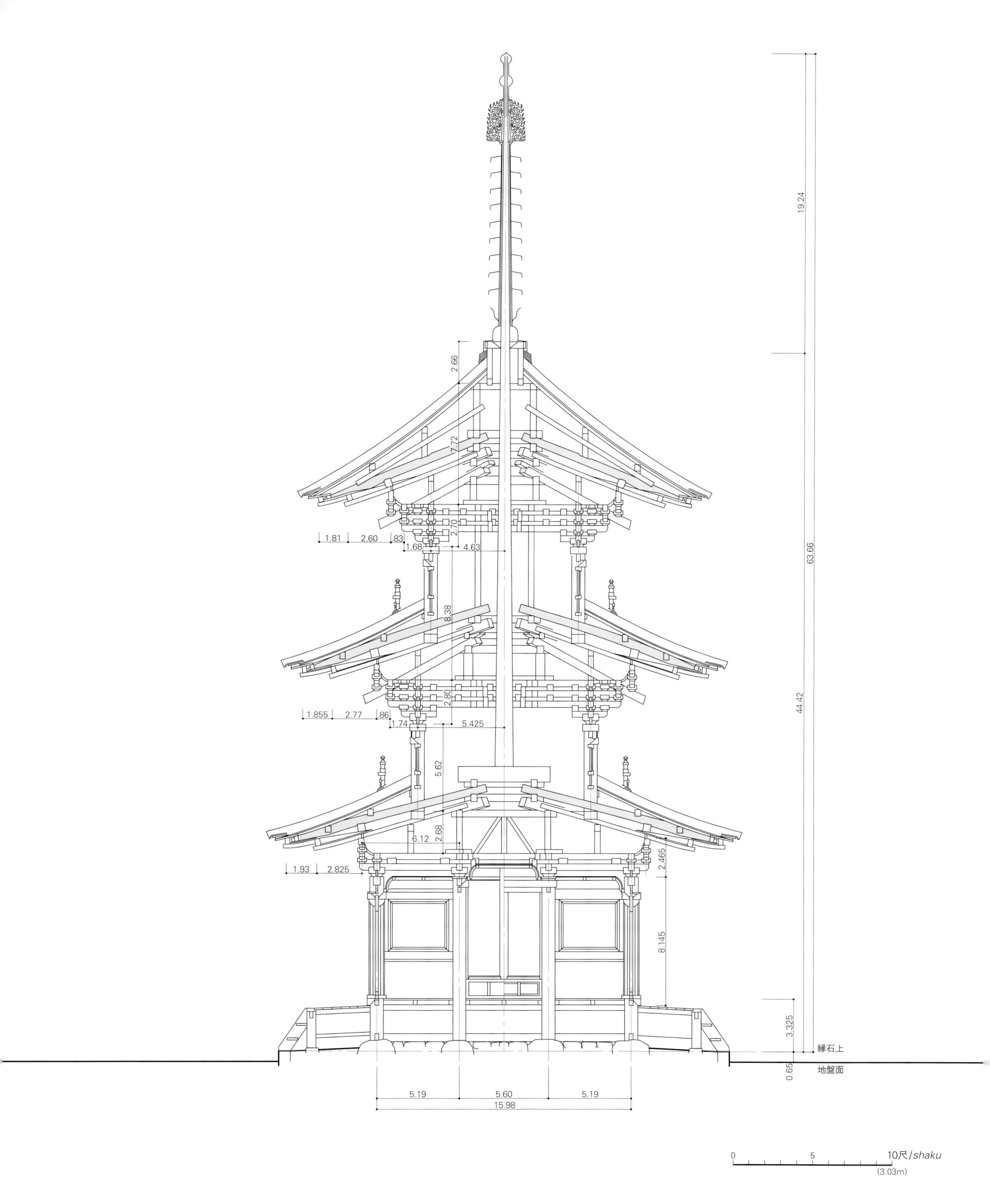

三重塔・断面図。基壇を築かず礎石の上に立ち、縁をつける。心柱は初重の桔木上に枠を組み、その上に置いた厚み30cmほどの柱盤の上から立てる。二重・三重の軸部に対して、初重の軸部が大きく、全体に安定感がある

Section of Three-story Pagoda. Rather than on a podium, the pagoda stands on foundation stones surrounded by a veranda. The *shinbashira* central pillar stands upon a roughly 30-centimeter-thick base set on a frame assembly over the first story's *hanegi* cantilevers. The framework of the first story is larger than those of the second and third stories, giving the whole a sense of stability.

二重目の三手先斗栱。斗栱間を三重の通肘木で結び、中央間に間斗束を入れる。
漆喰壁の余白と細い木割の木部が繊細な間合いで綾なす

The *mitesaki* three-step bracket complexes of the pagoda's second story. The gaps between the bracket complexes are connected by three tiers of *toshihijiki* bracket tie beams, with short struts and bearing blocks inserted at the central interval. The white plaster ground and finely proportioned wood members reveal a delicate sense of spacing.

垂木の打ち方は等間隔ではなく、端へ行くにつれて狭め、
羽ばたくような軽快感のある軒裏をつくる

The intervals between the rafters are not fixed-pitch but instead narrow toward the corners, imbuing the eaves with a sense of lightness that suggests outstretched wings.

浄土寺 浄土堂

国宝
建立　　1194年上棟
所在地　兵庫県小野市

Jodoji Temple Jododo Hall

National Treasure
Completed: 1194/framework
Location: Ono, Hyogo prefecture

時代背景

　東大寺南大門とともに、僧重源が手掛けた大仏様の遺構が、兵庫県小野市にある浄土寺浄土堂である。平安時代末の南都焼討ちによる東大寺伽藍の焼失にともない、再興の指揮を執った重源は、勧進活動を展開する現地拠点として7カ所に別所をつくった。この浄土堂はその内の播磨別所にあたる。1192（建久3）年から造営が行われ、1194（建久5）年に上棟、1197（建久8）年には完成総供養が行われている。

　東大寺復興の社会的使命を担っていた重源が、その目的と同時に推し進めたのが、浄土教の阿弥陀信仰にもとづく不断念仏の布教活動であった。念仏修行のために建てられたこの堂は、念仏者としての重源の側面を示す建物である。

　西に開けた小高い丘の上に立ち、大きな宝形造の屋根を被せたこの堂は、一間四面堂（1間四方の身舎に庇が四方にまわる形式）と呼ばれる典型的な阿弥陀堂の形式を取っている。内部の円形須弥壇には、雲に乗った阿弥陀三尊像（快慶作・1195年・国宝）が東を正面に安置されており、読経しながらその周囲を右まわりにめぐる不断念仏の場として空間がつくられている。西側の開口は全面を蔀戸とし、そこから入射する西日が須弥壇の三尊を背後から照らすと、堂内の朱塗りの反射と相まって、西方浄土からの阿弥陀来迎を彷彿させるような美しい光景が現出する。重源の活動の主眼は、具象的な宗教体験を通じて人々と交わる場と時をつくりだし、広く資縁と結縁（仏道に入り、成仏するための縁をつなげること）を結ぶことにあった。この堂は、重源の大仏様による数少ない遺構であるばかりでなく、その思想と生きざまの軌跡に思いを馳せ、たどることを可能にするものでもある。

特徴と見どころ

　日本の寺院建築の発展史から見ると、重源の大仏様は突然変異のようなかたちで現れたといっても過言ではないだろう。その特殊性は、重源の遺構のなかでも浄土堂にもっとも顕著である。

　まず、仏教建築につきものの屋根の反りがない。加えて、軒の出が短く、垂木には木口に鼻隠し板が打ってある。内部に入ると、天井は張られておらず、ピラミッド状の屋根裏がそのまま内部の空間ボリュームと等しくなる。内部では構造材がすべてそのまま見えるが、それは力学的な表現といえる域にまで高められている。部材の太さ細さのメリハリ、角材と丸材の明快な対比など、一つ一つの部材の寸法、形、組み合わせが、見せる要素としても統合的に構成されている。しかも、部材の種類が少なく、たとえば母屋桁と側桁の太さを同寸法にして、角垂木の力の流れをはっきりと視覚化している。

　上へと向かう高い空間構成と開放感、力強さ、光――みずからの意に即した念仏の場は、従来の和様による阿弥陀堂ではなく、宋の方式で実現したいという重源の思いが、ここでは純粋に貫かれているように感じられる。800年以上前の人々にとって、この堂を見たときの驚嘆はいかほどであっただろうか。

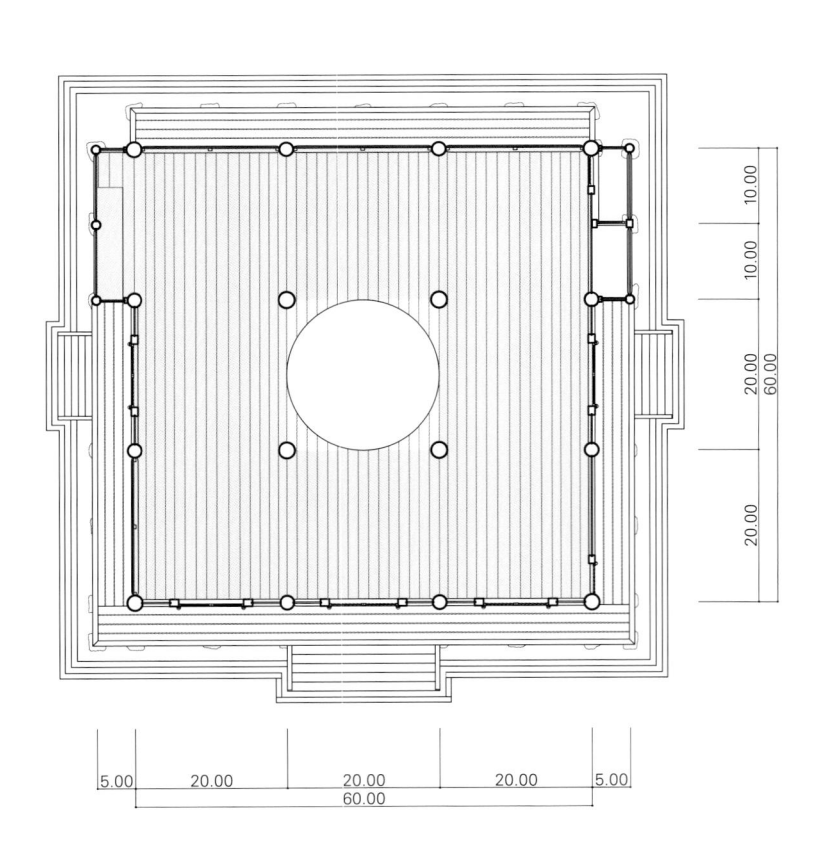

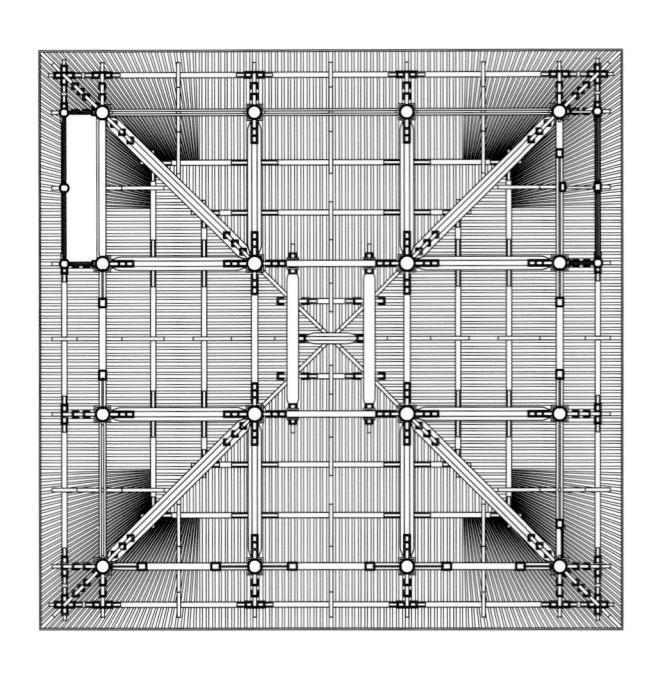

平面図　Floor plan　　　　見上図　Roof plan from below

Historical Background

Together with the Nandaimon gate at Todaiji temple, the Jododo (Pure Land) hall at Jodoji temple in the city of Ono, Hyogo prefecture is also a Daibutsuyo-style structure undertaken by Priest Chogen. Charged with leading the reconstruction effort after the Todaiji temple complex burned down during the siege of Nara by the Taira clan, Chogen established seven subsidiary temples to serve as regional bases for fund-raising efforts. The Jododo hall served as the subsidiary in Harima province; construction began in 1192, the framework was completed in 1194, and a ceremony to mark its completion was held in 1197.

In addition to seeking to fulfill his mission of restoring Todaiji temple, Chogen also sought to spread the Pure Land Buddhist practice of *nenbutsu*, or repetitive recitation evoking the name of Amida Buddha. Constructed for the purpose of this practice, the Jododo hall reveals something of what Chogen was like as a *nenbutsu* practitioner.

Standing on a small hill open to the west, this building with its large pyramidal (*hogyozukuri*) roof follows the classic "one-bay, four-sides" (*ikken-shimen*) form typical of Amida halls, with a one-bay-by-one-bay core surrounded by isles on four sides. The round timber altar (*shumidan*) at the center holds statues of the Amida triad (by Kaikei; 1195, National Treasure) riding on clouds, facing east. The space was designed as a place for *fudan nenbutsu*, or ceaseless recitation of the *nenbutsu*, with practitioners circling these statues clockwise as they chanted.

The entire west side is fitted with *shitomido* lattice panels that allow light from the setting sun to stream in, illuminating the Amida triad from the rear and reflecting the vermillion of the interior to create a beautiful sight reminiscent of Amida's descent from the Western Paradise to welcome the faithful. Chogen's chief aim was to create a space and time that would help people to enter the path of Buddhism and achieve enlightenment—through concrete religious experience. Not only is the Jododo hall one of the few remaining examples of Chogen's Daibutsuyo style, it also offers an opportunity to reflect upon his thought and retrace the path of his life.

Characteristics and Highlights

Seen in terms of the history of the development of temple architecture in Japan, Chogen's Daibutsuyo style arrived as a kind of sudden mutation, and its peculiarities are nowhere more evident in his buildings than in the Jododo hall. First, the roof lacks the characteristic upturn commonly associated with Buddhist architecture. It also has single eaves with a short overhang and rafter ends covered with fascia boards. Inside, there is no ceiling, so the pyramidal space beneath the exposed underside of the roof itself forms the spatial volume. All the interior structural members are visible in a way that rises to the level of dynamic expression; the rhythms of thick and thin, the contrasts between squared and rounded, the size and shape of each member—all are on display as visual elements of an integrated whole. Moreover, only a limited variety of members is used. For example, the core purlins (*moyageta*) and the outer wall purlins (*gawageta*) share the same diameter, thereby clearly displaying the flow of forces onto the squared rafters.

With its upward-reaching spatial composition, openness, strong lines, and light, this setting adapted to the practice of *nenbutsu* prayer suggests the purity of Chogen's desire to realize an Amida hall using Song Chinese methods rather than a conventional Japanese style. One can only imagine the surprise people must have felt when they first saw this building more than 800 years ago.

蔀戸の入る西面外観
West side with *shitomido* latticed shutters

背後から夕陽を受ける阿弥陀三尊。床に反射した光が堂内に満ち、高さ10.5mの天井頂部まで拡散して、空間に上昇感をつくりだす

The Amida triad illuminated from behind by the setting sun. Light reflected off the floor fills the interior, spreading even to the 10.5-meter-high peak of the ceiling and creating a sense of upward motion.

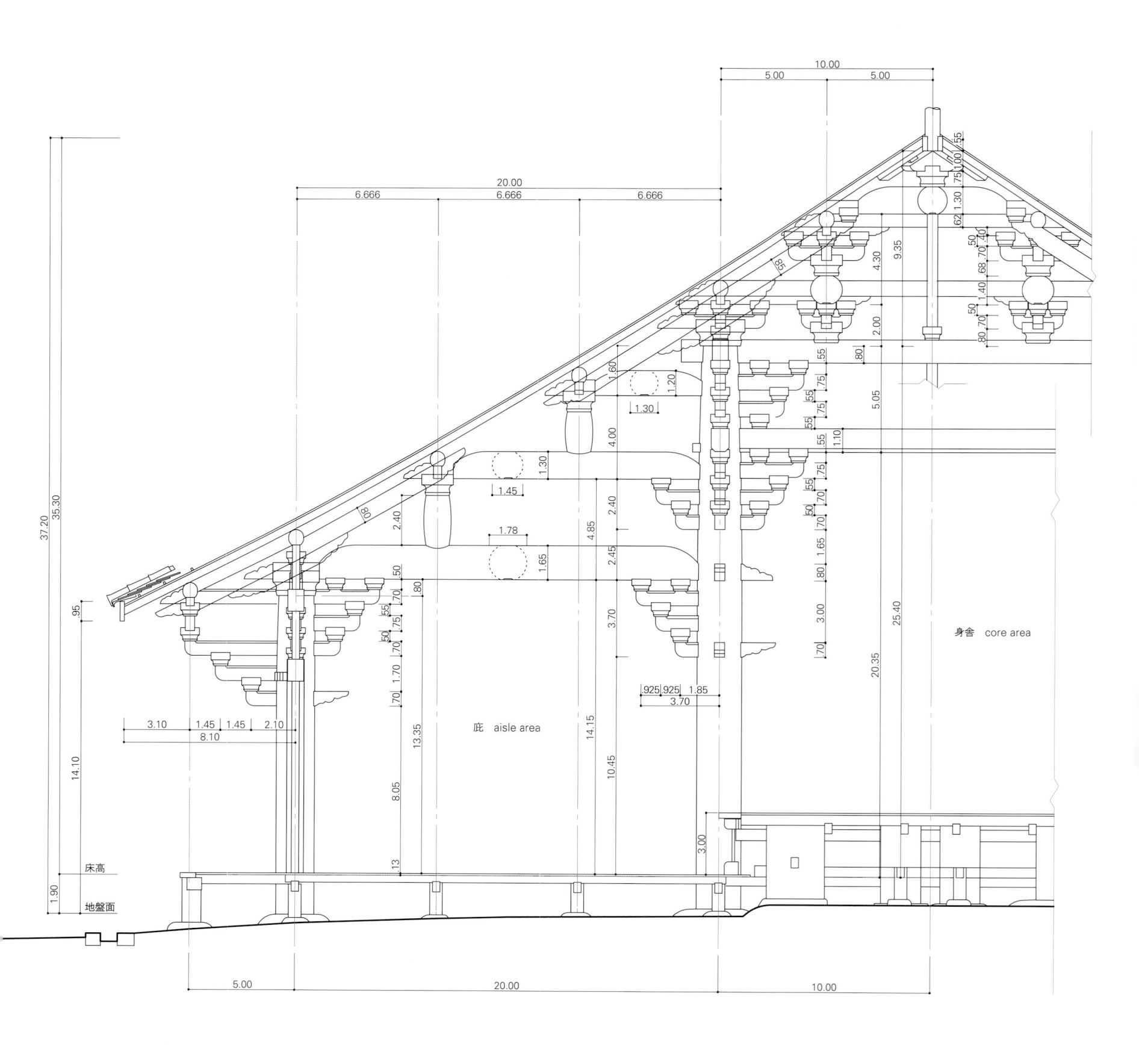

矩計図。挿肘木が梁を受ける。梁上に丸束を立て、桁を支えながら3段に梁を組み上げた構造。四天柱の間は2段の貫で固める

Sectional detail drawing. The transverse beams are supported by *sashihijiki* bracket arms inserted into the shafts of the pillars. In supporting the purlins, the structure incorporates three tiers of transverse beams upon which stand cylindrical struts. The four central *shitenbashira* pillars are firmly joined by two tiers of penetrating tie beams.

(右)梁の端部を肘木と同じ断面に細めて柱に抜き通し、鼻先に繰形をつけた大仏様独特の形式。柱間には板蟇股を入れ(奥・白壁)、それを支点に遊離尾垂木を載せる。遊離尾垂木は内外の桁を支える

(Right) The ends of the transverse beams are narrowed to the same size in cross-section as the bracket arms and drawn through the pillars, their ends embellished with molding characteristic of the Daibutsuyo style. *Itakaerumata* solid-board frog-leg struts are positioned between the pillars (see white walls in background) to serve as fulcrums for the *yuri odaruki* separated tail rafters that rest upon them and support the interior and exterior purlins.

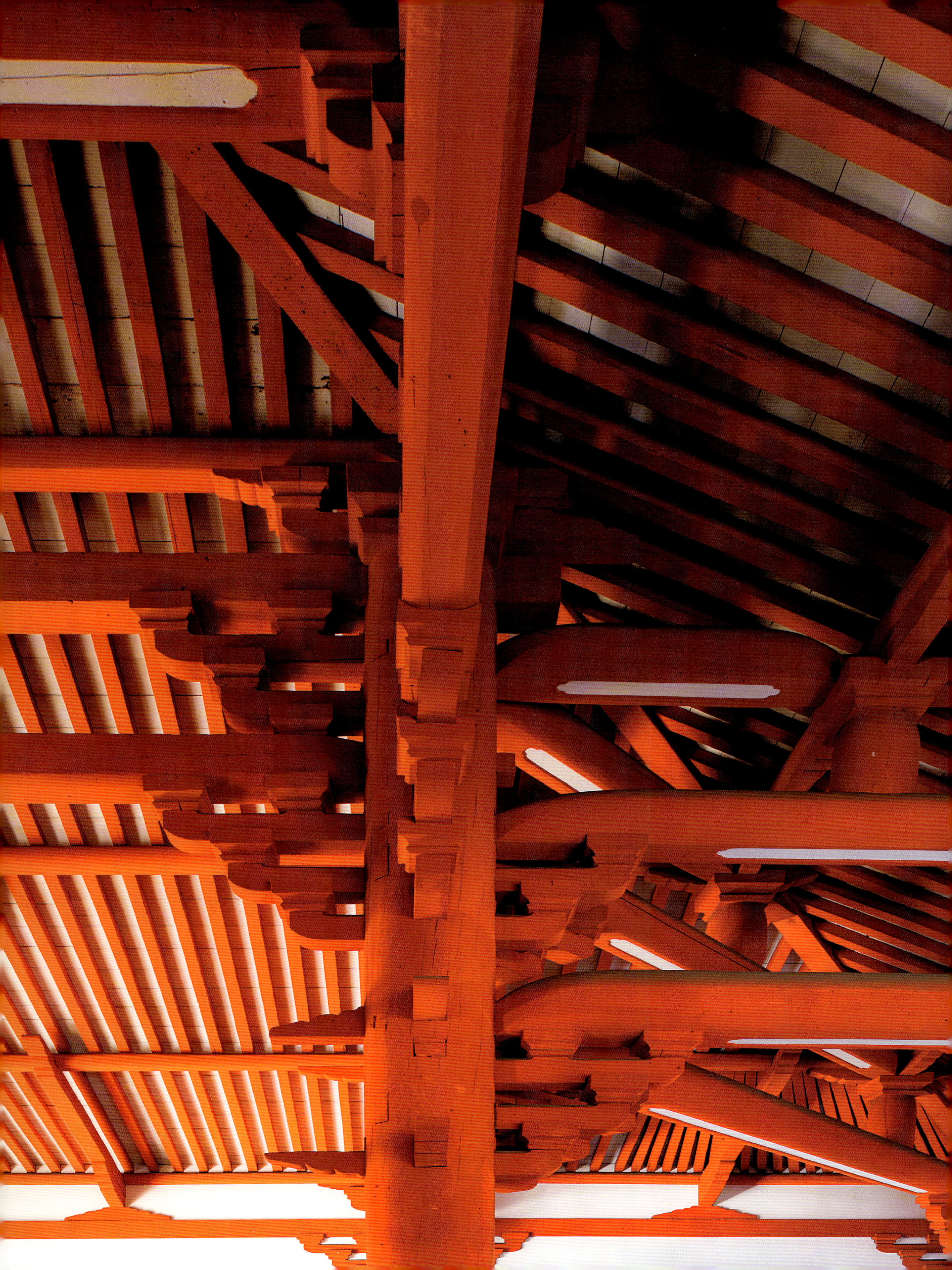

構造材をすべてそのまま見せた内部空間。天井がなく、四天柱は
屋根まで延びる。1本の柱から3方向に3段の梁が渡る

The interior space leaves all structural members exposed. There is no ceiling so the four central *shitenbashira* pillars stretch up all the way to the roof. Each pillar is fitted with three tiers of transverse beams extending in three directions.

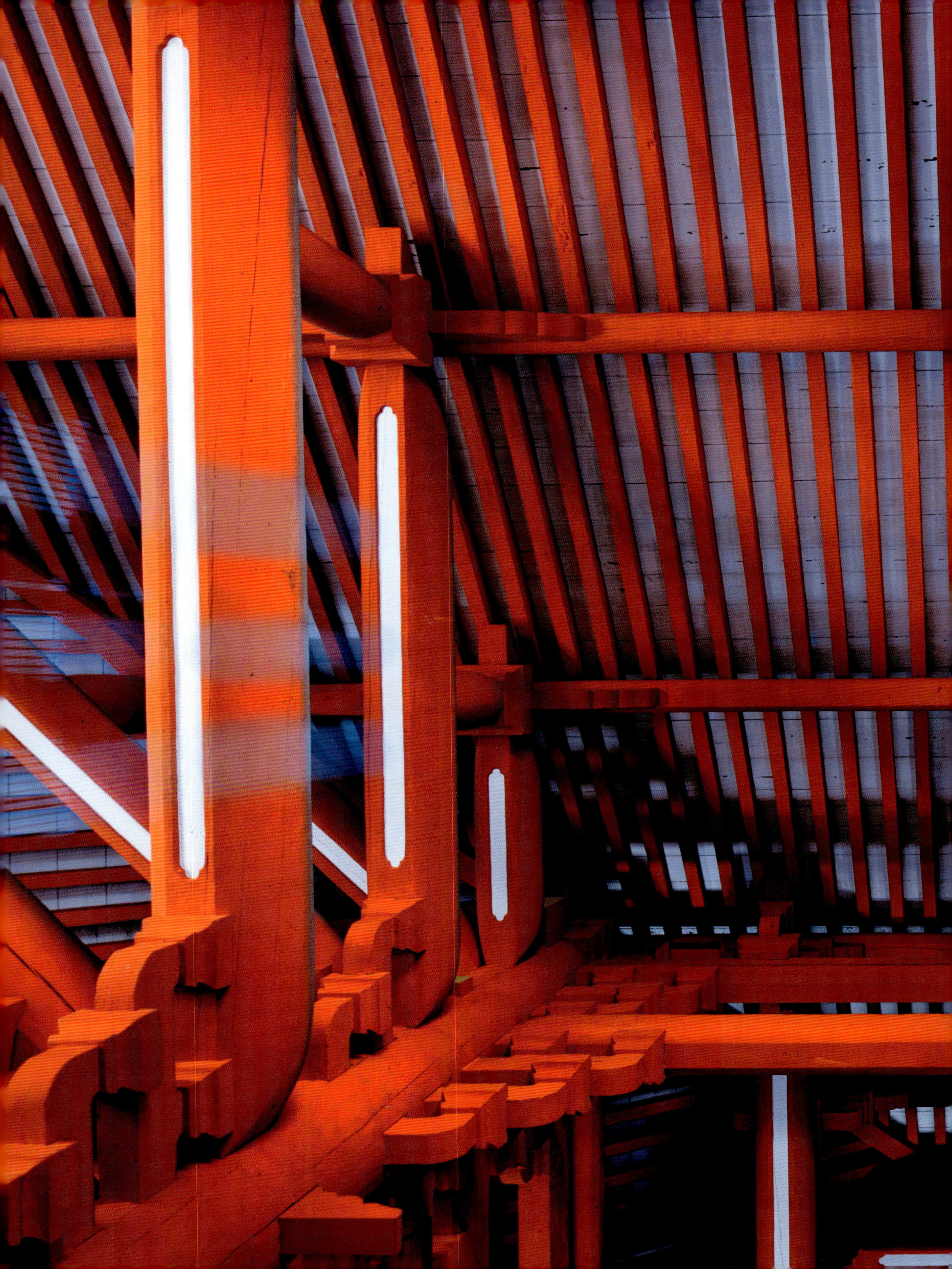

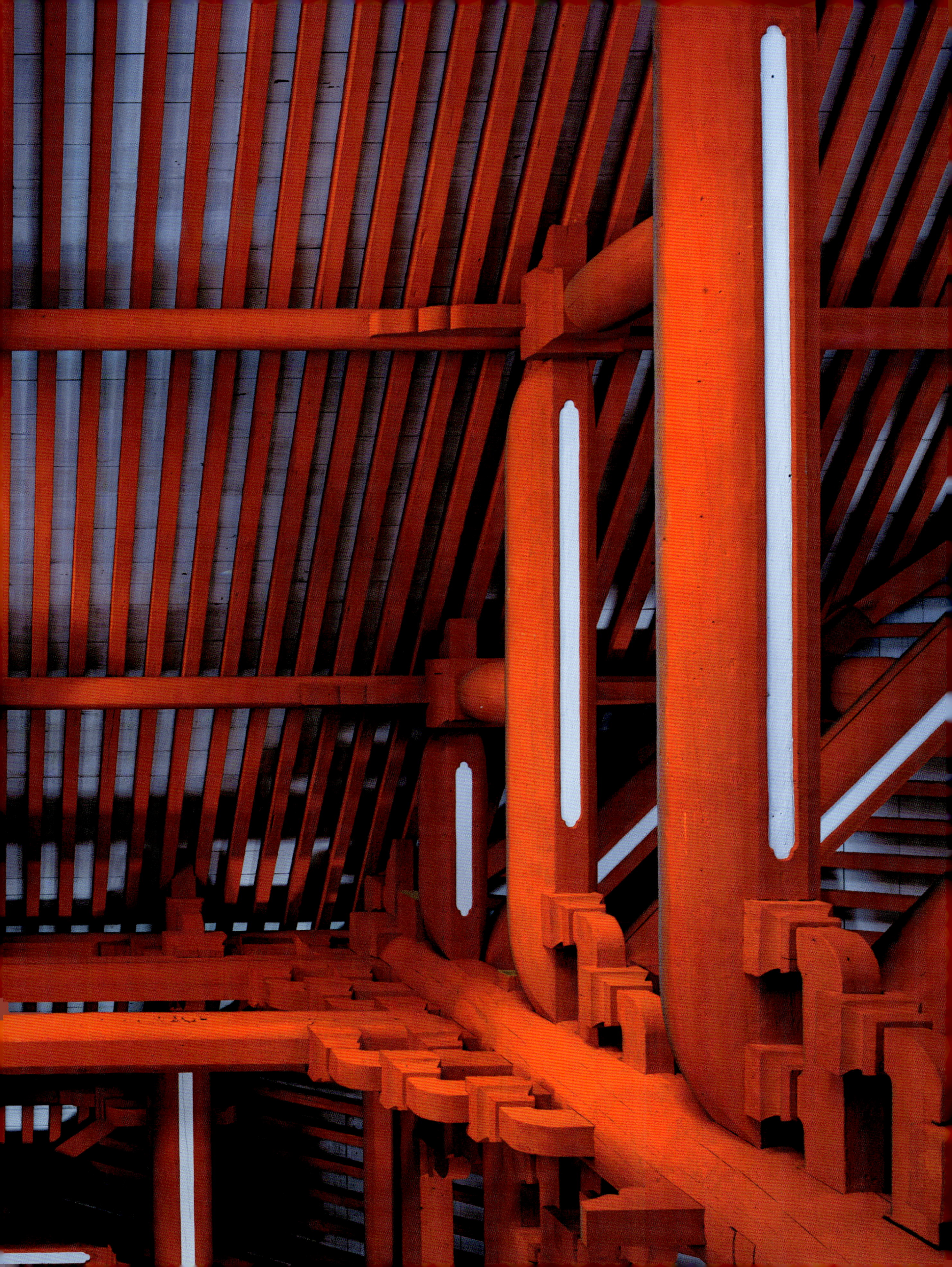

挿肘木。三手先目には斗を二つ載せ、梁の荷重を分散して受ける

Sashihijiki bracket arms inserted into the shafts of the pillars. At the third step of the bracket complex, each bracket arm carries two bearing blocks that disperse the weight of the transverse beams.

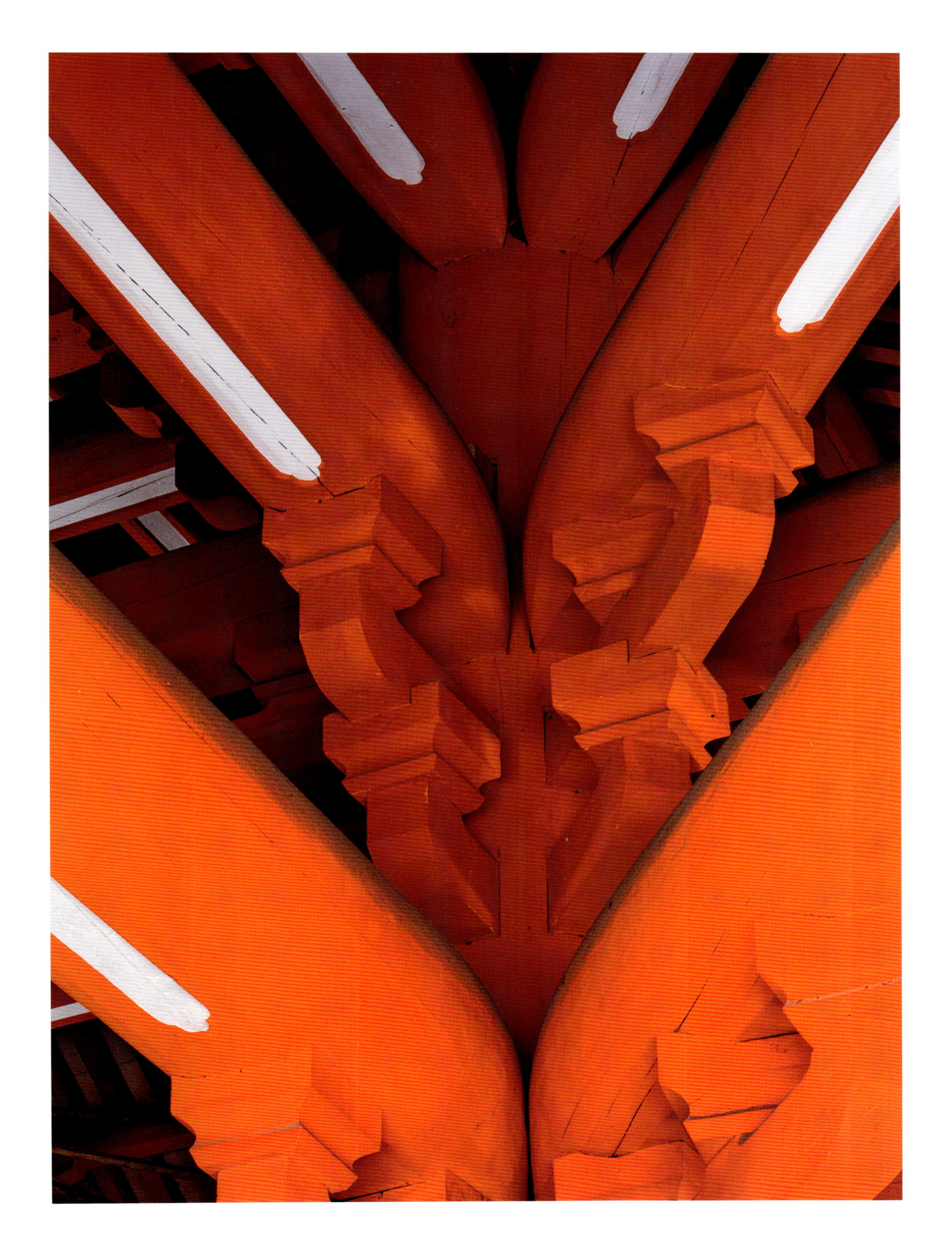

梁の下部には、白く塗られた彫りの装飾がつく。梁は上段へと徐々に細くなり、1段目の径は54cm（1.78尺）、2段目44cm（1.45尺）、3段目39cm（1.30尺）

The lower face of each transverse beam is decorated with a carved-away area painted white. Higher transverse beams grow successively thinner, with those on the first tier measuring 54 centimeters in diameter, those on the second tier measuring 44 centimeters, and those on the third measuring 39 centimeters.

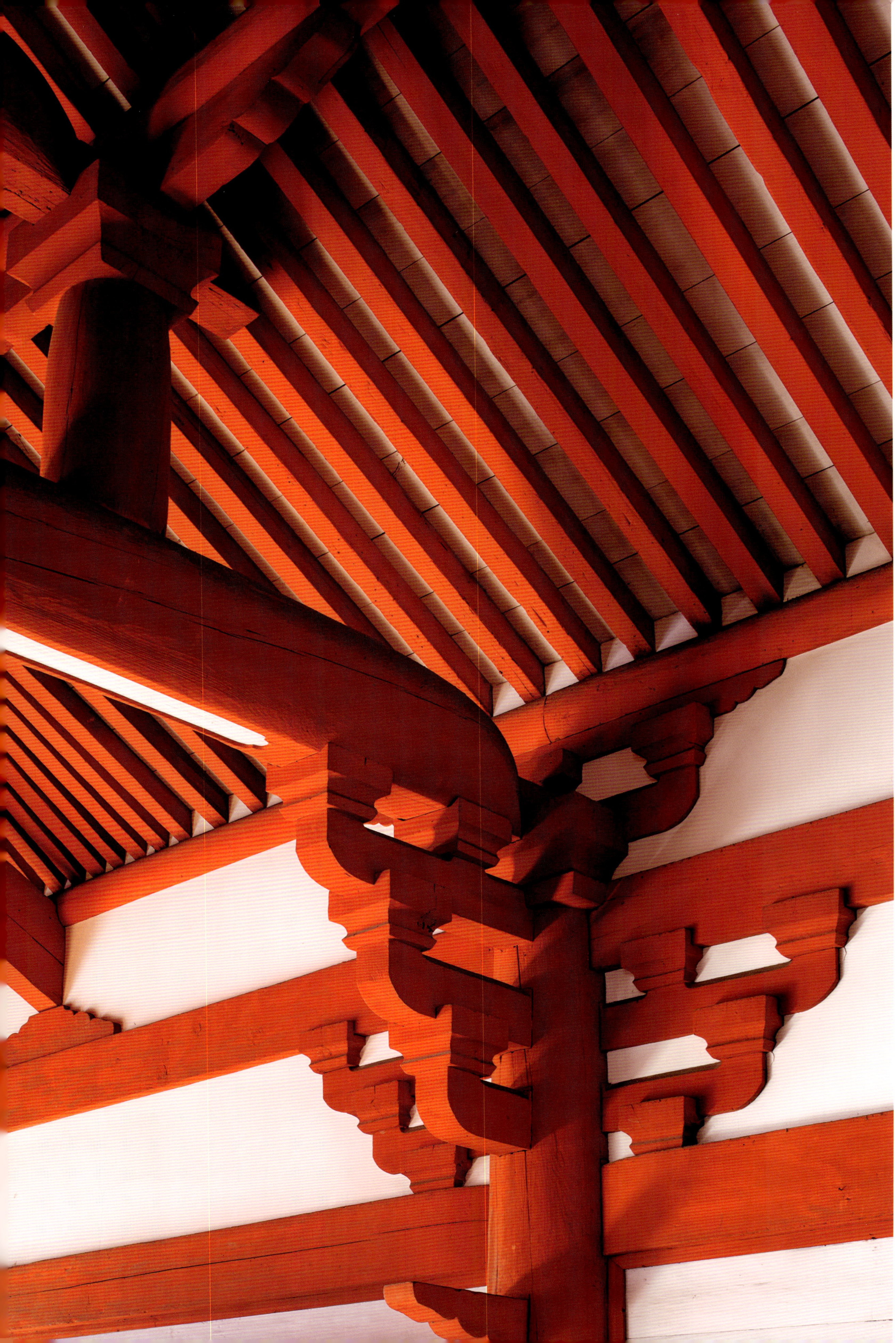

(左)母屋桁と側桁とも同寸の材で、幅21cm(7寸)、成が22.7cm(7.5寸)の楕円断面。桁と束の交点には肘木(左上)をつけ、力を分散させるとともに、ここで材を継ぐ

(Left) The core purlins (*moyageta*) and outer wall purlins (*gawageta*) use timber with the same measurements: 21 centimeters wide, 22.7 centimeters high, and elliptical in cross-section. Bracket arms incorporated where the purlins and struts intersect both disperse the load and provide a place for joining the purlins together.

(上)垂木の角材と桁の楕円材の明快な対比。垂木は化粧材ではなく、屋根荷重を直接受ける。9.7cm(3.2寸)×10cm(3.3寸)、約25cm間隔(10尺の12分割)で打たれている

(Above) The squared rafters and elliptical purlins contrast clearly. The rafters are not decorative but bear the load of the roof directly. The rafters measure 9.7 × 10 centimeters and are spaced at intervals of about 25 centimeters (a distance of 10 *shaku* divided by twelve).

天井見上げ。隅は垂木を放射状に配する(扇垂木)。3段の梁が
中央に向かって高く組み上げられていく空間は見事

Looking up at the underside of the roof. The rafters are arranged radially at the corners (*ogidaruki* rafters). The three tiers of transverse beams reaching higher toward the center form a magnificent space.

東大寺 金堂

国宝
建立年代　1705年／上棟
所在地　　奈良県奈良市

Todaiji Temple Kondo (Great Buddha Hall)

National Treasure
Completed: 1705/framework
Location: Nara, Nara prefecture

時代背景

「一枝の草、一握りの土であっても捧げて、造立の助けたらんことを願うものがあれば、その望み通りに受けいれようではないか」[*11]

743(天平15)年、聖武天皇は盧舎那仏(大仏)造顕の詔を発し、広く人民に寄進を呼びかけた。一人一人が大仏造立という国家的大事業と何らかの結びつきを持つことで、大仏をシンボルに人心の統一を図り、国を治めんとする意図がこの言葉には表出されている。この時代、仏教に望まれた社会的機能は、鎮護国家、すなわち国家の繁栄と安泰であった。同時に、この詔はその後の東大寺の歴史を暗示する。平安、戦国時代と、2度の兵火で大仏殿は焼失し、大仏も焼損したが、その度に傑僧が主導する勧進によって、この堂宇は民の寄進に力を得て再興を果たしてきたからである。日本最大の仏像と建築が、民衆の小さな寄付や奉仕の積み上げを頼りによみがえる歴史は、じつに躍動感にあふれている。巨大であるがためにあまねく社会に協力を働きかけざるをえず、その圧倒的な大きさゆえに、大仏のイコンとしての力は飛び抜けて大きく、いつの時代も人々の祈りや願いをすくいあげて、世の中の混迷を打開する社会事業となりえたのである。

東大寺金堂の歴史は、三つの時代に大きく分けられる。まず、天平時代の創建(751年)から、平安末期に南都焼討ち(1181年・治承4年12月28日)で平家に焼かれるまでの第一期である。創建当初の大仏殿の規模は、正面11間(約86m)×側面7間(約50m)で、間口は今の大仏殿より4間(約29m)広い。ヒノキの大柱84本のうち、50本を播磨(兵庫県南西部)から調達し、柱の径は110cm前後、入側柱は約21mの高さがあったとされる。その後の再建でも、天平創建のこの規模を再現することが目標となった。

次の時代は、重源が大仏様を採用して再建(1190年上棟・1195年落慶法要)した鎌倉時代初頭から、松永・三好の乱(1567年)でふたたび焼失するまでの第二期である。重源が大仏殿を再建するにあたり、従来の日本建築の構造技術や様式をそのまま踏襲せず、国内では先例のない中国の構法で、この巨大木造建築の建設に挑戦した。中国大陸の先進的な文明を直接学んだ重源と、平家を滅ぼし、日本最初の武家政権を鎌倉に開いた源頼朝からの支援。ここに新たな時代の新たな建築が胎動する。

鎌倉再建で使われたヒノキの大柱は92本で、柱の径は150cm前後と、創建時より40cm太く、入側柱の高さは約27mというから、およそ6mも長い。これほどのヒノキ材の入手は困難をきわめたが、重源は周防(山口県東部)の国で伐採し、幾多の難関を乗りこえて奈良へ運びこんだ。この時代の大仏殿の姿は、重源の貴重な遺構である東大寺南大門(1199年上棟)や兵庫県小野市の浄土寺浄土堂(1194年上棟)を参照しつつ、拡大して思い描くしかない。南大門同様、合理的で簡潔な架構をそのまま見せた、豪快な建築空間であっただろう。

第三期は、僧公慶(1648-1705)による江戸時代の再建(1709年落慶法要)から、現在にいたる300有余年である。1567年の兵火から142年間も経て金堂が竣工していることからしても、再建がどれほど苦難の道のりであったかがうかがえる。創建期・鎌倉期と同規模のものを目指したものの、途中で断念し、間口のみ11間から7間に変更して建てられた。大きな問題は、財政的困窮と大径長尺材が入手できなかったことである。そこでケヤキ材などで継ぎ柱をつくり、そのまわりに一重から三重に周辺材を打ちつけて金輪で締めつけて1本の柱にする、いわば今日でいう集成材に近い方策を取った。

1906(明治39)年から1915(大正4)年まで解体修理が行われ、大屋根の虹梁の補強に鉄骨トラスを導入するなど、近代建築の素材・手法で構造が強化された。また、1974(昭和49)年から1980(昭和55)年まで、雨漏りのために瓦の葺きかえ工事などが行われ、現在にいたる。時勢の追い風、向かい風を受けながら、それぞれの時代に即した建築技術を考案しつつ再建されてきたこの仏堂は、木を軸組にどこまで巨大な建築をつくりうるかという挑戦の歴史であった。

柱と挿肘木ディテール
Detail of a pillar and *sashihijiki* bracket arms

Historical Background

"Let us receive even a tuft of grass, a handful of earth from whoever wishes to donate to the construction." In 743, Emperor Shomu issued an edict ordering the construction of a great image of Vairocana Buddha and calling on the people to contribute to the project. His words expressed his wish that each and every person would connect in some way with the great project of erecting the Great Buddha, thereby unifying the hearts of the people and government of the country around the symbol of the great bronze statue. At that time, the role of Buddhism in society was to "protect the state" (*chingo kokka*), in other words, to promote the prosperity and stability of the country. At the same time, the edict foreshadowed the subsequent history of Todaiji temple. For, although the Kondo (Great Buddha Hall) was reduced to ashes twice and the Great Buddha image itself was destroyed, first in an armed attack by the Heike clan in the Heian period and second in a battle in the Warring States (Sengoku) period, each time, the Great Buddha Hall was reconstructed, the statue recast or repaired, thanks to a country-wide campaign soliciting contributions from the public at the initiative of some leading members of the Buddhist clergy. The history of Japan's largest image of the Buddha and its hall, the reconstruction of which relied on the accumulation of small contributions from the people, offered both in kind and in labor was impressive and energetic. The huge size of the project made the cooperation of society as a whole indispensable. Because of its immense size the Great Buddha exerted an overwhelming presence as an icon, able to answer people's every prayer and wish in any given era, and made possible a public project that brought society together in times of turmoil and trouble.

The history of the Great Buddha Hall can be divided into three periods. The first stretches from its founding (751) in the Tenpyo era until 1181 (twenty-eighth day of the twelfth month, Jisho 4) when the Heike clan attacked and burned Todaiji, Kofukuji, and other temples in Nara. At the time of its founding the hall measured 11 bays (approx. 86 meters) wide in front and 7 bays (approx. 50 meters) wide on the side. It was 4 bays (approx. 29 meters) wider than the present hall. The pillars measured some 110 centimeters in diameter and the *irikawabashira* pillars surrounding the inner sanctum were about 21 meters tall. Each time the hall was subsequently reconstructed, every effort was made to maintain these measurements used at the time of the temple's founding.

The second period spans from the early Kamakura period, when Priest Chogen reconstructed the hall in the Daibutsuyo style (the ridge-raising ceremony in 1190; the completion ceremony in 1195), until it was again burned down during the warfare in 1567. In the reconstruction of the hall, Chogen did not follow the traditional architectural style and techniques as they were but ventured to build this huge wooden building employing Chinese construction methods not attempted until then. Ninety-two massive *hinoki* cypress trees were used for the Kamakura-period reconstruction. The diameter of the pillars was around 150 centimeters and the height of those around the inner sanctum was about 27 meters; they were 40 centimeters broader in girth and 6 meters taller respectively than at the time of the temple's founding. Finding an adequate supply of such large cypress timber was no easy task. Chogen located the trees in the province of Suo (today the eastern part of Yamaguchi prefecture) and had them transported all the way to Nara, overcoming immense difficulties. One can get some idea of the scale of the Great Buddha Hall rebuilt at that time by looking at—and then expanding the size of—the structures seen in Todaiji temple's Nandaimon gate (framework completion in 1199) and in the Jododo hall ("Pure Land Hall"; framework completion in 1194) of the Jodoji temple in the city of Ono, Hyogo prefecture, both valuable extant buildings that were also built under Chogen's direction. Like the Nandaimon gate, the Great Buddha Hall of that time would have been a dynamic architectural space with the simplicity and rationality of its great framework in full view.

The third period lasts more than 300 years from the 1709 reconstruction of the hall by Priest Kokei (1648–1705) during the Edo period to the present. The hall was reduced to ashes in a battle in 1567, and it was not until 142 years later that it was rebuilt, suggesting something of the arduous path that led to its reconstruction. Although Kokei tried to reconstruct the hall on the same scale as that of the temple's founding and the Kamakura-period reconstruction, he was forced to compromise, and the number of bays at the front was reduced from eleven to seven. Among the major problems were financial constraints and the lack of large and tall trees such as had been available in the Kamakura period. In order to maintain the scale of the building with the timber available, the builders employed sophisticated lamination joinery such is used even today: zelkova (*keyaki*) shafts were spliced together to form the cores, which were then wrapped with one to three layers of planks that were fastened in place with tight metal bands.

From 1906 to 1915 the Great Buddha Hall was dismantled and repaired to strengthen its structure using modern architectural materials and techniques. Steel trusses were inserted, for example, to reinforce the curved rainbow beams (*koryo*) of the large roof. Also, over the period 1974 to 1980, repairs were carried out mainly by replacing the roof tiles. The history of this building buffeted by the favorable and unfavorable forces of each era and repeatedly reconstructed and repaired using the architectural techniques of each era is a history of pushing the limits of the scale of architecture that could be attained using a framework in wood.

特徴と見どころ

　富と権威と技術を象徴するのは、近代建築の洗礼を受けるまでの日本においては、空を支配するような大きな屋根がつくりだす景観であったろう。8世紀半ば以来、九折山(若草山)を背景に、奈良の空にはいつもこの仏堂の大屋根が威風堂々と浮かび上がり、大仏がここに御座すことを高らかに宣言してきた。だが同時に、技術面においては、この建物の歴史は屋根荷重との戦いの歴史でもあった。屋根に載せる瓦の総重量はとてつもなく重い。その負荷を受ける柱は巨大なものでなくてはならず、軒が下がらないための方策を要した。そして、焼失したとなると、木材の調達は困難をきわめ、いざ建てるとなると、地震や風、荷重に耐えうる構造技術が求められたのだ。

　創建期や鎌倉期とくらべると、正面規模が4間分縮小されたため、現在の金堂からは水平方向の安定感が確かに失われている。だが、身舎にかかるきつい勾配のついた屋根の軒と、それよりも大きく張り出した水平感のある裳階の軒との重なりは、絶妙な相殺効果をもって垂直性の強い外観に独特の均衡を与えている。

　鎌倉時代創建の重源の大仏様を踏襲し、柱には挿肘木が取りつけられ、そこから裳階は六手先、身舎は七手先の組物を出してそれぞれの軒を支える。内部には小組格天井が張られていて、おそらく重源の堂では仰ぎ見られたであろう仏像頭上のダイナミックな架構は望めないが、それでも長大な柱が林立し、その柱間に幾重もの貫が渡されて形づくられる大容量の木造空間の迫力は圧巻である。

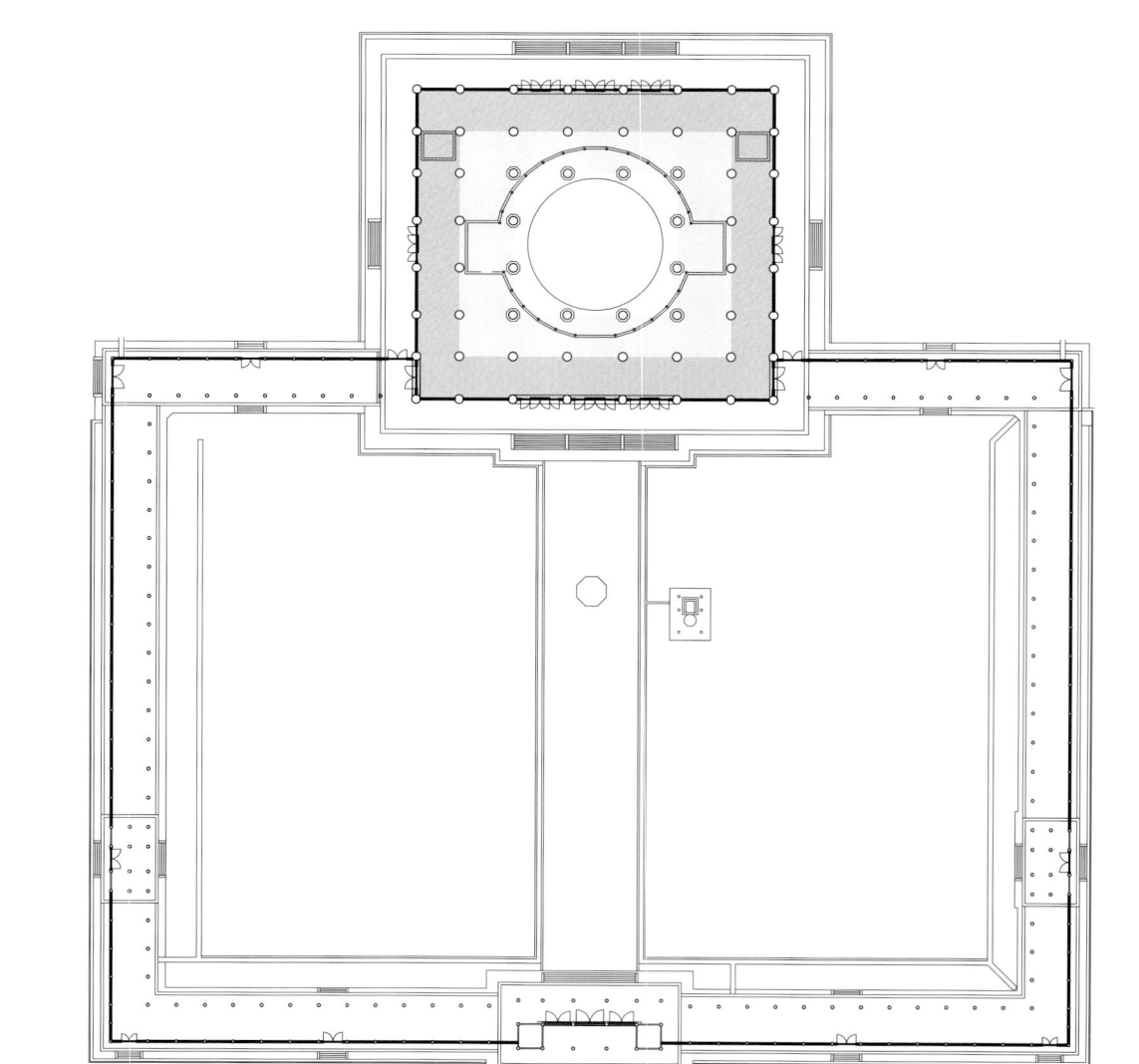

平面図　Plan

Characteristics and Highlights

The Great Buddha Hall's roof, so vast as to seem to rule the sky, remained a symbol of wealth, power, and technology until the introduction of modern architecture in the nineteenth century. From the mid-eighth century, its majestic proportions rose up against the backdrop of Mt. Tsuzurao (Mt. Wakakusa), proudly announcing the presence of the Great Buddha. In terms of technology, however, the history of this building has been a history of battles with roof load. The total weight of the tiles on the roof is tremendous. Pillars large enough to carry that weight and measures to prevent sagging of the eaves were required. With the original pillars burned to ashes, finding new timber in adequate quantity proved difficult, as was developing the structural technology needed for a massive structure that would withstand earthquakes, strong winds, and heavy load.

The decrease in the width of the building by four bays compared with the original hall or the Kamakura-period reconstruction did reduce the massive, horizontal grandeur of the Great Buddha Hall. However, the way the eaves of the steep-sloped roof over the *moya* core overlap the eaves of the horizontally extending *mokoshi* enclosure creates an excellent offset effect and achieves a distinctive balance with the overall verticality oriented shape of the hall.

Following the Daibutsuyo style used by Priest Chogen in the Kamakura period reconstruction, the *sashihijiki* bracket arms were inserted into the pillars, from where a system of supporting blocks and brackets was introduced to support the eaves of the *mokoshi* pent roof and the eaves of the *moya*, using six brackets and seven brackets respectively. In the *moya* interior, a latticed ceiling was installed which obscures what would have been the dynamic structure visible over the head of the Buddha statue in Chogen's time. Even then, the cluster of massive pillars towering over the expansive space of the wooden structure and the layers of tie-beams visible between the pillars makes a powerful and awesome sight.

山を背景に威容を誇る大屋根。寄棟造、棟の両端に鴟尾を揚げる。
本屋根の大きさは約55m×62mある

Making a magnificent sight against the backdrop of the mountains, the hipped roof measures 55 meters by 62 meters. The ends of its ridge are ornamented with *shibi* (acroteria).

中門から見た金堂正面。廻廊で囲われ、前面には儀式のための庭が広がる。内部は一層だが、立ちの高い身舎に裳階をまわし、屋根の見え方は二重となる。間口約57m、奥行き約50m。唐破風をつけ、正面性を強調する

The façade of the Kondo (Great Buddha Hall) seen from the Chumon gate. Enclosed by corridors, the open space in front of the hall is used for ceremonies. Although the interior has only one story, the *mokoshi* encircling the structure's towering core gives it the appearance of having two stories. The *karahafu* undulating gable draws attention to the frontality of the 57-meter wide, 50-meter deep building.

金堂内部。天井高は約29m。60本の柱が貫で連結され、
壮大な内部空間がつくりだされている

Great Buddha Hall interior. Sixty columns are joined by penetrating tie beams to create a magnificent interior space with a ceiling that rises 29 meters.

正面の唐破風と観相窓。唐破風で裳階屋根を切り上げている。観相窓は、本尊・盧舎那仏に屋外の儀式を見せるためにあるという

The façade's *karahafu* undulating gable and *kansomado* window (center) installed to show the Buddha the ceremonies being held outside. The undulating gable cuts in to raise up part of the *mokoshi* roof.

裳階の軒裏。大仏様による六手先の組物。梁の木鼻には禅宗様の影響を受けた繰形がつく

The underside of the *mokoshi* eaves. The *mutesaki* six-stepped bracket complexes follow the Daibutsuyo style in their use of *sashihijiki* bracket arms inserted into the columns, while the carving on the tips of the transverse beams shows the influence of the Zenshuyo style.

六手先の五手目に通肘木をまわし、斗栱を連結する

The *mutesaki* six-stepped bracket complexes are connected at their fifth steps by *toshihijiki* bracket tie beams.

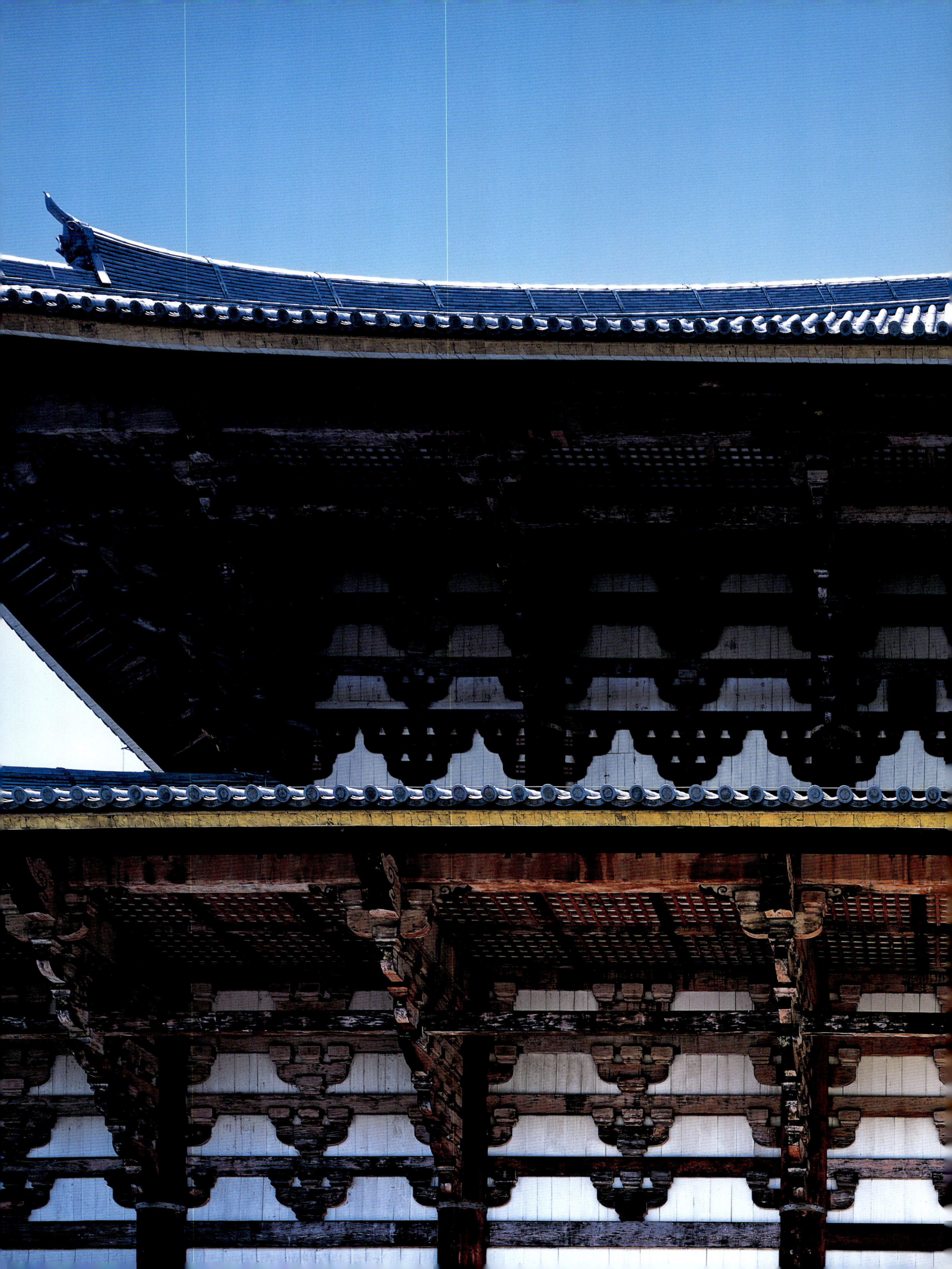

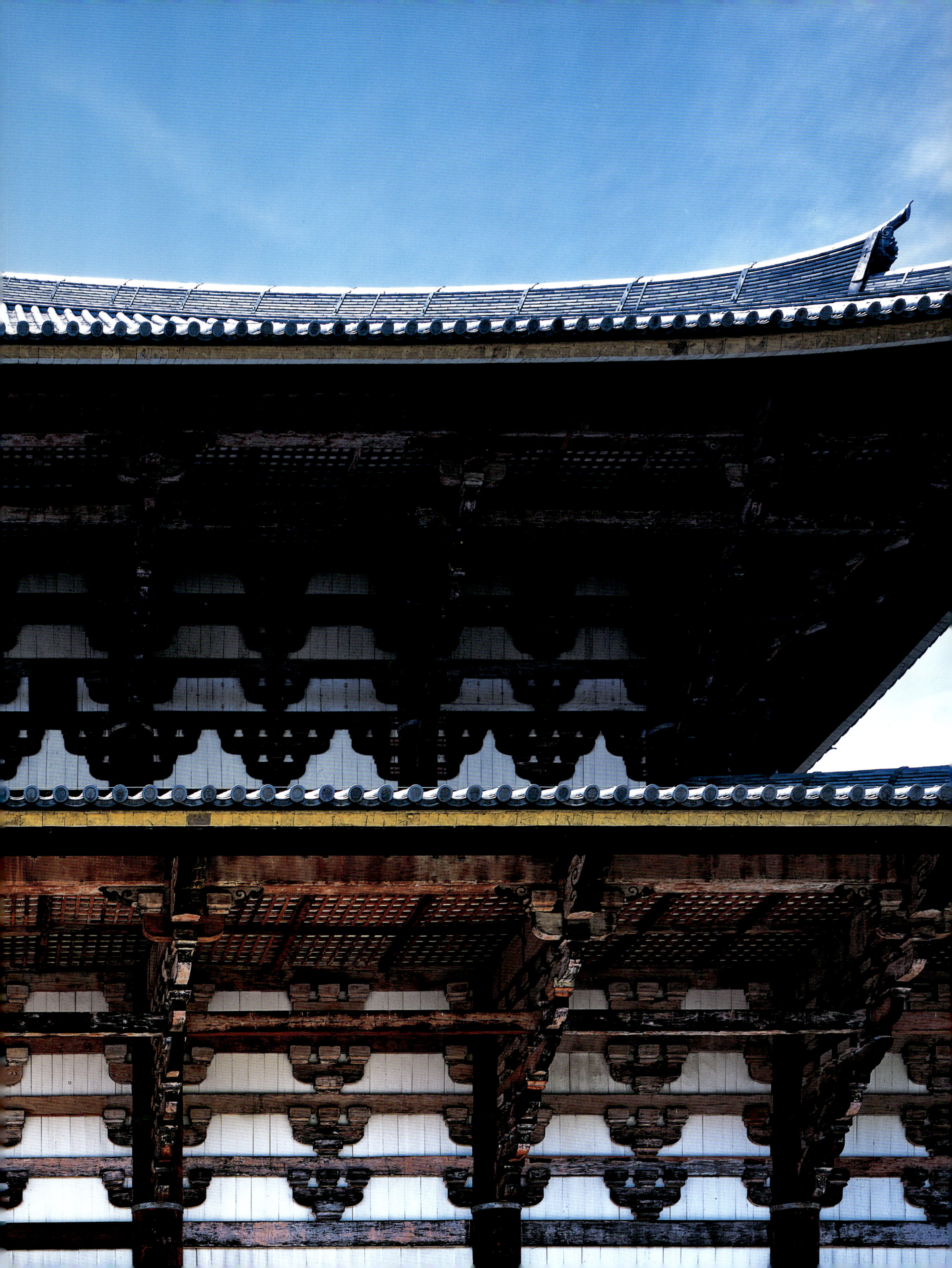

寺 南大門

1199年上棟
奈良県奈良市

Todaiji Temple Nandaimon (Great South Gate)

National Treasure
Completed: 1199/ framework
Location: Nara, Nara prefecture

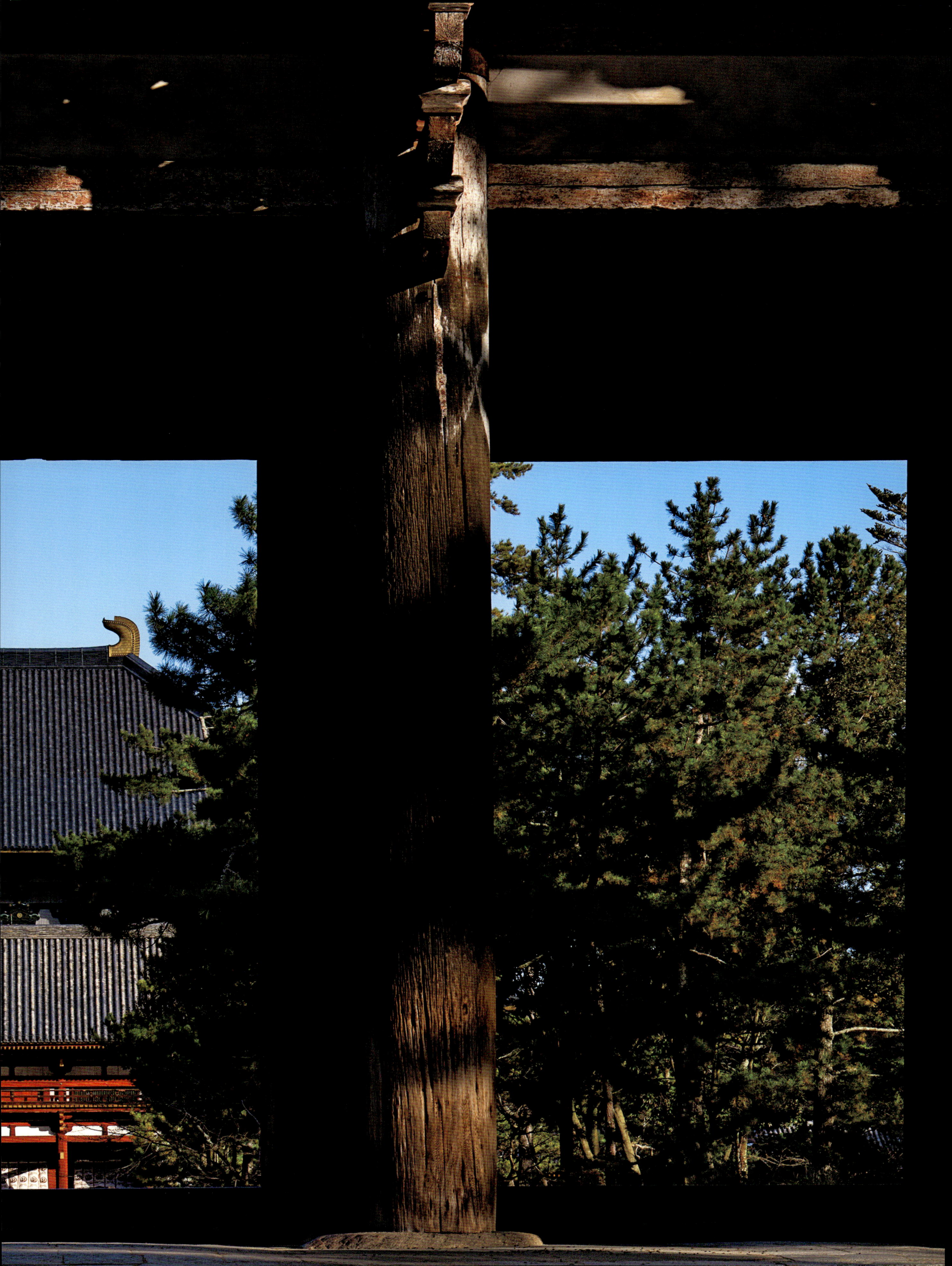

時代背景

　建築史の視点からは、平家による南都焼討ちで焼失した東大寺の再興が中世の起点となる。国風化を深めた400年間の平安時代を経て、鎌倉時代とともに始まる東大寺の復興は、日本の建築がふたたび中国の新たな建築技術・様式に接し、それを採り入れ、進展していく契機の一つとなった。

　この平家の兵火で、東大寺は奈良時代以来、日本の仏教信仰のシンボルである盧舎那仏（大仏）と金堂（大仏殿）をはじめ、広大な伽藍に立つほとんどの建物を失う。喫緊の課題は、大仏の大々的な修造とそれを収める大仏殿という巨大建築の再建であり、次に伽藍全体の復興である。この大きな使命を、勧進というかたちで担った僧侶が重源であった。宋（中国）に渡った経験をもつ重源は、建設にあたって当地の構法をこの機会に採用する。長大な柱を立て、貫（水平材）を多用し、がっちりと軸固めをしたこの構造は、全体がきわめて堅固となり、地震に強く、巨大建築の架構に適していた。大仏様と今日呼ばれる様式である。この構法で、1195（建久6）年には創建当初と同規模の大仏殿の落慶法要が行われ、1199（正治元）年には南大門が上棟する。しかし、重源が心血を注いで建てた大仏殿は、1567（永禄10）年、松永・三好の乱でふたたび兵火にかかって焼失してしまう。幸いにして南大門は火難を逃れ、現在も当時からの威容を誇る。大仏様の豪快な表現とともに、この門は重源の進取の息吹と軌跡を今に感じることができる貴重な遺構の一つである。

特徴と見どころ

　長大な通し柱（長さ約19m、下方の直径約1m）が林立するなか、柱と柱は幾段もの貫が貫通してがっちりと固められている。柱には肘木が直接挿しこまれ（挿肘木）、肘木の先端に置いた斗を支点に一手ずつ上方前方へと延ばして六手先に組み上げ、さらに肘木間を水平材（通肘木）でつなげつつ、大きく張り出す軒を支える。組物が整然と並ぶさまは圧巻で、軒下はじつにリズミカルである。

　天井を張らずに、合理的な構造をそのまま露出させた簡潔な表現は、ほかには見られない豪快さに満ちており、大仏様ならではの醍醐味がある。また、貫や肘木など、大量に必要となる水平材の断面寸法が統一されており、部材寸法を規格化することで工事の単純化と工期短縮が図られたと考えられている。いわば標準規格化された工法の先駆けである。構法、表現ともに今も新鮮味に満ちた南大門は、巨大モニュメントであると同時に、いたって現代的な建築である。

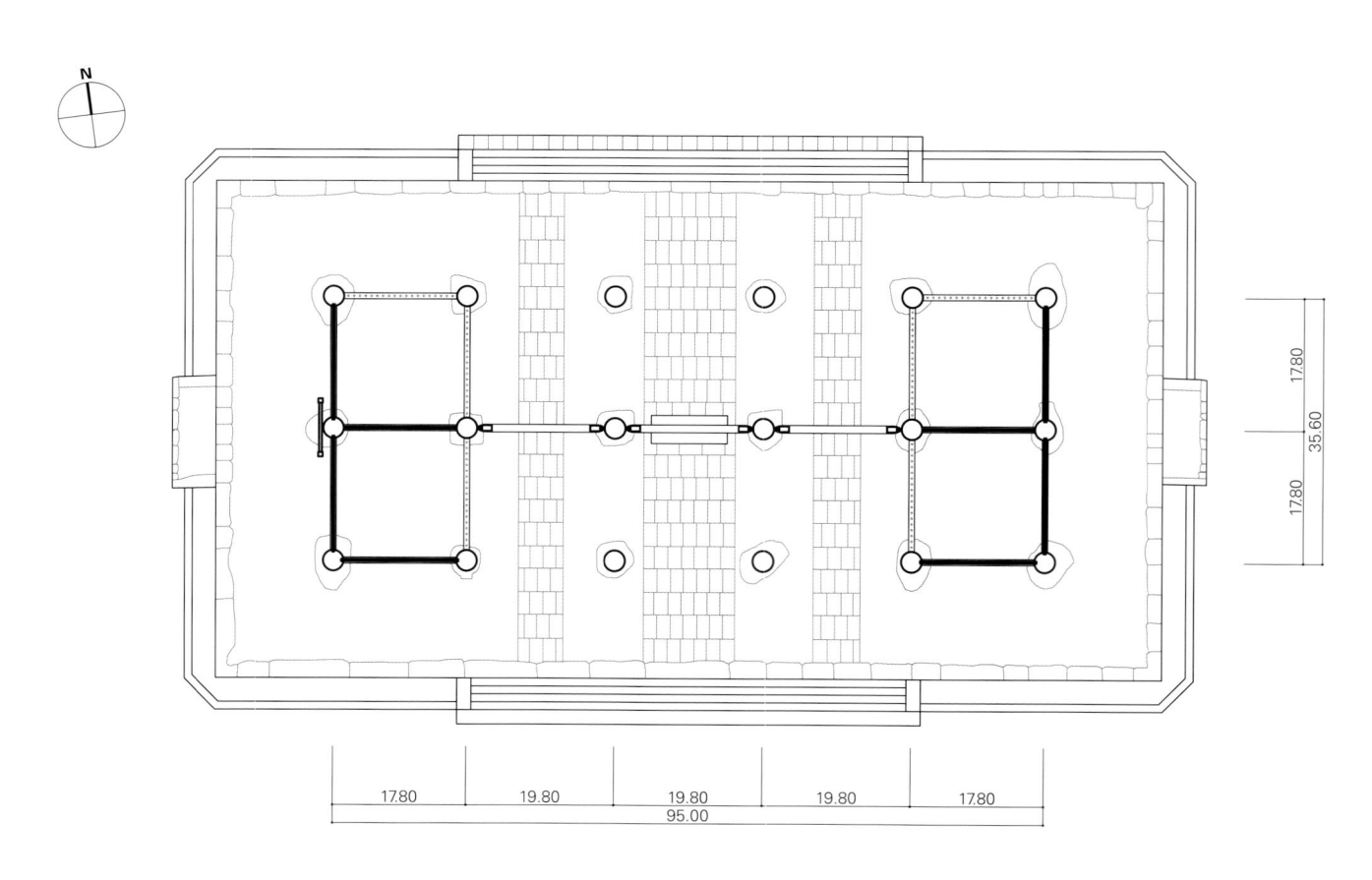

平面図　Plan

Historical Background

In architectural history, Japan's middle ages began with the reconstruction of Todaiji temple after it was reduced to ashes during the siege of Nara by the Taira clan in the late twelfth century. After the 400-year Heian period during which a sense of national identity in culture and art had deepened, the reconstruction of Todaiji provided another opportunity for Japanese architecture to come into contact with—and to incorporate and develop—the latest techniques and styles from China.

The Taira assault destroyed almost all of the buildings in Todaiji's vast temple complex, including the Great Buddha Hall (Kondo) and the Great Buddha statue that had symbolized Japanese Buddhism since the Nara period. The most pressing issue was to restore the statue and to rebuild the massive main hall needed to house it; next in importance was the reconstruction of the rest of the temple complex.

The rebuilding mission was undertaken by Priest Chogen, supported by the *kanjin* system of fundraising through solicited donations. Chogen took the opportunity to adopt a construction method that he had observed during his travels in Song dynasty China. Well suited for framing massive buildings, it is known today as the Daibutsuyo style and involves the use of huge, tall columns and many *nuki* (penetrating tie beams) to create a solid framework that results in an extremely robust and earthquake-resistant structure. This style was used for the new Great Buddha Hall, built at the same scale as the original; its dedication ceremony was celebrated in 1195. It is also the style of the Nandaimon gate, for which the ridge-raising ceremony was held in 1199. Unfortunately, the Great Buddha Hall into which Chogen had poured his heart and soul was again lost to fire during a battle between the Matsunaga and Miyoshi clans in 1567. The Nandaimon gate escaped destruction, however, and displays its original magnificence even today. In addition to being a bold expression of the Daibutsuyo style, the gate is also cherished as a monument to Chogen's memory and achievements.

Characteristics and Highlights

Penetrating tie beams connect a line of mighty columns (approximately 19 meters high and 1 meter in diameter at their base) at multiple levels, binding them firmly together. Bearing blocks placed on the ends of bracket arms inserted directly into the columns (*sashihijiki*) act as fulcrums for building out successive bracket sets, each projecting one step higher and further out than the last, to form *mutesaki* six-stepped bracket complexes, which are then further reinforced by horizontal bracket tie beams (*toshihijiki*) that run between the bracket complexes to support the overhanging roof. These orderly bracket complexes are a highlight of the structure and give the eaves a distinctive rhythm.

This concise expression of a rational structure—one that is fully exposed in the absence of a ceiling—is the essence of the Daibutsuyo style and has a dynamism not seen elsewhere. Also notable are the uniform dimensions in cross-section of the *nuki*, *hijiki*, and other horizontal members that were required in such enormous quantities. This uniformity of measurements, which is thought to have been an effort to both simplify and hasten construction, can be seen as an early example of standardized construction methods. The Nandaimon gate, so richly innovative in its structure, construction methods, and expression, is both monumental in scale and a startlingly modern work of architecture.

冬の朝。金堂・中門・南大門と南北の軸線上に立つ。身近に見られる重源の
大仏様の遺構。基壇から棟までの高さ25.5m、正面28.8m、軒幅約40m。
礎石の位置は創建時と同じで、柱間は中央3間各約6m（20尺）、両端間・
側面は各約5.4m（18尺）

A winter morning. The Great Buddha Hall, Chumon gate, and Nandaimon gate are aligned along a north–south axis. Seen at the foreground, Chogen's Daibutsuyo-style Nandaimon gate stands 25.5 meters tall from podium to roof ridge; it measures 28.8 meters wide at the façade and about 40 meters wide at the eaves. The foundation stones are positioned as they were when the structure was originally built. The pillars of the central three bays are spaced about six meters apart, while those of the bays on each end of the façade and along the side of the building are about 5.4 meters apart.

18本の柱は高さ約19m（63尺）、太さは下方径約1m（3.3尺）。六手先斗栱・挿肘木によって、5.4m持ち出して深い軒をつくる。軒の荷重の多くを両側各6本の柱で受けている

Each of the 18 columns stands about 19 meters tall and measures roughly one meter in diameter near its base. *Mutesaki* six-stepped bracket complexes and *sashihijiki* bracket arms inserted into the columns are used to project the eave purlins out from the columns to create 5.4-meter-deep eaves. Most of the load from the eaves is borne by the six columns standing at each end of the building.

Labels (diagram)

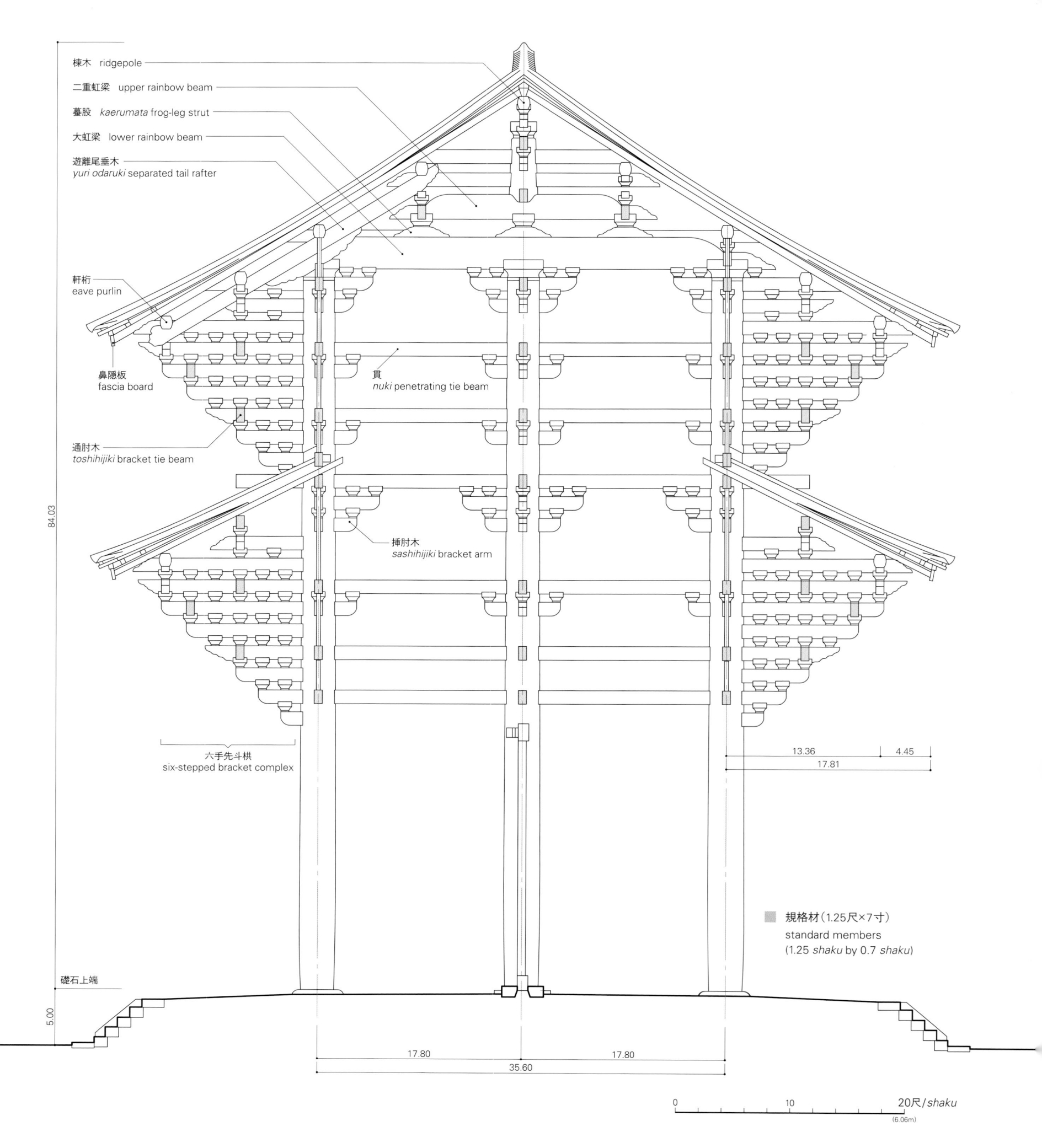

- 棟木 ridgepole
- 二重虹梁 upper rainbow beam
- 蟇股 kaerumata frog-leg strut
- 大虹梁 lower rainbow beam
- 遊離尾垂木 yuri odaruki separated tail rafter
- 軒桁 eave purlin
- 鼻隠板 fascia board
- 通肘木 toshihijiki bracket tie beam
- 貫 nuki penetrating tie beam
- 挿肘木 sashihijiki bracket arm
- 六手先斗栱 six-stepped bracket complex
- 礎石上端
- 規格材（1.25尺×7寸）standard members (1.25 shaku by 0.7 shaku)

0 10 20尺/shaku
(6.06m)

Caption

断面図。下2段の横材は1本で貫通する貫になっているため、中央柱に斗栱はついていない。3段目以上は貫を中央柱内で継ぎ、左右の緊結を補強するために斗栱をつける。4段目の貫には、地震時に水平力が大きくかかり、本来ならばもっと太い梁が必要となるが、ここでは同寸規格材の使用を方針とするので、2段組みの斗栱で強化する。上部は二重虹梁蟇股式で棟を支える

Section. The two lowest horizontal tiers are *nuki* penetrating tie beams made with a single timber, so there are no bracket complexes at the central columns. Beginning with the third tier, the penetrating tie beams consist of two timbers joined at the central columns, with bracket complexes at both sides to reinforce the connection. The penetrating tie beams at the fourth tier, where compressive and tensile forces intersect during an earthquake, would normally require a thicker beam; since the principle here was to use timber of common dimensions, however, two-stepped bracket complexes are incorporated as reinforcement. At the top, the roof ridge is supported by a system of double rainbow beams and frog-leg struts.

（右）連続する貫。内部は天井がなく、吹き抜けになっている。4段目には2段組の斗栱が見える

Multiple tiers of *nuki* penetrating tie beams. The interior is a great void with no ceiling. Two-stepped bracket complexes are visible at the fourth tier.

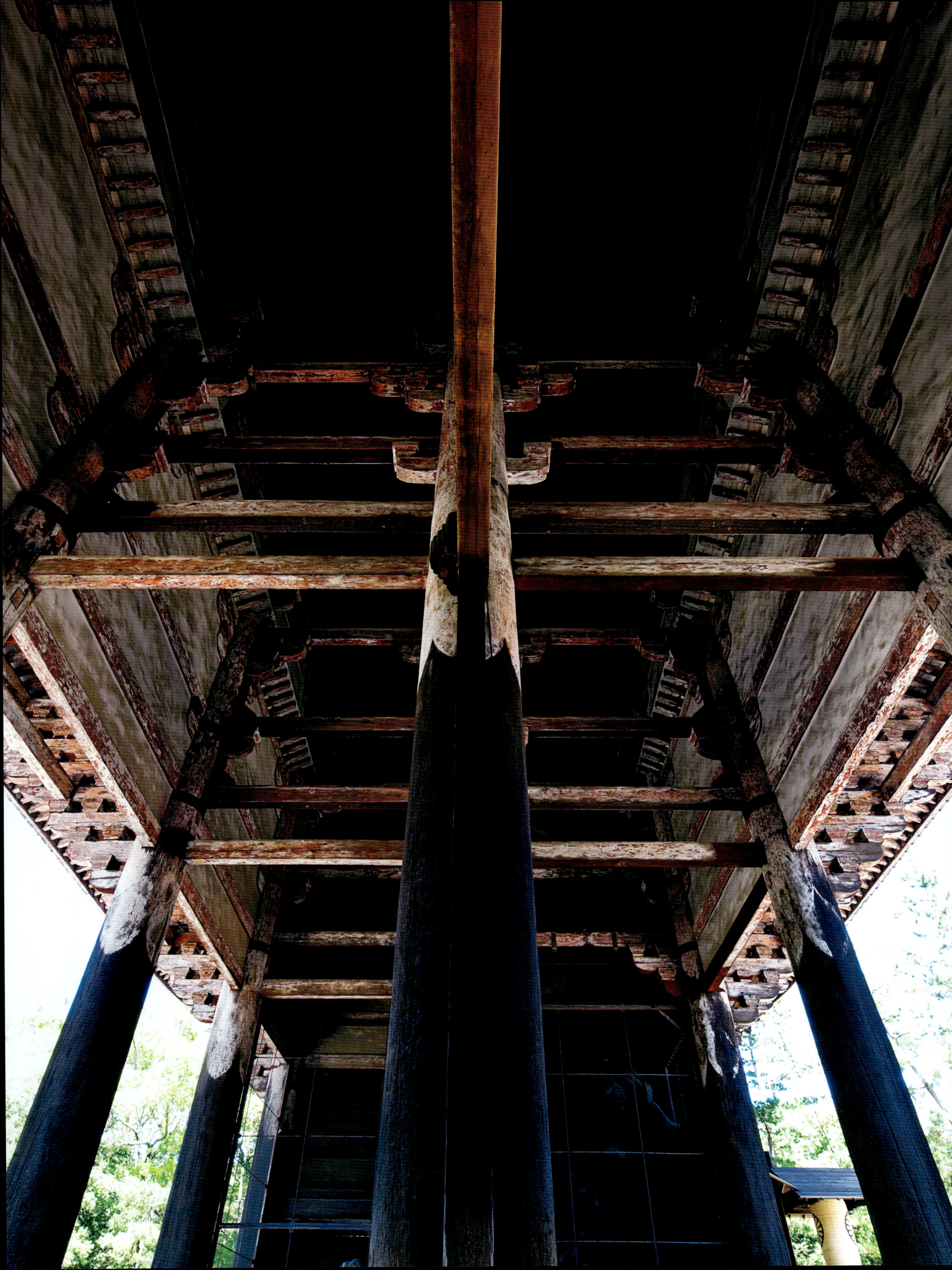

挿肘木の部材寸法は37.9cm（1.25尺）×21cm（7寸）。片持ちに有利な縦長の断面とする。六手先肘木は21cm（7寸）間隔、約2,000個の斗はすべて同一寸法で等間隔に並べられ、整えられている

The timbers used for the *sashihijiki* bracket arms measure 37.9 centimeters by 21 centimeters and are vertically rectangular in cross-section, as is advantageous when cantilevering. The structure is well ordered; the bracket arms of the *mutesaki* six-stepped bracket complexes are spaced at intervals of 21 centimeters while the roughly 2,000 *masu* bearing blocks all share the same measurements and are arranged at regular intervals.

西日を受けて赤く輝く。六手先斗栱の横ぶれを防ぐために上下層とも通肘木を各2段取りつける。垂木の先には大仏様の特徴である鼻隠し板がつく

In the reddish glow of the setting sun. To prevent lateral vibration in the six-stepped bracket complexes, both the upper and lower stories incorporate two tiers of bracket tie beams. Fascia boards are attached at the rafter ends.

東大寺 法華堂

国宝
建立年代　正堂：8世紀　礼堂：12世紀末-13世紀
所在地　　奈良県奈良市

Todaiji Temple Hokkedo Hall

National Treasure
Completed: Image Hall, 8th century;
　　　　　 Worship Hall, late 12th–13th century
Location: Nara, Nara prefecture

礼堂内部。化粧屋根裏で二重虹梁が
連続する豪快な空間

The worship hall interior, a magnificent
space whose exposed ceiling incorporates
a series of double rainbow tie beams

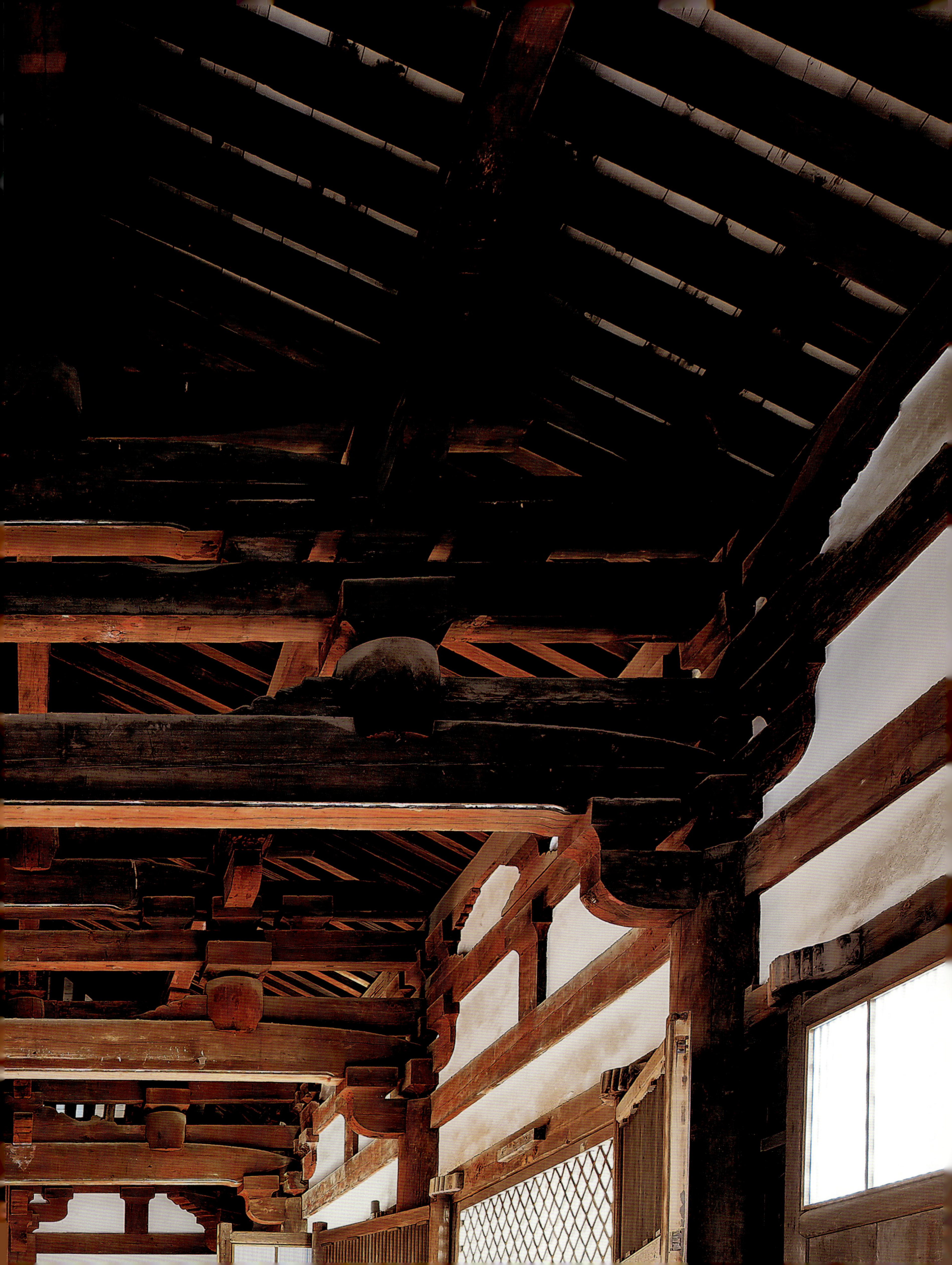

時代背景

　東大寺の堂宇のなかで、今に遺された最古の建物が、伽藍東方の高台に位置する法華堂(三月堂)である。東大寺に2度の壊滅的な打撃を与えた兵火を逃れた数少ない建物の一つである。

　平面的には礼堂と正堂の二つの部分に分けられるが、架構と天井構成から見ると、礼堂と正堂に、両堂をつなげる「造り合い」と呼ばれる三つで構成されている。正堂部分は奈良時代の建築で、本尊・不空羂索観音立像(8世紀・国宝)をはじめとする見事な仏像群とともに、天平文化の粋を今に伝える。堂の創建年は確定できないが、『正倉院文書』の天平勝宝元年(749年)の項においては、この堂が本尊にちなんで「羂索堂」という名ですでに記されているため、建立はそれ以前と考えられている。一方、平安後期に作成された寺史『東大寺要録』においては、建立は733(天平5)年と記される。

　かなり早い時期から現正堂の前(南側)に、軒を接して別棟で礼堂(礼拝読経するための空間)が並んで建てられており、奈良時代から記録に現れる双堂の形式を取っていた。双堂とは、本尊を祀る正堂の前に別棟で礼堂を並べて建てた形式である。奈良時代には両堂が構造的に独立していたが、平安時代には両堂が造り合わせとなって一体化されるものが現れた。法華堂では、鎌倉時代に礼堂が建てかえられ、正堂と礼堂の屋根をつなげて二つの堂が一体化された。西側から見ると、正堂と礼堂をつなぐ軒先には木樋が残されているのがわかる。

　なお、礼堂の建てかえ時期については、南都焼討ちのあとに東大寺の再興を任された重源による1199(正治元)年とする説と、東大寺僧でやはり堂宇の復興に尽力した円照(1221-1277)による1264(文永元)年とする説がある。

特徴と見どころ

　この堂は8世紀の天平文化の香りが充溢する正堂と、鎌倉時代の豪快な大仏様の特色をもつ礼堂をあわせもち、天平様式と大仏様式という東大寺を象徴する二つの建築様式が並置された形で明快に提示されている。その間の差は450年以上ある。今にたとえれば、16世紀の室町時代の仏堂の前に21世紀の礼堂を建て、大きな一つ屋根をかけて新旧を一体化する感覚である。法華堂の礼堂に挑んだ鎌倉時代の工匠も、奈良時代の正堂に対してはそれに近い感じを抱いていたのかもしれない。その際、今も昔も課題となるのは、保存修復と新旧の調和であり、さらには、その時代の最先端の技術と様式を駆使した建物全体の再生である。

　新旧を調和させる意図は、西側外観に顕著である。全体8間のうち、北側4間が奈良時代の正堂、南側4間が鎌倉時代の礼堂と造り合いを合わせた部分で、一見そこに450年以上の時間差があることを予備知識なしで感知するのは難しい。屋根は正堂部分の寄棟造に礼堂部分の入母屋造を連結した変則的な形ではあるものの、同素材で葺かれているせいもあり、さほど違和感はない。また、共通の高欄がまわることも統一感を強めている。柱、組物、扉など、一つ一つの構成要素に目を向ければ明らかに様式の違いがあるが、その違いを控えめにとどめ、正堂との調和に配慮して全体をまとめあげた印象がある。

　一方、礼堂の内部は大仏様独特の活気に満ちている。それは架構の派手さからくる活気である。2間×5間の細長い空間ではあるが、化粧屋根裏にして架構をそのまま見せ、天井高7.7mの上昇感ある空間に二重虹梁が豪快に連続する。なかでも注目されるのは、二重虹梁の上に何段も横架材を延ばし、厳重に構造の強化をはかっている点で、過剰ともいえる意欲的な構造表現が、礼堂の空間を力感あふれるものにしている。躍動感ある明るい礼堂と、陰翳に包まれた穏やかな正堂。新旧の鮮やかな対比と調和が両立している。

正堂と礼堂の間に残る木樋

A wooden trough at the intersection of the image hall and the worship hall

Historical Background

Of the buildings of the Todaiji temple complex, the oldest surviving today is the Hokkedo (also called the Sangatsudo), which stands on a rise in the eastern precincts. It is among the few buildings that survived the fires of war that ravaged the temple twice in its history.

The building is divided into two, the image hall (*shodo*) and the worship hall (*raido*), but when we examine the structure and roof composition, we can see that it is composed of three elements, including the *tsukuriai*, or "connecting" structure between the two parts. The image hall part built in the Nara period and, along with its principal image of Fukukensaku Kannon (eighth century; National Treasure) and surrounding guardian statues, distills the essence of Nara's Tenpyo culture. The year the image hall was built is not certain, but as the Tenpyo-Shoho 1 (749) section of the *Shosoin monjo* (Documents of the Shosoin) mentions a "Kensaku hall," referring to the principal image of the hall, it is believed to have been built before that time. The *Todaiji yoroku*, a history of Todaiji temple compiled in the late Heian period, records the hall as having been completed in 733.

From quite an early stage, a separate worship hall (space for prayer and sutra recitation) was built in *narabido* (aligned-hall) fashion on the south side of the image hall. The *narabido* is a style that first appeared in Nara-period documents, a style in which a worship hall is built in alignment with an image hall (sanctuary) with the former in front of the latter. In the Nara period the two halls were structurally separate from each other, but in the Heian period, in some temples the two halls were brought together with adjoining roofs. In the Hokkedo, during the Kamakura period the worship hall was rebuilt and the two halls were united as the single building we see today. The wooden trough that in the past drained off rainwater where the *shodo* and *raido* roofs meet is visible at their intersection.

Characteristics and Highlights

The Hokkedo is a building that combines an image hall embodying eighth-century Tenpyo culture with a worship hall displaying the bold features of the Daibutsuyo style from the twelfth and thirteenth centuries (Kamakura period). It presents in clear juxtaposition the two great architectural styles for which Todaiji temple is known.

More than 450 years separate the construction of the two parts. It is as if we of the twenty-first century were to build a worship hall in front of an image hall built in the sixteenth century (Muromachi period) and sought to unify the new and the old by spanning the two with one roof. The Kamakura-period craftsmen who undertook to build Hokkedo's worship hall must have felt at least the same degree of distance in time from the Nara-period hall before them. Their greatest challenge, which would be the same today as it was back then, was to preserve and restore the new and the old in harmony, bringing into being a whole building that employed the most advanced techniques and styles of their time.

On the exterior, the intent to harmonize old and new is evident especially on the west side. Of the building's eight spans, the four on the north end are the Nara-period image hall and the four on the south end are the Kamakura worship hall and *tsukuriai*, but few without prior knowledge of this building would guess that four and a half centuries passed between the construction of the two parts. Although the roof is of an irregular shape with its connection of the hipped roof over the image hall and the hip-and-gable roof over the worship hall, it is roofed with the same material, so the difference is hardly noticeable. The railing around the building adds an additional element of unity. If we examine the posts, bracket complexes, doors, and other elements, we can see clearly the differences in style, but the differences have been restrained, and effort made to achieve harmony between the two parts.

The interior of the worship hall, meanwhile, is alive with the distinctive vigor of the Daibutsuyo style, a quality that derives from the complexity of the framework. The hall is long and narrow, 2 bays by 5 bays. Spanning the 7.7-meter high space is a grand series of double tie-beam complexes. What is notable about these complexes is that the builder was not satisfied with just using sets of double tie-beams, but stacked up more horizontal members above each one in a determined, almost obsessive, effort to strengthen the structure. This structural feat resulted in a worship hall that is bright and full of energy, and together with the image hall creates a bracing harmony and contrast of old and new, light and shadow.

正堂（手前）・礼堂の棟
Ridges of the image hall (foreground) and the worship hall

西側。北側（左）4間が奈良時代の正堂、南側（右）4間が鎌倉時代の造り合いの間と礼堂。450年以上差のある二つの建物を屋根でつなげる。北側は寄棟造、南側は入母屋造

West side. The four bays on the north end (at left) are the image hall from the Nara period while the four bays on the south (at right) are the worship hall from the Kamamura period and the *tsukuriai* space that connects the two. Constructed more than 450 years apart, the two buildings are joined by their roofs: a *yosemune* hipped roof at the north and an *irimoya* hip-and-gable roof at the south.

正堂の軒裏。長押をまわし、頭貫を通し、出組で軒桁を受ける

Underside of the eaves at the image hall. The structure has head-penetrating tie beams connecting the pillars, *nageshi* tie beams wrapped around the outside, and one-stepped bracket complexes supporting the eaves purlins.

礼堂の軒裏。長押はなく、内法貫を通し、その木鼻には大仏様繰形をつける。頭貫でつなげ、挿肘木による組物で軒桁を受けた鎌倉時代の大仏様による構成

Underside of the eaves at the worship hall. *Nuki* penetrating tie beams—with nosings incised in the Daibutsuyo style—are set over doors and windows instead of using *nageshi* tie beams (see opposite page). The structure, using bracket complexes that incorporate *sashihijiki* bracket arms inserted directly into the pillars to support the eaves, is typical of the Kamakura period Daibutsuyo style.

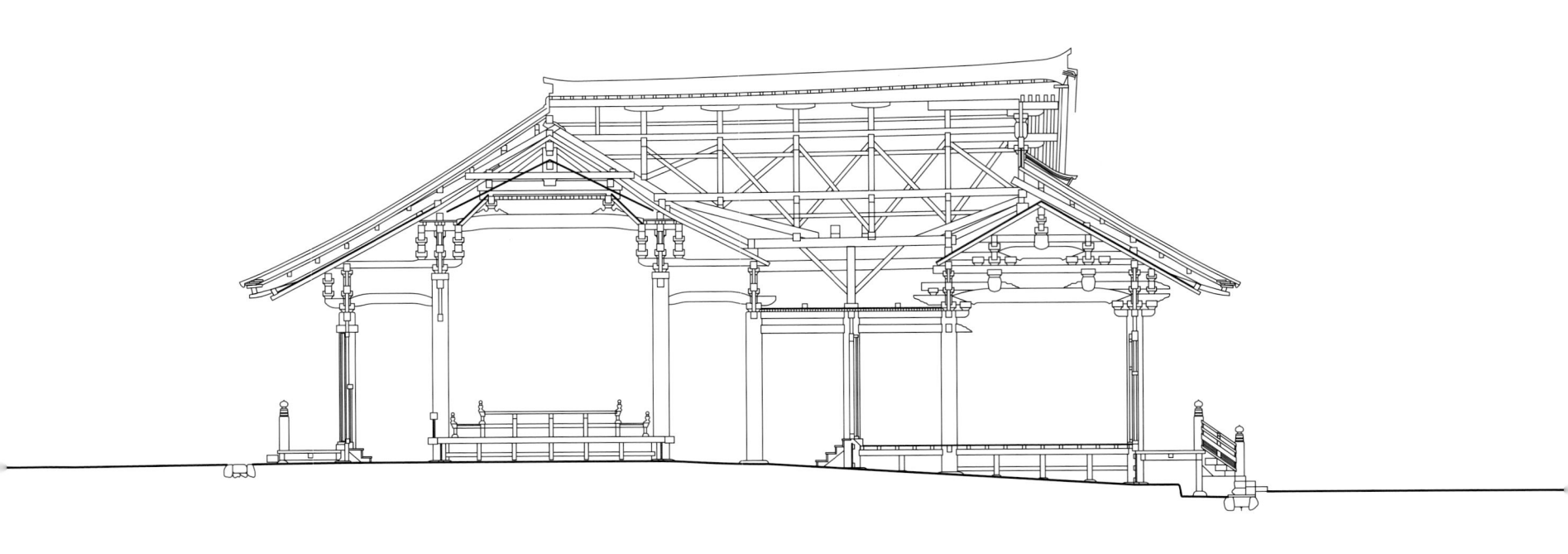

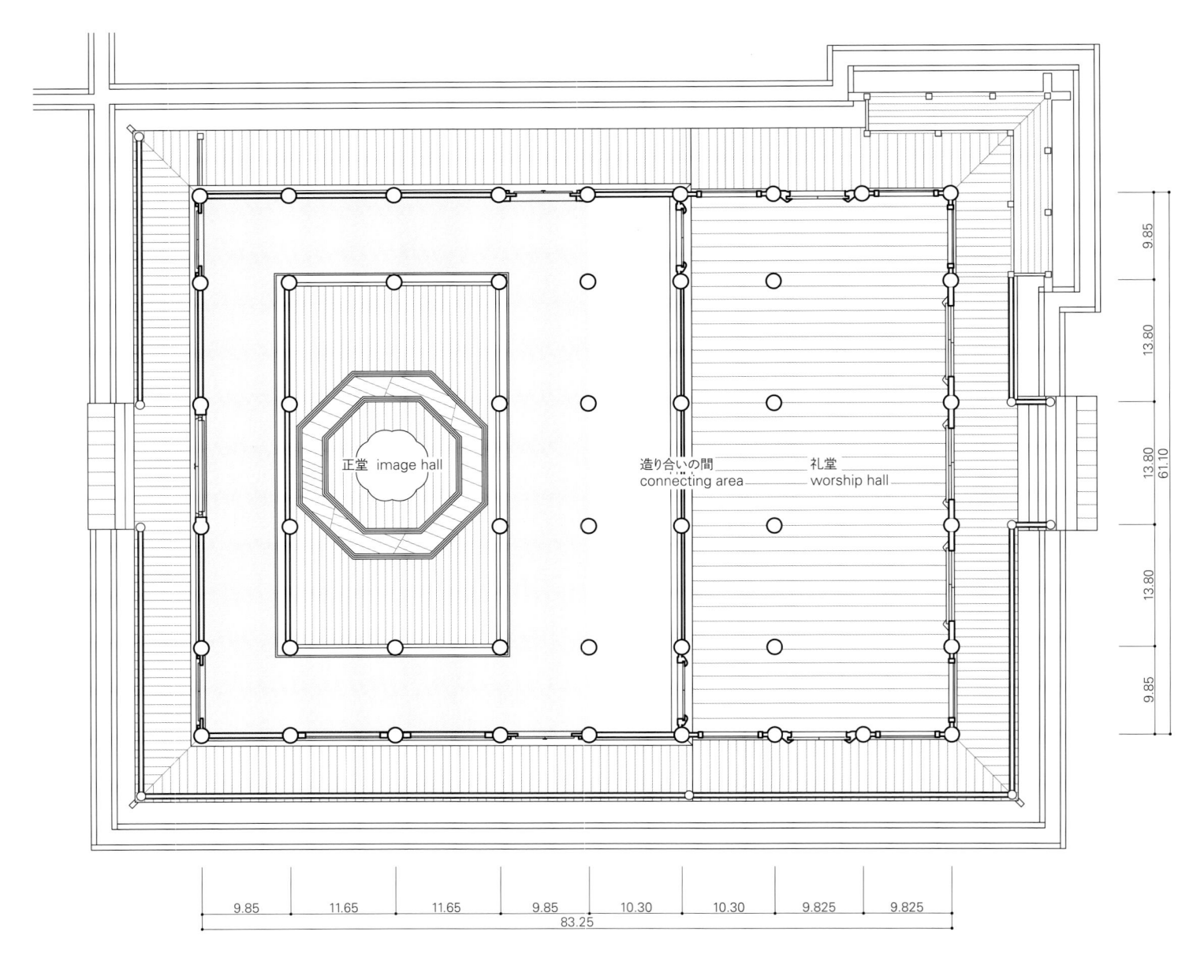

正堂 image hall　造り合いの間 connecting area　礼堂 worship hall

(上)南北断面図 (下)平面図
成立過程の異なる非対称形の建物2棟をつなぎ、その上に大屋根をかけており、力のバランスを取る必要がある。そのため、礼堂の小屋組の構造は横架材を何重にも用いて、とくに堅固にしている

(Top) North-south section. (Bottom) Floor plan.
Using a shared roof to connect two asymmetrical buildings built at different times required finding a way to achieve a balance of forces. This is why the structure of the roof framework in the worship hall is particularly solid, using multiple tiers of horizontal members.

礼堂ディテール。虹梁上に手先肘木を重ね、横架材の重複が力強い構造表現となる

Worship hall details. With tiers of bracket arms above the rainbow beams, the overlapping horizontal structural members convey the building's structural strength.

およそ1,300年前に華開いた天平文化が息づく正堂内部。中央の本尊・不空羂索観音立像は一切の衆生を救う観音とされる。左右に見えるのは金剛力士立像(阿形と吽形)で、仏法を守護する神。堂内は折上組入天井を張り、中央柱は幡、長押下は華鬘で荘厳されている

The Tempyo culture that flourished 1,300 years ago lives on in the image hall interior. The principal image is a standing statue of Fukukensaku Kannon, said to be the manifestation of Kannon that leads all living things to salvation. Visible to the left and right are statues of Agyo and Ungyo, the Kongo Rikishi guardian kings who protect the teachings of the Buddha. The ceiling over the image of Kannon is latticed; banners (*ban*) hang on the central pillars, and a decoration (*keman*) dangles from the tie beam between them.

東大寺 大湯屋

重要文化財
建立年代　1408年
所在地　　奈良県奈良市

Todaiji Temple Oyuya (Great Bathhouse)

Important Cultural Property
Completed: 1408
Location: Nara, Nara prefecture

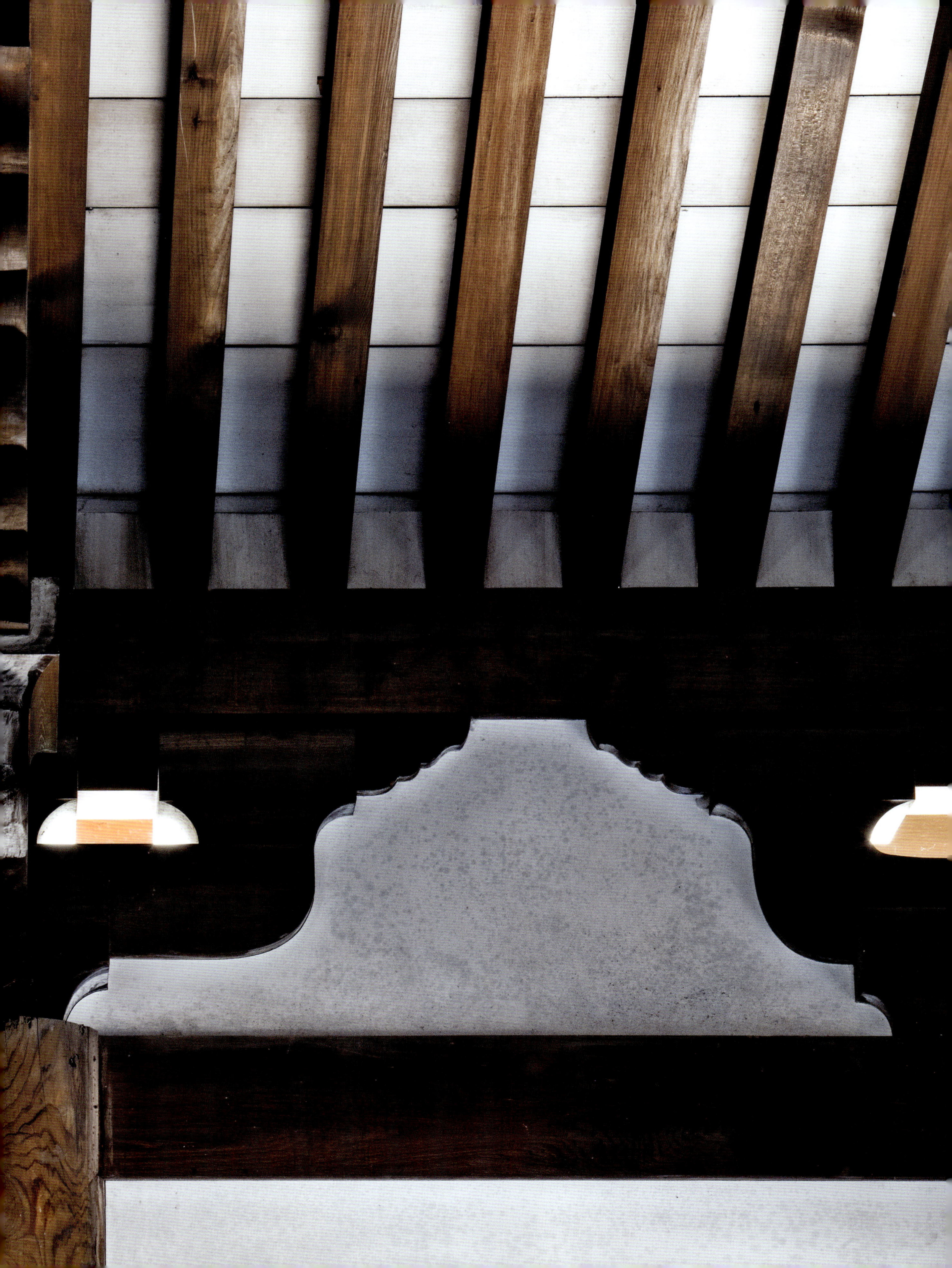

時代背景

　仏教寺院と風呂との関係は、古く深い。沐浴して身を清めることは、仏に仕える者の大切な修行の一つとされ、古くから寺院の境内に湯屋が建てられてきた。東大寺では、古くは「温室院」と記され、1104（長治元）年に「大湯屋」と記録にある建物は、『七大寺巡礼私記』に従えば、現在の建物とほぼ同じ場所に立っていたと考えられている。平家による兵火でこのあたりも焼けたが、湯屋を再興したのは重源で、1197（建久8）年に湯船を鋳造している。これが現在、大湯屋内に残る重要文化財の鉄湯船である。建物の方は重源が関わったものは現存せず、1239（延応元）年に「新造」されたと記され、その後1408（応永15）年の修理の際、浴室まわりの部分が大きく改築・増築された。架構・様式は大仏様を基本に、一部ディテールに禅宗様が加えられている。

　この大湯屋は寺内の僧侶のために機能した建物で、僧侶間の結束を図り、重要な決議なども行われる空間であったという。「永代不朽の寺物」「大湯屋の宝物」と『東大寺造立供養記』に誇り高く記録されて今に伝えられる重源の鉄湯船や、その亡き後にも、やはり大仏様を色濃く継承して建てられた格調高い建物から、この湯屋が実用に資するとともに、ある種の神聖な空間として位置づけられてきた歴史が感じられる。

特徴と見どころ

　幾重にも透けをつくりだす連子窓と格子に、光の洩れ入るリズミカルな組物。湯屋には湿気がこもらないようにすることが重要だが、ここでは換気・通風に配慮した合目的性が、そのまま美しいデザインとなり、爽やかで現代的な光の空間をつくりだしている。ものとものを離し、くっつけない。そうしてつくられた隙間への美意識。そこには、現代に通じる磨かれたデザイン力が発揮されている。

　前室と浴室との間には板扉を入れて仕切るが、その上は連子の欄間とし、その空隙からは奥の唐破風の曲線が垣間見える。これは浴室のなかにつくられた風呂屋形の屋根で、室内のなかに、さらに室内を囲いこんだ入れ子状の空間になっている。機能面から見れば、湯の熱気や蒸気を逃さぬための工夫であろうが、風呂屋形の前面は「てりむくり」のついた立派な唐破風造となっており、そこが日常とは異なる特別な空間であることを暗示している。この風呂屋形の部分については江戸時代の補修が入り、材もすべてその頃のもので、室町時代の状態は不明という。しかし、唐破風と湯屋とのシンボリックな組み合わせが、古い起源をもつこのような遺構で見られることは興味深い。

東西断面図　East–west section

Historical Background

Buddhist temple connections with baths are old and deep. As performing ablutions to cleanse the body is considered to be part of the training of a devotee of Buddhism, bathhouses have been built on temple grounds since ancient times. The great bathhouse at Todaiji temple was originally called the Onshitsuin ("Hothouse Hall"), and the building that was recorded as Oyuya (Great Bathhouse) in 1104 is believed to have stood in the same location as the current building. The bathhouse, after the attack by the Taira army, was rebuilt by the monk Chogen and the iron tub was cast in 1197. Chogen's iron tub is designated an Important Cultural Property but the building currently housing it is not Chogen's. The present building was built in 1239, and the dressing and bathing room underwent major remodeling and expansion during repairs done in 1408, during the Muromachi period. Structurally the building is basically of the older Daibutsuyo architectural style introduced by Chogen, but it incorporates details in the later Zen style (Zenshuyo).

Todaiji temple's Oyuya was built as a functional amenity for the temple's priests, but it was also considered a place for strengthening the solidarity among them, and it is said that sometimes very important decisions were made there. Noting the descriptions in old documents hailing the iron tub as an "eternal and enduring temple fixture" and "the treasure of the Oyuya," and judging from the elegant structure of the building deeply imprinted with the Daibutsuyo style in remodeling done even after Chogen's death, we can sense how this building not only served a practical purpose but through its long history was thought to be a kind of sacred place.

Characteristics and Highlights

The transparency of the building afforded by layers of latticed windows and transoms and the rhythmic play of light shining through openings in the bracket complexes testifies to the need to keep air moving and moisture released so important in a bathhouse, but the contrivances for ventilation and airflow resulted here in a beautiful design, creating a space with a bracingly modern sense of light. Elements are kept separate from one another, leading to an aesthetic of crevices and gaps. One feels the application of a highly polished sense of design that feels right at home in the present day.

The anteroom is separated from the dressing and bathing room by wooden doors with lattice transoms. Through the spaces between the lattice boards, we can see the undulating lines of the *karahafu* bargeboard of the bathing enclosure, forming a kind of nested structure within the dressing room. Functionally the bathing enclosure serves the purpose of retaining heat and steam, but the *karahafu*, with its elegant curves at the front, marks the space within it as special, setting it aside from the ordinary and everyday. Repaired during the Edo period (1615–1867), the material of the bath roof is entirely from Edo times. How the building looked during the Muromachi period is unknown. It is of great interest, nevertheless, that the symbolic combination of a *karahafu* roofline and bathhouse can be found in the remains of such an ancient structure.

透けの重なり。湯屋に必要な通風への配慮が、美しいデザインへと昇華する

Overlapping openings. Attention to the need for good ventilation results in a beautiful design.

5種類もの連子で光を濾過した空間。各場所で連子子(棒)の太さや間隔を変え、風通しの量を調節するとともに、変化に富んだ光と影の景をつくりだす。庇1間通りは化粧屋根裏とする

The space is illuminated by light filtered through five different varieties of *renjimado* slatted windows. The thickness and interval between the slats varies at each location, both adjusting the level of air flow and creating a rich landscape of light and shadow. The one-bay perimeter space has a sloping ceiling.

斗と斗の間を閉ざさず、開放して通気口とする。構造体に風を通し、上部にこもる湿気を逃す工夫は湯屋らしい爽やかなディテール。桁を支える実肘木には大仏様の繰形がつく

The spaces between the *masu* bearing blocks are left open for ventilation rather than closed off as part of the wall, drawing fresh air into the structure and permitting moisture that would otherwise linger at the upper part of the room to escape—a refreshing detail befitting a bathhouse. The *sanehijiki* purlin-bearing bracket arms incorporate Daibutsuyo-style carving.

桁と梁が交差する隅までも、通気のデザインを徹底する。
虹梁端部は断面を細くし、上部小壁の余白を生かす

The incorporation of ventilation into the design extends even to the corners where the purlins and transverse beams intersect. The narrowing at the end of the rainbow beam makes room for more of the white wall above.

前室の扉を開けると、着替え室、さらにそのなかに唐破風のついた風呂
屋形がある。両側の壁面には粗い連子窓を入れ、風と光を多く入れる。
壁には腰板を張り、白壁を美しく保つディテールとなっている

Opening the doors from the anteroom leads to the dressing room and—within it—the enclosed bathing room with its *karahafu* undulating gable. Fitted along both sides of the room, *renjimado* slatted windows with widely spaced slats draw in abundant air and light. The walls are a beautiful white plaster above; below, wooden wainscoting protects the lower parts from the soiling of daily use.

室内のなかに室内(風呂屋形)を囲いこんだ
入れ子状の空間

The bathing enclosure is surrounded by interior space.

風呂屋形には唐破風がつき、そこが特別な空間であることを表わす。柱は下部を石柱とし、その上に木を継ぎ立て、水気に対処したデザイン

The roof of the bathing enclosure includes a *karahafu* undulating gable, marking it as a special space. The pillars are designed to address water issues by joining stone sections at the bottom to the wood above.

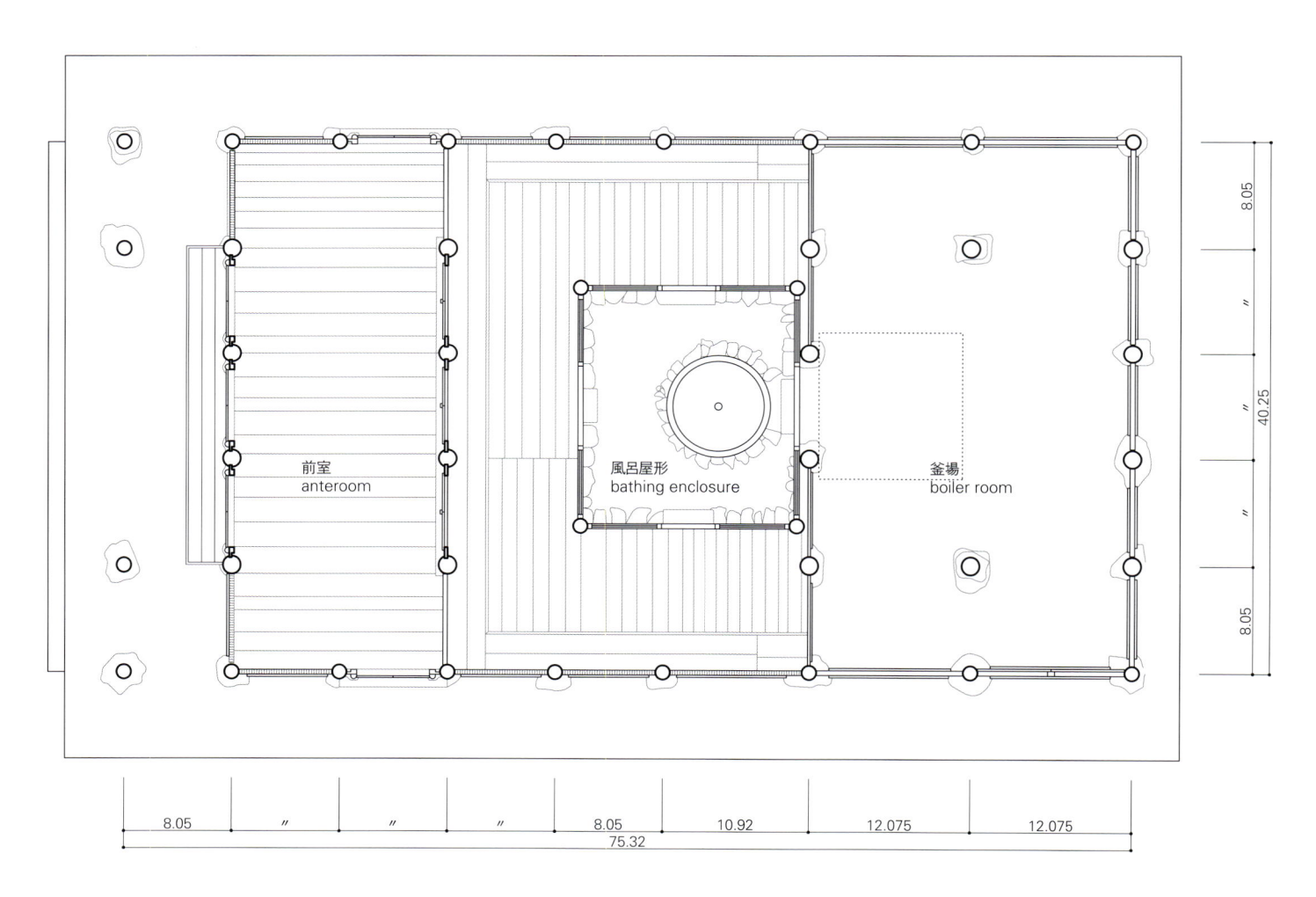

(上)釜場の煙出し
(下)平面図。風呂屋形のなかには重源が鋳造させた
鉄湯船(直径約2.4m・重文)が収められている

(Top) The smoke louver above the boiler room.
(Bottom) Floor plan. The bathing enclosure contains the iron bathtub that Chōgen had cast (2.4 meters in diameter; Important Cultural Property).

釜場。風呂は直焚きではなく、ここで湯を沸かし、裏扉（左下）から鉄湯船に注ぐ。日本建築は煙突をつけない。そのため天井を高くし、煙出しを取って上昇気流をつくりだし、薪の燃焼を促す。屋根瓦に当たった光が煙出しから入射し、白い天井裏に反射した光が降り注ぐ

Boiler room. Rather than heating the bathtub directly, water is boiled in the boiler room and fed to the bath through a rear door (at left). Japanese architecture does not use chimneys. Instead, smoke louvers are installed in high ceilings to create an updraft that promotes the burning of the firewood. Sunlight striking the roof tiles enters through the smoke louver, reflects off the white ceiling, and spills down into the room.

北側から見た大湯屋。正面(右)が入母屋造、背面(左)が
切妻造となり、煙出しをつける。田んぼと土塀を前にして、
変則的な屋根の形が印象深い佇まいをつくる

The Oyuya seen from the north. The front of the building (at right) has an *irimoya* hip-and-gable roof while the back of the building (at left) has a *kirizuma* gabled roof with smoke louvers at its peak. The irregular shape of the roof is striking when seen with the earthen walls and rice fields in the foreground.

東大寺 二月堂

国宝
建立年代　1669年上棟
所在地　　奈良県奈良市

Todaiji Temple Nigatsudo Hall

National Treasure
Completed: 1669/framework
Location: Nara, Nara prefecture

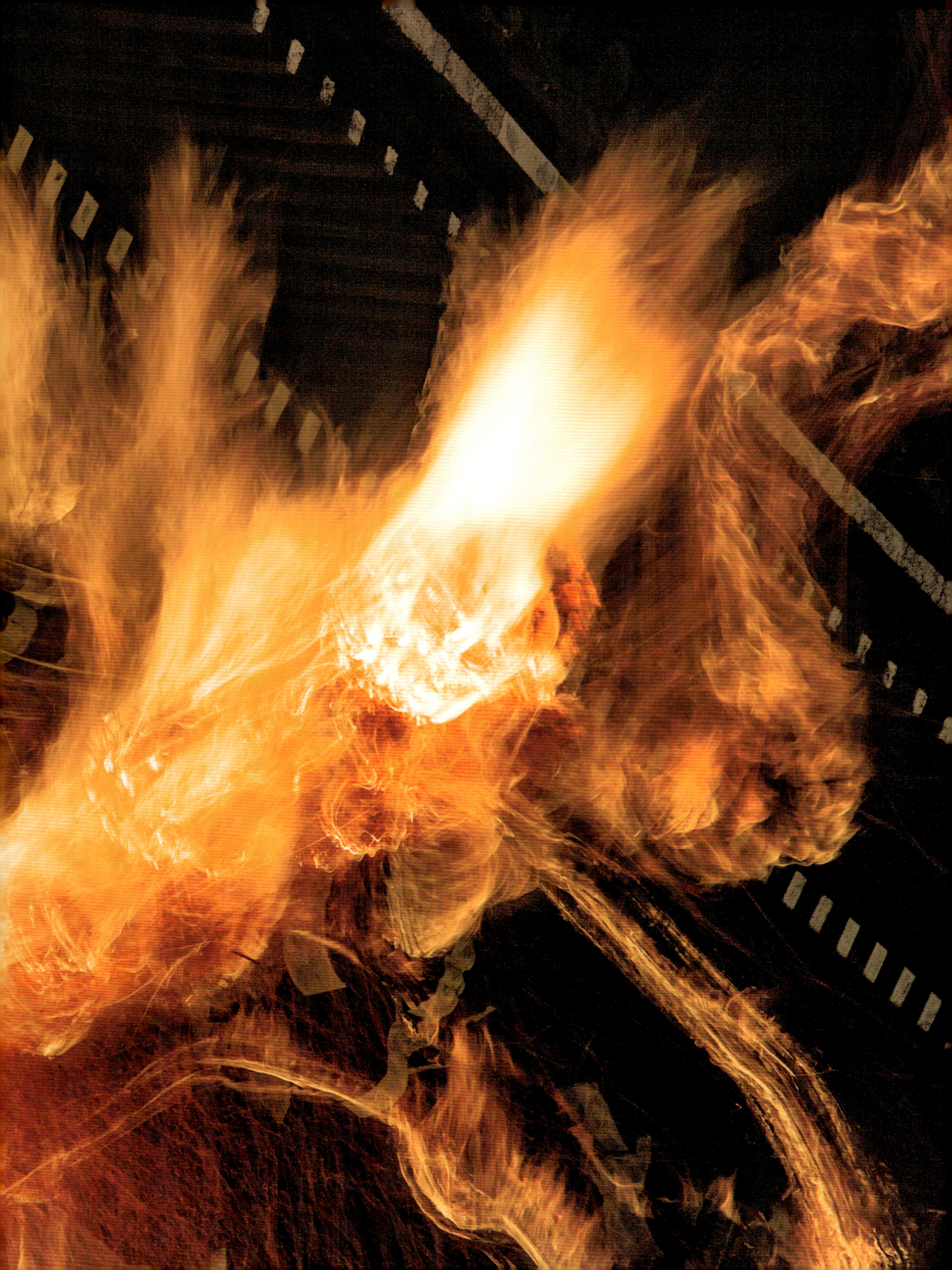

時代背景

修二会（お水取り）の建物として知られる二月堂は、法華堂の北東、観音山の斜面に位置する。大仏殿より40mほど高い立地で、西向きに立ち、高欄のついた吹放ちの広縁からは東大寺伽藍や奈良市街地の眺望が広がる。二月堂は東大寺を襲った2回の兵火を法華堂とともに逃れたが、1667（寛文7）年、修二会の最中に火災で焼失した。その2年後に再建されたのが現存する建物である。

二月堂の起源は古く、その成立は修二会と不可分の関係にある。修二会は、正式には十一面悔過といい、過去に犯した過ちを二月堂の本尊である十一面観世音菩薩像の前で懺悔する行法である。記録の初出は大仏開眼供養と同年の752（天平勝宝4）年にさかのぼり（『東大寺要録』）、現在まで途絶えることなく毎年旧暦2月に行われてきたと伝えられる。その行法のためにある建物がこの堂で、創建は752（天平勝宝4）年よりは下らないとされ、『要録』の記述*12からは、正面3間、側面1間、前後一間通り庇つきと解釈できることから、初期はごく小さな堂であったことがわかる。時とともに修二会道場として拡張が重ねられて、現建物は正面7間、側面10間、内部は外陣・内陣で構成され、そのまわりを聴聞所となる局と呼ばれる小部屋が取り囲み、その前面に礼堂を付設した複雑な平面形式へと発展した。現二月堂は前身建物の礎石を再利用し、ほぼ忠実に焼失前の間取りを踏襲して再建された。

特徴と見どころ

山を背負って際立つ単純明快な寄棟造の屋根。その大きなボリュームに対して、片持ちで突き出した縁と堂の主要部分と、さらにその下の懸造の架構部分からなるこの建物は、正面から見たとき、これら三つの構成要素における配分の比率がじつに素晴らしい。縁を支える腰組の組物は、挿肘木を用いた三手先組物とする。組物の木口に塗られた胡粉の白が、質実な感じのするこの堂に爽やかで小気味好いリズムを刻んでいる。

懸造の広縁が提供する素晴らしい眺めが人々を呼び寄せる親しみやすさとは対照的に、内部空間はひっそりと閉ざされ、俗界を寄せつけない。内陣の本尊は絶対秘仏である。修二会の際、北側の登廊から松明に導かれた連行衆が入堂し、行法の活気が漂うひととき、およそ1250年の間、厳格な修二会道場として機能してきたこの建物の本来の顔が浮かび上がる。

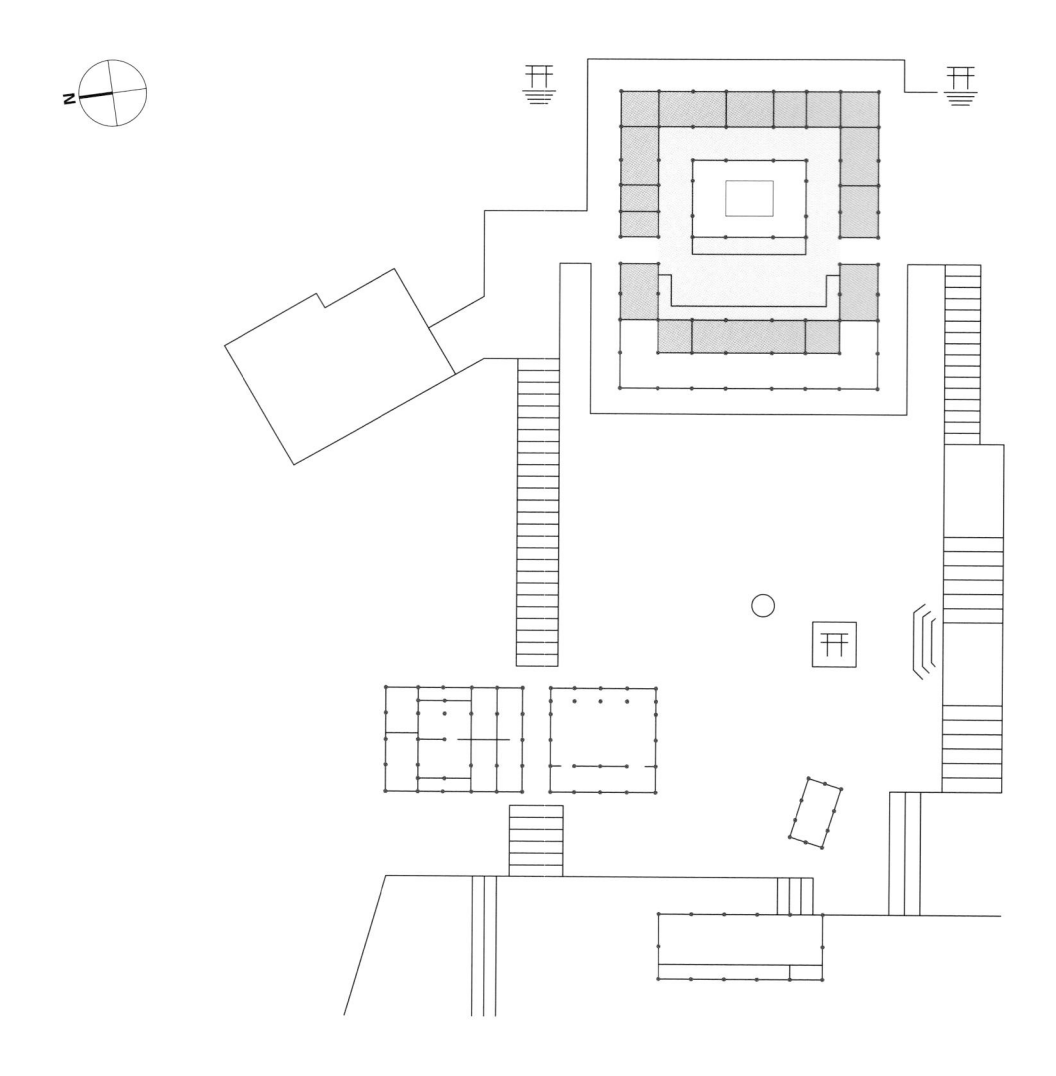

二月堂・付属施設配置図　Site plan of Nigatsudo Hall and its facilities

Historical Background

Nigatsudo hall, known as the site of the *shuni-e* (or *omizutori*, water-drawing) ceremony, stands northeast of the Hokkedo hall on the slope of Mt. Kannon. Located approximately 40 meters higher than the Great Buddha Hall and facing west, Nigatsudo's wide, open-air veranda surrounded by handrails, commands a panorama of the Todaiji temple complex and the city of Nara below. Along with the Hokkedo, the old Nigatsudo escaped the ravages of war that struck Todaiji twice, but it was consumed by fire during the *shuni-e* ceremony in 1667. Two years after the fire, the current building was built on the old foundations, and is believed to have closely followed the plans of the former structure.

The Nigatsudo's origins are ancient, and its founding is inseparable from the *shuni-e* ceremony. The ceremony, officially called Juichimen Keka, is for the confession of sins (*keka*) before the Juichimen (Eleven-headed) Kannon statue, the principal image enshrined in the sanctuary. The ceremony is first recorded as having been held in 752, the same year as the consecration of the Great Buddha, and has been conducted continuously every year to the present day during the second month (*nigatsu*) of the year following the lunar calendar. The original hall, which is thought to have been first built sometime before 752, was quite small. The *Todaiji yoroku* (Digest Record of Todaiji Temple) written during the Heian period, shows it to have been 3 bays wide, 1 bay deep, with a 1 bay roof extension in front and back. Expanded several times as the hall for the practice of *shuni-e*, the current building measures 7 bays wide in front, 10 bays wide on the side, and has a complex plan comprised of an outer sanctum, inner sanctum, and *raido* worship area, with a number of small rooms surrounding them.

Characteristics and Highlights

When viewed from the front, the three elements of the building—the simple and straightforward hipped roof rising against the mountain backdrop, the body of the building with its veranda jutting out into space, and the *kakezukuri* support structure composed of tall posts and penetrating ties—create a perfect proportional harmony. Long *sashihijiki* arms with three-stepped bracket complexes stretch out, supporting the broad veranda. The white wash (*gofun*) applied to the cut ends of the wood members adds a brisk rhythm to the otherwise function-centered beauty of the structure.

In contrast to the inviting quality of the wide overhung veranda offering a breathtaking view of the city, the interior space is silent and closed to the mundane world. The principal image enshrined in the inner sanctum is a *hibutsu* or image that is kept hidden from public view. The *shuni-e* ceremony is conducted in strict adherence with tradition, and when the *rengyoshu*, the eleven priests participating in the ceremony are led up the stepped corridor on the north side and across the veranda by bearers of flaming pine branch torches, the true face of the building that has functioned as the place for ceremony for more than 1,250 years comes back to life.

二月堂参籠所・食堂南面（鎌倉時代・重文）
Nigatsudo Sanrosho (Kamakura period; Important Cultural Property)

山腹の斜面に立ち、急勾配の大きな寄棟造屋根に覆われている。
西面・妻側を正面とする。下部は縁がまわり、懸造となる。屋根の軒
幅は約30m、軒から棟までの高さは約9m

Standing on a slope on the mountainside, the building is covered by a huge, steeply sloping *yosemune* hipped roof. The west end of the building, at right angles to the ridge, serves as the front. The building has an overhanging veranda in the *kakezukuri* style surrounding its lower portion. The roof measures about 30 meters wide at the eaves and about 9 meters tall from eaves to ridge.

(上)削ぎ上げた形のよい挿肘木。三手先で懸造の縁を支える。木口には腐り止めに胡粉を塗る

(Above) The *sashihijiki* bracket arms are planed in a finely shaped upward curve. *Mitesaki* three-stepped bracket complexes support the *kakezukuri* overhang style veranda. To prevent rot and cracking, the cut ends of the wooden elements are coated with *gofun*, a whitewash made from ground shells.

(右)北の登廊の石段。全86段。修二会本行の際、二月堂への動線となる

(Right) The stone steps of the covered corridor on the north. There are a total of 86 steps. Participants in the *shuni-e* ceremony pass up this corridor on their way to the Nigatsudo hall.

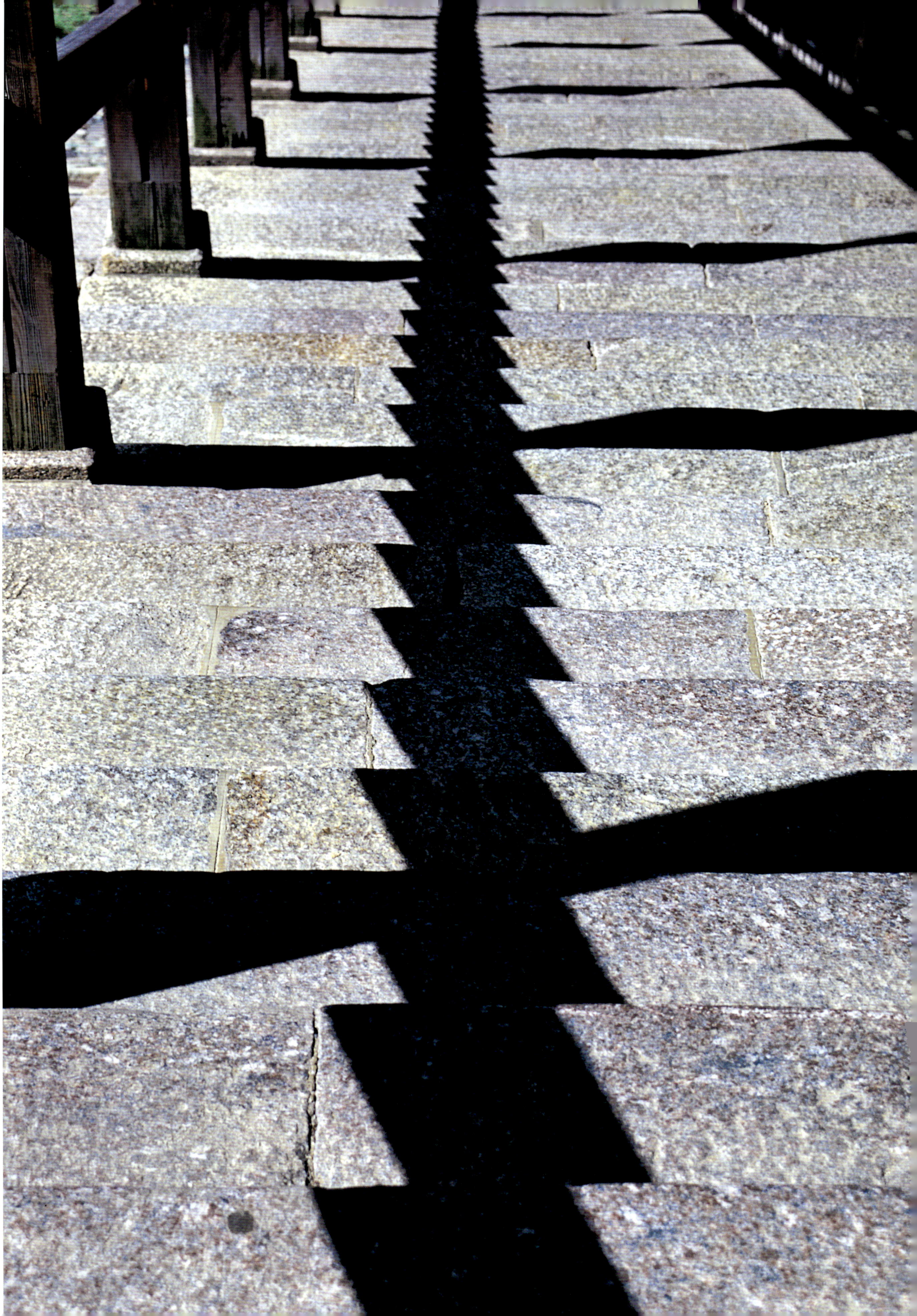

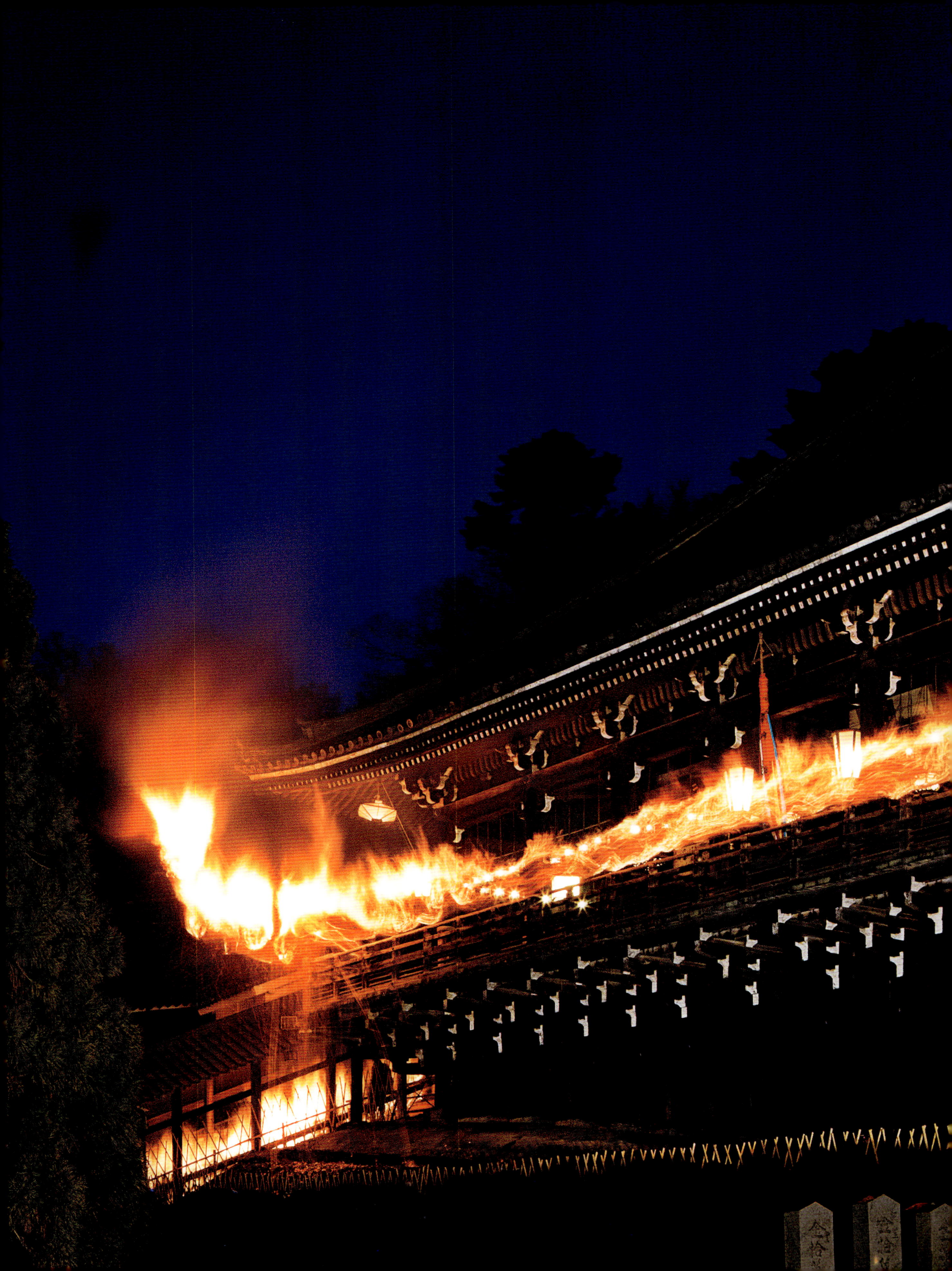

二月堂で行われる修二会の「お松明」
The *otaimatsu* (torch) portion of the *shuni-e* ceremony at Nigatsudo hall.

掲載建造物データ　Data of the Buildings

伊勢神宮
所在地　　三重県伊勢市
建立年代　2013年造替
形式　　　神明造・萱葺

法隆寺 金堂・五重塔・廻廊（国宝）
所在地　　奈良県生駒郡斑鳩町法隆寺山内
〈金堂〉
建立年代　7世紀−8世紀初頭（飛鳥時代）
規模形式　桁行5間・梁行4間・二重・初重裳階付・入母屋造・本瓦葺・
　　　　　裳階板葺
〈五重塔〉
建立年代　7世紀−8世紀初頭（飛鳥時代）
規模形式　3間五重塔婆・初重裳階付・本瓦葺・裳階板葺
〈廻廊〉
建立年代　7世紀−8世紀初頭（飛鳥時代）
規模形式　東廻廊：折曲り延長42間・一重・本瓦葺
　　　　　西廻廊：折曲り延長40間・一重・本瓦葺

正倉院 正倉（国宝）
所在地　　奈良県奈良市雑司町
建立年代　8世紀（奈良時代）
規模形式　桁行9間・梁行3間・一重・高床校倉・寄棟造・本瓦葺

唐招提寺 金堂（国宝）
所在地　　奈良県奈良市五条町
建立年代　8世紀後半（奈良時代）
規模形式　桁行7間・梁行4間・一重・寄棟造・本瓦葺

新薬師寺 本堂（国宝）
所在地　　奈良県奈良市高畑町
建立年代　8世紀（奈良時代）
規模形式　桁行7間・梁行5間・一重・入母屋造・本瓦葺

元興寺 極楽坊禅室（国宝）
所在地　　奈良県奈良市中院町
建立年代　1200年前後（鎌倉時代前期）
規模形式　桁行4間・梁行4間・一重・切妻造・本瓦葺

室生寺 五重塔・金堂・灌頂堂（国宝）
所在地　　奈良県宇陀市室生区室生
〈五重塔〉
建立年代　800年頃（奈良時代末−平安時代初期）
規模形式　3間五重塔婆・檜皮葺
〈金堂〉
建立年代　9世紀（平安時代前期）
規模形式　桁行5間・梁行5間・一重・寄棟造・
　　　　　正面1間通り縋破風付葺き下ろし・柿葺
〈灌頂堂〉
建立年代　1308年（鎌倉時代後期）
規模形式　桁行5間・梁行5間・一重・入母屋造・檜皮葺

醍醐寺 五重塔（国宝）
所在地　　京都府京都市伏見区醍醐伽藍町
建立年代　951年（平安時代中期）
規模形式　3間五重塔婆・本瓦葺

三徳山三佛寺 奥院（投入堂）（国宝）
所在地　　鳥取県東伯郡三朝町大字三徳
建立年代　11世紀後半−12世紀（平安時代後期）
規模形式　懸造・桁行1間・梁行2間・一重・流造・
　　　　　両側面に庇屋根および隅庇屋根付・檜皮葺
　　　　　愛染堂：懸造・桁行1間・梁行1間・一重・切妻造・檜皮葺

平等院 鳳凰堂（国宝）
所在地　　京都府宇治市宇治蓮華
建立年代　1053年（平安時代中期）
規模形式　中堂：桁行3間・梁行2間・一重裳階付・入母屋造・本瓦葺
　　　　　両翼廊：各桁行折曲り延長8間・梁行1間
　　　　　　　　　隅楼二重3階・宝形造　廊一重2階・切妻造・本瓦葺
　　　　　尾廊：桁行7間・梁行1間・一重・切妻造・本瓦葺

法界寺 阿弥陀堂（国宝）
所在地　　京都府京都市伏見区日野西大道町
建立　　　1226年頃（鎌倉時代前期）
規模形式　桁行5間・梁行5間・一重裳階付・宝形造・檜皮葺

宇治上神社（国宝）
所在地　　京都府宇治市宇治山田
建立年代　本殿：11世紀末−12世紀（平安時代後期）
　　　　　拝殿：13世紀（鎌倉時代前期）
規模形式　本殿：桁行5間・梁行3間・一重・流造・檜皮葺・内殿3社・
　　　　　　　　各一間社流造
　　　　　拝殿：桁行6間・梁行3間・一重・切妻造・両妻1間通り庇付・
　　　　　　　　向拝1間・檜皮葺

嚴島神社（国宝）

所在地　広島県廿日市市宮島町
建立年代　13世紀前半－17世紀前半（鎌倉時代前期－安土桃山時代）
規模形式　本社
　　　　　本殿：桁行正面8間・背面9間・梁行4間・一重・
　　　　　　　　両流造・檜皮葺
　　　　　幣殿：桁行1間・梁行1間・一重・両下造・檜皮葺
　　　　　拝殿：桁行10間・梁行3間・一重・両端縋破風付入母屋造・
　　　　　　　　檜皮葺・背面両端庇間付
　　　　　本社祓殿
　　　　　　桁行6間・梁行3間・一重・入母屋造・妻入・
　　　　　　背面拝殿屋根に接続・檜皮葺
　　　　　摂社客神社
　　　　　本殿：桁行5間・梁行4間・一重・両流造・檜皮葺
　　　　　幣殿：桁行1間・梁行1間・一重・両下造・檜皮葺
　　　　　拝殿：桁行9間・梁行3間・一重・切妻造・
　　　　　　　　両端庇屋根付・檜皮葺
　　　　　摂社客神社祓殿
　　　　　　桁行4間・梁行3間・一重・入母屋造・妻入・
　　　　　　背面拝殿屋根に接続・檜皮葺
　　　　　廻廊
　　　　　東廻廊：折曲り延長45間・一重・切妻造・檜皮葺
　　　　　西廻廊：折曲り延長62間・一重・東端切妻造・
　　　　　　　　　西端唐破風造・檜皮葺

春日大社 摂社若宮神社（重要文化財）

所在地　奈良県奈良市春日野町
建立年代　17世紀（桃山時代）－19世紀（江戸時代）
規模形式　本殿：一間社流造・檜皮葺
　　　　　拝舎：桁行2間・梁行1間・一重・切妻造・正面御廊に接続・
　　　　　　　　檜皮葺
　　　　　細殿および神楽殿：桁行10間・梁行3間・一重・流造・檜皮葺

高山寺 石水院（国宝）

所在地　京都府京都市右京区梅ケ畑栂尾町
建立年代　13世紀（鎌倉時代）
規模形式　桁行正面3間・背面4間・梁行3間・正面1間通り庇・一重・
　　　　　入母屋造・妻入・庇葺き下ろし・向拝1間・柿葺

石山寺 多宝塔（国宝）

所在地　滋賀県大津市石山寺
建立年代　1194年（鎌倉時代初期）
規模形式　3間多宝塔・檜皮葺

興福寺 北円堂・東金堂・三重塔（国宝）

所在地　奈良県奈良市登大路町
〈北円堂〉
建立年代　1210年（鎌倉時代前期）
規模形式　八角円堂・一重・本瓦葺
〈東金堂〉
建立年代　1415年（室町時代）
規模形式　桁行7間・梁行4間・一重・寄棟造・本瓦葺
〈三重塔〉
建立年代　12世紀末－13世紀（鎌倉時代）
規模形式　3間三重塔婆・本瓦葺

浄土寺 浄土堂（国宝）

所在地　兵庫県小野市浄谷町
建立年代　1194年上棟（鎌倉時代初期）
規模形式　桁行3間・梁行3間・一重・宝形造・本瓦葺

東大寺 金堂・南大門・法華堂・二月堂（国宝）

所在地　奈良県奈良市雑司町
〈金堂〉
建立年代　1705年上棟（江戸時代中期）
規模形式　梁行5間・桁行5間・一重裳階付・寄棟造・本瓦葺・
　　　　　正面唐破風付・銅板葺
〈南大門〉
建立年代　1199年上棟（鎌倉時代初期）
規模形式　5間3戸二重門・入母屋造・本瓦葺
〈法華堂〉
建立年代　正堂：8世紀（奈良時代）
　　　　　礼堂：12世紀末－13世紀（鎌倉時代）
規模形式　正面5間・側面8間・前部入母屋造・後部寄棟造・本瓦葺
〈二月堂〉
建立年代　1669年上棟（江戸時代中期）
規模形式　懸造・桁行10間・梁行7間・一重・寄棟造・本瓦葺

東大寺 大湯屋（重要文化財）

所在地　奈良県奈良市雑司町
建立年代　1408年（室町時代）
規模形式　桁行8間・梁行5間・一重・正面入母屋造・背面切妻造・
　　　　　妻入・本瓦葺

注　Notes

*1　西岡常一・小原二郎『法隆寺を支えた木』（NHKブックス318）日本放送出版協会　1978年
　　Tsunekazu Nishioka, Jiro Kohara, *The Building of Horyu-ji: The Technique and Wood that Made It Possible*, (Japan Library), Michael Brase trans., Japan Publishing Industry Foundation for Culture, 2016.
*2　奈良六大寺大観刊行会編『奈良六大寺大観』（1, 法隆寺1）岩波書店　1972年　p.19参照
*3　平成の大修理の際の発掘調査により、金堂創建時の基壇版築土層から出土した土器から、その版築の上限年代が8世紀第四四半世紀とされた。「史跡唐招提寺旧境内 2014年度発掘調査出土 三彩瓦について」（奈良県立橿原考古学研究所・報道発表資料）奈良県立橿原考古学研究所　2014年10月9日
　　〈http://www.kashikoken.jp/from-site/2014/toshodaiji_sansai_press.pdf〉（参照2016-1-19）
*4　奈良教育大学編「新薬師寺旧境内―奈良教育大学構内遺跡の埋蔵文化財発掘調査報告書―」2012年3月30日
　　奈良教育大学〈http://near.nara-edu.ac.jp/handle/10105/8554〉（参照2016-1-18）
*5　大岡實『南都七大寺の研究』中央公論美術出版　1966年　p.139参照
*6　松田敏行「国宝室生寺五重塔 災害復旧工事について」（月刊文化財440）第一法規　2000年
*7　窪寺茂「塗装と飾金具、国宝・三仏寺投入堂の荘厳」（奈良文化財研究所紀要2007）奈良文化財研究所　2007年
　　〈http://repository.nabunken.go.jp/dspace/bitstream/11177/634/1/BA67898227_2007_050_051.pdf〉（参照2016-2-29）
*8　大岡實『日本建築の意匠と技法』中央公論美術出版　1971年　pp.100-104
*9　小松茂美編・解説『春日権現験記絵 上』（続・日本の絵巻13）中央公論社　1991年　p.64, p.85
*10　仏書刊行会編「高野春秋編年輯録オンデマンド版」（大日本佛教全書131）2007年　p.17
*11　『続日本記』天平15年10月15日詔
　　「一枝の草、一把の土を持ちて像を助け造らむと情（こころ）に願はば、恣（ほしきまま）に之を聴（ゆる）せ」
　　黒板勝美『續日本記』（國史大系2）吉川弘文館　1966年　p.175参考
*12　羂索院に付属する建物として「三間二面庇瓦葺二月堂一宇」と記述される（諸院章第四）。筒井英俊編・校訂『東大寺要録』国書刊行会　1971年　p.94

主要参考文献　References

[全般]

浅野 清編『日本建築の構造』（日本の美術245）至文堂　1986年
伊藤ていじ・ほか編『名建築選』（日本名建築写真選集20）新潮社　1993年
伊藤延男編『鎌倉建築』（日本の美術198）至文堂　1982年
伊藤延男編『日本建築の装飾』（日本の美術246）至文堂　1986年
井上充夫『日本建築の空間』（SD選書37）鹿島出版会　1969年
太田博太郎『日本建築史序説』（増補第3版）彰国社　2009年
川上 貢編『室町建築』（日本の美術199）至文堂　1982年
神代雄一郎編『日本建築の空間』（日本の美術244）至文堂　1986年
工藤圭章編『平安建築』（日本の美術197）至文堂　1982年
鈴木嘉吉編『飛鳥・奈良建築』（日本の美術196）至文堂　1982年
中川 武『建築様式の歴史と表現―いま、日本建築を劇的に―』彰国社　1987年
中川 武編『日本建築みどころ事典』東京堂出版　1990年
西澤文隆『日本名建築の美―その心と形―』講談社　1990年
濱島正士『寺社建築の鑑賞基礎知識』至文堂　1992年

［神社］

伊藤ていじ・ほか編『厳島神社』（日本名建築写真選集8）新潮社 1992年
稲垣栄三『神社と霊廟』（原色日本の美術16）小学館 1968年
稲垣栄三編『古代の神社建築』（日本の美術81）至文堂 1973年
太田博太郎・稲垣栄三編『日本建築史基礎資料集成』（2, 社殿2）中央公論美術出版 1972年
太田博太郎・稲垣栄三編『日本建築史基礎資料集成』（1, 社殿1）中央公論美術出版 1998年
福山敏男編『中世の神社建築』（日本の美術129）至文堂 1977年
福山敏男・岡田英男編『春日大社建築史論』綜芸舎 1978年

［寺院］

浅野清『奈良時代建築の研究』中央公論美術出版 1969年
秋山光和・ほか編『平等院大観』（1, 建築）岩波書店 1988年
伊藤ていじ・ほか編『室生寺』（日本名建築写真選集1），『東大寺』（同2），『平等院』（同3），『法隆寺』（同4），
　『唐招提寺』（同5），『醍醐寺』（同9）新潮社 1992年
伊藤延男編『密教建築』（日本の美術143）至文堂 1978年
井上靖・葉上照澄『高山寺』（古寺巡礼 京都15）淡交社 1977年
今西良男「国宝 唐招提寺金堂保存修理」（GBRC, 138）日本建築総合試験所 2009年
大岡實『南都七大寺の研究』中央公論美術出版 1966年
大岡實『日本建築の意匠と技法』中央公論美術出版 1971年
太田博太郎・澤村 仁編『日本建築史基礎資料集成』（4・仏堂1）中央公論美術出版 1981年
太田博太郎・工藤圭章編『日本建築史基礎資料集成』（11・塔婆1）中央公論美術出版 1984年
太田博太郎・濱島正士編『日本建築史基礎資料集成』（12・塔婆2）中央公論美術出版 1999年
太田博太郎・澤村 仁編『日本建築史基礎資料集成』（5・仏堂2）中央公論美術出版 2006年
太田博太郎・ほか編『大和古寺大観』（6, 室生寺）岩波書店 1976年
太田博太郎・ほか編『大和古寺大観』（3, 元興寺極楽坊・元興寺・大安寺・般若寺・十輪院）岩波書店 1977年
太田博太郎・ほか編『大和古寺大観』（4, 新薬師寺・白毫寺・円成寺）岩波書店 1977年
久野健・ほか編『室生寺と南大和の古寺』（日本古寺美術全集8）集英社 1982年
国立歴史民俗博物館編『中世寺院の姿とくらし 密教・禅僧・湯屋』山川出版社 2004年
佐和隆研『醍醐寺』（寺社シリーズ1）東洋文化社 1976年
杉山信三「高山寺石水院の建築について」（月刊文化財, 211）第一法規出版 1981年
鈴木嘉吉「南都の新和様建築」（大和の古寺3）岩波書店 1981年
杉本秀太郎・中田聖観『新薬師寺』（古寺巡礼 奈良4）淡交社 1979年
中尾 堯編『旅の勧進聖 重源』（日本の名僧6）吉川弘文館 2004年
奈良六大寺大観刊行委員会編『奈良六大寺大観』（補訂版, 7, 興福寺1）岩波書店 1999年
奈良六大寺大観刊行委員会編『奈良六大寺大観』（補訂版, 12, 唐招提寺1）岩波書店 2000年
奈良六大寺大観刊行委員会編『奈良六大寺大観』（補訂版, 9, 東大寺1）岩波書店 2000年
奈良六大寺大観刊行委員会編『奈良六大寺大観』（補訂版, 1, 法隆寺1）岩波書店 2001年
濱島正士『塔の建築』（日本の美術No. 158）至文堂 1979年
山崎正和・岩城秀雄『法界寺』（古寺巡礼 京都29）淡交社 1978年

［その他］

阿部 弘「正倉について」（正倉院紀要25）宮内庁正倉院事務所 2003年
　〈http://shosoin.kunaicho.go.jp/ja-JP/Bulletin/Pdf?bno=0000000009〉（参照2016-1-21）
清水真一編『校倉』（日本の美術419）至文堂 2001年
和田軍一『正倉院案内』吉川弘文館 1996年

謝辞

ご協力に深く感謝申し上げます

神宮司庁
法隆寺
宮内庁　正倉院事務所
唐招提寺
新薬師寺
元興寺・元興寺文化財研究所
室生寺
醍醐寺
三佛寺
平等院
法界寺
宇治上神社
嚴島神社
春日大社
高山寺石水院
石山寺
興福寺
浄土寺　歓喜院　宝持院
東大寺
(掲載順)

写真提供　法隆寺
　　　　　平等院 p.177

翻訳　リン・E・リッグス
　　　武智 學
　　　ハート・ララビー

図面制作・画像オペレーション　丸谷晴道 (齋藤裕建築研究所)
レイアウト・デザインデータ制作　勝田亜加里 (デザイン実験室)

プリンティング・ディレクション　勝又紀智 (図書印刷)

Acknowledgements

Jingu Shicho
Horyuji
The Office of the Shosoin Treasure House/Imperial Household Agency
Toshodaiji
Shin Yakushiji
Gangoji/Gangoji Institute for Research of Cultural Property
Murouji
Daigoji
Sanbutsuji
Byodoin
Hokaiji
Ujigami Shrine
Itsukushima Shrine
Kasuga Taisha
Kosanji Sekisui-in
Ishiyamadera
Kofukuji
Jodoji　Kanki-in　Hoji-in
Todaiji

Photograph credits:
　All photographs ©Yutaka Saito except the mentioned below.
　Horyuji temple Kondo, Five-story Pagoda, and Corridors
　Byodoin (p. 177)

Translation: Lynne E. Riggs
　　　　　　Manabu Takechi
　　　　　　Hart Larrabee

Drawing and image processing:
　Harumichi Maruya (Yutaka Saito Architect & Associates)
Page layout and design data processing:
　Akari Katsuta (Design Laboratory)

Printing direction:
　Noritoshi Katsumata (TOSHO Printing)

著者紹介　　About the Author

齋藤 裕　建築家

1947年	北海道小樽市生まれ
	独学で建築を学ぶ
1970年	齋藤裕建築研究所を設立
1986年	日本建築家協会新人賞を「るるるる阿房」で受賞
1992年	吉田五十八賞を「好日居」で受賞
1993年	東京アートディレクターズクラブ・原弘賞を『ルイス・バラガンの建築』で受賞
1998年	日本建築学会・北海道建築賞を「曼月居」で受賞
2000年	日本建築学会・学会賞および作品選奨を「曼月居」で受賞

建築作品集に、『齋藤裕の建築』(TOTO出版　1998年)、
『現代の建築家シリーズ 齋藤裕』(鹿島出版会　1994年)がある。
また、写真を媒介として建築空間を探求し、写真集を出版する。
既刊写真集に、
『ルイス・バラガンの建築』(TOTO出版　1992年／メキシコ・ノリエガ出版　1994年／
TOTO出版・改訂版　1996年)、
『フェリックス・キャンデラの世界』(TOTO出版　1995年)、
『建築の詩人 カルロ・スカルパ』(TOTO出版　1997年)、
『カーサ・バラガン』(TOTO出版　2002年)、
『ルイス・カーンの全住宅：1940–1974年』(TOTO出版　2003年)、
『ヴィラ・マイレア／アルヴァ・アールト』(TOTO出版　2005年)、
『AALTO: 10 Selected Houses アールトの住宅』(TOTO出版　2008年)がある。
そのほかに、エッセイ集『STRONG』(住まいの図書館出版局　1991年)、
対談集『建築のエッセンス』(A. D. A. EDITA Tokyo　2000年)が出版されている。

Yutaka Saito　Architect

1947	Born in Otaru City, Hokkaido, Japan.
	Studied architecture independently.
1970	Founded Yutaka Saito Architect & Associates.
1986	Won the Japan Institute of Architects Prize of the Best Young Architect of the year for "Rurururu Abo."
1992	Won the Isoya Yoshida Prize for "Kojitsu-kyo."
1993	Won the Tokyo Art directors Club Hiromu Hara Prize for *Luis Barragan*.
1998	Won theArchitectural Institute of Japan Award for "Mangetsu-kyo."
2000	Won the 2000 Selected Architectural Design Award of the Architectural Institute of Japan for "Mangetsu-kyo."

The collection of his architectural works has been published:
Gendai no kenchikuka shirizu Saito Yutaka [Contemporary Architect: Yutaka Saito] (Kajima Shuppankai, 1994), and *Yutaka Saito: Architect* (TOTO Publishing, 1998).
Along with his architectural practice, he has begun to photograph architecture as part of his study of space and published photographic books including;
Luis Barragan (TOTO Publishing, 1992, Noriega Editores, 1994; revised edition, 1996), *Felix Candela* (TOTO Publishing, 1995), *Casa Barragan* (TOTO Publishing, 2002), *Louis I. Kahn Houses* (TOTO Publishing, 2003), *Villa Mairea/Alvar Aalto* (TOTO Publishing, 2005), and *Aalto: 10 Selected Houses* (TOTO Publishing, 2008).
He is author of books entitled *STRONG* (Sumai-no-Toshokan Shuppannkyoku, 1991) and *The Essence of Architecture* (A. D. A. EDITA Tokyo, 2000).

©Nacása & Partners

日本建築の形 I

2016年9月21日　初版第1刷発行
2018年7月20日　初版第2刷発行

著・写真　齋藤 裕
発行者　加藤 徹
発行所　TOTO出版（TOTO株式会社）
〒107-0062　東京都港区南青山1-24-3
TOTO乃木坂ビル2F
［営業］TEL: 03-3402-7138　FAX: 03-3402-7187
［編集］TEL: 03-3497-1010
URL: https://jp.toto.com/publishing

編集　三輪直美
デザイン　工藤強勝
印刷・製本　図書印刷株式会社

落丁本・乱丁本はお取り替えいたします。
本書のコピー・スキャン・デジタル化等の無断複製行為を禁じます。
本書を代行業者等の第三者に依頼してスキャンやデジタル化することは、
たとえ個人や家庭内での利用であっても著作権上認められておりません。
定価はカバーに示してあります。

©2016 Yutaka Saito

Printed in Japan
ISBN978-4-88706-361-7